Juliusz Słowacki

# FOUR PLAYS

MARY STUART, KORDIAN,
BALLADYNA, HORSZTYŃSKI

GLAGOSLAV PUBLICATIONS

# FOUR PLAYS

## MARY STUART, KORDIAN, BALLADYNA, HORSZTYŃSKI

by Juliusz Słowacki

Translated from the Polish and introduced by
**Charles S. Kraszewski**

This book has been published with the support
of the ©POLAND Translation Program

Cover image "Stańczyk" by Jan Matejko (1962)

Publishers
Maxim Hodak & Max Mendor

Introduction © 2018, Charles S. Kraszewski

© 2018, Glagoslav Publications

www.glagoslav.com

ISBN: 978-1-912894-13-0

A catalogue record for this book is available from the British Library.

This book is in copyright. No part of this publication may be reproduced, stored in a retrieval system or transmitted in any form or by any means without the prior permission in writing of the publisher, nor be otherwise circulated in any form of binding or cover other than that in which it is published without a similar condition, including this condition, being imposed on the subsequent purchaser.

Juliusz Słowacki

# FOUR PLAYS

MARY STUART, KORDIAN,
BALLADYNA, HORSZTYŃSKI

Translated from the Polish
and introduced by Charles S. Kraszewski

GLAGOSLAV PUBLICATIONS

# CONTENTS

INTRODUCTION: THE EARLY PLAYS OF JULIUSZ SŁOWACKI . . . . 7

MARY STUART . . . . . . . . . . . . . . . . . . . . . . 29

KORDIAN . . . . . . . . . . . . . . . . . . . . . . . . 117

BALLADYNA . . . . . . . . . . . . . . . . . . . . . . . 242

HORSZTYŃSKI . . . . . . . . . . . . . . . . . . . . . . 424

BIBLIOGRAPHY . . . . . . . . . . . . . . . . . . . . . . 567

ABOUT THE AUTHOR . . . . . . . . . . . . . . . . . . . . 568

ABOUT THE TRANSLATOR . . . . . . . . . . . . . . . . . . 569

JULIUSZ SŁOWACKI

1809 – 1849

# INTRODUCTION:
## THE EARLY PLAYS OF JULIUSZ SŁOWACKI

As any younger son will testify, it's not easy being number two. The subtle rights of primogeniture are an ever-present burden. The accomplishments of the cadet are always being compared to those of the elder sibling, and rare it is that they ever surpass them.

It is worth considering what would be the position of Juliusz Słowacki (1809–1849) in Polish literature, had Adam Mickiewicz (1798–1855) never never been born. Considering the fact that Juliusz's father Euzebiusz, who died when the boy was six, was a fairly well known poet in his own right, and that his mother Salomea, who outlived her son by six years, kept a literary salon in the eastern marches of Poland, it is probable that he would have reached for the pen anyway. We would certainly not have had *Kordian* (1834), his crowning achievement. For that play is a riposte of sorts to Mickiewicz's *Dziady* [*Forefathers' Eve*] — to Part III of which, published in 1832, Słowacki took exception due to the way in which his stepfather, August Bécu, was portrayed. A Russian toady in Mickiewicz's play, inimical to Polish independence, he is struck down by a lightning bolt as a sign of divine judgement.

It is possible that we would not have the unfinished *Król-Duch* [*King-Spirit*, 1847] — for hadn't Mickiewicz shown the path toward the esoteric, mystical hagiography of Poland with his para-evangelical *Księgi narodu i pielgrzymstwa polskiego* [*Books of the Polish Nation and Polish Pilgrimage*] back in 1832? Would Słowacki have arrived at the curious etymology of the name Polska — Poland — as a derivative of the phrase "na ból skale"* ["on the scale of pain"], had not Mickiewicz beat, and beat, and beat again the drum of "Poland as the Christ of Europe" before him?

Such hypotheses are as fruitless as they are entertaining. But even if Mickiewicz had not been around for the younger poet's emulation and rivalry, others would have drawn him from his father's neoclassicism toward the new Romantic trends bleeding into Poland from the West; he still would have read Antoni Malczewski's *Maria* (1825) and the poems of the slightly older

---

\*     *Król-Duch*, I.iii.316.

Józef Bohdan Zaleski (1802–1886) anyway.[*] More importantly, he would still have been captivated by Byron, and so his marvellously entertaining digressive epics *Podróż do ziemi świętej* [*Journey to the Holy Land*, 1836-1839] and *Beniowski* (1841) would still have been written. He would have still travelled to London — more of that later — and still have submerged himself in the pan-European enthusiasm for Shakespeare.[**] And this — especially his fondness for the great dramatist — would have assured him a prominent place in the history of Polish letters. For unlike the other "two bards" of the Polish tradition — Mickiewicz and Zygmunt Krasiński (1812–1859), Słowacki, eschewing the enormous stage of the monumental tradition — a stage so wide as to almost foreordain works like *Forefathers' Eve* and *Irydion* (1836) to solitary reading as closet-dramas — Słowacki chose Shakespeare as his mentor and patron, and thus created, in works like *Mary Stuart, Horsztyński, Balladyna*, and others not included in this present volume, verse dramas that are made for acting.

The first of the plays included in our translation, *Mary Stuart,* was composed when Słowacki was just twenty-one. The play is remarkable to the degree in which it is not derivative. Surely Słowacki knew Schiller's play, written three decades before his own. Yet the young Polish poet resisted the dramatic tension of Fotheringhay — the dynastic conflict Mary had with her cousin Elizabeth, the Catholic plottings to unseat the twice-illegitimate Tudor queen and replace her with Mary, the show trial (with its falsified evidence)[***] and the execution — a prime opportunity for pathos if there ever was one. The whole topic of Mary's execution — or judicial murder — is dramatically compelling. For better or worse, England, and the world, enters the modern age with this startling precedent of an anointed sovereign — of a foreign

---

[*] Out of fairness to Euzebiusz Słowacki, it is appropriate to note that, as Dorota Staszewska reminds us, "in the Literature Department [of the University of Vilnius ... Euzebiusz] Słowacki already knew and took into consideration the German theoreticians." See her *O sonetach polskich romantyków* [*On the Sonnets of the Polish Romantics*] (Łódź: Acta Universitatis Lodzensis, 2005), "Folia Litteraria Polonica 7:240.

[**] As he wrote in an 1834 letter to his mother: *Szekspir i Dant są teraz moimi kochankami — i już tak jest od dwóch lat* ["I am now in love with Shakespeare and Dante — and have been now for two years."] Cited by Alina Witkowska, *Literatura romantyzmu* (Warsaw: Państwowe wydawnictwo naukowe, 1986), p. 154.

[***] The interested reader is referred to Stephen Alford's *The Watchers. A Secret History of the Reign of Elizabeth I* (New York: Bloomsbury Press, 2012). Chapter 14, "Sleights of Hand," describes the falsification, by government agent Thomas Phelippes, of Anthony Babington's "bloody letter," which was used as the primary piece of evidence to prove Mary's "guilt" at her questionable trial.

nation, to boot — subjected to common law and subsequently penalised capitally — a fate her grandson Charles was also to face. Instead of all that, Słowacki presents us with a young and vulnerable queen, at a crucial moment of her reign, when her devotion to the ancient faith was being challenged by the new currents of Protestantism favoured by her husband Darnley, and when the idea of a female sovereign with a male consort was new and rankling to some. Whether or not Mary is in love with the courtier Rizzio, the favour she shows him is more than enough to infuriate Henry, in an age when men didn't cotton much to playing second fiddle:

> Now I'm slain!
> The sharp words of a jester pierce my chest.
> I am a king — I am no king — I stand
> Amazed myself at how long I have suffered
> This blot upon my honour. Now, enough!
> Enough humiliation! Wherever I be
> I hear the smallest children say, "O, look —
> The husband of the queen!" Why not "the king?"
> "The husband of the queen." Such is my fame?

The space given to questions of Mary's love interests — something we have no right *not* to expect — at times fleshes out her character nicely, and at times shades (but only just shades) into melodrama. But the core of the young Słowacki's dramatic genius is not so much his depiction of Mary as a woman, as it is his depiction of Mary as a person born to the ermine. Consider her interview with Rizzio, whom she is trying to save by banishing him to his native Italy:

> Your Majesty! Repeat those words!
> No — say them not again — I shall not heed,
> Here on the very lip of the abyss,
> Although I merit your anger thereby;
> My death cannot dishonour you, indeed?
> Nor sadden you? Your Majesty — Mary!
> I shall remain! I seal this with an oath,
> And nothing shall deflect me from my resolve.
> Your words sentence me to a death more bitter —
> Although your sweet lips spoke them; even though
> Your voice trembled when shaping them — Mary,
> Listen...!

MARY
> Rizzio! Deign address the queen.
> The words you spoke were formed for someone else.

Her reply is magnificent. Whatever she feels for him, as soon as he inches a bit too close, stepping within her pale, the lioness inside her rears and she reminds him, angrily, of the distance that necessarily separates her, a crowned head and public figure, a symbol erected for the veneration of the people, and him, a commoner who, ironically, enjoys more individual freedom.

Although he may overdo it a bit with Mary's sudden, and purple, admission of love to Bothwell following the fainting fit after Rizzio's murder, Słowacki toys with Mary's sexuality in a very mature, teasing way. Sexual innuendo abounds, from Nick's biting insinuation of Rizzio's "back [being] covered by [Mary's] royal robe," to the light, risky banter between Rizzio and Mary just before his murder. Rizzio, who is about to sail abroad at Mary's command, first asks for a flower from the garland that adorns her head, and then for her fan. It is a very gentle amorous dialogue; almost a strip-tease, in which Mary — at her ease for once in the play — participates happily:

> RIZZIO
> My lady! I am your page, and your page begs
> You for your fan. For your fan's breath
> Has such a sweetness in it, which recalls
> The Scottish mountain air. When I'm abroad,
> In some far country, it will bear the scent
> Of roses, which surround you, to my nose.
> Then, for a while, I shall close my eyes
> And travel to your presence in a dream...
>
> MARY
> *Smiling.*
> The queen forgives her page. But Rizzio
> Would never dare direct such words at her.
> Page! Would you take the very crown from me?
> It's well you don't demand this robe of purple;
> It's well that you content yourself with fans.

This is all high quality dramatic writing. It is interesting that Słowacki, given his nationality and the times into which he was born, should launch his dramatic career not with a Polish theme, but rather with a story from the world's historical heritage; a story which appeals to all in its universality. Here too Słowacki is imitating his Shakespeare, and very skilfully indeed. In the introductory letter to *Balladyna,* addressed to his friend Zygmunt Krasiński, Słowacki makes reference to his early years in Krzemieniec, gazing wistfully at the castle up on Bona Hill:

> [...] However many times I would gaze up at the old castle, the ruins of which crown the hill in my hometown, I would dream of someday spilling spectres, spirits, knights into its jagged wreath of battlements; that I would reconstruct the grand halls and illuminate them with the fire of a night filled with lightning, and that I would make the vaults ring with the echoes of ancient Sophocles' "Alas!"

The vividness of his childhood imagination gave birth in his young adulthood to dramatic characters of brilliant tangibility. Nick, Darnley's jester, is a witty clown who would fit perfectly amongst the company of the Bard's best comic creations:

> NICK
> Besides the clothes, will Nick get anything?
> Poor Nick is poor...
>
> HENRY
>                 What would you have besides?
>
> NICK
> *Thinks.*
> Give me, my sire, a portrait of the queen.
>
> HENRY
> I'll give you mine.
>
> NICK
>                 I don't want yours! A shilling!
> For there she's pictured in her crown. Not you —
> Your face is on no shilling.

The old Astrologer, — like Marlowe's Faust, sick of a lifetime of study that threatens to result only in despair — is another character that throbs with life. He is present in three scenes only, in the same act, as a secondary motor for the revenge tragedy that will culminate in the killing of Rizzio. And yet he is so well drawn by Słowacki that, despite his rather meagre time on stage, he *exists* in a real way. He is one of those characters that so grabs the spectator or reader, that even when he is off stage, one has the sense of his continued existence — pottering around back in his lab amongst his alchemical goblets and telescopes, while the stage is occupied by others. His scene with Nick is especially vibrant:

> NICK
> 
> Greetings, Father.
> 
> ASTROLOGER
> Father? Whence our consanguinity?
> 
> NICK
> Wisdom is sired by foolishness, and in turn,
> Wisdom sires madness. Thus I am your son,
> And all these books, my sisters, sired by you.
> 
> [...]
> 
> NICK
> *Looking through a telescope the wrong way round.*
> Aha!
> 
> ASTROLOGER
> What do you see?
> 
> NICK
> 
> The earth.
> 
> ASTROLOGER
> 
> And there?
> 
> NICK
> 
> Nothing.
> 
> ASTROLOGER
> But you must have seen me, is that not so?
> 
> NICK
> Yes, but far off — like a speck of dust.
> Look not aloft — you'll lose yourself amongst

>       Immensity. Look to the earth, but look
>       The wrong way round. How small they seem! Fame! Learning!
>       The best of lenses make distances greater.
>       Thus the king's clown sets forth his Q.E.D.s.
>       The king's wiseman...
>
>       ASTROLOGER
>                         Lets the king's clown prate as he please.

Characters like Nick and the Astrologer come close to stealing the show. But they never succeed in this, for Słowacki, as young as he is, always keeps the tragic figure of Mary front and centre, before our eyes. This is Mary's tragedy. As often happens with the tragedies of Sophocles, referenced earlier by the poet, this tragedy does not need to end with the heroine's death. Indeed, Alina Witkowska perceives political stalemate as the motor of this play:

> This story of a palace revolution is actually the tale of the impossibility of carrying out a revolution, whether that be the seizure of power by Mary's adversaries, or Mary's consolidation of power despite her adversaries, and over the dead body of her husband. In this drama of court intrigue [we have...] the disease of the incomplete act, the act not carried through to the end.*

That's one way of looking at the play. As far as the character of the queen is concerned, there are many facets to the tragedy of Mary's young life in Słowacki's telling. They range from her emotional troubles as a wife in a highly problematical marriage to a man who both despises and desperately worships her, a desirable woman who cannot help but attract the attentions of Rizzio, Bothwell, and even her young Page, as a flower attracts bees, and a woman with so outraged a sense of justice at the murder of Rizzio that she herself resorts to murder, while never losing her tragic — yet maybe salvific? — grip on her faith.

    Above all, though, as we have noted earlier, Mary's tragedy is that of a woman forced into the office of sole sovereign, years before it was common, if feasible. Perhaps nowhere do we feel more strongly for Mary than we do in situations such as her frustrated dealings with Douglas, who outrages our sense of propriety by not tendering Mary the respect she merits, as head of state:

---

\*    Witkowska, p. 147.

MARY
Douglas, a moment's not passed since I spied
Morton down by the palace gate. Quickly,
Take this command to him, for it requires
The seal of the chancellor.

*Douglas takes the paper from the queen, looks it over, and waits.*

What's this?
The virtue of a knight is blind obedience —
Do you deny this to a woman? A queen?

DOUGLAS
A queen? O, no — there's not a treacherous fibre
In all of Douglas' frame. But — you'll forgive me;
What's on this paper, ma'am, was writ in haste,
At such a sudden moment, and it lacks
The name of Henry, and his title, King —
Whom all the people hold in holy awe;
Whose name was always paired with yours. Perhaps —
Forgive my boldness — you might deign correct
The oversight?

MARY
                 The queen overlooks nothing
When she commands!

DOUGLAS
*With contempt.*
                         And so, from the queen's lips
I'd be commanded, and dismissed.

MARY
                 Do it!

Whatever we think of the Tudor cousin who was to lop off her head, this is not some imperious Elizabeth fulminating from the throne. It is rather a young woman placed in a position of power that is — still — too unwieldy to her hands; a ruler cognisant of what is owed her, and shocked when that is unjustly withheld. It is a person new to the métier, grappling with large problems, learning on the job. In short, it is an image of the young dramatist

Słowacki, who, unlike his tragic heroine, even at this early stage of his career mastered the tasks at hand.

Speaking of queens, there is none in the royal pantheon of Polish literature who equals Balladyna, the fantastic creation of Słowacki's imagination, conjured from the mists of Slavic pre-history. The play, composed in 1834, is entirely the work of Słowacki's fertile pen. The elements of Polish legend that the play contains — enchanted Lake Gopło and the cruel ruler Popiel, reigning from the first capital of the Polish nation, Gniezno, some forty miles to the west of the lake — are meagre. Słowacki completely passes over the legend of Popiel being devoured by mice in his castle tower; in fact, Popiel doesn't appear on stage at all.[*] As in a Greek tragedy, his death at the hands of the hero Kirkor is related to us by a messenger. Instead, Słowacki artfully ransacks the tragedies and fantasies of Shakespeare for his characters and themes, which he then blends, from truly disparate sources, into a tragicomedy that is both gloomy and charming.

Goplana, the pagan spring deity of the lake, and her imps Skierka and Chochlik, emerge as if from the pages of *A Midsummer Night's Dream*. Rake ("Grabiec" in the original Polish, whose name we modify in order to approximate the punning that goes on in Słowacki's play) is the Polish Bottom. These characters provide us with some lighthearted scenes — especially Rake's first speech to his "subjects" when, transformed into the King of Diamonds, he assumes rule over the flora and fauna of the lake region:

> Oyez, oyez, give hear and memorise
> The codex of the king — eternise it
> Within the rotting bark of some old willow.
> From now on, we shall draft into our ranks
> Bison and rabbit, boar and all the elk,
> Who proudly bear their halberds on their brows.
> Henceforth, should flowers wish to dip their leaves
> Into the dew, let them pay per the ounce;
> The Jews are hereby granted letters patent
> Over the usufruct of dew. Starlings
> Are hereby strictly forbidden to think
> While they are chattering. We too forbid
> The swallow senate free association
> To discuss politics among the reeds.

---

[*] The cruel Popiel of legend, that is. The Hermit, who plays a central role to the story, is also a Popiel. In fact, he is the true king of Poland, who was deposed by his evil brother, banished to the woods after the slaughter of his family.

> The House of Sparrows is henceforth abolished.
> Judgement and hanging and the distribution
> Of favour shall be centred in our hands.
> The swallows are forbidden to leave our borders
> Without a passport, such as which includes
> A nice description of beak, claw, and wing,
> As well as tail and characteristic marks.
> No bird shall dare henceforth enrol his chicks
> In German institutions, where parrots
> Are headmaster and beadle — we except
> From this law magpies, who enrich thereby
> Our native tongue.

But this is neither the carefree bucolic playground that might be painted by a Fragonard or a Watteau, nor the humorous cavorting of Shakespeare's romance. The smell of blood, introduced at the very outset of the play, with the Hermit's tale of the butchering of his daughters by Popiel the usurper, taints the air in Słowacki's enchanted forest. "The forest smells of carrion," declares Kirkor at a key moment in the play. It is delightful when Goplana, frustrated at Rake's fixation with a human girl, decides to teach him a lesson and transforms him, drunk, into a weeping willow. But the mood changes dramatically when Rake, still quite conscious as a human, though his outward form is changed, must witness the brutal murder of Alina by Balladyna, which takes place at his feet. Literally rooted to the ground, he is unable to do anything but watch the crime unfold, and express his horror by whispering "Jesus and Mary!"

The other Shakespearean inspirations come from *Macbeth*, obviously, through the bloody and conniving character of Balladyna, and *King Lear*, whose howls are borrowed here by the widow, Balladyna and Alina's sorely tried old mother.

Is Słowacki overreaching here? Does he ask us, in these two characters, to swallow more than we can handle? Who kills a girl over a jar of raspberries — even in the context of a competition, the winner of which gets a ticket out of rural poverty to the nearby ducal estate? Well, Balladyna does, as do — let's admit it — other people we read about in the newspapers, who end the lives of their brothers and sisters over trivial matters. And Słowacki does provide a backstory, if in shorthand, that prepares us for Balladyna's actions. When Rake admits to Goplana, at the start of the play, that he is in love with Balladyna, Goplana is taken aback in surprise. How can he be in love with a girl who has an evil heart? And so (despite Rake's humorous, and how predictable, for a man!, objection that a girl with such pretty legs must have a pretty heart, too), there were, in Balladyna's case, warning signs.

What we are not quite prepared for, perhaps, is the way this village girl suddenly blooms into an eloquent, capable lady, as if she had been to the manor born. Upon returning from the Hermit's cottage, where she had sought in vain a concoction to wipe the stain of guilt from her brow ("out, out, damned spot!"), this girl, from a village in the middle of the Polish woods, who, considering the time period, would probably have been illiterate, starts speaking like Hamlet:

> Perhaps by now he's forgotten it all,
> And it's but I, who needlessly rehearse
> These thoughts which no more through his mind revolve?
> For who am I that others should regard,
> And spy upon, and seek to ruin? Hell!
> Why can't the pressure of one thousand words
> Squeeze out the life of these mere two: "He knows?"
> What drove me to his cell to speak with him?
> What Satan took me by the hand and led
> Me there to speak with the hermit of the woods?
> If I am ruined, 'tis I that ruined me;
> And just think — if not for that sick visit,
> He'd be no different from the million souls
> Throughout the world whom I have never met!
> To think, this present hour so full of fright
> Would have been like the calm of yesterday,
> And even calmer, maybe... Hours pass,
> And with each hour more of this my secret
> Is rubbed by silence, till it's near erased —
> And now the scab is torn from off the wound
> Which shows itself more horrid, for having been
> So close to healing! How I envy her,
> The she that I was just this morning past!

And a little later on, in her tent while Kostryn and her troops are about to do battle with Kirkor, she speaks with a "stomach" that sounds like Richard III... It may be for this reason that, in the Epilogue, the Public accost the chronicler Wawel with the question, "where does she come from?" Because it sure can't be some unnamed hamlet in the middle of ninth century Poland...

But drama doesn't have to be naturalistic, and the best drama often isn't. It would be nitpicking to call Słowacki to task for his lack verisimilitude. To paraphrase Eliot, Słowacki "is not Zola, nor was he meant to be." *Balladyna* is, above all, a fairy story, and holds to the conventions of the fairy story — narrative shorthand, suspension of disbelief in deference to the moral, etc. It is great literature because it is a fairy tale that doesn't fully satisfy our sense of justice. It is true that the bloody queen gets her comeuppance at the end. Forced by custom of law to pass sentence as a judge upon the complainants who come before her — the last one being her blind mother charging her unnatural daughter with cruelty and neglect — Balladyna must pass a verdict of death "in absentia," after which she is immediately scorched by a lightning bolt. It is a fairy-tale ending which we saw coming, just as we watched "all the clouds of heaven" gather above the cupola beneath which she is sitting. As Eugeniusz Sawrymowicz puts it:

> When, after having achieved her goal, Balladyna determines to have done with her criminal past and swears "herself, to be righteous in the eyes of God," the poet has us understand that this is quite improbable. Balladyna might only remain in power by remaining a criminal; as a righteous queen, she must die, pronouncing a sentence of death against herself.[*]

Of course we saw this coming. It had to end like that: are there any fairy tales, happy or sad, which are not predictable? Yet that being the case, why must it be that, if justice triumphs in this one case, it fails in all the others? For *Balladyna* ends bloodily for everybody. First of all, Alina falls victim to Balladyna's jealous rage. The Hermit, and authentic inheritor of the "crown of Lech," is murdered by Fon Kostryn before the battle to restore him to his throne even begins. The just Kirkor, who is literally fighting the good fight, dies in the battle won by that repulsive pair — the "son of the hanged man," Fon Kostryn, and his adulterous paramour Balladyna. Good old Rake, who in his tippling is just as much Falstaff as he is Bottom, is murdered in his bed just like Duncan in *Macbeth*;[**] in an extreme display of motherly devotion, the Widow is put to torture for refusing to reveal the name of her impious daughter, and dies on the rack; even Goplana is "exiled to the land of pines

---

[*] Eugeniusz Sawrymowicz, *Juliusz Słowacki* (Warsaw: Wiedza powszechna, 1973), p. 147.

[**] In her interesting article, "*Balladyna,* czyli o próbie karnawalizacji literatury romantycznej" ["*Balladyna,* or Concerning an Attempt at the Carnivalisation of Romantic Literature"] (Łódź: Acta Universitatis Lodziensis, 2015), "Folia litteraria polinica" 1:72, Anna Kurska describes the character of Rake as created along the lines of the vigorous, potently erotic and "meaty" character type of carnival literature, exactly so as to have that familiar character type undermined. For virility, which usually guarantees health and safety, stands for nothing in this case.

and snow" for her role in setting all the tragedies afoot by mixing in where she doesn't belong: among the fates of humans.

In *Balladyna*, Słowacki raises more questions than he answers. Why, for example, did Balladyna not recognise her old boyfriend, Rake, when he arrived at her castle for the feast, disguised in wild kingly garb? Just because of his beard? And when she searches for the crown in the darkness of his tower room, after she has killed him, and runs her hands over "that table top with the features of a man's face," surely her fingers, which (we assume) stroked that face in the darkness of the aspen copse more than once, would recognise its familiar contours? Yet they don't — and this fatal mistake, or decision, would have made for an engaging Sophoclean reflexion on fate and tragic flaws. In this aspect of *Balladyna*, Słowacki shows himself, consciously or not, more a student of Christopher Marlowe than William Shakespeare. For, like Marlowe, that poet of experience and testing, who doesn't preach to us as much as he confronts us with problems intended to shock us out of our complacent devotion to assumptions and a priori statements, Słowacki doesn't teach us anything about justice in his play. Rather, he portrays injustice as well as justice, tossing them both on the table like the tangled horse's manes that Chochlik enjoys plaiting, and has us do battle with the strands ourselves.

One thing that does stand out in *Balladyna*, and it is a characteristic of most, if not all, of the plays included in our volume, is that desire to break with the past, mentioned by Sawrymowicz above. He is referring to the first part of Balladyna's speech upon assuming the throne, in which the protagonist suggests that what went before has no significance for what is to come:

> A life that's filled with labour has been split
> In two halves by the crown. My past age falls
> Away as viper's venom from a blade
> Half smeared therewith — when it divides an apple,
> One half remains whole, healthy, while the other
> Blackens and rots. None of you knew me such
> As I have been — let not my people seek
> To delve into my history. You know
> What I have told you. For the rest, the priest
> Who shall absolve me of my sins shall hear,
> And no one else.

In the unfinished play *Horsztyński*, the character of Felix (Szczęsny in the original), one of Słowacki's vacillating Hamlets (Kordian is another), hovers between obeying his harsh father's will, thus engaging in a *rokosz* (aristocratic uprising) that will set him on the Polish throne, and enjoying the peaceful life of a philosopher. When word arrives that all of Poland has erupted in a popular uprising proclaimed in Kraków by Tadeusz Kościuszko, he is roused from his melancholy torpor:

> Warsaw, Vilnius, all of Poland, the nation — Me — A procession of gigantic events is passing before my eyes. How can I mix in with them? How can I stand to? And where? What am I to become? What will my father become? O! I will cast myself at his feet and weep like an infant, begging him on behalf of the poor people thrashing about in the great net of events. I seem to hear the revolutionary cries of rubble and stone coming to life. Great God! I haven't prayed to You in quite a while, but right now, I can feel my heart crying out from the depths to You: Have mercy upon us!... Upon us? What am I? I did not rise in rebellion...! I am crying out here, safe within these walls, while others are dying in silence... I will look upon the battling people as if upon a gladiatorial slaughter! I the name of God, I go to perish!

Biographical criticism is a risky thing. However, it may not be too farfetched to suggest that, like Felix here, and Balladyna earlier, Słowacki himself saw his life fall into two distinct halves, split by a regret. In his case, the decisive event was the eruption of the November Uprising of 1830, which he witnessed at first hand in Warsaw — but from the sidelines, due to the endemic poor health that was to eventually take his life before he'd quite turned forty. His "orientation to the active struggle," as Sawrymowicz puts it,

> was manifested above all in poetic terms: he published a few poems, in which he took the side of the insurrectionists with enthusiasm, and in which he described his position in regards to the battle being waged between the [insurrectionary] government and the democratic opposition.

Yet Słowacki's great twentieth-century biographer and editor does not entirely dismiss the possibility that there might be emotional or mental reasons, rather than physical problems, at the bottom of his decision not to take up arms. Discussing the poet's flight abroad, as the doomed insurrection was tending toward its eventual defeat, Sawrymowicz notes:

> There seem to have been several causes for this unexpected decision. One of them was the still as yet unsolidified [*nie okrzepły jeszcze*] character of the youth raised in the hothouse environment of his childhood hearth, where all unpleasant things were kept from him,

above all on account of his weak constitution. From this there resulted the sense of his own physical incapacities, which certainly elicited a fear of putting himself at risk of difficulties and dangers.*

Is it this guilty conscience — which was to result later in his unsuccessful attempt to actively join another Polish insurrection shortly before his death in 1848 — that is at the bottom of Balladyna's determination, and Felix's Hamletism? It may certainly be at the bottom of young Kordian's anxieties, expressed after listening to the war stories — both glorious and horrifying — of his old faithful servant Grzegorz, who had been a Napoleonic soldier:

> Dear God, how that old man has grown
> Into a giant! But I... lack belief...
> Where men respire freely, I cannot breathe.
> From men's sublime thoughts my mocking eye brings
> Me back down the path to the muddied springs —
> I shall not overstep the barricades
> Set up on the roads by superstition...
> Now is the time for youth to seize its mission,
> To figure out: To live? Or not to live?
> And I? am helpless. I'm not made to strive
> Against the Sphinxes like killer Oedipus,
> Unravelling their riddling speech, because
> Today they're many — the Sphinxes have multiplied.
> Time was, with threefold riddle they mystified
> Their prey; now, like weeds their riddles expand —
> Riddles as numerous as grains of sand.
> Everywhere, mystery. The world has not been stretched
> Any wider, but it has grown in depth.

Hamlet? For sure, right down to the "To live? or not to live?" allusion. But his wavering is not that of the indecisive. What Kordian expresses here is, in the first instance, a jealous regret at not being a man of action, proving himself on some battlefield, and then... in the second instance, a self-serving rationalisation of the world having become more complicated, suggesting thereby that, had he lived in the good old days, say, twenty years previous to the present moment, he would have found it easy to join the ranks along with Grzegorz, whereas today, the "Sphinxes" have so multiplied, that even Grzegorz would not be able to "breathe freely" if push came to shove.

---

\*   Sawrymowicz, pp. 72; 78-79.

Yet of course he knows, at the bottom of his heart, that he *could* act if he wanted to. That the fault lies within him is at the bottom of his failed suicide attempt — something which also motivates the decision of that other vacillator, Felix, in the concluding scenes of Horsztyński, when he decides to remain in his dead father's castle as the vengeful crowd approaches, to be blown skyward by the load of powder he has stockpiled so that the castle should not be taken.

Słowacki is, as we have mentioned, a disciple of Byron as well as Shakespeare. Yet the marks that his characters bear on their foreheads — Balladyna's raspberry stain, and the scar left on Kordian's brow by the bullet which failed to kill him — are more than just "marks of Cain." As both these characters are literally ashamed of these all too visible signs of villainy and weakness, is it not possible that Słowacki himself was ashamed — whether he had reason to be, or not — of his abandonment of Poland after the uprising, in which he took only tangential part?

Not everyone is cut out for soldiering — that's certainly true of the writer of these lines (so let no one assume that I am pointing fingers) — Witold Gombrowicz, who left Poland for Argentina just before the outbreak of World War II, counted himself among the number of Poles like Mickiewicz and Chopin, who lived afar from their nation at its time of trial, not out of cowardice, as much as from the conviction that, as artists, they could do more for the cause of Poland by living, than by dying uselessly on a battlefield.<sup>\*</sup> This is also considered by Słowacki's biographer:

> Another [reason for leaving Poland] was his deep-seated conviction of his poetic vocation as his only true path, which led him to seek out those conditions that would foster the development of that path.<sup>\*\*</sup>

*Kordian* is, however, a complex play. On the one hand, it acknowledges the value of active individual engagement with the problems of the world, such as oppression and injustice. "So I set out — and this shall be my task: / To fell all wood gone rotten, with my axe." Sure, he makes this statement before his

---

\*    See Witold Gombrowicz, *Dziennik* I (Paris: Instytut literacki, 1957), I: 169. Gombrowicz acutally says that these "patriots" were motivated by a desire "not to make fools of themselves" [*nie chcieli się zbłaźnić*]. For historical accuracy, we should point out that Mickiewicz took part in the mustering of legions for armed battle against the Russian Empire, dying in Turkey while doing just that, and Słowacki himself travelled back to Wrocław in 1848, in an unsuccessful attempt to join the active struggle in the Prussian Partition.

\*\*    Sawrymowicz, p. 79.

attempted suicide, but later, after returning from his ironic, Byronic journeys through England, Italy and Switzerland, he takes it up again on the heights of Mont Blanc and determines to (literally) hurl himself into the struggle on behalf of "Poland, the Winkelried of the nations." During his lonely soliloquy (the equivalent to the Great Improvisation in *Forefathers' Eve,* Part III), he cries:

> To think this, and not wish it!
>     O shame! Disgrace!
> To think this, and be impotent?
>     I'd rather flay
> My breast with my own hands!
>     Hell is impotence!

This is perhaps why, during the scene in the crypts of St John's Cathedral in Warsaw, when the conspirators' votes are tallied up 150 — 5 against the assassination of the Tsar, Kordian decides to go and kill him anyway. For those burdened by a strong sense of the imperative of "manly" action, impotence must certainly be Hell.

Słowacki took some part in the November Uprising, travelling to London as a secret courier for the rebel party headed by Prince Adam Czartoryski. From the distance of London and Paris, he was able to consider the Uprising coolly. Perhaps this was not the time to strike; perhaps these were not the leaders to prosecute an armed rebellion to its successful conclusion.* He is withering in his estimation of the insurrectionary and military leaders of the Uprising, especially in the marvellously Goethean opening scenes of the play, when the devils gather near Piotr Twardowski's cottage in the Tatra Mountains to concoct their monstrous figures in their cauldrons. Even Czartoryski is not spared his acerbic pen, nor is the elder statesman/poet Julian Ursyn Niemcewicz — although Niemcewicz's words in the crypt scene were to prove much more closer to the poet's thought, than those of his hero, Kordian.

*Kordian* is a response to Mickiewicz's *Forefathers' Eve,* part III. It was partially written to rebut Mickiewicz's characterisation of Słowacki's stepfather as servile to the Russians, whose death by lightning was (as in the case of Balladyna), a visible act of divine justice. It seems that Joachim Lelewel, Mickiewicz's professor, and one of the insurrectionary leaders

---

\* See, for example, Julian Krzyżanowski, "Duch — wieczny rewolucjonista" ["Spirit — the Eternal Revolutionary"] in *W świecie romantycznym* [*In the World of the Romantics*] (Kraków: Wydawnictwo literackie, 1961, p. 204.

parodied by Słowacki in the opening scenes of the play, was of the same opinion.[*] Yet it would be misguided to suggest that the younger poet was motivated by feelings of vengeance. *Kordian* was published anonymously. It is so stylistically similar to *Forefathers' Eve*, that the Poles who first read the work assumed it to be the fruit of Mickiewicz's pen — something that, as the poet wrote to his mother on April 27, 1834, *nie jest mi niemiłą [...] pomyłką* ["is not for me an unpleasant /.../ error"].[**] That Słowacki was perhaps aiming at this "not unpleasant error" might be divined from the very name of his protagonist, as Kordian is an approximate anagram of Mickiewicz's Konrad.

But the stories of the two characters are quite different. Kordian is not possessed of a megalomania that has him do battle with God himself; he does not wish to deprive men of their free will (as Konrad suggests in his raving Great Improvisation); both during the soliloquy on Mont Blanc and in the crypts of St John's he expresses his desire to convince his fellows to "entrust themselves into his hands," not to force them to his will. Kordian, unlike Konrad, is not possessed. Although frightened and tempted by devils, he is, above all, someone punching above his weight. Słowacki, who earlier expressed the desire to be involved in real, significant, individual action, now, at a distance, shows the futility of such desires. An individual man cannot — as Mickiewicz suggests in his play — overturn thrones by the power of his will. As he traipses the corridors of the silent palace toward the Tsar's bedroom, at the threshold of which he will faint into unconsciousness, short of his murderous goal, Kordian is plagued by the bugbears of his own mind (as most normal people would be):

> KORDIAN
> *Moving forward with his carbine.*
> Let me go! Let me go! I'm the murderer of Tsars;
> I go to kill... Who restrains me, by a hair?
>
> IMAGINATION
> Listen! I can see what's there!
>
> FEAR
> Listen! My voice — the beating of your heart!

---

[*] See his 1831 brochure *Nowosilcow w Wilnie* [*Novosiltsov in Vilnius*], cited by Sawrymowicz, p. 78.

[**] Juliusz Słowacki, *Korespondencja* ed. Eugeniusz Sawrymowicz (Wrocław: Ossolineum, 1962), Vol. I, p. 239.

KORDIAN
No one is there;
I hear some gibbering.

IMAGINATION
Don't look at me — look where I'm fingering!

KORDIAN
I cannot see your finger, but my sight falls
There, where you're pointing. I can see faces,
Arabesques, painted on the walls.

FEAR
Look closer! see? Those are the traces
Of reptiles! See them scurry? Disgusting!
Each snake has a sting of fire...

Although he does his best to bravely soldier on toward the act, despite the ever more horrifying images conjured up by his Imagination and his Fear, they will overcome him in the end. There are certain tasks that men are simply not made for.

This is similar to the lesson taught us by Mickiewicz in part III of his monumental drama. Konrad cannot "create a happier Poland" by the mere force of his individual will, fixing the poor, botched job of God Himself [*sic!*], any more than he can actually "stop the cranes in flight" with the power of his eye — another claim he puts forward in his frenzy. At the end, as he is being led off to Siberian exile, Konrad presents Fr Piotr with his ring to sell, directing him to spend the proceeds in charity. It is a simple, small act — but a significant one; one that cannot change the entire world, but one that can make it somewhat better.

Słowacki's point is similar, but not identical. He also shows the inevitable failure of all Manfred-like or Faustian overreaching, one man putting his shoulder to the world and nudging it into a more positive groove. In one of the most Konradian passages of his Mont Blanc soliloquy, Kordian muses:

And can we not, like God Himself, when He
Created the world, with this one hand of ours
Toss in one mighty sweep myriads of stars
And so mark out the paths of destiny
That never should these poor vessels of clay
Err in their navigation, mistake their way

And shatter on the infinite deep?
>	I can — I shall! I go, to jar,
To wake the slumbering people from their sleep!

The answer is, no, "we" can't. But whereas Mickiewicz shows us what we *can* do with Konrad's touching donation on behalf of the suffering souls in Purgatory, and the poor among us, Kordian offers us only bitterness. He moves — justly? — from the impotence of the "great souled individual" such as Kordian to the impotence of the nation, doomed to failure in its armed uprising. He does this near the final scenes of the play when Kordian, sentenced to death for his attempt on the Tsar's life, is led out onto the Saski Square and, given a horse by Grand Prince Constantine, is encouraged to gallop towards a high picket of bayonets and leap over the impossible barricade, in exchange for his life. It is of no small significance that he only agrees to do it after the Tsar has countermanded the Grand Prince's offer and has assured Kordian that, even if he clears the hurdle, he will be shot. In this way, it becomes a disinterested act, and an empty one:

> GRAND PRINCE
> O, let him make it! I want him to win out!
> The Tsar will recognise by what great heights
> My soldiers overtop his Muscovites!
> Look! Here he comes — he stops... He turns his glance
> Upon the people... who wait in silence,
> Black, muddy...
> *Frowns like a tiger.*
>> O, I do not like this folk —
> They toss their hats and hankies... Any hope,
> Kuruta?
>
> KURUTA
>> If you say so, Your Excellency.
>
> GRAND PRINCE
> *Violently.*
> Look! What a cloud of dust he kicks up! Ah —
> I can't see... Come on, boy! He made it!
>
> SOLDIERS
>> Hurrah!

PEOPLE
*From afar.*
He lives!

So he makes it, against all probability. Along with the "heroic" Polish soldiers, none of whom were brave enough to take the challenge for a hefty reward when it seemed as if Kordian was going to refuse it, we cry "hurrah!" relieved that horse and rider are safe — perhaps more relieved that the poor horse, who had no choice in the matter, cleared the deadly barricade without having his belly torn open. Yet however "brave" or "heroic" Kordian's jump seems, in reality, it is silly, frivolous. A mad stunt signifying nothing. And this symbolises, for Słowacki, the November Uprising.

It is a curious, cynical, and perhaps none too justified ending for a serious dramatic work based on recent history, a recent national tragedy. Of course, we do not know how Słowacki intended to continue the story. The play ends with Kordian standing at the wall, facing the firing squad, with a rider bearing a pardon rushing in... Will the adjutant get there in time, or not? That the poet intended to continue the story is made clear by his signifying the work as "Part I." Unlike other Romantic mystifications, *Kordian* truly is a "magnificent torso." We know that a Part II was written by the poet, and then destroyed by his own hand. And so we are left hanging in this uncertainty.

We began our brief discussion with a reflection on Słowacki as a younger brother of sorts to Mickiewicz, constantly in his shadow. Mickiewicz was first interred amongst the crowned heads of Poland in the royal crypts of Wawel Cathedral. Early in the twentieth century, a petition was circulated in support of transferring Słowacki's remains from the Montmartre Cemetery in Paris to that same crypt. Not only was he first refused the honour by the Archbishop, but two decades later, it took an edict from the Polish strongman Marshal Piłsudski to effect the transferral. While the two bards lie side by side in the crypt (and not, as in the case of Mary and Elizabeth Tudor in Westminster Abbey, with the latter triumphantly on top of the former), it is somewhat ironic that even the boat that carried Słowacki's coffin down the Vistula to Kraków was christened the "Mickiewicz..."

But Słowacki should not be considered a second-rank poet. For Polish literature, he is an important cardinal figure. On the one hand, he would not have been the poet he is, were it not for a youthful enthusiasm for his fellow Lithuanian, Adam Mickiewicz. His early verse is strongly imitative of the father of Polish Romanticism, eleven years his elder, and a frequent visitor to the Wilno salons hosted by his beloved mother, Salomea. On the other hand, Słowacki was not afraid to take issue with Mickiewicz. The great example of this is his play *Kordian*, which we have just discussed. It was not purely a personal grudge that determined the composition of Słowacki's most famous play. It is a critical comment on the political and philosophical thrust of Mickiewicz's work.

Just as Mickiewicz leads to Słowacki, so Słowacki leads to later epigones of Romanticism, such as Stanisław Wyspiański. For Słowacki not only confirms the importance of Mickiewicz to the poets who come after him, he also encourages them not to accept his directives blindly. If it were not for Mickiewicz, we would not have Słowacki; we certainly would not have the *same* Słowacki, and of course, we would not have *Kordian*. If not for Słowacki, we would not have had Wyspiański's *Wyzwolenie* [*Deliverance*], *Legion*, or *Noc Listopadowa* [*November Night*].

If, in a statement often quoted without context, Mickiewicz said of Słowacki's poetry that it was a *piękny kościół, w którym nie ma Boga* ["a beautiful church, in which there is no God,"] it is worth noting that Słowacki answered for himself, and all the Polish poets who were to come after him, when he described himself and Mickiewicz as *dwa na słońcach swych przeciwnych — Bogi* ["two, on their own suns in opposition — Gods"]. It is with this demand for respect, on his own terms, that we leave the reader, encouraging him and her to consider the four plays included in our translation for what they are: fine pieces of poetry, the well-chiselled cornerstones of the modern tradition of Polish drama, which could have arisen from none other than the Shakespearean genius of Juliusz Słowacki.

*

As always, I would like to thank Ksenia Papazova and everyone at Glagoslav for their continued support of Polish literature.

*Także, jak zawsze, pragnę wyrazić swoją wdzięczność swojej ukochanej żonie, Oli. Jej tę książkę poświęcam — tak jak zresztą wszystko, co piszę, co robię.*

20 June 2018
*Kraków*

# MARY STUART

*a historical drama in five acts*

**PERSONS:**

Mary Stuart, *Queen of Scotland*
Henry Darnley, *her Husband*
Morton, *Chancellor*
Rizzio
Bothwell, *Mary's lover*
Douglas
Lindsay
Mary's Page
Nick, Henry's jester
Astrologer

## ACT I

### Scene 1
*A hall in Holy Rood Palace*

PAGE
*Running in.*
Alas, I bear you more bad news, my queen.
The fickle people of the town insult you
Again, as they have done so many times.
Today I witnessed a new travesty
Flung at your royal chapel. Early this morning
I watched, beyond the garden wall, a troupe
Of jolly maskers — Robin and his train
Of morris dancers; Friar Tuck in's cowl,
The bowmen, Little John, Maid Marian,
Pale as if cut from ivory, the gay lass,
And with the crowd, I followed them, until

They halted — all the jangling bells fell silent —
And there we watched some strange man, threatening,
Haranguing, until he went into a house
Where, at a high window, as if at pulpit,
He once again appeared, to preach his treason
Against you, sovereign Lady.

RIZZIO

                                        From what's been said,
I recognise the preacher. Knox, my lady,
Who day and night rails from that corner window,
The while the crowd below listens and prays,
Sucking in every word that falls from's lips,
Expecting miracles. O, it's Christian doctrine!
One time he pointed here and cried aloud:
"Destroy the nest, and watch the crows fly off!"
As if the Pope himself, he thundered out
Anathemas from that window, and the mob —
They bow before him like he were a saint.

PAGE
The bolder ones, my Queen, thirsty for crime,
Rushed in your chapel, shrieking wildly,
"O pit of papal vipers!" tearing down
The holy images, the candles; setting fire
To all their hands despoiled. And then, dressed up
In priestly robes, that clown of Darnley's stood
Upon the altar, preaching blasphemy.
The people joined in sinful antiphony,
The while the jester stripped the church of gold.
I drew my sword, despairing and enraged,
And threw myself upon him. That put paid
To his bells' tinkle! Did I spill his blood?
I don't know. For soon I was surrounded,
And, pressed against the wall, made to submit.
If not for Bothwell, and the royal guardsmen
Who came to my aid — your page had been no more.

MARY
You hear that, Rizzio? On this lonely throne,
By all abandoned, I'm hated by my people,

The while this Knox insults a woman's crown,
And boldly! Have I now fallen so low?
He curses me, he jibes — it tears my heart!
Even today I offered prayers for them;
Does my faith differ so from theirs? O, Scotland!

RIZZIO
They'll stop insulting you, my queen, and soon.
A well-deservéd punishment will fall
Upon those criminals. Allow me, ma'am
To write a rescript. Let the guilty pay
With loss of freedom — or loss of their head.
Take pen in hand, page, write out the command —

*The Page sits down with pen and parchment.*

Unworthy are they all of clemency;
I'd burn them all to ash upon one pyre.

MARY
You'd slaughter all the people? What wild vengeance!
The people have betrayed me...

PAGE
*Writing.*
                            To your name,
Is it your wish I add that of your husband?
Henry? And add to that the title King?

MARY
Yes, as you've always done — our names together.
No, wait! What am I doing? Perhaps the people
Have acted in accord with his command?
For, after all, you said his jester led
The mob in their blasphemous rioting?
Set down no King! I, Queen, am sole monarch!
But, Rizzio, what's your thought? Will he grow wroth,
Insulted with this first sally against him?
The missing title will envenom life
Between us — for I granted him that title

In happier days, and, more than once, the crown
Was placed upon his brow with my own hands.

RIZZIO
My queen! You have an angel's face, and heart!
Why do you sow blooms in so rank a soil?
In Rome, I've watched the sun sink in the Tiber,
Casting its last glance on a cross of gold...
Now, you are like that sun. Your crown now sinks
In the dark waves of this misguided nation,
And only you behold the light of faith.
My lady, crime cries out for punishment
Deserved — as eclipsed virtue: champions —
The sun that sets today, rises tomorrow.

MARY
Faith's rule is to forgive.

RIZZIO
                    'Tis God's to punish;
But you, enthroned, must punish in God's name.
Indifference smears your name with infamy.
Arouse your lazy ire! The nation looks
To you and sees a lamp no longer burning.
Re-kindle in its heart an ardent flame —
Let it shine forth, and blaze!

*To the Page, who has finished writing, and has arisen.*

                              Page, are you finished?
Who leads the watch tonight? Go, call him here.

*Exit Page.*

Now, let the nation read your verdict plain,
And let the angry thunderbolt of vengeance
Strike down upon the traitors; like the plume
That bobs here on my hat, let them all bow
Before your feet in meek obedience!

## Scene 2

MARY
Douglas, a moment's not passed since I spied
Morton down by the palace gate. Quickly,
Take this command to him, for it requires
The seal of the chancellor.

*Douglas takes the paper from the queen, looks it over, and waits.*

                        What's this?
The virtue of a knight is blind obedience —
Do you deny this to a woman? A queen?

DOUGLAS
A queen? O, no — there's not a treacherous fibre
In all of Douglas' frame. But — you'll forgive me;
What's on this paper, ma'am, was writ in haste,
At such a sudden moment, and it lacks
The name of Henry, and his title, King —
Whom all the people hold in holy awe;
Whose name was always paired with yours. Perhaps —
Forgive my boldness — you might deign correct
The oversight?

MARY
              The queen overlooks nothing
When she commands!

DOUGLAS
*With contempt.*
                        And so, from the queen's lips
I'd be commanded, and dismissed.

MARY
                    Do it!

DOUGLAS
*Ardently.*
For God's sake, please, your Majesty! Recall
This bloody order! Will you have a stream
Of blood lead, like a carpet, to your throne?

A woman's throne? Who was it set alight
The torch of discord in the palace walls?
Some hidden enemy? Or does the wind
Blow pestilence from France beyond the sea?
This verdict — comes it from some barcarolle
That's crooned in Venice? Or a Papal hymn
So loud it's heard in Scotland? Thirst for blood!
What's to be done? The chancellor — give way,
Remain...

MARY
Enough! Remember this well, Douglas!
I am unharmed by your insulting words,
But you've set out on unchivalrous paths.
Look that you not lose spurs or velvet sash.
Should Morton's trembling hand let fall the seal,
Then that shall lift it, that shakes the commonweal.
I am the queen!

DOUGLAS
              Am I to lose my spurs?
You'd merely scrape the gold from them; the iron
Beneath will shine more brightly. They were not
Won by deceit, nor harping, nor by song;
Nor did I find them at this royal footstool.
The fields of Albion can tell you how
I came by them — in clashes, through sleepless nights,
Both mine, and those of noble ancestors —
A long and noble line, and every sword
Of theirs — like mine — served Stuart faithfully.

RIZZIO
Sometimes the sword, and sometimes... the stiletto...

DOUGLAS
You speak, wretch? You'll declare how Douglas repays
An insult? My spurned ancestors avenged
Themselves upon the Stuarts, upon the court!
Upon whom shall I wreak revenge? Come, puppet, coward,
With all your ringlets and your powdered cheeks;
Here, boy — I toss my gauntlet.

*Throws down his glove.*
Now, pick it up, indeed, if you've the strength.

RIZZIO
*Picking up the glove.*
I do, and so I repay you in kind.
*Picks up some flowers lying on the table near the queen, and throws them at Douglas' feet.*
Pick up the blooms — if you like flowers, sir.
Only such weapons ought to be unsheathed
Before the queen…

MARY
*To Rizzio.*
                Set now his glove aside!
That is an order.

RIZZIO
                Gladly. I've no sword,
And I find iron heavy for my hand…
Lend my your fan, my lady.

DOUGLAS
*Furious*
                    Yet again
He insults me, tossing my glove aside?
Your Majesty — though he may hide beneath
The shadow of your throne, still I shall find him!
He shall not sleep beneath a roof in flames!
I'll harry him, I swear. He will not fight?
Then I'll become a vulgar murderer,
But he'll be murdered! Always shall I chase,
And never cast the line until the kill
Which shall come sure as sunrise.
He will find me in the palace where he dared
To spread treason; he'll find me at the gates,
And in the courtyard; he'll find me in church;
He'll find me at the French court, the Papal throne,
Though he spread flowers before his feet, as now,
And cringe upon them, I shall seize his neck
And lift him up — I swear, a knightly oath…!

*Coldly, with contempt.*
Some day, your Majesty, when you are encircled
By courtiers, all at ease, the bitterness
Of rule set by for a moment's relaxation;
Some day when you are smiling — you'll behold me,
And, smiling like a flirty courtesan,
I shall present you with these blooms — dipped in his blood!

MARY
Rizzio! Get you from this room! Retire!
Douglas, behold: I am of Stuart blood
And know how to contemn.

*She exits, Rizzio following. After a moment, Rizzio returns.*

RIZIO
                    Tomorrow, Douglas.
I will await you in the gardens — there
Where the cool pantries stand — and by the sword
You'll lose your life, or gain your satisfaction.
*He runs off after the queen.*

## Scene 3

DOUGLAS
Tomorrow! Thank you! — for now wiping clean
The foul stains of the insult you'd just smudged there.
Tomorrow! — you will rest in a still grave...
Who would have thought he'd such courage in him?
He seemed so cowardly! His very hand
Trembled, throwing down the flowers before me...
Was that contempt? It cannot be, for him
To hold a Douglas in contempt! He knows
I threaten him with sure death...
*In thought, then, more calmly.*
                            Does he know
The swordsman's art? That base strummer of harps?
I couldn't make myself strike a naked chest...
I'll give him a well-tested sword, one longer
Than mine... I can defend my honour with
A shorter blade... O that the night would fall!

I'd like to sleep — the hours fly by in sleep...
When I awake, the heavens will be bright.

## Scene 4

*Enter Morton.*

DOUGLAS
Greetings, Grand Chancellor — I was just looking for you;
Come see how conjugal love develops
When a harp's sweet voice resounds.
*He shows him the command.*
                                        Your seal, please.

MORTON
*Looks at the document.*
But where is Henry? There's no mention of him?
And I'm to seal this? But If I refuse,
The queen will say...

DOUGLAS
                    The queen has said already:
"Should Morton's trembling hand let fall the seal,
Then that shall lift it, that shakes the commonweal."

MORTON
She said that? In your presence?

DOUGLAS
                    I heard her
With my own ears.

MORTON
                    Her Majesty said that?

DOUGLAS
Ha, ha! I see the chasm that now yawns
Beneath your feet! You'd better seal it, then.

MORTON
But when the king finds out? What will he say?

DOUGLAS
That isn't hard to guess:
"The seal that from Morton's hand, trembling, fell
Is picked up by that hand, jangling with bells."
*Laughing, he exits.*

MORTON
Wait, Douglas, wait! This news — so frightening!
Should I go to the queen? No — to the king!
*Exits.*

### Scene 5
*Henry Darnley's apartments.*

NICK
Reward me, Sire.

HENRY
              For what?

NICK
                    For, like a knight
Returning from the fray without his arms,
So I return from battle sans my bells.

HENRY
*Laughing.*
O, what a loss!

NICK
                Should Morton chance upon them,
He'll take them for his own, and my daily bread, too.
So how will you repay me for my loss?
All that I know of you is in those bells —
Just like old Midas' secret, in the earth:
Thou shalt no longer laugh, Nick — mirth is dead!*
*After a moment's thought.*

---

\*     In Polish: Śmiać się nie będziesz, wesołość zabiłem. "You shall not laugh, I have killed gaiety," with the subject of the second clause unclear.

Take the biretta off of Knox's head,
And Douglas' helmet from his. Let there be
No difference between men. This I ask.

HENRY
Ha, ha! What will you not dream up! Let Knox
Forever preach from pulpit in his cap,
And Douglas — let him defend the fatherland
Armed cap-à-pie. I'll have some new bells made;
You'll soon be prancing in new livery.

NICK
Besides the clothes, will Nick get anything?
Poor Nick is poor…

HENRY
                What would you have besides?

NICK
*Thinks.*
Give me, my sire, a portrait of the queen.

HENRY
I'll give you mine.

NICK
                I don't want yours! A shilling!
For there she's pictured in her crown. Not you —
Your face is on no shilling.

HENRY
                Now I'm slain!
The sharp words of a jester pierce my chest.
I am a king — I am no king — I stand
Amazed myself at how long I have suffered
This blot upon my honour. Now, enough!
Enough humiliation! Wherever I be
I hear the smallest children say, "O, look —
The husband of the queen!" Why not "the king?"
"The husband of the queen." Such is my fame?
*Falls to musing.*

NICK
*As if to himself.*
He gave me no coin... I can take no more!
I'll find somebody else. This time, no miser.
I'm Henry's servant, Rizzio serves Mary,
And which is better off? When I arrived
Here at the court, unknown, with a sealed bag
Of laughter, I was given a motley suit,
A stick with a two-faced head for a knob,
A cap-and-bells, a belt, pendant therefrom
Two empty purses — empty still today,
And hanging at the same now threadbare waist.
At the same time as I, that Roman came —
His travelling bags — like mine — were filled with wind;
Two-faced himself (like my wand), on his back
A poor thin coat — thin as his purse was poor,
And now? He's brilliant in the finest velvet;
He's a plume at his cap and spurs at heel;
His purse is bulging with coins from which Mary
Sends him her constant smile of amity;
His back is covered by her royal robe —
If only he'd a jester like me, why
There'd be no telling between him and... that king.

*He nods at Henry with a malicious grin.*

His mind's a-slumber. Come, let's wake him up.
Your Majesty, is that a harp I hear?

HENRY
Where?

NICK
　　　　In the throne room...?

HENRY
　　　　　　　　　　You're a devil, Nick!
I hear it, and it torments me, that harp!
O, let the castle crumble into ruin,
And bury throne and harp...! Where can I rest?

I hear it in my sleep! I wake unrested,
And hear it at my rising! What's to do?

NICK
Put on my cap-a-bells. They'll drown it out.

HENRY
I'll slice those harp-strings with my own stiletto!

## Scene 6

*Enter Morton.*

MORTON
I've urgent news, your royal Majesty,
Important news... I'm well-disposed, you know,
Noble...

HENRY
      Who doubts it?

MORTON
                    O hear me out, my prince!

HENRY
Prince?

MORTON
      King! Hear me out! I cannot find the words...
This rescript — here — my seal is demanded...

HENRY
*Looks it over.*
What is this? Where's my name? On whose command?
No, there's been some mistake...

MORTON
*Smiling.*
                For sure! The king's
Been left out by mistake...

HENRY

                                  You doubt it, age?
I'll go and see the queen — It all shall change!
I'll go, and lash her for unfaithfulness...
No, I'll beseech her... Living long apart,
Our feelings had to shift; our disaccord
Is — almost my fault. Empty jealousy
Tore us apart, and then deceitful minds
Betrayed us — but the queen loved me once,
And still she does. Where is Queen Mary now?

MORTON

In her apartments, with Rizzio at her side,
Urging her, certainly, to change the order.

HENRY
*With violence.*
Rizzio! Rizzio! Has he risen so high
As now to snatch my crown? Who will deliver me
From Rizzio?

MORTON

                    Sire, I'm capable of that...
I offer myself. Accuse him of some crime.
You be the prosecutor, I'll defend him,
And he shall die.

HENRY

                      You wretch! That's your advice?
You want to seem guiltless in the queen's eyes —
As white as snow, your hands washed clean of blood!
I am to go to court? In purple? Crowned?
I, Henry, in some vulgar suit with Rizzio?
That vile Italian might just win acquittal
And have all the more license to insult me!
No! I will stain these hands of mine with blood —
His blood, which shall provide me a fat harvest:
Peace in my home, again... Yes, let me think...
What good is thinking? I've thought overmuch.
And my thought is as clear and bright as heaven,
As black as hell. I've pondered long, and coldly —

Today I'll act upon my thought, and boldly!
Furiously! Before the day is through
The grave that's dug today will have its due.

NICK
*Spying Morton's joy, which he cannot conceal.*
What is it, Morton? You've not found my bells?
For you were witty, now you're jubilant;
Give back my bells — be chancellor again.


## Scene 7

*Enter Lindsay.*

LINDSAY
My king, today I've got another king —
The king of birds! A young Norwegian falcon!
His mail and beams all silver — When he soars,
The eye can't spy him, on the roads of heaven!

HENRY
What? is he handsomer than my own falcon?

LINDSAY
Ha, ha! There's no comparison. He's lighter,
A trifle smaller — a toy for a woman's hand.
Once, Lady Hamilton, hunting by the Clyde,
Bore him upon her wrist; he hunted well —
Never returning without prey, his claws
Gilded with blood, like the spurs of a knight.
Come hunt today!

MORTON
          The king is occupied.

HENRY
Indeed, my friend. I'm after other game
Today — and I must hold my quarry's scent.
Lindsay, the crown has fallen from my brow!
I am a woman's toy, a laughingstock!

I am denied both rule and ancestry;
I am a hollow king! Can you believe it?

LINDSAY
Such being the case, be off then to fierce vengeance.
Let someone thus insult my hunting skills,
And he would pay!

HENRY
     Before this day's sun sets,
Help me, my Lindsay, to set out my nets.
You know the traitor's name? It's Rizzio!
That wretched foreigner! Tonight the moon
Will shine upon his fresh grave. He arrived
A vagrant, as a criminal he dies.
Will you aid me?

LINDSAY
     With all my heart, I will.
'Twas he forbade me hunt in my own brakes!
I'll have my own revenge.

HENRY
     And a reward —
His deer parks, for your hunting pleasure.

## Scene 8

*Enter Douglas.*

LINDSAY
*To Douglas.*
How is it Rizzio so cheated death?
The echo of your quarrel carried wide.
I heard…

DOUGLAS
   You may have heard. But lest you bruit
The matter further — mind: a bell grows mute
When its tongue is torn out…

LINDSAY
                        Then join with us!
Today stilettos; today fresh revenge
Removes the enemy that's stained your honour!

DOUGLAS
Who dares entrust his honour to other blades?
I warn you — I desire that Rizzio live.
Tomorrow I'll hand you your vengeance; today
Is his to live. Today the breast of Douglas
Repulses your stilettos from his own!
If blood's to flow today, it shall be yours.
I don't suppose you itch to fight me, Morton?
And I'm no stag for you to aim at, Lindsay!
And you, Henry, would do well to remember
That your crown is of thinner metal forged
Than Douglas' sword! Put off until tomorrow
All thought of vengeance. He who does not do,
Is Douglas' enemy.
*Exit.*


## Scene 9

LINDSAY
What was that? Has Douglas gone mad from despair?

MORTON
Let not his threats cause you to waver, sire!

HENRY
No — But still, let's leave it till tomorrow.
I'm satisfied our anger should mature.
The hasty-blooming flower wilts too soon.
My knights, let no fear make you start your covert;
We hold our victim's life safe in our grip.
*To Nick.*
And you, my little clown, run to consult
The star-gazer about our bloody plans.

[END OF ACT I]

# ACT II

*The apartments of the Astrologer. In the centre, a table piled with books. At the windows, telescopes point toward the skies.*

## Scene 1

ASTROLOGER
*Solus.*
All science is vain. Its fruit is bitterness!
To teach, to delve — and then to disbelieve,
In constant torment to expand the range
Of dreams — but ah, to read the constellations!
The stars, O, are they not the book of fate?
Predestination... madness to fight against it;
You who wring your bloodied hands — lift up
Your pale brows — curse your fate, if you so please,
But cease tormenting yourself with your conscience.
The stars are guilty of the blood you shed!
Your cradle rocked a murderer to sleep;
Your mother's milk was spiced with bitterness!
And you, O virtuous one, will die a wretch,
But cease your wailing. That merit was not your own.
If only, in your final agony,
You realise the vanity of virtue:
Virtue without one freely willing it —
What? All your life long you struggled... for nothing!
Thus it is to be lonely on the earth.
And can there be another world?

## Scene 2

*Enter Nick.*

NICK
                              Greetings, Father.

ASTROLOGER
Father? Whence our consanguinity?

NICK
Wisdom is sired by foolishness, and in turn,
Wisdom sires madness. Thus I am your son,
And all these books, my sisters, sired by you.

ASTROLOGER
What do you know, wretch, of the power of wisdom?
Your thoughts never overleap the bounds of earth!

NICK
So, lead me farther, Father, I beseech you.
*Squints through a telescope.*
Ha, ha!

ASTROLOGER
  What do you see?

NICK
      The sky.

ASTROLOGER
        And there?

NICK
*Coldly.*
Nothing at all.

ASTROLOGER
    But it's sown thick with worlds.

NICK
*Looking through a telescope the wrong way round.*
Aha!

ASTROLOGER
  What do you see?

NICK

                        The earth.

ASTROLOGER

                               And there?

NICK

                                       Nothing.

ASTROLOGER
But you must have seen me, is that not so?

NICK
Yes, but far off — like a speck of dust.
Look not aloft — you'll lose yourself amongst
Immensity. Look to the earth, but look
The wrong way round. How small they seem! Fame! Learning!
The best of lenses make distances greater.
Thus the king's clown sets forth his Q.E.D.s.
The king's wiseman…

ASTROLOGER

                    Lets the king's clown prate as he please.
Why have you come here?

NICK

                        The queen's husband would
Inquire after the fate of Rizzio.
But — don't let stuff and nonsense trouble your head —
I've read his fate. Tomorrow he'll be dead.
And you will tell the king… just what I've said.

ASTROLOGER
Be off with you! I do not need your aid.
Take this note to the king — it's confidential —
I've read the fate of Rizzio this night.
All of his stars grew pale, their silver cheeks
Buried in clouds. Begone now!

NICK
>One more thing_

What's in my stars?

ASTROLOGER
>A quick death.

NICK
>And thereafter?

ASTROLOGER
I've no idea.

NICK
>Till we meet again,

My peer in wisdom.
*Exits.*

ASTROLOGER
>O sordid human flesh,

That clothes profundity in foolishness!

## Scene 3

*Enter Page.*

PAGE
The jester's gone? That's good. At your summons
I've come, wise master.

ASTROLOGER
>Listen, young sirrah —

Do you love the queen?

PAGE
>How can you even ask?

Do I love the queen? What sort of evidence
Do you require? I love her as a mother,
A sister... I love her as an angel.
My happiness entire's to spend each hour
From sleep to waking at her feet, so close

A rose petal will fall upon my knee,
Half-wilted from the chaplet on her brow;
Sometimes, I cool her heated countenance
That glows with blushing, with a gilded fan;
Sometimes, at humble prayer before the altar
I'll hold her missal open — and at times
I'll hold her robe's hem as she goes. So happy
Am I!

ASTROLOGER
       Then wait not a moment longer,
But rush off to the queen, and, secretly,
Tell her: the man she holds more dearly
Than throne or life itself will die today.

PAGE
What's this you say? Bothwell will die today?

ASTROLOGER
*With surprise.*
Bothwell? I was to warn another man?
I wasn't thinking of Bothwell at all!

PAGE
*In despair.*
O, I've betrayed her! Into such a pit
I've fallen! Don't believe me; she herself
Never confessed so much, never put in words...
I've read her blushing merely... I have erred!
No, she's not in love with Bothwell! Forget it!
O, let my pleas, my despair, move you to mistrust
My light words! Hush! Defend the queen's honour!
I drank in all your words with thirsty soul —
No wonder that they jarred this out of me?
O, my misfortune! With one touch you've sprung
The darkest secret, from the deepest pit
Of my unwary heart. Forget it! I beg you!
*Unpinning a brooch from his cap.*
Here: take this bauble, and forget it all.
You have already, right? As I forgive
My debtors — at once — you're no different?

ASTROLOGER
Come child! Can learning make an old man vile?
The queen has smothered me in grace and honour.
She wouldn't favour so a traitorous wretch.
Keep you your gems — I pardon you the offer —
Which shows your too light estimation of me.
Look round the room. All this my Lady gave me:
The priceless books... and gold, and manors, too.
Someday I'll pay her back her many favours —
You see the black juice brimming in these goblets?
The embryo of gold matures therein —
The very sort of ore Peru brings Spain.
At the queen's feet I'll spill far greater treasure,
In such largesse, she'll purchase continents.

PAGE
Bu who is going to die, then?

ASTROLOGER
      Rizzio!
A pack of dirks is speeding towards his heart.
Tomorrow, you'll bedew his shroud with tears.
His murderers are strong — so say the stars.

PAGE
Father! I go!
*He runs off.*


## Scene 4

ASTROLOGER
*Taking in hand one of the goblets.*
     Herein are poured my hopes.
I dare not broach these goblets. Ha! When shall I?
Perhaps tonight the gold will flash to me?
*Gazes into the goblet.*
None yet — it's still too early — but tomorrow?
And so, tomorrow. But what's gold to me?
Ask yourself, old man, what for? Fame? What's fame?
Glory to the contrivance! Doggedness,
Devotion is a virtue — Can't the same

Be said about the tiller of the soil?
All my life long I've dreamed... So near the grave,
Shall I now learn the emptiness of dreams?
That art leads to no end? O, that would kill me!
No, in a manner strange, the page's words
Enweave themselves with the idiom of the stars.
The queen! And Bothwell! These two names, together?
The queen loves Bothwell? This day, over his head,
Mars and Saturn are in conjunction: signs
That mean... O Bothwell! The stars speak!

## Scene 5

*Enter Bothwell, in thought.*

BOTHWELL
Why have I come here? I must be insane!
To sip the future? To quaff it to the lees!
The drapes of hope enshroud my future not —
But ah, the silent curtains that obscure
My death — O, death has always made me smile.
But should the drapes part — will my smile fade?
What is it I've desired? Yes, who knows
What that old man might read writ in my soul?
Perhaps he shall reveal what I've not dared
Reveal unto myself. Shall he uncover
The chasm that yawns at my feet? In the morning,
I shall awaken, and hurl myself therein.
I'd know the future? Ha! May I survive
The present merely! Why have I come here?
I shall retire, yes, I'll go back... And yet...
What is to happen, has already happened.
I shall remain. Old man, can you foretell
The future?

ASTROLOGER
          What is written in the stars,
That have I studied.

BOTHWELL
     Then — sincerely — say:
Do you believe in what you spell out there?

ASTROLOGER
As certainly as I believe in death.

BOTHWELL
You've never been mistaken?

ASTROLOGER
        Never.

BOTHWELL
         Vain, then,
The science of the world! The promises
Of this day are deceived in their results.
Will I live long?

ASTROLOGER
   Three years.

BOTHWELL
*Contemptuously.*
       Three years? That end
Is far too distant — your mistake's too great.
Three days are overmuch! Three years? O, vain!
Look at me, astrologer. On my pale face
You see a bitter and contemptuous smile.
But dare not look inside me — Who's so bold
As to inspect the contents of a tomb?
Crimes have not charred me; here is fullness of life;
My heart has burned hot since I first was born —
But now I'm tired, cold, and I must die.
*Holds out a crystal vial containing poison.*
Behold: I've poison, and nought to stop my hand,
Unless it's shunted by the fixedness
Of your predictions wise? What if I drink it,
And fall dead, now, here, at your aged feet,
And free myself from long pain, with one spasm?
For I am dying.

ASTROLOGER
*Takes Bothwell by the hand and leads him to the table upon which the horoscopes are spread.*
                      No, Bothwell. You'll live
Three years yet. See what's written in the stars.
You shall be king…

BOTHWELL
                              King? What is this you say?
I shall be king? Is this a goal to aim at,
When tottering at the grave, wherein is rest?
I shall be king… Shall I curse you, or thank you?
I don't know. Tell me, old man, will I know more pain
Enthroned or entombed? For the grave swallows
All men. Perhaps my life will sprout
Bitterer fruit. And for what reason, man?
Why should one chase such evanescent dreams?
I'll drink the poison… No, I'll pour it out…!
But why? Maybe I'll want it later on;
It's good to be well packed for such a journey…
And have I not dreamt crowns before? You've won!
Astrologer, I shall live!

ASTROLOGER
                    I have won.

BOTHWELL
On to the goal. I shall not die before
My time. Astrologer, lead me into
Your high-ceilinged chambers and show me
The worlds that rule my fate.
*Exit both.*


## Scene 6
*The queen's chamber. To the rear, a Gothic window.*

PAGE.
Soon Rizzio will be here.

MARY
                       What's keeping him?
From once so many friends, just he remains,
And soon he is to die.

PAGE
                     Ma'am, you're unjust!

Calling to mind your friends, remember Bothwell.
I haven't the right to say, "remember me..."

MARY
You're growing up, my dear, and soon shall leave me,
Exchanging fan for sword. Fame beckons you.
And who will then make bright this wilderness?
Bothwell? I know him not. Oh, my beloved!
You weep, my page?

PAGE
                     These are but childish tears...
Pardon me, ma'am — I just thought I might win
My spurs here at your court, defending you.
The thought of parting never roiled my sleep;
And now for the first time, I sense it might
Just come about — and this mere thought deprives me
Of half my knightly valour. Ah, but Bothwell
Has spurs? And he is here at court,
And might be closer, closer still, to you.

MARY
*Echoing the thought, pensively.*
Bothwell, yes, might be closer to the queen...

PAGE
So was he yesterday, amidst the court,
When he squired you, my lady, at the hunt.
I saw strange sadness etched upon his brows.
And then, when you stepped on the gilded bark,
Bothwell stood at the helm, and then grew pale.
He gazed in the deep water, as if he saw
There, some strange, unnerving wonder;

Low he bent, lower still... I've never seen
Such thought fixed on a person's face... I shivered,
And still can't understand it. Even now
It grips me like a bad dream...

MARY
                                        Guiltless child!
I understand it clear enough — the wild
Thoughts of the frenzied...

PAGE
                                    O, your Majesty!
The winds that filled your sails then, on the water,
Sent forth a bolder gust which, from the wreath
That wound your bright-haired brows, cast down
A rose, which fell upon the waves, and bobbed
Behind us — Bothwell then uprose
And, shivering, nodded to his servants;
A skiff made ready, he jumped in, alone,
And went off after the torn bloom. I watched him
For a long time until he disappeared
In the mist.

MARY
*Impatiently.*
                        Go now. Be off, my faithful servant!
But leave the fan to cool my brows... It's hot...
Be off with you! It's time for evensong.

*Page exits.*

## Scene 7

MARY
*Sola.*
That page has sharp eyes — but he can't believe
That love is criminal, and leads
To errant paths. Long have I tried to stifle
This love that will not be put down. O, Bothwell!
I shall see him — I shall depart the court.
The slightest breath will stain the looking glass...

What? I'm guiltless! Must I fear appearances?
I have been slandered long with dark suspicions —
They think that I love Rizzio! O, childish fear!
Who has the right to judge me? I myself.
The people are at my feet — God is above me.
　　　　　Such was I yesterday... Today I'm guilty.
I love Bothwell! I love him! May God judge me.
This crown lies heavy upon me — the French crown
Was poured of lighter metal... For a while,
I'll set it down.
*Takes off the crown.*
　　　　　And thus, now am I freed
Of all the ties that bind me — You burden!
O, how you weighed upon my brow! Your sheen,
Seductive, many a man has terrified,
And many a man repelled... Now I am free.
No — I still have this heavy wedding band...
*Takes it from her finger.*
And now, my Bothwell, come to me! Appear!
I have no crown, I wear no wedding ring,
Come, Bothwell! I fear neither slander nor Hell;
Your gloomy face casts on me such a spell —
Your bitter smile, your cloudy moodiness...
I'll chase away the thought of death that slumbers
Deep in the furrows of your brows,
With smile sincere and tender. For too long
Trudging a round of gloomy thought, from now on
You shall be handsomer still, being happy.


## Scene 8

RIZZIO
You summoned me, my queen?

MARY
　　　　　　　　　　　*In fear and trembling*
I've called you, Rizzio, to these private rooms.
You are in danger. For the flowers you threw
At Douglas' feet have gone to deadly seed.
Listen to me in patience, my errant knight —
You can stay here no longer. Against the swords

Of enemies a buckler will protect you,
But you are threatened by stilettos — sharp,
Treacherous death. Believe me: He does ill
Who puts his life into the hands of foes
Unknown. You must evade the blow. Today
You must leave here. I shall entrust you with
A message to the Pope of great import.
Your ship awaits, its sails well-nigh unfurled.
Farewell!

RIZZIO
      Your Majesty! Repeat those words!
No — say them not again — I shall not heed,
Here on the very edge of the abyss,
Although I merit your anger thereby;
My death cannot dishonour you, indeed?
Nor sadden you? Your Majesty — Mary!
I shall remain! I seal this with an oath,
And nothing shall deflect me from my resolve.
Your words sentence me to a death more bitter —
Although your sweet lips spoke them; even though
Your voice trembled when shaping them — Mary,
Listen...!

MARY
      Rizzio! Deign address the queen.
The words you spoke were formed for someone else.

RIZZIO
Where is your crown then? 'Tis not on your brow;
The rosy chaplet that you bear instead
Makes you my peer — and so I boldly spoke.
Forgive me! For I thought... I thought... Madman...!
That you had doffed it for me.

MARY
                You were wrong.
You know I wear no crown when I'm at prayer —
And I've been praying.

RIZZIO
                          Forgive me my mistake.
But do not place it back upon your front —
It wearies you, and covers some gloomy mourning.

MARY
I am not used to speak to the people uncovered.
I speak thus only with God, or
*More softly.*                  with myself.

RIZZIO
You've stolen my courage. All right, I'll be gone.
*Sits down at the Gothic window. With studied indifference.*
The weather's nice — it's a good day for travel;
The sky is clear and blue: soft, pale clouds,
They indicate my road, threatening no storm.
Come see, your Majesty, how calm outside —
Your flowers, freshened with the dew, in bloom;
The Scottish mountains, bordered with such blue,
And distant as a dream... And hear the sea!
It roars! The ships, in mist enveloped, rock...
*Rizzio turns from the window and covers his face with his hands.*
With sails unfurled... O, I can look no longer!

MARY
Rizzio — You are as weak as a child!

RIZZIO
                                My Lady!
Do you wish to preserve my life, indeed?
But life has lost all comeliness for me.
Soon I shall watch this castle fade away
Into the blue haze, from ship's deck, a sea
Beneath me — Ha! Who knows whither I sail?
I'll throw myself into the bustling world;
Oblivion shall wrap me in its cloak...
O, dark! And ever darker! Shall I not
Return here, ever? I am quite consumed,
And overcome with pain — Shall I return?
Why? To choke back my tears and sighs? And she

Cannot, she will not, understand. And so
I go, lonely, but wish her happiness.

MARY
*Moved.*
Rizzio!

RIZZIO
   Say my name again! Once more!
The language of your soul breaks through your words.

MARY
*Coldly.*
And thus, I ask you, when you are in Rome,
Request the Holy Father that he send
Bread of the Lord's Table to me, enclosed
In a gold pyx...

RIZZIO
*With consternation.*
     O pious sovereign!
Abusing hearts and killing: these are virtues!
And after such good deeds, you still can pray?
All smudges can be blotted out.\* Farewell.

MARY
We all are buffeted by the winds of Fate.
Farewell! I shall ever think well of you.

RIZZIO
Then I'm to go?

MARY
   Why do you ask?

---

\* The original Polish reads: *Wszystko zgładzić można*, which, in the context, suggests that "all rough spaces can be smoothed." However, the Polish verb *zgładzić* can mean "exterminate" as well as "wipe out" — a sinister sort of double entendre for such a bloody drama.

RIZZIO
                              Forgive me,
But yet there was a sadness in your voice,

A tenderness — more tender than your words.
Permit me one more day. I'll leave tomorrow.

MARY
*With irony.*
Remain! Remain! Today you may, and sinless —
There is a ball at court, there will be masks,
I will wear one myself: the Happy Queen.
Come then — We'll have a new round of farewells,
And jolly ones, from a smiling, laughing queen!

RIZZIO
Madame, goodbye. Forever!
*Exits.*

MARY
                              I wound him
With words. He fears my laughter. He'll stay no more.
One word will save him from a certain death:
The bitterest pills most surely work our health.

[END OF ACT II]

# ACT III

## Scene i

*A garden — night — amidst the trees and flowers, Holy Rood Castle may be seen, along with the chapel of the Holy Cross. The windows of the palace are lit; the moon is shining.*

BOTHWELL
*Solus.*
That old man held me back at the grave's lip —
He dreamed, and I believed in his dreaming;
To die... to be the king... I'd have been dead...
Now, am I one step closer to the throne?
I am — who I was — deceived with fantasies.
Perhaps I move too quickly toward my goal?
I wish to check this morning's prophecies
Tonight; today it's early — tomorrow,
Bothwell, you'll seat yourself upon the throne.
O star, to which my destiny is hitched,
You shine as yet too weakly on my path.
Perhaps it's stained with blood... shine out more brightly!
I'm not afraid of blood... The gloomy chapel
Of Holy Cross... Will they pray there for me?
When I am in the grave — or on the throne —
When I secrete my hands incarnadined
Within the purple folds of a king's robe...
Will they pray for me then? Here at this court
There are so many flirting parasites
Bloated with hope and ardour... I am like
A beggar at the gates... The windows glow
With light — and there — a shade flits by the panes...
Yes, it is she! The queen! I saw her crown!
Closer, ah closer! Heaven! Have I the strength?
My eyes are fevered with flashes of colour...
If any man should see me in this state
He'd cry with pity, "Bothwell, you are sick!
Off to the hospital! Listen! You're mad...!"

## Scene 2

PAGE
I've been all over looking for you, Bothwell —
And here you are, strolling the queen's own gardens?

BOTHWELL
Seeking refreshment in the evening cool.

PAGE
It's pleasant here, is it not? Among the poplars,
The flowers breathe more sweetly, all the blooms...
And yet the handsomest rose of all is there,
Inside the castle. Would you like to see her?

BOTHWELL
What? Will the queen permit it?

PAGE
                                        She has already.

BOTHWELL
Me? In her presence? When?

PAGE
                                        In one hour's time.

BOTHWELL
You have this from her lips?

PAGE
                                        'Tis her command.

BOTHWELL
*[Bitterly]*
Shine on, my star! I'll strike out for the sea...
May I, against the teeth of rocks submerged
Bottom out — what care I? The auguries were true!

PAGE
My lord, my lord, chase your sadness away!
With such bugbears, the queen you'll terrorise.
From your dark brow, the gloom will snuff her eyes.

BOTHWELL
*With irony.*
You'd have me chase the sadness from my brow?
I'll spend an hour before the glass, right now
Since it's so easy, to arrange one's face…
This bitter smile — 'tis not the fruit of pain?
I'll wipe it off, if it's just a child's game…
My face was guiltless once, just like a child's!
I'll grin like one to whom the world is mild.
And this brow, furrowed with such lines of care —
Like love-letters on parchment writ, no doubt
One scratch will suffice — they're no longer there!
Or if not, ink will serve to blot them out.
Farewell!
*Exits.*

PAGE
      He chills me with such bitterness…
So. Off to Rizzio, at the queen's behest.


## Scene 3

HENRY
And so it's true? Rizzio eludes our grasp?

MORTON
It's not good news, this trip. So of a sudden —
His men have brought his kit aboard the ship,
Which is to sail — under the colours of France.
We must make haste — we know not his intents.
But those French lilies provide him with good shade.

HENRY
And so he shall evade just punishment
Before he sets a foot aboard that ship,
Let him die on the shingle.

LINDSAY
            Haste then, haste!

HENRY
Hold on, hold on, let me give it some thought —
Haste has not served us well thus far. Should I,
The king, stain these my royal hands with blood?
There on the beach are crowds of witnesses —
So many: sailors, and the vulgar sort,
Who later might shoot an accusing finger
In my direction — What a frightful thought!
They'll point, or they'll insult me to my face
If it should pale — who knows how it would end?
Rizzio sails? Well, let him sail away!
His corpse entombed, here, so nigh to the queen
Would cause me more harm than Rizzio alive
And far away.

LINDSAY
            My lord, finish the chase!
We've nearly got the timid stag at bay!

HENRY
No — let him sail.

MORTON
                Yes, let him go with God!
And let him spread your fame about the earth.
You're still not all that well known on French soil?
That harper, in voluntary exile
Will introduce you to the French. At court,
They'll cense him piously! In the royal halls
His friendship will be much sought after — he
Might be of aid, you know! He holds the heart
Of Mary in his palm. And thus the beam
Of Scotland's scales of power. And as for you...?

HENRY
What would you say?

MORTON
                    That Henry is the king...
In Scotland.

HENRY
                    Lindsay! Hear you what he dares
To say? I am the king!

MORTON
                    O, Lindsay hears
My words and gives them credit. And when Rizzio
Drinks to satiety the paltry fumes
Of incense, shall he not go to the Pope?
Then will you see him come back here, from Rome,
Wearing a wide brimmed red hat. Well, you know —
He even looks like Wolsey! We shall fall
Prone at his feet — Darnley himself will say
All hope of vengeance now has flown away.

HENRY
Enough! I go!

*They make to leave, but suddenly meet with Douglas, and halt.*


## Scene 4
DOUGLAS
                    Stop! Rizzio has already sailed.

HENRY
He goes! And with him, my hopes for revenge!
Now would I waver no more! ... I'll to the strand
And have them hold the boat.

DOUGLAS
                                    It's under weigh.
This is my fault. Revenge yourselves on me.
I bear my breast to you, and sheathe my sword.
This blood is worth a Rizzio. I'm so degraded,
I trust no person. I trust not myself.
I would have cut the thread of life myself,

But — who knows why? Was it fear restrained my hand?
I feared to strike him down in the queen's presence,
And feared to kill myself before my God.
That vagrant's life lies heavy on my conscience;
I trusted in the word of a lutenist,
To take the field of honour like a knight.
Will you trust any man, now? I'm burdened with
A heavy shame — And seeking my way out
Of this immensity of misfortune
I see but one step from shame to the grave —
Which one of you will hide me from the eyes
Of a contemptuous world? If only he'd —
Before leaping abroad — declared his fright
Was not of your stilettos, but this sword —
I might still live.

## Scene 5
*Enter Page at a run; Douglas grabs him by his shirt.*

DOUGLAS
      The page! The page must die —
And I shall kill him. The page loves the queen
No less than Rizzio.

*Douglas spies a paper in the Page's hand. He tears it from him.*

        But what do we have here?
I see some unclear signs here on the parchment —
Read it...

PAGE
     It is a letter to the queen!
You have no right to read it!

LINDSAY
*Takes the paper from Douglas.*
        Might is right.
*Reads.*
"I thank your Majesty, for permitting me

To spend this evening in your presence." Signed:
Rizzio.

DOUGLAS
    Rizzio? You're eyes are not deceived?

LINDSAY
The monks taught me to read, and I learn well.

HENRY
So Rizzio is to spend this night at court?
This is betrayal — some Italian ruse...
But no — He must have  stayed — our ambuscades
We're wrongly set. Lindsay, confine the page
To my apartments, lest the boy betray
Our plans, and hinder their accomplishment.

PAGE
You fear betrayal? You teach me it yourselves!
Douglas! The mark of shame's burnt on your brow!
Hand me a sword as long as that you carry,
And I will wash it clean in your heart's blood!

LINDSAY
You're still a child, page! O, you new-fledged tercel —
You're yet to moult in your first spring. Come with me.

PAGE
Remember — all of you — I'll grow to manhood.

*Lindsay exits, leading the page.*

DOUGLAS
So Rizzio must die!

HENRY
                When?

DOUGLAS
                        Today?

HENRY
                                          And where?

DOUGLAS
Do you still hesitate? In the throne room!
At the queen's feet! Even should she hide
Him in her royal robes, I'll hunt him there,
And pierce him with this steel.

HENRY
                             But if you do,
And in the very presence of the queen,
With that same blade you slice me from her side,
Forever!

DOUGLAS
        Ha! Then bear contempt and shame
Forever. Since you're not emboldened by
Disdain, nothing will spur you to revenge!
Go! Cower at her feet in meekness feigned!
But be aware: no woman loves a man
Whom she once dared despise.

HENRY
                           Despise? She never!
Today I shall be bold — today I'll prove
My manhood — Come, let us take our stilettos
Blessed at Loreto, then, by secret stairs
I'll lead you to him.
*Exit, with Douglas.*

MORTON
They're gone. I'll stay. Mary shall never know
I too had pacted to kill Rizzio.
*Exits opposite.*

## Scene 6

MARY
*Sola, as in II. 4. She sits at a loom.*
Where is my page? He tarries. I'm alone.

How might one prick on time that crawls so slowly?
My best-loved business occupies an hour:
Fleshing out blooms upon the canvas, like
A village girl here at the loom and shuttle;
But such hours are so few in number, always!
Always surrounded by unfeeling crowds
Ever suspicious, whose tears are not tears,
Whose smiles are no smiles; none who understand me...
Were I to take myself to some low cottage
Amongst my people, crowned, bedecked in jewels,
To ask some goodman, "Is the queen of Scots
Happy?" He'd say, "Why yes, she must be happy!
I was in town once — I saw palaces;
I saw the windows of her castle, bright,
While a dark grave awaits me, a poor wretch;
And years of toil before that — my low roof
Green, overrun with moss and mouldy thatch;
A poor refuge after my daily labour
Wrenching my bread from out the flinty highlands.
A poor man's grave is covered with wild heather;
I've seen the tombs of kings in marble dressed;
The queen? Happy? She must be happy. Yes."

### Scene 7

RIZZIO
How can I thank you? For, with my own eye,
I still behold your majesty; at your feet
I'll spend my final hour. And for each moment
I'd pay with half the span that yet remains me —
Mary! I am so happy! I shall sail
Tomorrow — but, tomorrow is tomorrow —
And that tomorrow is still far away.
My lady! O, my Mary! Thus I fool
Myself with happiness, as if this joy,
This evening of joy were to last ages...
O, when shall I be waked from this blest dream?

MARY
My heart is seized with unused anxiety ...
Even this joy of yours saddens and affrights.

RIZZIO
My queen — be not insulted at my words;
I'd always stay with you until the dawn —
But this next morning I am sworn to meet
With Douglas, and I shall hold to my oath.

MARY
Rizzio — that cannot be...?

RIZZIO
                        It can. It must.
But that's too sad a theme for us tonight,
And I am full of joy tonight, my lady;
A frenzied joy! I've pondered leaving here
And smiled — I hear the song of Tasso echoing,
As — so it seems — I'm borne on the canal
By a gondola festooned with black crepe,
As if in a long coffin... As I pass,
The windows of the palaces shine bright —
Casting columns of light upon the waves,
House after house; my gondola speeds on,
Borne by the current, and above me, high
Aloft, the golden moon sheds her sad light,
While in my bosom, a wild yearning is born
For a heart burnt through by flames unrequited...
Which needs such suffering — let it feed on tears.

MARY
O, Rizzio — and you say your heart is happy?
As long as we are young, all is before us!

RIZZIO
All is now past for me — will these my lips
Smile ever again? If so, that smile will die,
And quickly; like an autumn-blooming rose
Sheltered by rocks; how sad the bloom, and pale...
Exhausted... But why should I be sad?
All will change, some day! I'll return. Why not?
Why should I not return? The world's a pit,
And he who casts himself therein is lost,
Never to climb back out... No, that can't be.

I shall return to Scotland, to these rooms;
This hall that now seems draped about with mourning
Shall once again resound with joy; these walls
Will glow again with brightness, as a crowd
Of maskers fills them, dighted in bright robes.

MARY
O Rizzio, look! Behold this gloomy palace!
Such guiltless games the people call a sin.
Even the courtiers murmur.

RIZZIO
*With ever more jollity.*
                                And their sniping
Will be drowned out with laughter! Let even half
The courtiers show up here without a mask,
And when any among them should so ask:
"Do you know me?" "I do not know you, mask,"
They will hear in reply — and they won't err
Who make such answer, for those who laugh
Are always victorious over those who weep.
The youth of France will journey to this palace,
And then it shall be gay!

*A clatter of weapons is heard.*

MARY
                    Did you hear that?
Swords!

RIZZIO
          Ah, no, ma'am. My harp upon the wall,
Swept by a breeze, gave out a mournful tone.
My harp! I shall take with me your sad adieu —
You alone bid me farewell with a sigh.

MARY
*Uneasily.*
Where is my page?

RIZZIO
                    Cheer up, your majesty!
I'll take your page's place. All my life long
I've never been this happy — Like a child!
*He sits down on the Page's stool, at Mary's feet.*
I sit down at your feet — how splendid here!
Now I don't wish to die...

MARY
                    What did you say?
To die so young, a heart so filled with hope!

RIZZIO
With hope? I'd like to read that in your face —
I've read every emotion writ thereon,
But never hope... My lady, don't cloud over
Your face with anger as your page looks on —
The page is but a child, who'd fish the moon
From the pond's surface... O, your majesty!
How beautiful that chaplet blooms there, on
Your forehead! Give me some of those roses.

MARY
Rizzio, what would you do with flowers?

RIZZIO
                                    In Italy,
I'll hang the dear gift on the blessed marble
Of summer altars; more priceless than gold,
I'll point to it — Ah, look: those blooms, a gift
Of Mary Queen of Scots, an angel crowned!

MARY
*Gives him some roses.*
I won't deny you what you ask of me.
Take you the roses, but offer them not
On consecrated altars. They are unworthy.

*Enter Henry via secret stairs. He places himself behind Mary's chair, unseen.*

RIZZIO
My lady! I am your page, and your page begs
You for your fan. For your fan's breath
Has such a sweetness in it, which recalls
The Scottish mountain air. When I'm abroad,
In some far country, it will bear the scent
Of roses, which surround you, to my nose.
Then, for a while, I shall close my eyes
And travel to your presence in a dream…

MARY
*Smiling.*
The queen forgives her page. But Rizzio
Would never dare direct such words at her.
Page! Would you take the very crown from me?
It's well you don't demand this robe of purple;
It's well that you content yourself with fans.
*Gives him the fan.*

RIZZIO
I thank you!

## Scene 8

DOUGLAS
*Armed with a stiletto, he grabs Rizzio by the shirt.*
This morning too he held flowers and fan —
Tonight he takes them with him to the grave.

RIZZIO
My queen!

MARY
*Rising.*
      Stay your hand, Douglas! Whence this boldness?
These are the private chambers of the queen!
You hold her in such disrespect? Stop! Stop!
Douglas, be gone! It is the queen implores you!
No, I'm the queen, and you're at my command!
Away! Or you shall pay for this with your head!
To me, Rizzio!

DOUGLAS
                    In vain you call him near —
'Tis Douglas holds him fast — His death is certain.
*To Rizzio.*
Pray now — a minute more, you'll meet your God.[*]

MARY
Be off, Douglas! Be off! You desecrate
The throne with your near presence. Thank man, think!
In vain you'll beg me in your agony;
The hangman soon will spoil you of your spurs
And shame you with a spurn of his rough hand —
Insulting you in public, on the rack!

DOUGLAS
In vain you threaten, ma'am! I have a sword,
And all I need do is but light a torch
Upon the palace walls, and you shall see
It stormed with armed ranks of my retainers.
Shall Douglas fear a skirt? But why fight?
On that same ship that was to bear him hence,
I'll sail to France, and there shall set aside
My sword, to clothe myself in his silk jerkin;
To cap myself with just such ostrich feathers
And dangle his gold toy from my sword belt;
I'll learn the role of base Italians
And win thereby a flock of flattering Frenchmen;
I'll set out comely nets of treachery
At royal courts. The first place at the banquets,
A warm nest in the favour of the great —
These shall be mine! I'll learn to twang the harp!
Unless a drop of blood upon my forehead
Or bloodied velvet, broken plume, betray me...
Die, Dago! ... No, I cannot kill you thus;
I'd never thrust with a stiletto...
*He tosses away his dagger.*

---

[*]    In Polish: *Za chwilę będziesz lub w piekle, lub w niebie.*

MARY
>                                God!
Douglas! O Douglas! No, I'll not believe
That you could dare to kill him.

DOUGLAS
>                                    Watch and learn —
Insulted by a tongue, Douglas, avenged
By steel.

MARY
>        Douglas! See how unfortunate
I am abased to beg you for his life!
I've never set my eye on bloodletting!
Depart — and with you take these scenes of horror!

DOUGLAS
I wish that we were walled around with mirrors,
So that you'd see his death a thousand times!
I wish the moans of Rizzio would echo
One thousand times in the chambers of your ears!
O, let this blood sink deep into these stones
As an eternal testament to this crime!

*He takes Henry's sword and runs Rizzio through.*

RIZZIO
Mary! O, Mary! Lord have mercy on me!
O! O!
*Dies.*

MARY
>            Rizzio...! God, have mercy on me!
Hold off! I beg you! — O, I hear him moan
Again! Ah! If only Henry were here...!
How silent is the tomb... Henry! Where's Henry!
Henry! My husband!

HENRY
*Softly, bending near.*
>                    I am at your side.

MARY
*Turning around slowly.*
Here? All the while? Henry, my husband? God!
*Sinks onto the armrest of her chair.*

HENRY
She's fainted. Take away the corpse.

DOUGLAS
*Gloomily.*
                                        I came
To kill, not to lug corpses. Call your diggers.

*Lindsay drags the corpse from the room, and then returns.*

HENRY
*To Douglas.*
Douglas, you grow so pale! Is this the way
The manliness of knights is used to fade?
You were to dress yourself in his cap and jerkin…?

DOUGLAS
They're black with blood.

HENRY
                        You feel the tooth of conscience?

DOUGLAS
*Comes close and looks him directly in the eye.*
Henry! And you do not? Your hands are stained
As red as mine with Rizzio's blood. You killed
A man! Now, look inside yourself as well!
Had you a cause for rancour and revenge?
And yet you can be calm! O what a difference!
I but avenged a black stain on my honour
And am so knocked askew… Make bright your cheeks!
We are so different… Be now off to bed;
You'll have a good night's sleep, but, when you wake,
I hope that, when the sun ascends the skies,
It shall behold the ruddy face of Darnley,
As ruddy as it is today. My queen!

Forgive me! I'm off to a distant land,
Exiled, a cutthroat base, the mark of crime
Indelible on my forehead.
*Exits.*

LINDSAY
                  Such a knight!
Unworthy the honour.

HENRY
                  Listen, man —
The queen will soon come round; let us escape
This chamber.

LINDSAY
                  Come my friend. We'll go hunting.

HENRY
Lindsay — You know the feelings of the queen?
Will she despise me?

LINDSAY
                  It's too early to fear.
Shh! Lord, I hear steps… Let's get out of here.


## Scene 9
*Enter Bothwell, to Mary, still in a swoon.*

BOTHWELL
The queen —is she asleep? No — she's out cold…
What is this blood? I set foot in these chambers
For the first time, and already I wade
Through gore? Some crime has been committed here …
Some reckoning dark's been settled, a nameless crime…
The dying torchflames burn blue — stilettos?
Stilettos on the floor! Whose throat's been cut?
Perhaps the king's?

MARY
            O!

BOTHWELL
                        The queen is coming round.

MARY
*Confusedly.*
Douglas? Have mercy... where am I? O God,
It is so dark! I've waked up late! Ah, yes —
It's far too late... I'm at your side... O God,
Have mercy on me...! He was here at my side,
Henry, my husband — Here at my side... he killed...

BOTHWELL
*Shocked.*
Henry...? He killed?

MARY
                            Perhaps these robes are stained
With blood? I see him! How he suffered, pierced...
Through and... Away! O tear pernicious! Now,
Should I beweep the loss? I'll be avenged!
Tremble ye killers! Can tears pay for blood?
Only blood pays for blood! Tremble, ye cutthroats!
Tremble before the vengeance of the queen!
As death has come to court, there'll be more crime!

BOTHWELL
What is this horrid pain that sears the queen?

MARY
And you — are you stained with the blood of Rizzio?

BOTHWELL
No! With my own, perhaps...

MARY
                                 You? At this hour?
Why? Douse the torches and the lanterns, all!
My shame must not be seen... I love you, Bothwell!
Now's not the time emotion to dissemble —
I fall upon your breast... And now I'm lost!

BOTHWELL
O Mary! Nothing now shall ever tear you
Away from these two arms, save death itself!
It's vengeance you desire? Say? Murder? Poison?

MARY
No, I desire nothing. Listen — come;
We shall approach the altar of the Lord —
Let me there join my hand with yours, just as
We're already united in my heart...
But no — that other hand, beneath the blood,
Still pulses with its own life... O dear God!
What have I said?

*She tears herself from Bothwell's embrace and runs off.*

### Scene 10

BOTHWELL
*Solus.*
He's living still...? It's late? I'm right on time!
I'd have to wait whole ages on such an avowal,
But now she's been betrayed by her despair
And frenzy — Now, the thought of retribution...
I must develop it until it bloom
Into a bonny flower — with venomous fruit —
Unless the devil tear her from my power!
No woman shall soften my heart with tears...
She wants me to guess at her wishes? Ha!
No — She must command me: "Bothwell, kill the king!"
I shall not kill for any less reward.

[END OF ACT III]

# ACT IV

## Scene I

*The queen's apartments.*

MARY
Today I'm calm. The government of pure
Prayer sets all worry to rest, smooths all pain;
Both time and patience heal the deepest wounds.
Everything can be endured.

BOTHWELL
                        Everything?

MARY
All cares and miseries...

BOTHWELL
                        Contempt as well?

MARY
Enough! I've suffered more than any woman!
I'm on the throne — and still my heart is broken.

BOTHWELL
Mary, you place too much trust in both throne
And splendour... What's a throne but planks of wood
Covered in scarlet? Just remove the plush
And cover it with mourning crepe, and see:
Before you know it, the throne becomes a tomb.
In France I've seen, when a great king has died,
His figure fashioned at once in wax.
Dressed up in scarlet, it's lain on a bier:
How strangely rests the crown on that soft brow!
The people, stirred, turn from it in disgust,
That wax puppet decked out in jewellery
During the funeral... Madame, take no offence

At my words, but you, Mary, Scotland's queen,
Are not much different from that figurine.

MARY
What must I do?

BOTHWELL
    Ha! Pray. Pray and forgive!

MARY
Forgive? Whom?

BOTHWELL
   Everyone.

MARY
        Explain your words.
*Bothwell makes the sign of the cross.*
Why have you blessed yourself?

BOTHWELL
        I'm praying, ma'am.
I hear a tolling bell.

MARY
     A bell? For whom?

BOTHWELL
For Rizzio.

MARY
    I but lay low my pain,
Stifle in prayer the moan within my breast,
And Satan jostles me awake again.

BOTHWELL
*Looking through the window.*
Look there, my lady — the funeral trains,
With the paid keeners singing the deceased's
Virtues; behind the coffin file his friends,
A long, sad troop, but the most faithful lies

Within that coffin. Each, leaving his house,
Carried a candle burning — half are snuffed —
The other half will soon extinguish theirs.
They'll not illuminate the grave for him —
And with the candle flames, their mourning
Of him will be snuffed out as well. Sleep, sleep
Rizzio — everyone has forgotten you!
Enough? Yet, *in aeternum requiescat...*

MARY
O Bothwell — what will a woman not dare?
Look at that portrait hanging on the wall:
How well it figures Henry's pale face,
Those eyes... They follow me! I cannot bear it!
Look — everywhere I turn, they follow me!
And their gaze pierces me through — O, those eyes!
That image is not the work of human hands;
Satan transferred my conscience to that canvas,
And with it, cruelly he torments my heart.

BOTHWELL
Ha, ha! And so, Darnley's glance does not please you?
Perhaps I'll drape it?

MARY
      No, tear it in twain!
Slit it from top to bottom with your dirk!
What good are pictures? I have him in my heart.

BOTHWELL
My lady, if I carry out your orders,
Will you be calmer?

MARY
      Carry out my desires?
What are you saying?

BOTHWELL
      Destroy Henry's image.

MARY
*With bated breath.*
His image...!

BOTHWELL
     Is that not what you wish?

MARY
          Yes,
I had forgotten I wished the picture's death.
*Aside.*
All hope is gone, he doesn't understand
And I dare not speak plainly.

BOTHWELL
        Madame, farewell.
Today we part forever. I wish you well.

MARY
*In despair.*
What did you say? My dear man! Such a blow's
Too much for a poor woman to bear! Too much!
I won't endure it!

BOTHWELL
    Then, ma'am — shall I stay?
So you command me? You're the queen. You may.
But have a grave dug for me next to Rizzio;
Courage alone is a wretched defence
Against stilettos.

MARY
    O, you tear my heart!
There is a hell writhes in me now — revenge!
Revenge! What other course is left to me?
Revenge!

BOTHWELL
   On Douglas? That's an empty hope...
Along with Lindsay, he has fled abroad.

MARY
Go, find them! No, stay here. Stay! Have mercy!
Deign understand me, Bothwell, I beseech you!
Must I express my soul in words? Although
I know these words will weigh my conscience down,
And will not pass away with the mere echo...
He ought to perish!

BOTHWELL
                Who?

MARY
*Struggling with herself.*
                        He!

BOTHWELL
                        Who?

MARY
                                The king!

BOTHWELL
And so he shall.

MARY
Just like an echo, you repeat the words
That I would not wish to hear reverberate.
But as it is, now I have tipped the scales —
My inclination shows in their decline —
Onwards! I must move on this — Onward! Onward!
Where will this path lead me? O, you are pale!
As if you would reproach, abandon me?

BOTHWELL
My queen, I have grown pale? Such are the traces,
Perhaps, of old pains.

MARY
                    Bothwell, let your front
Not be a mirror in which I might read
With mute terror the blackness of my crimes.

Must I your shining thoughts eclipse with shadows
Of crime? Forget my unguarded words!
I spoke as if dreaming. Forget my dreams!
And dare not repeat them!

BOTHWELL
                Lady, he dies this day.

MARY
*With terror.*
Today? That's far too soon!

BOTHWELL
                Where's Henry now?

MARY
Not far from here — a cottage in the country.
They say he's ill.

BOTHWELL
                Perhaps incurably...
Fear not — today he goes under the knife;
There shall be no suspicion. He is ailing.
But I'll need help... You, as his faithful wife,
Ought to go visit him this very evening.
You'll take with you a draught to help him sleep.

MARY
O, what you ask is far beyond my power!
I am to visit him tonight? I saw him
But yesterday, and tomorrow morning
I am to see him dead... See him today?
I cannot!

BOTHWELL
           But you must! For in this way,
You'll shatter all suspicion and dread —
Without this, he won't sleep. He'll escape death.

MARY
Give me the draught, then. I'll descend the throne
And for the space of this dreadful night alone,
None of my vilest subjects will be my peer
In wickedness and sleights...

BOTHWELL
*Extracts the vial of poison he had at the Astrologer's.*
                                            Your majesty,
Here is a draught of herbs well known to me.
Let Henry drink it down; it may taste foul,
But it's a sovereign medicine for pain.
The sick man will find sleep through its ministry.

MARY
So, when he drinks it...

BOTHWELL
                     He will fall asleep.

MARY
For how long?

BOTHWELL
                That I cannot tell you.
*Aside.*
Since the venom will be given by the queen,
I'll keep my dagger sheathed, my own hands clean.
*To Mary.*
Farewell, your majesty!
*Exits.*

MARY
*Sola.*
I watched him closely — striving in his face
To read his inner heart. The slightest trace
Of treason there I could not find. He's sad?
Whenever was the face of Bothwell glad?
He's pale? His face has ever been so white...
It can't be poison! would he not show fright
— Even a shiver — were he to proffer

Poison, to his unsuspecting lover
Or can he have no feeling in his whole
Heart; with my soul's eye, searched I not his soul?
*Exit.*

## Scene 2
*A cottage in the country. Henry's abode.*

HENRY
I wander like one cursed. Just punishment
Of God. While through my sickened fancy range
Pale spectres — at the four posts of my bed
Stand bitter pangs of conscience.

NICK
        Ah no, sire.
It's only me, the clown.

HENRY
        Only the clown
Remains with me, abandoned by all else.
But then the pale torch of imagination
I shine upon the spectres — Look! each stone
In my royal crown is encrusted with crime!
Their burden weighs my head down to the grave;
The crown's weight pulls me in!

NICK
        I'm astray too.
Behold the cap I frayed in royal halls.
I used to hang upon it all the coin
I'd conquered — soon the cap will be worth more
Than the head — Then it too will pull me down.
It's not good to wear too much on the head —
Knowledge and foolishness quite suffice.

HENRY
        O Nick!*

---

\* In the original, Henry says *O paziu!* "O, page!"

In your words one can find more common sense
Than smiles upon your face, but when I'm wracked,
Tortured by the spectres that surround me,
How can I help but see them? 'Tis their sight
That crushes my heart. I would not see them, Nick!

NICK
Then close your eyes.

HENRY
                              They're not before my eyes —
They're in my soul! I see them — just as I
See you; just as I see the shadow there
Behind me, chasing me…

NICK
                        Snuff out the lamp.
Then you won't see me, sire. Snuff your conscience,
And you'll no longer see the ghosts.

HENRY
                                I can't!
It lies not in my power! You're insane!
How can one snuff one's conscience, like a lamp?
*He gazes into the depths of his room.*
See? There he stands, in gloomy mourning weeds!
As if he wished to lay bare to my eyes
The secret ways of death! Silent, and bloodied,
And pale, he waves, and calls me to himself…
And yet I saw him quartered with stilettos!
He's risen from the grave as if from sleep;
Just like a babe, fresh, rising from his cradle!

NICK
All his life long, Rizzio was fond of clowns.
Perhaps he's come to seek them, after death?
And so I wonder that he speaks to you,
And not to me — You must be like to me
At this hour, in his eyes.

HENRY
*Not hearing his words.*
                              Be gone! Be gone!
Rizzio, away! Your apparition makes
My heart to bleed! O, I'd give everything,
All that I have, that you should live again!
Blame me no more! Be gone! And let me sleep...
Is it my sleep you want? You sleep a-grave!
Or is there no sleep there either? My life —
I'll give my life to you — Just let me sleep!
Give me back sleep! Return not, take my life!
Your face so pale, your eyes stare so, Ha, ha!
*Wildly.*
Will you take nothing from me but my reason?

NICK
That ghost is better at this job than I.
So hire him as your clown. Never my jokes
Did coax from you a chuckle so sincere!

HENRY
What is it, Rizzio? You show your bloodied robes?
Was it I killed you filthy, unshrived of sin?
Tell me! I am a king! And I am rich —
How many Masses do you need? I'll buy them!
I'll buy a week of Masses, or a month,
A year, an age of Masses for your soul!
Though you were caked in blood, prayers can storm Heaven;
You'll hear the priests still chanting when you're dust,
Nothing but rotten dust, in your old grave.
Ha, ha! Again the harp!

NICK
                    Calm yourself, sire!
These visions spring from... The queen is coming...

HENRY
The queen! What shall this audience be like?
She kills despising, contempt her dagger-strike!

## Scene 3

MARY
Henry! I thought to find you here amidst
The rout of your retainers! Yet, alone, and pale...
Tell me, are you not ill? Your eyes are wild,
And in your face some sleepless nights are etched.

HENRY
*With despair.*
O Mary!

MARY
*Interrupting.*
     Calm yourself! You're ill, my dear.
Lay down and sleep. Insomnia is unhealthy.

HENRY
Mary, I'm guilty! Guilty of Rizzio's death!

MARY
*With seeming indifference.*
I know nothing of that. What's it to me?

HENRY
Do you forgive me? Tell me!

MARY
         Forgive you what?

HENRY
His death.

MARY
    Whose?

HENRY
      Rizzio's!

MARY
        Ah. I'd forgotten.

HENRY
I wanted to acquit myself, explain,
But that Italian's not worth your regard.

NICK
*To Henry.*
He wasn't worth your regard, your highness.
I'll echo back your words — your very own,
When you'll chase sleep in vain.

HENRY
*To Nick.*
                                      Be off, you wretch!
*To Mary.*
You have forgiven me, and now I'll sleep.

MARY
Sleep must be coaxed near when it flees your bed,
And I have here a draught — you'll prove its strength —
After you down it, sleep will wrap you round
With its soft wings; you'll slumber like a child,
And dream of pleasant things. Let me prepare it.

HENRY
*To Mary, who is pouring the liquid into his cup.*
Thank you, my queen!

NICK
                                She shivers! Now I see!
*To Mary.*
Madame, deign drink the liquor too, by half —
Who knows if, when the king has drank his down,
You too might not need help falling asleep.

MARY
*Glances at Nick, then turns away in contempt.*
What a hard role! But it must be played out!
Each look betrays me, every word I say —
As my thought has betrayed me before Heaven.
Ah, now be quick! And then, quickly away!

HENRY
O Mary, why are you dressed in mourning?

MARY
You're ill — it is a sign of my concern.

NICK
*Aside.*
And so, for this, an inky cloak is needed...

HENRY
*To Mary, tenderly.*
I do not suffer much — they amplify
My pains, who bring you news, to frighten you.
Now, all my weakness has quite fled away —
Chased hence by your forgiveness!

MARY
                              Fare you well.

HENRY
Farewell? O no, Mary; it is too soon!
Why must you go? Stay yet! But one word more!
Sometimes, I must confess, I'm tormented
With how I've treated you. Forgive me, ma'am!
*Kneels before her.*
Run through in thought our many times together.
Is there a black hour that pulls us apart?
I beg you — blot it from your memory!

MARY
*Turns away with a shiver.*
He begs my pardon — from his bed of pain,
As it were. A man who won't see morning,
Most likely, kneels here at my feet and begs
Forgiveness. If I don't forgive him, will God
Forgive me? Rise, Henry! Let us forgive
Each other.

**HENRY**
What must I forgive you for?
Of me you ask forgiveness? For what sin?
Behold, I spread my heart open to your gaze...

**MARY**
Be well — our hour has run its course so quickly...!

**HENRY**
*Tenderly.*
When shall we meet again?

**MARY**
*With trembling voice.*
Perhaps tomorrow?

**HENRY**
You take your leave of me so coolly? What?
Forgiveness... love — where have our fresh vows flown,
So quickly disappearing?

**MARY**
*Kisses his forehead.*
Fare you well.

**HENRY**
*Jolted.*
Your lips were so cold as they pressed my brow;
A shiver shot through me.

**MARY**
*With a bitter smile.*
You're fevered, my dear.
*Exit.*

## Scene 4

**HENRY**
Thank you, my dear! Mary, my angel! O God!
You have turned your heart towards me — She loves me!

NICK
And you believe that, sire?

HENRY
                              Yes, I believe it!
'Twas only Rizzio came between us; now
Rizzio lies in his grave... all things have changed,
And I am happy. Did you see her smile?
It was a sincere smile, a tender smile;
Soon I shall sit myself upon the throne
With peaceful countenance, at Mary's side.
Rejoice, Douglas! Rejoice! I'll win your pardon,
I'll cover you beneath my royal robes.
Rejoice, my faithful Nick! I've lain my conscience;
I dream no more of pale ghosts, but gladness!
I will reward you Nick, and generously!
I'll fill your cap with gold, and dress you up
In shining livery!

NICK
              Of raven black.

HENRY
For whom will you be mourning?

NICK
                        Drink down the cup
The queen's seasoned for you, and then your clown
Will dress himself in mourning for your sake!

HENRY
Be gone! Be gone! You're like some hag of Hell,
Base and suspicious, snapping, spitting venom!
Off with you, vagrant — off to beg and die
In misery! But no — your death shall be
Exemplary to others — Choose your death!

NICK
That's a tough choice, for foolishness, eternal,
Cannot die; from the world's dawn to its dusk.
I'd like to die at sword's point, but the hangman

Calls in my debt, "Nick, You owe me your head!
But, where've you hidden it?" Ha, ha! Isn't that droll,
My lord, to have no head? Ha, ha! And yet,
There is a noose to fit any size neck —
Yet I'm so feather-light, the wind would bear me
Aloft; I cannot hang; death's not for clowns
Unless it be the lightest death — that cup there.
Is it my death you want?

HENRY
                    Monster, be gone!
You wretch! Such is the gratitude you bear me?
Let your own conscience dictate your punishment.
I banish you from court.

NICK
                      And so I die,
By my own verdict.
*Drinks the cup poured by the queen.*

HENRY
                    What are you doing?

NICK
Nothing — I merely drank the cup prepared
By the queen's hand — I'll sleep now like a babe,
And dream of pleasant things.

HENRY
                          I shivered just now.
But what scared me? He shall but fall asleep —

NICK
I'll fall asleep upon my final bed.
And maybe even that will be denied me...
*He pales, sits down at the king's side, and rests his head in his hands.*
With such a long road stretching out before me,
I'll still return in thought to my home — there,
That hovel, poor, set at the village bounds,
Its walls blackened with soot, upon the wall
A holy picture hangs, with a lamp burning

Before it; near the gate, the guard-dog watches,
And there above the thatch, an ancient oak
Stretches its dead limbs, sifting rot. O, God!
I see — I see — my ancient father there,
Mending a plough at the porch steps, in prayer;
The while my tearful mother sets to distaff,
Singing the lullaby she used to sing
Above my cradle... Who had ever guessed
That under such a misery-thatched roof
A thing in love with laughter should be whelped?

HENRY
I've never seen you sad, Nick — whence this mood
Of longing? You who ever were so gay?

NICK
Yes — I was a vagrant — who would gather in
A whining orphan? Moans and damp lamenting
Are the prerogatives of the high-born.
The wretch must gambol, if he wish to eat.

HENRY
What's with you, Nick? Say? What was in that draught?
O God! Help —

NICK
            I don't need anything, now...
Listen, your highness, brought up at the court,
I was a toy — the courtiers all laughed.
But I saw contempt there curdling on their lips —
By God, I did! And, you know, I have a heart,
Like any mortal. Like the dog stretched out
Before your threshold — thus I loved you, sire.
And knowing well how rarely sovereigns laugh,
I wished that laughter always should be with you...
But now the king shall hear my voice no more,
Unless he deign to laugh over my grave,
Unless the bells that toll my funeral
— If there be such — remind him of my cap...

HENRY
He's dying! Treason! Treason by the queen!
Nick! Nick! What can I do for you? Your eyes
Are darkened, and your face is deathly pale!
NICK
Hang a few pennies on my cap-a-bells,
And send it to my parents. They'll be glad
Of copper, and perhaps they'll have a need
Of it in their poverty; my cap they'll hang
Upon the wall of their poor cottage; there,
It will remind them, at odd whiles, of me,
Their son — my mother will spin wool beside it;
May it remind her of that lullaby
She used to sing above my cradle, rocking...
O God, I grow weak — has it grown so dark...?

HENRY
O Nick, my heart is breaking! See my tears!

NICK
Never before was I the cause of tears
To you, my lord. Now, why should jollity
Depart the world along with me?
*[Chuckles]*

HENRY
                              No, no, laugh not!
That is forced laughter; that smile is too sad —
It runs me through! You die on my behalf
You faithful man, rewarded with contempt!

NICK
*Gaily.*
Reward me, then. Choose four most learned men
And have them bear the jester's catafalque.
Let them port foolishness on their wise shoulders,
And when they're burdened down with folly's weight,
Let them announce throughout the realm entire
That Nick, dead, weighs more than did Nick when quick.
You smile! O, now I'm happy. I so wished

To see a smile upon your face once more.
Forgive me my offences, lord. I close
My eyes and will not see you any more —
It seems I see... I am so weak...

HENRY
       Nick!

NICK
         Goodbye.
Forever and ever!

HENRY
    Nick, my friend! My son!

NICK
*Confused, raising himself up.*
Son? Who is it that calls me? My father?
In vain — it's grown so dark on every hand
I cannot see you — and now, I must go!
I must abandon you, but save a place:
I shall come home some day, I'll rest at home...
I always thought that I'd return to you...
O Mother! Mother! Give me other wraps,
Mother! I suffered so much in the world... O!
*He falls at the king's feet, and dies.*

HENRY
He's dead!
Thus has my last friend left me, tender wife,
Look — your sleeping draught it was that killed him!
You poisoned him — you meant to poison me
No! Henry lives! Although he lives alone
Upon the earth, now no different from a grave...
And this is why your lips kissed me so cold!
*He takes a lamp and lights up Nick's face.*
Let me see him again... How pale his face!
His lips are livid — O, how hard the bed
He chose to lie upon — Heavens! Sparks from the lamp
Fell on his face! I'll brush them off... But, madness!
He cannot feel a thing... He cannot feel...

Anything, any more. The end... In vain
Do I despair — I must to covert go,
Before a woman's treason. But, escape?
Where might I flee? The night is pitchy black —
Perhaps she's hidden cutthroats round the house?
What would they not dare? What not attempt?
There is no greater monster on the earth!
*After a pause.*
I shall remain! To see how she will greet me
When morning comes, and she sees a dead husband
Here on this bed. Her countenance will feign
Its paleness — Perhaps she will paint it pale?
Perhaps I'll hear her groan from the side chamber —
Sure of my death, before she's made certain
That I am truly dead! She'll weep her loss...
And then I'll... here alone...! My glance will kill her!
*Sets the lamp down at Nick's head.*
So God is watching over me, fending off death...
I'll set the lamp near, cover him with a shroud —
And through the night I'll pray here for the dead...
Alone thus, with the dead, through the dark night.
Alone, alone, God! Have mercy on me!

[END OF ACT IV]

# ACT V

## Scene 1

*A Gothic chamber. To the rear, a large ebony crucifix, before which a silver lamp is burning. It is night. Moonlight enters through a window.*

MARY
Has it gone midnight? Snuff out all the lamps,
And draw the drapes before the chamber windows.
No one should see that I'm watching tonight.

*The Page snuffs the lamps and then points to the votive lamp before the crucifix.*

PAGE
That one, too?

MARY
     No, let the votive lamp burn.
Its glow should not betray me to strange eyes —
To the Lord, yes, perhaps, but shades of night,
However black, cannot obscure the guilty
From God's eyes.

PAGE
    Who is guilty?

MARY
        Has the king
Drunk down his medicine? Is he asleep?
I've found a leaden-footed avenger
In Bothwell! Where's he dawdling so long?

PAGE
Bothwell? I saw him wandering among
The dark trees of the retreat, very near
The house where Henry lodges.

MARY
                          You saw him?
And did he have a dagger in his hand?

PAGE
He had no weapon with him, and his face
Was pale and terrifying.

MARY
How the time flies! And what a horrid change
Has poisoned the present — and perhaps the future!
Not long ago among the Franks at court
I loved and was beloved of everyone —
With childish laughter I looked upon new jewels;
With childish laughter I heard gentle sighs;
Smiling before the glass I brushed my hair,
Plaiting rosebuds among the golden curls...
Today...

PAGE
       Today, look once more in the glass —
Could you be any lovelier?

MARY
                       You wrong me,
To make me look upon these pale cheeks.

PAGE
Perhaps the flashing crystal smarts your eyes,
But here it's dark — only one lamp is lit;
Does the light hurt your eyes? I'll curtain it...
Madame!
You're scaring me! You're paling more and more —
How can I brighten this black melancholy?
Do you like stories? Here's a nice ballad
That still today the Scottish people sing —

Will you permit me? You're silent. So I'll dare...
Now listen: an old mother speaks to her son.

*Mary sits, deep in thought; the page begins to recite the poem in his childish voice.*

Why does your brand sae drop wi' bluid
Edward, Edward?
Why does your brand sae drop wi' bluid?
And why so sad gang thee, O?

O, I hae killed my hawk sae guid
Mither, mither.
O, I hae killed my hawk sae guid
And I had nae mair but he, O.

Your hawk's bluid was never sae reid,
Edward, Edward.
Your hawk's bluid was never sae reid,
My dear son I tell thee, O.

O, I hae killed my reid-roan steed,
Mither, Mither.
O, I hae killed my reid-roan steed,
That erst was sae fair and free, O.

Your steed was auld, and you hae more
Edward, Edward.
Your steed was auld, and you hae more
Some other duel you drie, O.

O, I hae killed my faither dear,
Mither, Mither.
O, I hae killed my faither dear.
Alas and woe is me, O!

And what penance will you drie for that
Edward, Edward?
And what penance will you drie for that
My dear son, now tell me, O.

I'll set my feet in yonder boat
Mither, Mither.
I'll set my feet in yonder boat
And I'll fare over the sea, O.

And what will you leave to your bairns and your wife
Edward, Edward?
And what will you leave to your bairns and your wife
When you gang over the sea, O?

The world's room, let them beg through life
Mither, Mither.
The world's room, let them beg through life
For them never more will I see, O.

And what will you leave your own mother dear,
Edward, Edward?
And what will you leave your own mother dear?
My dear son, now tell me, O.

The curse of Hell frae me shall you bear
Mither, Mither.
The curse of Hell frae me you shall you bear,
Sic councils you gave to me, O.

MARY
*Suddenly awakened from her musing.*
The curse of hell? What? Me? Accurst of hell?
For counselling the killing — What was that
You said? The killing of father — husband — king?
What have you said to me? Your curse has power
To kill me...!

PAGE
              It's a sad song — it moves me...
But has it frightened you? The queen is in pain
Today...

MARY
        Who set those words upon your lips?
It's me you curse! Who taught you how to curse?

Up until now I've hid this all from him,
The page; I dared not terrify him with it —
I dared not peep a word of it... Accurst!
Cursed I am for killing counsel— yes!
It's Bothwell saying this to me, my God!
It's Bothwell speaking!

PAGE
                      I don't understand...
How might I have offended her?

MARY
                      How's that?
He curses me and he can't understand?
He cast my guilt before me. Still a child,
Still such a youngster — already dissembling.

PAGE
My Lady — Bothwell's at the door.

## Scene 2

MARY
*Fixing Bothwell with her stare.*
                      Bothwell?
What is it? Why are you so silent?

BOTHWELL
                      Time...
That discovers all is a poor confidant.

MARY
Bothwell, he lives?

BOTHWELL
                    That I know not, my queen.
He may have died by now...

MARY
       What's that you say?
You couldn't see the crime once undertaken
To its conclusion?

BOTHWELL
      I saw not the king.

MARY
So he shall live?

BOTHWELL
      No, he shall perish.
Perchance he already has…

MARY
       But you've not seen him?
I don't understand.

BOTHWELL
      I haven't seen him…
But you have.

MARY
   What? Might I kill him with my glance?

BOTHWELL
Perhaps you wished to?

MARY
       No, that's what you wanted!
I am no basilisk to kill by staring —
Bothwell… It was on me that you were relying?
You've missed your mark. The only sin with which
I've stained myself is brash hypocrisy!
I smiled at him…

BOTHWELL
*Sardonically.*
       And killed him with your smile.
At any rate, you've killed him. Worry not

Your head with how — now is the time to blot[*]
Away the stains and traces of our crime.
The king is fast asleep — beneath his pillow
Sulphur is sprinkled, with saltpetre. Now,
Lend me a torch.

MARY
            The moon is high, my dear —
What need you with more light?

BOTHWELL
              He's dead, and now
It's time to bury him beneath the ruins
Of his lodging place. I'll bury King Henry.

MARY
But if he lives?

BOTHWELL
            Alive, he'll fly to Heaven.
I've mined an arsenal beneath his house
That only waits upon a spark, a flame!

MARY
O, woe is me! What shall I do?

BOTHWELL
                A torch!

MARY
But should the house fall on you too?

BOTHWELL
                    Fire!

MARY
The torches have been snuffed.

---

[*] Again, the verb in Polish is *zgładzić*.

BOTHWELL
*Pointing at the votive lamp.*
                                    There one yet burns,
And it shall serve me...

MARY
                    That's my votive lamp.

BOTHWELL
Give it to me.

MARY
              You'd take it from the altar?

BOTHWELL
Sometimes a blessed candle serves a burial,
And I am off to a cemetery now.

MARY
Have you never sought refuge in the Lord?
Look how the cross of bronze reflects its light,
And that Christ of ebon, suffering thereon!
He reads our thoughts; He hears our every word...
God...!
*Kneels at the altar.*

BOTHWELL
Is it the king's death that you're praying for?
Your prayers have been answered — perhaps even now
He's in his final throes...

MARY
*Starting up.*
                  What do you say?
His final throes? and I am praying? How?

BOTHWELL
*Taking the lamp.*
I must make haste to wipe the traces clean.

MARY
O Bothwell, Bothwell, that's a sacred lamp!

BOTHWELL
It shall return unto its sacred place,
Though stained in blood...

MARY
                            Though stained in blood, replaced
Upon the altar?

BOTHWELL
              Silly are your fears!
If you can stand before your God bloodstained,
The bloody lamp can stand upon His altar.
The lamp is nothing but an instrument,
And God won't mind it, for it's innocent.

MARY
O God, what shall I do in my distress?

BOTHWELL
Open your prayer book.

MARY
                    It's so dark in here!

BOTHWELL
*With sarcasm.*
So just pretend to read it — Play a role,
And if God won't applaud you, people will:
Let just one say, "Ah! Like a holy angel!
A living saint, that woman — you can see,
Almost, the halo round her head. Ah, look!
She's praying for her husband's death!" Come, Mary —
Toss off your superstition with your fear.
Be calm! Your dish, already's sunk so low,
By one small lamp its burden shall not grow.
Farewell!

MARY
>Stay, Bothwell!

BOTHWELL
>I must go.

MARY
>I swear!
All of his wrongs — forgot! Wiped clean, the slate!

BOTHWELL
You may forget — but may not hesitate.
*Exits.*

## Scene 3

MARY
He's gone — I couldn't hold him back... I could have!
O, my black heart! With one word I might have!
I chose not to. We shall no longer pledge
Our wedded troth before a holy altar —
O no, happiness is not for me! Page,
Tell me sincerely: I'm a horrid woman?

PAGE
You're pale, my lady.

MARY
>Kneel here at the altar
And say a prayer for me.

*The page goes before the altar, but looks back at the queen with unease.*

Upon my eyes a troubling darkness falls —
I sleep and wake — my dreams have taken colour.
A thousand lights and thrones... I am enthroned...
Now all is dark again... in purple, crowned,
I go — O God! O God! See? Prison walls!
Who has imprisoned me? Buried me alive?
Yet I am still ringed by a faithful troop...
But why are they weeping? Why dressed in black?

A priest before me recalls all my sins...
What sins? Those of this night! This sinful crime!
Now, all have gone — The priest now stands aside...
What place is this? I enter a throne-room;
A thousand torches glowing gloomily;
Who is this woman seated on my throne?
God! A throne room, and hung in black crepe?
Instead of flowers, it is festooned with yew...
They have me kneel... Why? Am I now to pray?
Ah!

PAGE
*Comes near.*
         My lady, these dreams roughly prefigure
The strange prophecies of your Astrologer.

MARY
But why do they now stand before my eyes?
My mind has dressed them in bright, living colour,
Stamped them with faces, fleshed them with sinews, bones...

PAGE
Your majesty! Your reason wanders, sick...

MARY
Can't you hear anything?

PAGE
         Your majesty,
It's silent as the grave. Your words echo
Throughout the empty palace, word after word...
The wind is blowing through the larch branches...
The moon stares dumbly through the Gothic panes...

MARY
The moon, you say? How pale must be his face,
Bothwell's, in the moonshine? On his gloomy cheeks
The thought of crime rests deeply, lulled asleep —
The moon pulls long his shadows behind him;
He errs about, shielding safe the lamp,
So that the wind's breath shouldn't snuff it out...

Would that it might! With dark face he'll return…
At least I won't see the crime written thereon!
Alas, the wick burns yet — it burns the brighter
For all the wind's bellows! Henry will die!
O God, have mercy on me!
*Pause. Then with growing terror*
                              Rizzio!
The words of Rizzio! Has that night returned?
Look — he is wrapped around in royal robes…
And I, who've never seen blood before! My robes,
Are drenched with it… Stop, Douglas! Stay your hand!
Look, page! Look there for me — there in the darkness…
Who stands behind me?

PAGE
                    Where?

MARY
                         Is it the king?

PAGE
My lady, these are dreams… You're suffering…

MARY
You hear his words? "I'm here! I'm at your side!"
He's by my side? Here in this room, right now?
I fear to glance behind me… He should rest
There in his grave… And here he stands beside me?
That cannot be! But there's still time — O, page!
He lives! The king still lives! Hasten! Stop Bothwell!
What? Did you shiver? Was it from joy, or fear?
Hurry now! Hurry! Woe is me — the king!
He'll kill the king! O, for the love of God,
Hurry!

PAGE
          But Bothwell will not heed my words.

MARY
That's true… But take from me this golden ring —
There is still time, am I not right? There's still time!

I can hear nothing... The king must not die...
I could not bear the guilt...

PAGE
                        I go, my lady...
*He runs to the door, but, at the threshold, totters, and stops there.*

MARY
Hurry, for God's sake, hurry!
What are you waiting for?

PAGE
                        Your Majesty!
I lack the strength. I am so suddenly weak...

MARY
Go on...

PAGE
      I go...! I go... ah! O my queen...
*Falls.*

MARY
Page! My dear child! Page! Speak to me! One word!
Is he to die, my Lord, so young a boy?
No...! He must not die!

PAGE
*In a weak voice.*
                             These pains... they pass...
I am so sleepy... Madame... Do you love me?

MARY
Like my own son! Wake up! A drop of wine
Perhaps, will give you strength?

PAGE
*In a trembling voice.*
                            I've had some wine
Today... my Mary... O, O!
*Dies.*

MARY

                              My page! My life!
My page! I call, I call, and he wakes not?
My God! And you punish him for my crimes?
The stench of death around me infects all,
Kills all, but can't harm me, for I alone
Unworthy am of punishment... My God!
*Kneels at the foot of the altar before the crucifix.*
I beg Thee, take me to Thy bosom, Lord —
I have been used to seek peace in the depths
Of faith; why hast Thou placed upon my brow
This crown? Why hast thou covered me in robes
Of earthly glory? the radiance of dreams
Dissolved as soon as I'd lived through this night...

*An explosion is heard.*

Ha!
*She gets up and runs to the window.*
                Look, ah Lord! Those clouds of smoke and fire,
And there — amidst the clouds — some horrid spirit
Rises to heaven, darkens and transforms...
It's Henry! Henry! I know him now... He's dead!
*Turns from the windows, then, again, in terror.*
Henry! Again, with me here in the room!
I saw him just now: he was pale and ill,
And now his face is shining bright with colour,
As if he were alive! His eyes, aflame...
Be gone! Be gone from me? You seek your ring?
Your wedding ring? Here — take it and be gone!
I am no longer yours. O Henry, Henry!
Have you no conscience? To torment a soul
So much tormented before your advent here!
Have mercy on me! So unfortunate...!
You want to look upon my misery?
Look at this face! I have no tears to weep,
But I do suffer, I swear! You don't believe
My oath? You trusted me an hour ago...

## Scene 4

BOTHWELL
*Enters, with the lamp extinguished.*
Mary, escape, escape!

MARY
      Look! There before me...

BOTHWELL
I see! Rivers of blood inundate the floor —
The blood of Rizzio!

MARY
       Where? No, I see no blood...
It's so dark in the room — but there! A figure —
A figure dead and pale... The king's treasons...
We blotted out them with still blacker treason.
I had to pardon him, but he, not me!
He won't forgive me — Look!

BOTHWELL
      The page is dead.

MARY
Dear God, the page is dead! What does this mean?

BOTHWELL
*With a wild laugh.*
Ha, ha! What does it mean? He knew our crime,
And now he's dead...!

MARY
      The poor unfortunate lad!
O Bothwell, Bothwell! You are no angel!
I had a different image of you once
Here in my heart, but now... Away from me!
You murderer, with your cold, pale brow!

BOTHWELL
Come with me!

MARY
                Where?

BOTHWELL
                              To find your rest upon
The wedding carpet... But first, we've wandering
Before us... Can you hear the growing cries?
Your vengeful subjects draw near; a wild mob,
With weapons! Soon they'll breach these royal halls,
O Mary, come away!

MARY
*Breaks away from him in fear.*
                            You frighten me!

BOTHWELL
Hearts made filthy with crime fear no crime —
You killed the king with poison! Now, you're mine!

MARY
Yours...? O, Bothwell, no — you're driving me insane!

BOTHWELL
Horrid the people's cries in this dark night,
This dark night of crime.

MARY
                          What hear you in them,
These cries, what do you hear?

BOTHWELL
                          Curses! Come, Mary!
We must escape! Come with me! Come with me!

                      [THE END]

# KORDIAN

*A Coronation Conspiracy*

And so I'll sing, and push on to my goal;
If flame remain in spark, I'll stir the fire;
Just as in aloes leaf, the Egyptian folds
The withered heart of one who has expired,
The words of resurrection I shall write
Upon the leaf. Although I lack the power
To make it beat again, my words have might
To keep it from corruption. When the hour
Strikes, to unravel my words' riddling thought,
The answer shall be found — deep in the heart.

—Juliusz Słowacki,
*Lambro*


## PREPARATIONS

*31 December 1799. Night*

*The cottage of the famous sorcerer Twardowski, in the Carpathian mountains. A large open space before the building. In the distance — cliffs. Down below, beech woods The darkness is split now and again by lightning. A witch combs her hair and sings.*

WITCH
From the stars that err,
From my combed black hair,
Sparks fly
As from Polish blades.
The devils gaze
And reply

With lightning flash;
A-wing — they dash
And the beeches cower.

SATAN
*Flies up in the guise of a beautiful angel.*
Ha, witch! Has it struck, the hour?

WITCH
Which hour?

SATAN
               That hour that no man
Will ever hear strike twice?

WITCH
Before ten times you blink your eyes
It shall strike, from the Babylonian tower.
And though I may be deaf, I can
And will hear it. But now, your
Eminence, why don't I spy
Your comrades riding through the lower sky?
How lazily they fly!
The tortoise, from whose shell the turner formed
My harrow more quickly roamed...!

SATAN
Show me that harrow, here! O, how my heart is warmed!
I can't refrain from weeping! 'Tis the currycomb
Twardowski used, my shaggy fur to dress
When I into a dog myself transformed
To gambol at his feet, and fawn, and press
Myself against his side! Be off, my lady —
On Bald Mountain, invited guests are waiting.

*Exit witch.*

*Crying out:*

Satans!

*Ten flashes, ten devils descend.*

The devils rain upon the earth — let it pour!
If from the saplings of Eden grow any more
Trees of good and ill and all that pother,
Let them grow!
In the fall there'll be fruit for men to gather.
Sit down! Sit down!
But I don't see Mephisto?

ASTAROTH
He's kneeling on the ground over there —
At Twardowski's tomb
Deep in prayer.

SATAN
How pious and tender he's become!
Just like a poet. But the horned moon
Is shining; it's time we'd begun
Our work.

DEVILS
What's your command, your majesty?

SATAN
It's time to check the cogs and gears
In the clock of the years;
With newborns' blood to oil the springs,
Assess the pendulum to the pennyweight
So that it strike precisely, hour, year, date
And not be off in anything.
Bring it here, set it up.
Well, it's not gone bust?

ASTAROTH
Not a sprocket, not a chain's
Been chewed at by long ages' rust;
The clock face — fashioned from a Host
(That choked a fellow, with much pain);
The mechanism underneath
Is quite precise, you know, most-

ly Leviathan's sting (but there's teeth
Of dragons, too); the hour hand's
Made of a hornet's stinger, and's
Never missed a beat; the rope's
A strand of Satan's pigtail, white
From terror when plunging from the height
Of heaven — ah, "abandon hope!"
Remember? (Sorry). The second hand
And spring come from John Calvin's land;
Both are fixed fast to a human eye —
Preciser than diamonds (so say I),
And there, amongst the springs the chimes
Are chirped by a damned soul that whines
In tempo to a spider's foot,
Who sets the springs in motion, but —

SATAN
Enough description!
Gehenna, Astaroth, sons of perdition
Worse than Tsar's lackeys, bend your ears,
And when the clock strikes, count the years
The days, the ages —

*The clock strikes, the devils count.*

Wholly, wholly, wholly
O world, the snake of ages winds you round, slowly
Squeezing you in its scaly crush;
With poisoned fang gnawing (faintly) at your sides,
While ages die above you, sifting down the dust
Of memories of those who've died.
When you were fashioned, I was there,
You handful of sticky grime
Belted with foetid air!
A corpse of chaos enclosed in the blue,
Burnt through with the rot of time,
Built up from rusty ore and the thew
Of granites — later came moss and bloom and wood,
And then those two-legged pests
That bore through your breast
And brood.

Woe to them, whose
Dreams end not with the earth's horizon;
Woe to them if — fleering that limit, beyond
They dare to go.

GEHENNA
The nineteenth century's struck, my king.

SATAN
Let Astaroth take care
As he counts the years —
Perhaps the fellow up there
Who wields the thunderbolt might wish to bring
Aid to some earthly nation, and I fear
Lest He should try to steal from us a day,
An hour — or for men's sake to tear away
A year entire from a century —
Should there be any shysting of that manner
I'll go to God and put him in His place —
I'll demand it of Him, right to His face!
Or else unfurl the rebellious banner.
In me, and violated nature, he has an enemy!

ASTAROTH
Eighteen hundred years have tolled.

SATAN
And so the rack of pain has made a whole
Revolution? Each screw tightens, each tooth bites,
And now with heaven flashing bright,
Each bolt lasts longer than all those past years —
The world's elapsed torments and tears,
And each year seemed to creep at snail's pace
For wretch, for lovers' hopes delusory;
The shiny silver path once traced,
Man slid back down it in skittish memory.
Those mad ever-erring sailors who roamed
The past's billows — so-called historians — wrote
(Such was their trade) immense tomes
Chock-full of royal names, dates... and footnotes;
Others in thought traced thoughts of others —

Philosophers (thought's hierophants),
At last, above the dark abyss they hovered,
Came to, and tossing their astounded glance
Into the depths, exclaimed "O dark! O murky! O dim!"
Tickling our ears with that Satanic hymn
To organ tones pumped by black cherubim.
Who's thought for an hour is, or will be, at my side.
This dawning age will be our joy, our pride.

MEPHISTO
*Enters.*
Tricked out, our chief prophesies and presages —
His cloak is patched with pages
Ripped from the works of Voltaire;
A plume of Rousseau's is bobbing above his hair!

SATAN
Mephisto! It's time to set our shoulders to the job.
Pick out some puppet from amongst the earthly mob;
Amongst the Krauts no more you'll find a pliant doctor;
Today no Manfred skips about Helvetian rock, or
Monk is to be found, cell-bound, growing thin with fasting —
So go and turn some soldier's head.

MEPHISTO
                                    Do you know what you're asking?
A soldier is a wise old fish — from hooks he holds aloof.
He's got his share of common sense, and by that lamp he'll see,
Try as I might to hide it, this deceiver's cloven hoof.

SATAN
So, only knights are to slip us with impunity?
Listen! To one nation out of the horde
Of earthly tribes, an august hour nears;
Go there — where knights wield a crooked sword,
Curved like the moon, or these horns above our ears —
Nor is their pommel shaped like the cross.
Go help them — for they're about to toss
Their fate upon the scales of battle, even
As we once waged war with the Lord of Heaven.
O! They will pray and kill and curse and cry;

Already round their father's graves they've pitched their tents,
Brooding and waiting for the hour of vengeance!
That nation shall arise, and be victorious... and die!
In the fierce battle they will come to wreck,
Later to slay their enemies with thought,
Because their thought's a weapon, fiery hot —
It, like a noose, they'll loop about the neck
Of their foes, and them to such a high pillory they'll hitch
That the whole world will reach them with their gaze — and their spit.

MEPHISTO
Sire, I have here Hell's Psalter — now, let me see...
"The Day Called Resurrection..." good, I'll say that prayer
For them. On this first day of the new century,
We've the right to create kings and wretches to spare
As the new age begins to unroll —
Some dignitaries now let us create
For that nation, with which to bung each hole
In the apparatus of the state,
Great powers for to get her;
We'll take the people then and spell 'em
Into a lovely book bound in old leather;
Their brows shall shine like vellum.

SATAN
That's good advice — come, form a ring.
It's time to make a government!
Summon the witches; let's begin:

*Under Satan's direction, the devils begin their labours.*

Earth, air, and all the elements
Bound by this atmospheric glass,
Oxygen and carbon gas
That chemists beak down from the whole
That shall be, is, and ever was,
I pour into this platinum bowl.
Breathe, spirits!

*Thunderclaps beat the cauldron.*
The cauldron boils, the cauldron churns,

With the element of earth now, pour
In something that thrones overturns —
Forty thousand lacquered brads,
Each one with a corporal's badge.

DEVILS
Forty thousand, no more, no less?

SATAN
No.

DEVILS
Perhaps some corporal's common sense?

SATAN
No.

DEVILS
There, it's finished —

SATAN
                    Let him fly!

*Thunderclaps, a spirit flies out.*

An ancient duffer, none too spry,
Paternal, doddering and tame;
So that the joke will be more pleasant,
Let's give him an ironic name.
Something that seems to rhyme with peasant;[*]
A village-headman sort of rotter...
Now from the heavens, let him plunge
To lead the village cannon fodder.

---

[*] Józef Chłopicki (1771–1854), Polish general, who took charge of the Polish insurrectionists during the 1830 uprising, although unenthusiastically. He was a cautious leader, who was more concerned with winning favourable terms from the Tsar than putting his all into the military campaign for Polish freedom. Słowacki puns on his name, which is similar to the Polish word for peasant (*chłop*).

DEVILS
Sire! Will you stop at just one?

SATAN
In the cauldron, diamonds sink!
The diamonds will melt therein —
Then squeeze some of the secret ink
From out of Tallyrand's cunning pen,
Which pales to invisibility
Beneath reason's most piercing lens —
Bring all to boil, and then we'll see
What creature makes its appearance.

DEVILS
It's finished! But, despite the hex,
Here we've some proper gentleman!
A faulty goulash, one suspects;
Too cold the bouillon, or too thin.

SATAN
That's nothing. Even such as these
Among the poor folk need be thrust.
Before him, they'll fall to their knees!
He looks like an old Roman bust —
His profile's like a Roman face
Faint on a Roman coin still traced...
To make more humorous our game,
Let's christen him with a hellish name.[*]
Now, let him fly! Unbind, unfetter —

DEVILS
The third one will be even better.

---

[*] This is Prince Adam Jerzy Czartoryski (1770–1861), the scion of a noble Polish family, he both fought against the Russians in his youth, and served in the Tsarist army at the rank of brigadier. He was a personal friend of Tsar Alexander I. A conservative thinker who often held pro-Russian views (during the Napoléonic Grand Duchy of Warsaw period, for example), during the November Uprising of 1830 he worked, on the one hand, for a compromise solution between the Insurrectionists and the Tsar, and then, in France, for the diplomatic intervention of the Western nations. Słowacki puns on his last name; in Polish *czart* means "demon, devil."

SATAN
Snap off the legs, and with an awl
Prick out the eyes; toss in cock-spurs
And from the timid snail that crawls,
Add the front horns — Now, what stirs
There in the cauldron?

DEVILS
                        It's a knight,
Or something like one...

SATAN
                       What a sight!
A leader! like the crab he goes
Backwards, and like the snail he knocks
His horns; into his shell retracts
As in a civic chest* he packs
The corpses of plans, with that box
He waits, until the rooster crows.
Now, toss into the melting pot
All of the Lechite lore you've got,
With rhymes from conjugations ripe
And million bits of printers' type,
And drowsy poppies... What's that? Hark!

DEVILS
An old fellow, like a sky-lark,
But frozen under memory's
Ice... putrid in parts thawed, unstuck,
A poet — a knight** — an old man — null...

---

\*    Jan Zygmunt Skrzynecki (1787–1860), whose name sounds like the Polish word for chest or box — *skrzynia*. He was a Polish revolutionary soldier, who joined the Polish Legion in Italy, fought with distinction in the Napoléonic Grande Armée (including the 1812 invasion of Russia), and was adjutant to General Jan Henryk Dąbrowski (famously mentioned in the Polish national anthem). Although Słowacki is perhaps too harsh in his assessment of Skrzynecki's military abilities during the November Uprising, it is true that he did not place too much faith in the Insurrectionists' chances of victory, and at one point opened a dialogue with the Russians on his own initiative.

\*\*    Julian Ursyn Niemcewicz (1758–1841). He was both a poet and a soldier, but Słowacki chiefly satirises him as the former. Niemcewicz comes of that cardinal period in

A harem guard, a sultan's tool,
A eunuch...

SATAN
Let's go — we've not much time to spare.
I hear the tones of Kraków's bells
That call the folk to morning prayer,
And through the breeze over Wawel swells
The incense from the cathedral nave.

WITCH
Damned your deeds, your windy spells!
The whole thatch from my roof you've shaved!
Who'll set me up with Hosts from Mass
To use for shingles? Those strong blasts
Of wind broke all the willow boughs.
What will become of Palm Sunday now?

SATAN
Silence, blindworm! Time flies, and
Still we must brew up a lot
Of greats. Whatever I command,
Fling now into the melting pot.
From the rust
On the Omphalus
Remaining
From the blood
When Hercules pricked his finger on the needle,

---

Polish literature that stretches between the Enlightenment proper, and the new Romantic movement. Although he did create some poems in a pre-Romantic, sentimentalist spirit, he is generally a Neoclassical poet — and thus, for Słowacki, dated, "impotent," and uninspired. (Hence the remark concerning his reliance on facile rhymes based on conjugations and declensions, in which a heavily inflected language like Polish abounds). He was a prodigious author, the most influential of whose poetic collections is Śpiewy historyczne [Historical Songs]. Based on characters and events from Polish history, these also irk Słowacki as quietist, backwards-looking compositions. He was a personal friend of Tadeusz Kościuszko, with whom he was imprisoned by the Russians following the unsuccessful 1794 Insurrection. During the period of the November Uprising, he was associated with the Czartoryski camp.

We'll be able to wheedle
Many a dandified cavalier-dud.

DEVILS
Dum, dum, dum — down they rain!
A proper flood!

SATAN
Hurry! New burdens and new pain
Let's brew before the gloomy matins
Are sung; before they ring for early Mass —
Before the dawn;
Get a move on!
Before the stew congeals and fattens
Toss in the tongue of Balaam's ass.
And the windbag culprits
That from him˙ derive
Will occupy the nation's pulpits —
An oratory tribe!

DEVILS
Dum, dum, dum, down they rain —
A flock of starlings ruffled by the gale.

SATAN
Good — do you see that figure, pale,
From the cauldron-dregs still shaping?
With sallow cheeks and eyes black ringed,
Whose maw-like mind, forever gaping,
Chokes on book, book-worm? Teetering
On crooked legs like wobbly governmental systems?
He wants to speak — What seeds will he sow? Let's listen.

---

\*        This description, and perhaps that of the head that emerges from the cauldron a few lines on, refer to Joachim Lelewel (1786–1861). Friend of Mickiewicz, Lelewel was a professor of history at the University of Vilnius — Słowacki was one of his students. During the November Uprising, he played a role in the administration led by Prince Adam Czartoryski.

CREATURE
*Poking his head out of the cauldron*
Is it better to have a king or not? Methinks...

SATAN
Away with that Sphinx
Who through such riddles delves
As devils can't disentangle themselves!
Be off with him! Let him torment
Scholastic minds with teaser and historic precedent;
Let him from some ministerial post, solemn,
Or on the blood-nourished delta of the Nile,
A stylite on some ancient broken column,
Jabber — in hieroglyphic style.

ASTAROTH
Sire! Look! The cauldron vapours stir!
Again some creature there begins to hatch:
His face is hideous — a real monster;
His bosom is crossed by a general's sash.

SATAN
Greet him triumphant! He's our man!
Like Asian hordes, a real devastator!
The capital artillery he'll command;
From the lake of blood he'll float to the top — a traitor!
When over the capital booms the cannonade,
He'll desert the perishing knights he betrayed.
Like a raven* he'll leap from the nation's ark,
Clapping his wings, flying off into the dark,
Never again to alight aboard.
He'll sell his nation — put it to the sword!

VOICE IN THE AIR
Be gone! In the Name of God, be off with you!

---

\* General Jan Krukowiecki (1772–1850). Słowacki reserves his harshest criticism for him, whose name he puns off the Polish word for raven, *kruk*. Governor of Warsaw during the November Uprising. A conservative, who has been blamed for not properly defending the city, and for a defeatist attitude of capitulation.

*Everything disappears.*

CHORUS OF ANGELS
The earth is a scar
That stains the limitless blue
Amidst so many shining suns, a dark star,
Eternal grave of Adam's issue.

ARCHANGEL
Ages ago, from the eternal firmament,
One of the stars erred — after which I chased.
It trembled in my palm, its heart in torment,
Like that of a bird, by a human arrow grazed.
I set it trembling before the throne of God,
Who spoke to me, with world-creating words:
"Your wings are blushing with human blood."
Before His feet, I fell prostrate, with my face
On the dust of stars, on the carpet of sunrays.
    "Lord! Lord! Lord!
I bloodied my wings against this world.
It was blood-soaked; I looked, and what I've seen:
A tribe, for their fathers' sins, into the grave hurled;
A people perishing, a star growing dim;
A whole people lost
These many years,
It's time, God, for resurrection,
Or for the coup-de-grace.
But if it's not Thy will
To save them, let it be more blood they spill,
Than tears."
And God replied, "My will shall be done."

CHORUS OF ANGELS
The earth is a scar
That stains the limitless blue,
Which God shall crush, or spark
As He once did Adam, that clay statue.

# PROLOGUE

FIRST PERSON OF THE PROLOGUE.
Lord, send upon Thy people, exhausted with the fight
Quiet sleep, restoring sleep, a joyful spring, and bright!
Let no succubus of despair disturb their rest;
Curtain them safe with the hem of Thy heavenly vest.
Let them not awake in tears before the Resurrection —
Deflect upon me their tears and sleepless affliction,
And give me the trump of the Angel of Judgement,
Then let each person by that trumpet's summon be sent
Before Thy throne of mercy. And grant me too such grace:
Upon the brows of the sons of perdition to place
A mark indelible. Grant me the hope, dear Lord,
To bend and crush golden calves by the power of the Word,
To cast down plaster idols from their thrones
And, in their place, erect statues of bronze.
Who am I? The spirit spoken of in the pages
Of the Apocalypse — turn here your faces
Sad, your clouded eyes — here to where I stand
Amidst seven candles, in the form of a man
In a long white robe, belted with gold, my hair
As white as snow, as wool as thick and fair;
My flashing eyes rain sparks of adamant;
My legs like copper fresh by furnace tanned;
My voice like great waters gathered, resounds;
I bear seven stars in my hand, and from my mouth
A double-edged sword flashes, shining like
The sun at zenith, waxing in its might —
And as yourselves here at my feet you cast,
I say, "I was the first... and I shall be the last..."

SECOND PERSON OF THE PROLOGUE
The ardour of the poet I'll unbraid
Strand by strand — do you laugh at my comrade?
At his enthusiasm? If you wish
To know him — he's like a Turkish dervish.

The seven candles, they are seven towns,
Seven nations bathed in gold ring him round;
An exile, he. His black hair has gone grey
Not from age, but worry. In his eyes play
Sparks of vatic vision; in his palm
Those stars are thoughts, as radiant as the dawn.
The sword in his mouth? Words, like stilettos,
With which he slays the stupid... or his foes.

THIRD PERSON OF THE PROLOGUE
I'll chase this feuding duo from the stage.
Now, give me some ashes from the nation's urn — dust
From which to raise the people; a cothurnus
I'll set upon the grave, and presto! Soon
I've made my actors taller by a tomb.
I'll tear the rotten shroud from my roused knights
And wrap them round with azure Polish skies;
I'll make each soul shine with dawns and sun-rays,
Hopeful; they'll pass before your eyes and ears;
Greet them with smiles — bid them farewell with tears.

# PART I

## ACT I

### Scene 1

*Kordian, a fifteen year old boy, is lying beneath a large linden tree on a village courtyard. Grzegorz, an old servant, is off to one side, cleaning a hunting rifle. On the one side we see a country house; on the other, a garden... Beyond the courtyard fence can be seen a pond, fields, and pinewoods.*

KORDIAN
*Musing.*
He killed himself — so young! Immediately,

Fear to my lips words of condemnation brought;
This was a gloomy warning to me —
To douse the fires of my fancy grown too hot.
Today, for the silly cautions of the folk
I've nothing but contempt. I flame, I burn —
And like a bloom stretching aloft, wide ope
To the air, I drink adventure, I yearn,
In earth's fair creatures I spell out God's runes;
I seek the spark hidden deep inside the stones;
And as that pond reflects the azure sky,
So does my thought reflect the blue on high.
The quiet fall that shakes the crowns of the trees
           Poisoning the leaves,
           Blasting with its breath
The tender forehead of the rose
           Is like to the angel of death,
           Whispering to these and those,
           "Die!" and with a shiver
           They curl and wither.
The thought of death, from nature, spills into my soul.
           Pale and yearning, glum with grief,
           I look upon the flower's dole
And seem to be helpless, like a dry, wind blown leaf.
So quiet. I hear the bleating of the flocks;
I hear them go, crunching the frosty stalks
Beneath their hooves, and searching with wet eye
The pale expanses of the leaden sky,
As if to ask, "Where have the flowers gone?
The blooming poppies, amongst which we would run?"
So quiet, cold, deserted... I hear the ring
Of bells that call to evensong on the air —
They will not rouse the clotted grass to prayer.
The earth will pray, at sunrise, in the spring.
I too am like a tree curdled by frost.
One hundred feelings, and emotions to spare;
One hundred leaves — all withered, through the air
Whole crowds of them fly off at the slightest wind.
The fate of feelings? Blight. Their noise — is din,
An unharmonious babbling... Lightning, strike!
One great thought, amidst so many, now — ignite!
God! Strip from my heart this swallow-like unease!

Enliven this heart! Let it heed Thy prophecies
And know its task! Let it burn bright and hot,
And I shall be the flywheel of that thought.
I'll show it on my face; with each heart-beat
I'll count it down, and mark each quarter hour
With ringing words, till Thou givest me the power
To Strike! And with my life, the task complete.
*Pause.*
Drop by drop
I've distilled my heart in a love unrequited.
Hey, Grzegorz — stop
Cleaning that gun...

GRZEGORZ
                I've just finished with it.
What would you wish, young master?

KORDIAN
                        Come here, old friend.
I'm bored.

GRZEGORZ
                Nothing new there! But how might I amend
Your boredom? How about a story? I'm able
To root through this grey attic for a fable,
A rich one, noble; or some old wise word
Of my old Gran, who now rests in the Lord;
An anecdote, a spell... I've everything
Ready. You prefer I gab? Or sing?

*Kordian is silent. Grzegorz begins his tale.*

Once upon a time, at school,
There was a lad named Jan. A dear
And pretty child, who, as a rule
Cared less for books, and more for beer.
Had he grown just a little taller
He'd have been a fine soldier, for
He wasn't a devoted scholar;
Indeed, his back was always sore
From birching. Till one day, at last,

At wit's end, Master called to Mother:
"Your son has been expelled from class!
Take him! He is not worth my bother!"
And so she took him. In despair,
They went to see the parish priest.
Weeping, she sobbed complaint and care
The while the vicar pouted, creased
His brow, and then, when the poor woman
Had finished with her litany,
He took Jan's chin in hand. "Come on,
Look me straight in the eye... Let's see...
This head's not made for books. A rake or
Spade's more fitting. My advice:
Trundle him off to the shoemaker.
He'll take him as an apprentice."
He stroked the urchin's pretty face,
Gave him a cake, and some five cents,
And then with blessing and a shrug,
Saw them both to the rectory fence.

And thus they heeded his advice.
The shoemaker's workshop was nigh;
But Jan was fed up in a trice
With leather thong and needle's eye;
Some devil tickled Janek's nape —
He dreamt of good times and of girls,
And one day, said, "So, I'll escape,
With my five cents, and see the world!"
And so, goodbye apprenticeship!
Contract and master aside he tossed
And off to Königsberg, on leaky ship
    He sailed...
The tub sank, and Jan was lost...

Jan's mother wrung her hands and wept;
At Sunday Mass, from the pulpit
The vicar fumed and warned and ripped
Into the perfidious culprit.
"And yet, my flock, have ye no fear,"
The good priest summed up, winding down,

"God fearing people, for it's clear:
Who's marked for hanging will not drown."

Now where it was that little Jan
Was hid in secret all this while
I know not — but he did hop on
A boat that struck port at an isle,
Where people lived, ruled by a king.
Then, walking into town, a crowd
He spied, vivating and singing;
The king's litter drew close, Jan bowed,
And did so with such pretty grace
The king was stunned. Putting on his specs
He cried, "Again!" And Janek traced
Such curtsies and such arabesques;
The king could not believe his eyes!
The courtiers too (as courtiers will)
Put on their glasses, rapt, surprised
(Just like the king) at the boy's skill.
The king was famed for inner sight.
For he could tell, at a mere glance
If one was fit to be a knight
Or draper. "That boy, he can dance!"
The awestruck king let fly the word —
And all the courtiers (of course) concurred.
"What is your name?"
                    "Jan."
                            "Jan, do tell,
What is it that you do?"
                        "I sew
Dog shoes."
            "And do you sew them well?"
"Do I sew good dog shoes, Pop? Ho!
Better you've never seen! No dogs
Have ever worn more comfy cogs!
My mukluks keep all canine toes
Warm in the harshest frosts and snows;
My summer sandals (with their soles
As thin as Hosts) are fit for strolls
In any palace garden, and
They're waterproof. Made by this hand,

They'll keep Portuguese water dogs
Dry shod through marshes, ponds and bogs!"
The monarch cried, "My lad! You're hired!
And from then on, his dogs, attired
In leather boots, and silk liveries
Sped out on hunts booted, and strode
The streets shod — setting off a mode
For clothing dogs there — all of which
Made little Jan obscenely rich.
From dog-shoemaker, he became
In short order, royal chamberlain,
With a palace all his own, and one
He bought to house his gushing mum...
The king made her, for all intents,
First lady of the realm.
      The priest?
He got back his five cents.

KORDIAN
Ha, ha! A splendid tale!

GRZEGORZ
      You see, my lord?
A tale to make you laugh. What's more, behind it —
A moral. Wisdom in every word.

KORDIAN
A moral? Tell me, old man.

GRZEGORZ
      Ah, who can find it?
For me it's enough the sense runs straight.

KORDIAN
I believe you.

GRZEGORZ
      O, that's a good thing, faith,
And necessary. When my boy asks for fish,
It's not a snake I'll set down on his dish.
I've wandered far and long away from home,

So sick with longing, my comrades in arms
Plagued me with jokes and wine and local charms —
It almost came to blows! I wanted none
Of their roistering. He who laughter sows
Will find from sterile soil no strong corn grows;
The sad man's heart is like a volume, full
Of learning — he won't rot like some toadstool
Beneath a pine, but grows wise, day by day
And crumb by crumb... When I was in Egypt... Say!
I've never told you about that battle...
With your permission?

KORDIAN
                      Speak, old man!

GRZEGORZ
                            Ah, devil
Take him, that Corporal! Every inch a man!
He led the army out into the field...
No, into the table-flat plains of sand,
Open on every side, empty and broad
Wherever you looked — they eye almost reached God!
The chief saw fit to form us in five squares,
Like five stars tossed onto the desert; there
I shone in one, and saw the other four.
As I recall, we had a laugh before
The fight — for you should know, sir, at the tail
End of the group traipsed donkeys with bales
Of baggage; there among them was a set
Of scholars (kept safe by our bayonets),
French wisemen out in search of ancient lore
With which to stuff their almanacs; we bore
No more love to them than we had for Krauts —
Those mutts out snuffling truffles with their snouts!
So, when it seemed the battle might begin,
We called "Take shelter, asses and learned men!"
Nor were they sluggish our advice to heed:
They raced — on two or four legs — at top speed!
Now, I'm a soldier, not adverse to fight,
But I was somehow glum that day, it's true;
I still can see the Nile afar, calm, blue...

Some city walls beyond it met the eye...
And far above our heads, the cloudless sky.
The air was clear, but shifty all the same:
It flickered, like the heat above the flame
Of tallow candles. But the greatest sight
That really struck the troops with awe, were those
Mountains of chiselled stone; so high they rose
You might see them from here on a clear day
If not for the Carpathians in the way...
And so the Chief rode up before his hosts;
At once a "Vivat!" thundered, like a toast,
Though we weren't drinking wine... And when he stopped,
He gazed at us, and pointed to the top
Of those pyramids, and cried, "Soldats!"
(That's French for "soldiers") "Behold, my champions!
From those high summits, one hundred aeons
Look upon you!" I looked and — I don't care
If I'm thought foolish — in the azure air
Above those tombs I saw, as clear and bright
As Michael on church vault, flashing with light,
An armoured figure, with a fiery spear,
Piercing a dragon which was flying near
Us over the boiling sands. Then did I hear
One hundred cannon thunder; their flash took
My sight from me; when it cleared: mamelukes
We're jabbing at us with their curving swords
Like ravens pecking; until those same hordes
Turned tail to run away; our bayonets
Prevented that, the monkeys!

KORDIAN
                    Then? What next?

GRZEGORZ
O, shame on you for asking! Everyone knows
We never lost a fight with such as those
Who break parole... If not for that damned plague...
But you're no longer listening, anyway.

KORDIAN
*In thought, to himself.*
I am ashamed! The old man's words set fire to my soul!
Sometimes, with wild thoughts whirling through my head, I go
Into the woods; amidst the noisy pines, I throw
Myself amongst swords clashing;
I see myself with mystic light aglow,
Heroic, flashing
Amongst shining troops; troops that spring from out the earth,
Which then erupts, like a volcano giving birth
To a city dug out of the magma... Idiocies!
Vain, childish daydreaming! With visions such as these
How dare I speak up amongst men with common sense!
So I seek out — whom? Elderly babbling servants
Who weave long, stupid tales...

*Pause, then to Grzegorz.*
                                        Grzegorz, you may go.
If the young lady goes out riding, let me know.

GRZEGORZ
Last night, perhaps, my lord did not sleep well?
For as if kicking some insistent beast,
So he spurns old Grzegorz... When I was held
Captive, I knew a bright young scholar... He at least
Did not despise me, or my tales — the mild
And noble boy thanked me for them! Pretty child...
But he ended badly...

KORDIAN
                    He died?

GRZEGORZ
                            Not... so...

KORDIAN
Then he's alive!

GRZEGORZ
                  He's not alive, O no!
There are worse things than death, is what I meant...

So, back in '12, we prisoners were sent
Off to Siberia by the Muscovites...
Two hundred of us; old campaigners, white
And grizzled, and a few young officers,
But "all for one" we were; we were brothers
Really — we broke bread like it was the Host.
There were no ranks among us; we were that close!
The young man that I'm speaking of was called
Kazimierz. Now, he suffered for us all
Whenever a Russian wanted to torment
A soldier, till once, in secret, he sent
Word to a group of us: he had a plan,
And it was a good one, all said and told;
A noble plan it was — for it was bold.
Don't smirk, young sir! For those who understand
Captivity — which greys fast youthful hair —
Will not condemn wild dreams born of despair.
He wished to take the pickets by surprise,
Slaughter the Cossacks with their Cossack knives,
And then to lead his faithful brothers home
To Poland... But the plot became known
To the Russians, who smelt the wolf that hid
Beneath the wool. And so the guardsmen led
All of us prisoners into the fields.
With Bashkirs before us, the Volga at our heels,
Their colonel then addressed us — a Tatar,
Reading aloud some edict from the Tsar.
Supposedly, the Polish prisoners
Were to be split in tens, to be dispersed
Amongst the armies of the Muscovites.
At this, we linked our arms and held on — tight!
And shouted — one and all — "We will not go!"
They... didn't shoot us, no. Leather lassos
Those Tatar devils tossed around our necks!
What I felt at that moment, I shan't forget
Until the grave! They treated us like flocks
For the shearing! We stood there with arms locked...
Tense, waiting for the massacre to start.
A man stood to my right... no, next my heart.
An older soldier, grey, he gripped my hand
As if it were a sabre. Too weak to stand,

He rested all his weight on me — a cruel
Tatar then galloped up, roped him, and pulled —
I saw his face grow livid as a corpse,
His eyes bulged — he was torn from me by force
When that knave lashed his horse, that reared, and sped
Off, tearing the man behind him, to be shredded
Against the flint and sandy waste — I found
A tuft of his scalp, bloodied, on the ground,
Torn living from his head. And on and on
The charger raced, grew smaller, and was gone…
The dust he kicked up long hung over the plain
And, though one couldn't see him, one's thought remained
At the poor fellow's side, torn, dragged, and ripped…
We stood like slumps of corn ripe to be snipped
On harvest fields; silent, full of dread,
With wild thoughts tumbling through our maddened heads,
While round us, whistling, pagans wheeled and leapt,
Killing time happily by dealing death…
'Twas then our brave young Kazimerz leapt, my lord,
Into the midst of that wild Bashkir horde,
And seizing that Tatar colonel by the collar,
He plunged with him into the ice-cold water.
He jammed the pagan so, that when two ice
Floes rushed together, his Bashkir head was sliced
From off his torso — and there it bobbed,
Eyes wide open, as if it had been lopped
Off by a sword-swipe.

KORDIAN
         And Kazimierz?

GRZEGORZ
             Was lost.

KORDIAN
Do you not know his family name, Grzegorz?

GRZEGORZ
I don't. I know Kazimierz was his name.
And after death? To him it's all the same.

*[Moved, Kordian grips Grzegorz by the hand.]*

You take an old servant's hand in your own
My lord...

KORDIAN
                    Dear God, how that old man has grown
Into a giant! But I... lack belief...
Where men respire freely, I cannot breathe.
From men's sublime thoughts my mocking eye brings
Me back down the path to the muddied springs —
I shall not overstep the barricades
Set up on the roads by superstition...
Now is the time for youth to seize its mission,
To figure out: To live? Or not to live?
And I? am helpless. I'm not made to strive
Against the Sphinxes like killer Oedipus,
Unravelling their riddling speech, because
Today they're many — the Sphinxes have multiplied.
Time was, with threefold riddle they mystified
Their prey; now, like weeds their riddles expand —
Riddles as numerous as grains of sand.
Everywhere, mystery. The world has not been stretched
Any wider, but it has grown in depth.
Man sails along its surface merely, and
If he's not measured out his road in knots,
He can't judge motion out of sight of land;
Perhaps the highway along which he trots
Has mileposts, set up by superstition,
The pale corpses of the centuries...
No, crosses, set along the hard-tramped ways,
Where simple men rein in their horse and pray
Before passing on. Till some wiseman sees
Fit some new straighter road to blaze.
The simple folk adopt it by degrees;
Only the storks abandon not the cross,
Building their nest upon it, while the moss
Covers its wood, which soon starts to decay...
Sometimes the cross falls, crushing kids at play
Setting flowers at its foot; the people moan —
How could they neglect to take the cross down?

So I set out — and this shall be my task:
To fell all wood gone rotten, with my axe.
And love? I shall forget,* amidst the press
Of the world's storms... It shall remain a fresh,
Wild song, like that of a belated crane
That soars above the empty, azure main...
The last bird, cut off from the happy crowds,
He needs new wings, new roads among the clouds —
Columbus, sailing unknown seas, for parts
Unknown, with sad thoughts, and a broken heart.

LAURA
*Calling from the porch.*
Kordian!

KORDIAN
That voice! it disperses the glowing light of dawn.
Enclosed within a ring of spells I'm caught.
I could have been something. I shall be nought.

### Scene 2

*A garden with intersecting paths bordered by linden trees, leading in different directions. Among the trees may be seen an abandoned house with broken window panes. It is autumn — leaves are falling — windy weather. Kordian and Laura get down from their saddles. Grzegorz remains with the horses, while Kordian and Laura enter one of the alleys. They do not speak for a long while.*

LAURA
*With a half sarcastic smile.*
Why are you so sad?

*Kordian looks at her with misty eye, but remains silent.*

---

\*     In Polish: *Miłość? zapomnę o niej.* "Love? I'll forget about it." However, because Polish words have three genders, and *miłość* (love) is feminine in gender, there is a subtle double entendre here, which cannot be reproduced in English. For Kordian actually says "Love? I'll forget about her," which pronoun grammatically refers to "love," but can also allude to another "her" — Laura, whom we are about to meet.

JULIUSZ SŁOWACKI

                        This morning I stole
A look into my book of autographs,
And there among the poems I found one...
I recognised the hand — ah, rather, the soul...
*Kordian blushes and bends low to the ground.*

Why do you bend down?

KORDIAN
                        I'm sweeping the path
Of thorns and weeds before your feet. You know,
The thorn that pricks my hand will harm no one!

LAURA
Do you forget your mother? A widow?
Why do you knit your gloomy brows, and blush?

KORDIAN
Ask the trees why, in autumn, when they're touched
By frost, their leaves turn purple. At most —
Well, such is the mystery of frost.

LAURA
Let's rest a moment. Which of us will see
First, the star we know so well?

KORDIAN
                        This I'll say:
If it's the star of hope, it won't be me!

LAURA
And if it is the star of memory?

KORDIAN
For me it is too early in the day
For such a pale planet!

LAURA
                        And Kordian's star?

*Kordian lifts his eyes to Laura, then looks away.*

What's its name?

KORDIAN

          Future.

LAURA
*Smiling.*

                    And where does it rise?
Where might I see it? What quarter of the skies?

KORDIAN
O! I don't know! I don't! It's not a fixed star —
Each day it must be lost, and then each day
It must be searched out again!

LAURA
Kordian
Has a bright future — talent, abilities…

KORDIAN
Yes, when I've been burnt through by miseries
I'll shine quite brightly — with the phosphorus
Of rotten bones. Such talents as are found
In madmen's hands are lanterns, bright enough
To lead them to the river where they drown.
Far better — shut the eyes, the lanterns snuff,
Or buy a pinch of reason, common sense,
The treasury of dreams' cold recompense!

LAURA
How bitter you are today!

*She sits down on a wooden bench, Kordian sits at her feet.*

KORDIAN
*Gazing at the sky.*

                    Such delight
Is nature! See that grey cloud there, in flight?
A horseman of the Apocalypse. You see?
Chased by the wind, it brews within its mind
The thought of lightning, yet, fainting with cold,

It cannot raise the spark. So, what's behind
Its gloomy brows, its ire, will never be told.
And so it sails on, its mind athrum
With shining thought. Let it sail on — cold, dumb...

*Picks a flower and turns to Laura with a smile.*

Accept this sprig of purple heather. Take
Care not to shake from it the jewels of frost...

*Lost in thought, he gazes at the sky.*

Look there, aloft — the spirits of Dante —
There — in that tree — a chattering
Of starlings alight, and settle down to sleep.
The wind at night will kill the leaves; their deep
Slumber will not be disturbed, the rocking
Branches, though dying, will hum a lullaby,
While their angel will teach them, through the night,
In dreams, the further paths of their long flight.
And when they wake, the tree will say, "Birds, fly.
I have no more leaves for you. I've grown old
This night, while you were sleeping..."

LAURA
                          And you've told
Me this for what reason? Has it some deep
Moral?

KORDIAN
      Ha, ha! A sad one: the tree didn't sleep,
But the birds did...

LAURA
                   Kordian, he who seeks the future
Should sleep well, too.

KORDIAN
                     Where's the angel to nurture
My dreams? Will she come to lead me? Thoughts, feelings —
These ought to be spent in a slow bleeding,

Like misers do — pinched out on yearly terms
And not cast out at once upon the storms
Of sense — you've got to win the present day
To see the next dawn. One's sparked on one's way
By a strange curiosity, for which
One pays with misfortune. One mustn't pitch
All one has to the storm winds.
*Violently.*
                                        But, you see —
I have! O good Lord, have mercy on me!

LAURA
Kordian!

*Kordian is silent.*

    It's cold and windy. Time we were gone.

KORDIAN
O no! Stay, yet...

LAURA
                    You promise to be calm?

KORDIAN
*Wildly, distractedly.*
Yes.

LAURA
The future's far away — it's not begun;
All lies before us while we still are young.

KORDIAN
*Lost in thought, gazing at the sky.*
The sky's dark azure sparkles through the mist,
And, ah! The moon! — look there — silver and full,
Has paused to gaze at us, through the bright wool
Of clouds that drape her; now she flies, as if
She'd broken free of them... A rotting bough
Of that tree split her in two halves, and now,
Behind the leaves she hides her disk in gloom...

Listen — if ever you should see the moon's
White face among the clouds of fall so shine,
The ghost you shoo away — it shall be mine!
*Pause.*
In endless works God made the soul incarnate;
Its ray then shattered, and the soul bestrewed
Amongst the feelings, in a million hues,
Of which five took our senses for its slaves;
The rest expired in the vacuum, hurled
Into the void. But there's another world!
And there these feelings, spilt, together ran,
From which arose an angel. White, than man
Smaller, perhaps, an atom, a mere mite,
Around whom wheel the shattered rays — but bright,
How bright! Unstained this angel's heart by human dyes.
By endless feeling the soul multiplies,
And God reveals the future to his eyes,
So that he ceases gazing in the graves;
A column of light before his feet He lays,
Upon which countless stars and suns are spread —
There shall the angel fix his gaze, his hopes;
And like a star, into the future fly —
O! My soul too would soar! Its weak limbs grope
The air; she leaps from burnt lips to the sky...
*His arms fall to his side in despair.*
But for one angel, one soul won't suffice —
Two are needed...!

LAURA
                It's bad to burn and strain
With dreams; I ... don't quite catch you...

KORDIAN
*With contempt.*
                                  I'm insane...!

*Laura moves off to the garden gate. She gets on her horse and goes off with Grzegorz.*
*Kordian remains alone in the garden, motionless.*

KORDIAN
*Solus.*
The stars of night in the sapphire heavens burn,
My thought has wandered in their midst, and wheels,
Fallen; the stars spin her, and toss, and twist,
Till gloomy, pale, exhausted, she returns
From dancing through the heavens into my breast,
My dull heart — Here I wait, at the abyss
Of heaven standing, shivering with concern
As she, caught in the starry eddies, churns…
Stars! Like a key of cranes you fly, somewhere —
I too would soar with you through the dark air!
*Takes out his pistol.*
It's loaded. Let the iron hammer fall…
A spurt of pain, then darkness… And then a flash
Of brightness… or not? What if that is all?
No brightness flashes, and the pain shall pass,
Then, darkness… and the darkness too shall die…
Nothing there, nothing, and not even I
Will be there to say: Nothing… is…
Nor shall I even question God for why
There's nothing… I'll be overthrown with this?
With nothing?… Ha! Death stares me in the eye
With her two faces — like that starry sky
And its reflection there upon the lake…
Truth or illusion? Difficult to make
A choice when you can understand nothing…
*He presses the gun to his temple.*
No — not here in the garden… A clearing
With flowers, but no other living thing.

### Scene 3
*Laura, alone in a room, by a lamp.*

LAURA
Eleven strikes… and Kordian's not returned.
Why is it that my heart is filled with fear?
What if I've killed that child with fickle jeers?
Blown petals off a rose the sun has burned?
And if his heart's been poured from such an ore,

That what I trace there, stays forever more
When hardened? And if — O dear God! — what's worse,
His eyes get used to tears, and I'm their source?
Get used to darkness? If, instead of tears
— As sometimes happens with boys of his years —

Who flame with ardour, pride should twist his lips
Into a mocking grin of bitterness?

*She falls to musing, then picks up her autograph book and begins to leaf through it.*

Dull, hackneyed niceness — This one likens me
To a flower; that, to a star, and number three —
The same as they. And then we have the fourth:
"Divine Diana." Oh well, as it is
He's godlike too. His head is like Apis'.
And this one here is ... Ah! it's Kordian!
By blind coincidence my listless hand
Turned to that page... I'll read it, to the end...

*Reads Kordian's poem.*

O! Someday I'll sail the sea of memories...
I'll stop — the images refuse to roll
     Until you say: "Troublesome soul,
Why over my spirit calm have you this sway,
Like to the moon when, gazing at the sea,
He'll draw her close, at times push her away...
Why are you everywhere, above, and within, me?"
Within you and without you; I've come here
    Neither to chide nor warn,
     I neither dare to bless, nor scorn,
But I've had strange dreams lately, in the grave;
I dreamt you happy. Happily engaged.
     Show me the golden ring you've got.
      It's tarnished? O! It's not my fault, it's not!

Why do you drape your face, tresses undone?
     And yet I glimpse behind their mist
     Something flashing out like the sun.

                    A string of pearls? An amethyst?
                         Cornelian? Or peridot?
Or maybe tears? It's not my fault, it's not!

             My angel! (Once I held you such),
             Once, with blooms you ringed your braids;
             There were so many blooms, so much,
             That wreath for wreath you would exchange
Before the first had even time to fade.
Why do I see you now, so muted? Strange —
The flowers on the meadows still must grow,
                    Surviving storm and sweltering heat,
Except one pale rose, withered at your feet
                    So long, O, so long ago!
                    But why
                         It withered for aye...
                         I've quite forgot...
             But if all of your flowers die?
             It's not my fault! It's not!

*Stops reading.*

A horse! It must be Kordian...! Let's see —
No, better leave the window closed.
It's better that nobody knows —
Especially him — that I've been worried...
But why does he not open the door?
*Opens the window.*
The horse — is by itself! And off it goes,
Without a rider! Something's happened! O Lord!

*Rings, Maid enters.*

Where's Grzegorz?

MAID
                    I don't know, Miss. He wasn't there
When we had supper. Nor did he share
A cup with me, or anyone of those
Who serve you. Just like the Jew with Jesus' clothes...

LAURA
Go! Look for him! I need him! Run!

GRZEGORZ
*Enters.*
Misfortune!
The young lord's shot himself!

### END OF ACT I

## ACT II

### 1828
### THE WANDERER

*London. St James's Park. Evening.*
*Kordian sits beneath a tree, green fields all around.*
*In the distance, the lake, shaded by trees. Flocks at pasture.*
*Nearby, St James's Palace and the two towers of Westminster Abbey.*

KORDIAN
Amidst these wastes of palaces, this green
Island, where I escape the seething mobs
Who rather drink the smoke, and visit shops,
The while this garden, London's Arcadian dream,
Set in the city's midst just like one jewel
Of verse in a dull epic by some fool...
People! These trees, the work of God's own hand
Are worth more than all your mansions on the Strand!
Untouched, the trees preserve their Edenic grace;
On foggy days, their leafy fans will chase
The clouds of soot away... There on the lake
The swans glide with their wings outspread, to take
The air like sails... The snaky paths, with sand
From the Pactolus... and the fields, all spread
With softer silk than that hawked by Flamand,
And there! The town... a clock whose cogs and wheels
Are human flesh and bone. Here in these peaceful fields
No people sprout; the gentle sheep flocks graze...
I used to dream, back in my childish days,
Of building capitals. Today I see
Them with my own eyes. But the fantasy
Of those days in my thought's still there —
Like images in tour-books, I compare
Them with what I look upon. Naked truth,
Reward the fondly fashioned dreams of youth!
If but with the same care I'd analyse
Myself as I do cities, even now

Might the world lead me back, away from pride
And moaning, to where I would fain belong:
O there, among the laughing, joyful cries,
The throngs of happy people, without a care?
..................................
I'd like to rub this Cain-mark from my brow!
Each eye that passes, scans the suicide...

CARETAKER
Good evening, sir. A penny for that chair...

*Kordian gives him a shilling and declines the change.*

The young gentleman pays just like a lord,
But doesn't sit like one.

KORDIAN
                    How do lords sit?

CARETAKER
Well, your true magnate doesn't seem to fit
On one chair. He needs three. He can afford
One for his... person, and one for his feet,
Another for his hat. Three pence.

KORDIAN
                         I see.
I'll keep that in mind.

CARETAKER
                    A noble way to sit.
I pray reform won't put an end to it...

*It grows dark.*

KORDIAN
There — just past the lake, in that dark glade,
A lonely man walks, gliding like a shade...
He gazes at the moon, sighs... Some poor soul
Whose heart's enveloped in a lover's dole:
Passion unrequited; vanished the golden dream,

He flees the world... Or so to me, it seems...
I'd like to meet him. Do you know that bloke,
Brother?

CARETAKER
             A bankrupt. Sentence passed. Still broke.

KORDIAN
So why is he not in gaol, but in the park?

CARETAKER
The law don't chase your debtor after dark,
And won't enter his house during the day.
So he sleeps at sunup, and walks the night away.
You will forgive me, sir, but I had thought
You also were shirking the law, with God's
Help.

KORDIAN
            Ah, the wretch!

CARETAKER
                     But you pay like a lord...
Allow me the honour of broaching a word
In recommendation of my brothers.
One sells chairs in Parliament, another,
Like me, in Westminster Abbey, sells graves;
The third heraldic seals and arms engraves.
On each he puts two towers, an ell, and scale
(Those towers remind one of a debtor's gaol);
The fourth is known as the poor man's Garrick
(His Punch to Judy takes the tragic stick).
Since he was but a tot he'd learnt to ape
And with his stories, entertain the gapes
Down in the street; through Punch's mouth he tells
Of murdering his wife, tossing his child
Out the window, hanging his justice, and while
The devils drag his poor soul off to Hell,
The people melt in tears, beneath his spell...

*Kordian exits.*

*Dover. Kordian sits on a chalky cliff above the sea, reading Shakespeare: a fragment of* King Lear.

KORDIAN
*Reads*
" Come on, sir, here's the place; stand still. How fearful
And dizzy 'tis, to cast one's eyes so low!
The crows and choughs that wing the midway air
Show scarce so gross as beetles. Half way down
Hangs one that gathers samphire, dreadful trade!
Me thinks he seems no bigger than his head.
The fishermen that walk upon the beach
Appear like mice; and yond tall anchoring bark,
Diminish'd to her cock; her cock, a buoy
Almost too small for sight. The murmuring surge,
That on th' unnumb'red idle pebble chafes,
Cannot be heard so high. I'll look no more,
Lest my brain turn, and the deficient sight
Topple down headlong."

*Stops reading.*

Shakespeare! Spirit! Thou hast made a hill
Taller than that which God himself had built,
Since thou describ'st to blind eyes an abyss
And draw'st mere mortal clay near endlessness!
I'd rather clouds darkened these eyes of mine
So I might look upon the world with thine!

*He stands.*

But genius gilds this world of ours in vain.
On each rung of the scale, reality lurks,
And, really, I and that man are the same,
Gathering weeds at cliffside. Such hard work!

*Konrad exits.*

*An Italian villa. A room hung entirely with mirrors. Carpets. Vases carved from lava, filled with flowers. Through the window, a charming landscape may be seen. Kordian, with Violetta, a young and beautiful Italian woman.*

KORDIAN
My soul!
Let me brush back the hair from your face.
I blossom with delight in your embrace;
Turn here your flaming, sparkling eyes, my girl —
Sapphires, their whites of snowy-azure pearl!
Those languid eyes! Ah! I fall at your feet...
Thus dies the golden butterfly on sweet,
Oversweet roses — those sparkling eyes — I rave!
And with but one kiss, I rise from the grave...

VIOLETTA
Release me! I faint.

KORDIAN
     And fainting, like a wave
Your swelling bosom pushes me to shore;
Then your lips part, those lips of fiery coral —
A flame ineffable, yet what you feel
They cannot help but to reveal,
Expressing all in such a tongue
As all love's voices are condensed in one:
The note of strings snapped, the murmur of shame,
Reproach, remorse, a child's laugh, and a sigh...
It's at such moments dear, I know you're mine,
I know you love me...

VIOLETTA
     I've abandoned name,
And lord, and God, for you! Who could deny
I love you more than life itself?

KORDIAN
     Not I!
Upon your lips I hang, a butterfly,
Upon a coral rose. Your neck's aflame —
But on your fiery bosom, all the same
Rest cold, cold pearls — I'll bite through the thread!

VIOLETTA
Alas!

KORDIAN
      Like water drops the pearls flow down
Your two breasts — tell me, love, are you afraid
Of the caress of pearls? Why do you frown
And tremble, like a leaf? ... Do you love me?

VIOLETTA
As I've told you, one hundred times or more,
Like the tears of the dawn I cling to you!
Shake your sleeve — and I'll be shattered, like the dew.

KORDIAN
*Ever colder, ever more pensively.*
Consider this vase. Once it seethed with living flame,
Chipped into shape when cold... and just the same
Is the heart of woman: lava grown cold,
The world its sculptor.

VIOLETTA
              Your words are sharp:
An unfair judgement of my faithful heart...

KORDIAN
My love! Far in the north a castle stands,
Ancient, my forebears' arms loom from the gate,
And in the halls, their portraits: rows of grand,
Worthy and venerable agnates;
They once trained upon me an eye severe,
And their harsh gaze pursues me even here —
For I melted down all to which I was heir
To form that golden chaplet that you wear.

VIOLETTA
You rack the heart with inopportune regret.

KORDIAN
If only one of your tears, love, would serve
To reclaim it all, I'd say no. You deserve

To flash and shine — a gem in jewels set,
Like to the star-encrusted Milky Way.
Here in this villa, I would gladly stay
Whole ages by your side amongst the flowers,
The laurels, mirrors, bronzes, waterfalls —
And yet, who knows? Tomorrow when you rise,
The spectre of misery may meet your eyes...
For... Curses! Everything's gone! I've lost it all!

VIOLETTA
What are you saying?

KORDIAN
                              In a few hours,
My creditors will be knocking at the door...
But who needs riches? I have so much more,
For I have you!

VIOLETTA
                Where are my gems?! My jewels?!

KORDIAN
You have my heart — my love —

VIOLETTA
                            Love is for fools!
My jewels! Where is the key?

KORDIAN
                              My love — alas —
Last night, striving to stave off our collapse,
I staked your jewels, and lost them. I must part
With all I own — except your angel's heart!

VIOLETTA
*Angrily, in tears.*
He staked my gems to cover his arrears!

KORDIAN
You slay me, love, with these untimely tears!
More than the world, your heart is worth to me!

VIOLETTA
You lost my heart along with the money!
Ah, misery!

KORDIAN
          My horse waits down below.

VIOLETTA
Go to hell!

KORDIAN
          I haven't far to go.
The horse is shod with gold — one thousand
Ducats apiece... I won at the last hand
Last night, and so I'll smuggle in those shoes
At least so much, safe from my creditors.
All night long through meadow and brake I'll fly;
The golden hooves beating the silver dew,
Until at the first hamlet I arrive.
I'll have the blacksmith unshoe the horse
And I'll fund four banquets — one with each shoe —
And then, like fashionable heroes do,
I'll shoot myself... Madame, you would not lack
An invitation, if I might be so bold...
That is, if you would deign to dress in black —
Indeed, it suits you well, the truth be told...
Madame? Will you go with me?

VIOLETTA
*Pause.*
                      Yes, my dear...

*They exit.*

*A public highway. Kordian and Violetta on horseback, galloping, Kordian in front.*
*The horse slips and falls. Kordian gets off and helps Violetta down.*

VIOLETTA
What happened?

KONRAD
                No fear. The horse was unshod,
And slipped, and fell.

VIOLETTA
                The horse, unshod?

KONRAD
It's nothing. I had explicitly asked
The smith to fix the shoes with rotten wire,
Not nails. So shod, we left, and in a flash,
The shoes came loose...

VIOLETTA
*Angrily.*
                You snake from Genesis!

KONRAD
Ah, Eve! There will be other Adams! As for this,
I'm truly happy that my servants now
Are scuttling over my tracks with lowered brow,
Searching for gold there where your teardrops run!

VIOLETTA
I hope they've stolen the bullets from your gun!
I hope you die from hunger, parched with thirst!

*She runs off, retracing their road. With a smile of contempt, Kordian watches her go.*

KORDIAN
I've never been loved with with a love quite like hers!
She seeks her lover's traces over the plain...
Giddup, my friend! Wherever. You have free rein.

*Kordian rides off.*

*The Vatican. A hall hung with damask. The Pope, in golden slippers, sits upon a golden throne.*

*Near him, the papal tiara rests upon a golden tripod, and on the tiara sits a Parrot with a red neck.*
*A Swiss Guard opens the doors and admits Kordian.*

SWISS GUARD
Graf Kordian, a Pole!

POPE
I greet the scion of the noble race
Of the Sobieskis! Surely many a grace
Showers from Heaven upon your happy land?
I lift prayers of thanksgiving for Poland,
For, like an angel with an olive branch,
The Tsar extends his frank fraternal hands
To our faith. Hosannah! It's clear he...

PARROT
*Thinly squawking.*
Miserere!

KORDIAN
I bring you, Father, this holy relic:
A handful of my native soil, thick
With the blood of myriads of men,
Women and children, cut down unshriven,
Uncomforted by the Eucharist. Please
Place it among your most treasured gifts. We
Ask in exchange but one tear...

PARROT
                    Lachryma Christi!

POPE
*Smiling at the parrot, shooing it with a handkerchief.*
Enough of that, Luther! Well now, Poland's son,
You've seen St Peter's? And the Pantheon?
The Circus Maximus? O, come Sunday,
You'll hear our new black tenor sing. The Dey
Sent me him as a gift... One thing more — be
Sure to hear my next Urbi te Orbi
Tomorrow — what a sight! The people lie

Prostrate before me. Tell the Poles that I
Bid them to pray and hold fast to the faith,
And honour their rightful Tsar unto the death...

KORDIAN
This clod of bloody earth no one shall bless?
What shall I say...?

PARROT
           Clamavi! From the depths!

POPE
*Laughs in consternation, trying to hide his embarrassment; he shoos away the parrot.*
Away, little Satan! Or I'll close your
Beak for good! Look — see him flit from crozier
To tiara; damned beast! I'd almost say
That Luther's soul's inside the vermin pent
To do the penance owed for his dissent,
The bird's so full of aphorisms, Q
E D's... D'you know, once he fell to dispute,
Hidden behind a hanging, with a Prince
Of the Church! A quaestor, who was convinced
That he was arguing with a professor!
The beast ran circles round him; the poor
Fellow tore a second tonsure on his head!
At last the parrot made him flee. He said
(In Hebrew?) At any rate, he chanced to say
"Papa Satan! Papa Satan! Aleppe!"
Stupid creature! Sometimes, the Lord permits
Davids to overcome Goliaths' wits...

---

\*     A line spoken in panic by Pluto, upon Dante and Virgil's penetration to the fourth circle of hell in the former's *Divine Comedy*, Canto VII. Often interpreted as mere gibberish, various theories have been put forward through the years based on phonetic similarities to living languages from Arabic through French. Abboud Abu Rashid, an early twentieth century Arabic translator, suggests *Bab al-Shaytan, Bab al-Shaytan, ahlibu*, meaning "The Gates of Satan! The Gates of Satan! Go Downward!" Some fifty years earlier, Ernesto Manara suggested the similarity of the phonemes to Hebrew words, which would travesty Christ's statement in Matthew XVI: 18 that the Gates of Hell would not prevail against His Church.

Well, go, my son, with God, and tell your nation
To take up psalter, hoe, and mind their station...

KORDIAN
*Throws the handful of earth into the air.*
I toss the martyrs' dust unto the winds!
And turn back homeward, my lips stained with sin...

POPE
Upon the conquered Poles I'll be the first,
If they be restive, to impose my curse...!
May faith's olive tree grow thick as a thuya,
To shade your humble people...

PARROT
                Alleluia!

*Konrad exits.*

*Kordian, alone.*
*With arms folded across his chest, he stands on the highest summit of Mont Blanc.*

KORDIAN
Here is the peak... Below, the abyss. It appals
Me to cast my eye into the dark chasm... And yet...
Below my feet — the heavens, and above my head
The heavens... I am enclosed in a crystal ball.
If this peak of ice were to fly off through the sky,
Higher — to Heaven itself — I'd not sense that I fly.
From here, the black wings of my thought, above the broad
World, I'll unfurl... Ha! What's that I hear? Hush!
      Against the ice, the prayers of mankind brush
      As they rise in thought to God.
The unclean sounds of mankind's tongues here die;
The sound of thought still sails on through the sky.
If this crystal sphere of heaven were to fall
      I'd be the first to die;
The firmament, shattered with a sigh,
In azure ripples spreading wide, from small
To ever greater rings, until it's flown

> To starry regions yet unknown...
> I'll try —
> I'll sigh,
> And die...

*Gazes downward.*

> Ha! again you thrust
> Yourself into my thought — grave of the peoples!
> The clouds now rush
> Apart and flee,
> And from the burly mist soar icy steeples,
> And there among the first
> Of Alpine ranges — that gigantic wood
> Of oaks and pine
> Seems a mere pinch of moss.
> And there — that white, pale stain
> Is the sea.
> And now I'll strain
> These eyes of mine,
> I'll sharpen my sight as much as I can,
> For I'd like to have a look at man.
> Around one peak a convocation whirls
> Of eagles — like a ring
> Of mourning
> On an icy finger of pearl;
> Beneath my feet an azure river springs
> And breaks in twain,
> Dividing again among the cracks
> Of granite, each stream rushing hurled
> Into the icy main...
> ....................................
> I — am man's image, set on the image of the world.
> ....................................
> O, if only to clamber over the steep tracks
> And stand upon the summit of all sense,
> To conquer the apex of human thought,
> To pierce the clouds of shibboleth,
> And be the greatest thought now become flesh —
> To think this, and not wish it!
> O shame! Disgrace!

To think this, and be impotent?
        I'd rather flay
My breast with my own hands!
            Hell is impotence!
May I not, by force of feeling, pour
Upon the legions of men, my own
Heart's blood, so that theirs might overflow the shore,
Flow on like rivers, and overturn thrones?
And can I not set off an avalanche,
          And then, before it plough
              Into the town, restrain it with my brow,
                  Or with my hands?
And can we not, like God Himself, when He
Created the world, with this one hand of ours
Toss in one mighty sweep myriads of stars
And so mark out the paths of destiny
That never should those poor vessels of clay
Err in their navigation, mistake their way
And shatter on the infinite deep?
          I can — I shall! I go, to jar,
To wake the slumbering people from their sleep!

*Pause, then, with a sigh of discouragement:*

Or maybe it would be better just to leap?

*Pause, then, calmly again; and then with enthusiasm.*

As on the byways of the world I've run,
My feelings have flagged, fallen off one by one;
I've had bitter women's kisses — at a price;
My childlike faith has been slain by the Vicar of Christ...
Nothing... Nothing... Nothing... until I arrived
        Here in the blue sky,
           Where I've come alive,
              Bathed in the sky, I feel life!
Yet before I burst into a gigantic thought,
I've a statue's beauty, but its lamp — I have not.
And so I'll wind my crown from all the stars — their light
Forged in the blue sky, alloyed with this flesh,
Will remake me like marble, like sunlit ice, bright...

Then, with some fabled spirit's comeliness,
I'll go into the chill world, and there,
A thousand stars circling my shining hair,
And in my eyes one thousand more, I swear:
My statuesque grace will set the nations afire!
        The people I'll inspire;
Into their hearts, like thought I'll thunder,
        Like a miracle of God, a wonder...
. . . . . . . . . . . . . . . . . . . . . . . . . . . . . . . . . .
No — a great thought's from the earth, or from the skies.
Here from the summits of these cliffs
        I see a knightly spirit arise
            From the ice —
              Winkelried! Who lifts
        His enemies' spears and darts
And sets them against his own breast...
People! He's raised to life again, indeed!
Poland is the nations' Winkelried!
Self-sacrificed, though he falls as of old
        And more than once;
Come, clouds, and winds, birds, come!
Bear me away!

*A cloud lifts him from the summit.*

CLOUD
Sit here on my mist, I'll carry you...
Look — there is Poland down below.
        Act now...!

KORDIAN
*Throws himself upon his native soil, with arms outstretched,*
*Calling:*
Poles!!!

                END OF ACT II

# ACT III

## The Coronation Conspiracy

### Scene 1

*Before the Royal Castle in Warsaw. The windows round about are festooned, and full of people. A large platform has been erected, covered in red cloth, and takes up most of the space on the square.*
*Elegantly dressed women are sitting there, in rows. In the immediate foreground is Zygmunt's Column; people are sitting on its base. Crowds, of various estates, stand around, gazing toward the castle and talking.*

FIRST PERSON OF THE PEOPLE*
Well then, my friend, what a feast for the eyes!
Last night, our merciful Tsar, so I'm told,
Had the joiners build this dais — or scaffold —
For should the nation not applaud, but rise,
He'll have a ready block to snip their heads.

SECOND PERSON OF THE PEOPLE
What rubbish you toss out, so carelessly!
It's a dais set up for the toffs of our nation,
From which they can look down upon the coronation.

FIRST YOUTH
The estrada is covered with beauties — like flowers...

SECOND YOUTH
Estrada?! What a word! Use rather one of ours:
"Wschodniowidownia."**

---

\*      The Polish phrase *z ludu* can suggest someone being "of the common people," or "of the Polish people."

\*\*      This is a Polish calque, built upon the words *widownia* (platform) and *wschód* (entrance). On the one hand, Słowacki is making fun of linguistic purism, à la the French Academy. On the other, however, he is making a bitter joke: *wschód* also signifies "East" in Polish; the East, associated with Russia, is almost never a propitious direction in Polish

FIRST YOUTH
          All right, my purist, agreed.
But look: feathers, flowers, tulles and parasols; you know,
I'd like to be the worm that crawls over that meadow...

SECOND YOUTH
Say that you'd rather be the Tsar instead,
To tramp over their heads.

SHOEMAKER*
Uff! So sticky! And crowds? Look at all of 'em!
Ha — that brewer there has shed some pounds
Since last I saw him here round Zygmunt's Column!

NOBLEMAN
That's the same fellow who was made to drag around
A cart, for some misdeed, harnessed like a draught-horse,
On the prince's orders. He slimmed so, if you please,
That when, for the first time in years, he saw his knees,
He burst out weeping.

SHOEMAKER
                    Who advised him to come here?
Those drums and trumpets must sound shameful to his ear...
Or perhaps he's stuffed that gut of his with a load
Of sulphur and balls,
So that when he falls
At the Tsar's feet in homage, he'll explode?

NOBLEMAN
That shoemaker's taken the measure of revenge...
Taken the measure..." The shoemaker... Get it? Look —

---

history. Thus, the Youths and People are looking, somewhat sarcastically, upon an "Eastern spectacle" (*widownia* also has theatrical connotations, as the "house").

\*      A character perhaps based on Jan Kiliński (1760–1819), a shoemaker by trade, who rose to become a Warsaw councilman and a revolutionary military leader during the Kościuszko Uprising of 1794.

\*\*     The Nobleman makes a pun on the word *prawidło*, which can mean "pattern, rule, law" as well as an instrument used by a shoemaker to measure a person's foot.

Ah, no one gets my pun! Bah! Fools! But that's not strange:
Who buys your sceptre, dunces, buys a shepherd's crook!

SHOEMAKER
Ha, ha, ha! My lord whines — he's turned red as the dais...

FIRST OF THE PEOPLE
Hush now! Listen — the first row erupts in cries!
The Tsar is coming! Let's join them...

SEVERAL OF THE PEOPLE
                        Hurrah, hurrah!

FIRST OF THE PEOPLE
I can't see a thing. The flag battles with the wind
And moves on so slowly...

SECOND OF THE PEOPLE
                  There — I see some old grandpa
All grey — As grey as early March — Look there, neighbour:
He carries a golden pillow. And on it, pinned
There lies a sabre.

SOLDIER
A lucky omen for the Tsar, when Polish swords
Are pinned to golden pillows, where they snore...

FIRST OF THE PEOPLE
Look at the Grand Prince! How quickly he goes...
Sing! he commands, Sing!

*Voices begin to sing, to the tune of "God Save the King."*

SOLDIER
Ha, ha! How they bellow. Their throats like oboes!

FIRST OF THE PEOPLE
Look how the chamberlains in green buzz and swarm!
Embroidered with gold, they look like drones awing...
Ha! Here he comes...

SEVERAL
> Who?

FIRST OF THE PEOPLE
> The king.

SOLDIER
*Sings.*
Such a knave our gracious King...

SHOEMAKER
You're out of tune and miss the tempo!

SOLDIER
It's not my fault! See, not too long ago
At Maciejowice the cannon's roar
Made me go tone-deaf. What's more, I admit
I'm at a loss, as in *mariage*,* when it's
The King's place to unite with the Queen,
How kosher must the suit be? As for me,
At least I'll toss down forty...

SHOEMAKER
> Shut your mouth!
You dare to speak about kings so boldly,
As if there were no spies walking about
Who know how to take measure of a foot
Just by glancing at the boot?
Believe me, my good man — Don't cut your leather
Till you've got the thong to hold the shoe together.

SEVERAL
Ha, ha, ha!

FIRST OF THE PEOPLE
He cut him short with leather snips!

ELEGANT HUNCHBACK
Pardon me, good people, let a person see...

---

\* A card game popular at the time.

SEVERAL
Quasimodo! Hey, here — set him on your knee!
Or on your shoulders...

SHOEMAKER
                    Willingly —
This dwarf is famous! Am I not right?
He's known all round the world... One night,
He couldn't quite overstep the gutter
(It seems he didn't want to spatter
His cloak of fine-cloth); then, who walks
Up, but this chap with music box!
The little imp asks for a ride
And up he's hoisted! Thus, bestride
His jangling charger, he's born round
From inn to inn, from town to town,
But for the ride he has to pay:
To sing and dance, to crank and play...

SEVERAL
Ha, ha, ha!

SOLDIER
Stop that! If you like, come, make fun of me,
An old soldier. But at deformity
To jest, that you may not!

FIRST OF THE PEOPLE
                    Well, the bean-stalk's
Gone off, anyway...

SECOND OF THE PEOPLE
            Look — we joke and talk
Of dwarves and cripples, and we've missed the Tsar!

FIRST OF THE PEOPLE
Big loss. Let's go hoof it in the streets, rather.
I hear that the wine's flowing there like water.
*The people disperse.*

## Scene 2

*The interior of the cathedral. The high altar is brightly lit. The Primate, assisted by other clergy in festive vestments, is celebrating Mass. Music. The Tsar stands under a scarlet baldachin; Polish state dignitaries and Muscovite generals stand around the steps leading to the throne... The Primate blesses the people and then, moving to the Tsar, hands him a crown, which the Tsar then sets on his head. The Chancellor presents the Tsar with a cushion bearing the sword of state. The Tsar lifts the sword and, with it, makes the sign of the cross in each of the four cardinal directions. The Primate extends the Constitutional Tome to the Tsar.*

TSAR
*Placing his hand on the book.*
I swear...!

*Again a deep silence... The Primate moves away from the altar and intones the "Te Deum."*

## Scene 3

*The square before the Royal Palace, with the people there, as it was in Scene 1.*
*The anthem "God Save the King" is being played.*

FIRST OF THE PEOPLE
And so the Tsar is crowned. They heard him swear
To hallow the Constitution like a prayer.

SECOND OF THE PEOPLE
Back in the Castle, he'll sit down to feast?
The King must eat, like any other beast.

NOBLEMAN
You know what's on the menu?

SECOND OF THE PEOPLE
                                  Well, it won't
Be table-scraps and half-gnawed bones.
There's piles of dainties for the royal maw.

NOBLEMAN
First — pheasants. Then, for dessert: the rule of law.*

SHOEMAKER
The Courier should print your riddles, my lord.
What was that cry?

FIRST OF THE PEOPLE
      Some gendarme parts a ford
Through this sea of people, surely.

MAN STANDING ON THE COLUMN
        No, the Prince —
The Grand Prince Constantine himself, in a wild
Row with some women...

WOMAN'S VOICE FROM AFAR
      My child! O! My child!

FIRST OF THE PEOPLE
*To the Man on the Column.*
What's going on? Your face has turned all white.

MAN STANDING ON THE COLUMN
There was an old woman with a child, there...
The Grand Prince struck her, and the child fell
Into the gutter. The crowd ran away,
Escaping from the Grand Prince in a fright;
Only the old woman stayed behind. She lay
Down upon her child to shield it — such rare
Courage!

DISTANT VOICE
  A child's been killed!

---

\*  *Będzie jadał bażanty, a na wety — prawa.* Literally: "He will be eating pheasants, and for the last course — laws." There is an untranslatable pun here. "Wety" signify the last course of a meal. The word is close cousin to *weto* — veto — bitterly prognosticating the authoritarian approach of the Tsar, who, the speaker feels, will ignore the laws when it suits him, despite his oath to the Polish constitution.

NEARER VOICE
                    A child's been killed!

MAN STANDING ON THE COLUMN
*Passing this on.*
Killed...

PEOPLE
      And the mother?

MAN STANDING ON THE COLUMN
                    Who says she's the mother?

PEOPLE
She must be! If she were any other,
She'd've run away too. What's happening?

MAN STANDING ON THE COLUMN
Wait! Something's going on there — two gendarmes
Have torn her from the gutter by the arms...
While others sweep the blood from before the king...

*A part of the crowd goes off, gloomily... The coronation procession returns to the Castle... The thinned crowd is silent. The music continues to play. It grows dark. Then the people throw themselves upon the platform and tear away the red cloth.*

PEOPLE
Cloth! It's left for us! Tear it to pieces!

*It grows darker and darker. The people have torn away the cloth and, wrapped in its red fragments, they disperse along the streets... A few drunken people can still be seen around the wine barrels. Then, a man wrapped in a black greatcoat mixes in among them, singing.*

THE STRANGER'S SONG
Drink the wine! Drink the wine!
It's not the miracle it seems —
Although you didn't plant the vine,
The wine still gushes forth in streams.
Drink, my friends! Drink deep and long —

Christ turned the water into wine
When he heard the bridal song
Back in Cana!
*Louder.*
            When the time
Came round for the dead to rise,
Jesus turned wine into blood...
The star of faith shines in the skies
Of morning... Drink! And then a good
Night's sleep. These wine cups now we'll take
And melt them down, a blade to form —
Entrusted to some doughty arm,
To pierce a tyrant's breast, and break!
Drink up! Then go to bed. It's late —
But when the dawn begins to flood
The sky, the wine must become blood!
Drink deep, wine transubstantiate!

*The song ends and the stranger goes off.*

FIRST OF THE PEOPLE
Who sang that?

SECOND OF THE PEOPLE
            I don't know. I felt it ring
Within me, and below me.

THIRD OF THE PEOPLE
            Frightful thing!
Let's go home. It's getting dark.


## Scene 4
*The crypts of St John's Cathedral. All around are the tombs of Polish kings. In the depths stands a small altar. A round table is placed before the altar, with chairs and a lamp. The President of the conspiracy sits at the table, alone. He wears a black mask; his hair is as white as snow. Stairs can be seen leading up to the naves of the church. On the stairs a sentry stands; he is visible up to his waist.*

PRESIDENT
*Solus.*
How well I know you, dark, sepulchral cave!
More than one spark I've cast into these graves
To wake the dust of kings, and search their hearts:
They sprang to action, they all played their parts
In history, like the bright celestial flames
That prink the heavens — never did they stain
Themselves or their realm with a crimson shame.
O, kings, if this were the resurrection day,
The people, upon seeing you, would say
"We know you! The old man would often tell
Us tales of you — as white as the angels
He painted you... We know you as our own!"
Now must I stain with blood the Polish throne
Immaculate? I've rushed unto these shades,
This cabal, where I rule the ready blades
Of youths enflamed — I have one hundred hands,
One hundred knives. Should I give the command,
I'd make one hundred wounds. Dim is my sight
With age, and yet my conscience still has bright
And healthy eyes, which see, gazing backward
From this dark place, toward the setting sun.
Far better had it been at Washington's
Side to die...

SENTRY
    Halt! What is the password?

VOICE
Winkelried!

SENTRY
    Pass.

*A masked man, in priest's garb, descends.*

PRIEST
    Already here, I see.

PRESIDENT
First to the graveyard. Where's the mystery?
My old age led me here.

PRIEST
              So, tell me sir,
How will it end?

PRESIDENT
              I don't know.

PRIEST
                    The wind won't stir
Stilettos like leaves... God grant us success!

PRESIDENT
God? Remember, Father, that you are dressed
In the white robes of the Saviour! You'll soil them.

PRIEST
Your voice trembles.

PRESIDENT
              I'm cold.

PRIEST
              And I'm boiling!

PRESIDENT
It's cold and dark... God, have mercy on me!
Father, how old might you be?

PRIEST
              I'm fifty.

PRESIDENT
When you were born, then, I was twenty-nine,
Fighting for freedom.

PRIEST
              And so?

PRESIDENT
                        Never mind.
It's just a memory.

PRIEST
                    You've jostled awake
My conscience... Made my soul to hesitate...
What's your command?

PRESIDENT
*With fervour.*
                        We must stop them, for God's sake!
May no thought of youth sink into these deep graves;
May black conspiracy never leave this cave
For there, above, shines God's untainted sun!
I've called the fevered here, because the graves
Are cooling, and here I can appeal
To the dust of kings to aid me. Once my breast
Swelled with poetic rapture. If I could,
Today I'd more than gladly tear my name
From out the pages of undying fame,
And burn my works to ashes, if that would
Give birth, phoenix-like, to a louder thought —
One louder than the din of youth, and riot,
A thought that breaks stilettos.

PRIEST
                            You might save
Yourself the fretting. Here upon these graves
They'll whet their bright swords.

PRESIDENT
                            Grind their blades
Upon the tombs of kings? Shame and disgrace!
The swords of regicides? Stilettos?

SENTRY
Halt! Who goes there?

CADET
Winkelried.

SENTRY
        Pass.

PRESIDENT
              Bishop, I need your aid!

PRIEST
I'm recognised... These corpse-like masks betray us.

CADET
How many worms fatten on royalty?
I'd like to lift the lids and take a peek...

SENTRY
Password!

VOICE
Winkelried!

*The First of the people descends, masked.*

FIRST OF THE PEOPLE
Ha! Our president's head may be grey,
But it's shrewd! The church is open all day
So people can come and pray for the Tsar,
And at the vestibule, informers are
Noting who enters, setting words of praise
By the name of each who enters and who prays —
Indeed, he's chosen a fine location,
For here we can kill two birds with one stone:
The Tsar's detectives take us for their own,
While we toil on behalf of the nation!

SENTRY
Who goes there? What's the password?

VOICE
Winkelried!

*Various people of different estates descend; all are masked.*

FIRST OF THE PEOPLE
What is this "Winkelried?"

SECOND OF THE PEOPLE
          Some spell, I guess.

CADET
He was a leader of the free-born Swiss.
Once, in a battle, with his hand he seized
The spear-heads of his nation's enemies
And, plunging them into his heart, he freed
A path for others, on to victory.

FIRST OF THE PEOPLE
We sure could use that knightly heart today!

PRESIDENT
Quiet! This is no place to jabber. Pray!
We've come here to pass judgement on the throne.
So, as for hearts, have a look into your own!
With starry truth may the Good Lord entwine
Our brows, that our descendants should not find
We'd acted foully ... Let some angel calm
Descend among us...

SENTRY
Who goes there?

VOICE
      Winkelried!

*Time and again one hears the Sentry's challenge, and the responses of the conspirators, who, masked, descend into the crypt and take their seats on the benches. The voices of sentry and conspirator are more and more infrequently heard, until they cease entirely... A deep silence ensues. The clock in the church tower strikes ten, slowly.*

PRESIDENT
          Brethren, I declare
The trial in session, in the Name of God.
*A moment of silence.*

FIRST OF THE PEOPLE
In the Name of God, I shall incise the word
Of vengeance with my blade.

SECOND OF THE PEOPLE
                    And so shall I.

THIRD OF THE PEOPLE
And I shall do the same as these, the third.

FOURTH OF THE PEOPLE
And I, the fourth.

PRESIDENT
People! I stand before you, my head grey
With age, and say to you: Wait! My old eye
Has looked upon great men, and here I say,
In all sincerity, you are not they;
You are not like them. Is God's holy faith
No longer in your hearts? By the Lord's death,
I beg you: Stop now! Exchange your stilettos
For the sanctified swords of heroes!
And one day we shall strike, and hear the tones
Of the great bell of resurrection ring,
Which shall make tremble our oppressors' thrones
Like rotten wood!

CADET
I cast my eye into the past, and see
A woman's shade — in mourning — who is she?
I look into the future: stars, whole swarms;
That shadow of the past stretches her arms
Toward them — and those stars are stilettos!
I see our nation, like a wild rose
Engrafted with another by wise men;*

---

\*    The Cadet's metaphor of a wild rose grafted to an older, cultivated bush by "wise men" signifies the Polish-Lithuanian commonwealth. The two nations first came together in a personal union, when Polish Queen Jadwiga was forced to renounce her betrothed, Wilhelm of Habsburg, and marry instead Lithuanian Grand Duke Jagiełło in 1386; in 1569 the Union of Lublin established the Commonwealth officially.

One young, the other ancient, growing on one stem;
Like two knights in identical armour
Who arm in arm set off to a common war;
Like two prayers sinking in the breast of God,
Each animated by the selfsame thought;
Like two swarms that a beekeeper unites
Within the battlements of the same hive.
   There was a time when southern titans, free,
Rose up against God, kings, and slavery;
God on His throne of sapphire merely smiled
But the kings fell, like poplars in a file;
The guillotine, covered in mourning rags,
Like a steel arm fell, and fell, and never flagged:
Each time it fell, the mob shrank by a head.
The kings looked on and shivered not with dread,
Those royal spectators, for they did see
The scaffold was the people's tragedy.
So, vengeance! That whore and Tsar named Catharine
Upon us trained her murderous eye malign,
Deeming us worthy of a martyr's crown,
Thought up a martyrdom, and, stooping down,
Picked up a skull fallen on the blood-drunk
Soil, a skull fallen from a Bourbon trunk,
Bloody and pale, and set it on her pet,
To give us a monarch with a death's-head.
She stole the very ground beneath his feet,
And he did nothing. Since no winding sheet
Could cover our dead Mother completely,
What did she do, but carve her into three.
Today — go ask the seagulls as they sweep
Here from Siberia, how many weep;
How many have been slaughtered in the mines;
How many have been into rogues remade,
And how many by these have been betrayed?
We all of us are tethered to a corpse,
For this land is a corpse. Then, in due course,
The Tsar, enraged at brother Constantine,
Sent him to Poland to drain off his spleen.
Let him foam with frenzy! Let him tear
With rabid teeth! Avengers, friends, I swear:
When at the altar's steps he took the crown,

Right then and there he should have been cut down
With the bright sword of state, tossed in the crypt,
And then the whole cathedral fumigated
As if the sanctuary'd been desecrated
By the Turkish plague; all entrances bricked,
And penitential palms endlessly hymned:
"Have mercy on us, Lord, for we have sinned!"
That's all, no more. By now, the Tsar is eating,
And our satraps their brows before him beating
The floor in homage; wine is overflowing
Goblets; music is booming, lamps are glowing,
The plaster's flaking off from the roaring sound,
Fresh, blooming girls are reclining around
The tables like bouquets of Sharon roses,
And more than one on Russian breast reposes.
*Strongly.*
Let's go there now! And on the walls we'll char
The words of vengeance — words of Belshazzar!
The half-drained goblet will slide from his hand;
By our blue flashing swords he'll understand
The prophecy of death more certain still
Than any voice of any Daniel.
And then we shall be free! The bright new day
Will see Poland stretch forth from sea to sea;
After the stormy night, she'll breathe and live.
O, Life! Have you ever gazed at that word? Deep
Into its soul? I have, and hear the beat
Of its strong heart — O, that strong syllable!
In each and every letter I hear the swell
Of its gigantic voice... As great, indeed
As the very day of our vengeance shall be!
A day that shall ring down the centuries!
When freedom dawns joyfully in the skies,
Heaven will shake with our people's glad cries.
Reflecting back on slavery's long, dark sleep,
The people shall sit down, and they shall weep —
Then shall be heard, from all three sections
Of our land, the great cry of resurrection.
*Murmurs of enthusiasm.*

PRESIDENT
The golden images you offer hide
Satanic thought — your conscience won't abide
To delve within and see it for what it is.
Your ardour swings you out over the abyss!
Look, boy — you kill the Tsar. His family
Is next, for that's the next step, naturally.
But then God's heavy hand fells you, and us,
For God is just!

CADET
It was a tyrant slaughtered by Brutus.*

PRESIDENT
And if there should be some Antonius
Who Caesar's bloody robe displays
To the stunned eyes of Europe, so to raise
Against Poland a large and vengeful host?
Of how many soldiers does your army boast?
And armed with what? Bandits' stilettos?

PRIEST
What shall the pulpits ring with at that time?
When he, whose sceptre thrones could undermine
Is borne out among tapers, and the sweep
Of thuribles, on a bier? O people, weep!
Fall prostrate to the earth in sorrow, for
The land of Lechites is become no more;
Put on sackcloth, sift penitential ash
Upon your brows, for Poland — land of Jael —
Whose weapon is the she-assassin's nail,
Has tumbled down a thorny, errant path,
Unworthy...

CADET
              By your cassock I can see
You are a man of God. A fine eulogy

---

\*    In the original Polish: *Z Cesarza karła weźmy zemstę Rzymianina.* "From the dwarf-Tsar let us take the vengeance of a Roman" [i.e. "let us avenge ourselves like Romans upon this dwarf of a Tsar"].

You've written for the Tsar...! Odd how the wind
Can turn a steeple-flag that's made of tin...
And so it is with your gloomy sermon!
It might as easily otherwise have run:
"The people, who so long had wept in chains,
Have cast them off, and they are free again!
Fall prostrate to the earth in homage, for
The land of Lechites is enslaved no more!
Don sackcloth, kings! Sift penitential ash
Upon your uncrowned brows, and wail, and gnash
Your teeth along the paths of exile!"

CONSPIRATORS
Ha, ha, ha!

PRESIDENT
Cursed is he, who like an apostate
Jeers in a royal crypt!

PRIEST
              Excommunicate!

FIRST OF THE PEOPLE
They called us here for this, to laugh our fill,
To rave and curse...

PRIEST
                    Don't think the Lord God will
Allow a crime brewed in this sacred space
Like lighting on the wings of thunder to race!
The Lord! — Who casts murderers into Hell! —
Grows wroth at sins concocted in His house!

OLD MAN OF THE PEOPLE
How much blood must be spilt to make us free?

VOICE FROM THE CROWD
The Tsar's...

OLD MAN
        One.

VOICE
> The Tsar's wife...

OLD MAN
> That's two.

VOICE
> And then,
His two brothers.

OLD MAN
> That's four... Keep counting, men;
I want a precise reckoning.

VOICE
> His son.

OLD MAN
That's five.

VOICE
> Five, then. For that is everyone.

OLD MAN
Then go and kill these five! And may their blood
Fall upon me...

PRESIDENT
> Old man, that head of yours
Is white!

OLD MAN
It's not to you I speak... Conspirators!
If insufficient for the deed be one
Man's blood, I offer my daughters and my sons.
I'll take the Tsarina and Tsarevich;
My sons will bear between them a Prince each,
And my two daughters, slight girls as they are,
I'll spatter with the thin blood of the Tsar.
And when God calls me on the Judgement Day,
I'll stand next to some blood-gorged potentate,

Who wades through gore each day, and boldly state:
"Behold us, Lord! stained with the blood we spilled!
We took this blood from people, that the tree
Of your Cross in that vale of tears should be
Lighter for the weight subtracted... Thy will
Be done."

CADET
    O, bless me, old man!

PRIEST
                      Blasphemies!
He insults God's justice...

CADET
                Be silent, priest!
Your eye can't follow his heaven-soaring thought.
In such a manner is true devotion taught!
This old man's filled me with new faith today —
Unless it be Satan leads you astray
With such words — and God means to punish me,
That, like some fruitless stalk broadcasting seed
I sow but sterile words... O, believe me,
People, for I am great, and full of might!
Only one weakness in my heart I hide —
I'm gnawed by the worm of sadness. Speaking here
Before you I would cease... and melt in tears...
But this sadness — an empty, childish grief,
Perhaps for my homeland... But worthy of belief,
The suffering man... O, rest not beneath a tree
From which ages flicks the sere and rotten leaf...
*With despair.*
Give me a lute! And I'll move you with song!
Give me a chronicle! and I'll find a page
That speaks of Poland blooming, happy, strong,
And thus I'll raise you, as if from shattered graves,
Avengers resurrected! Torn with rage,
I feel my bosom, as if ripped in halves —
You ought to see my heart! I have not come
Like some dark angel, leading you to doom;
Nor does my thought shiver in hesitation;

I'm whole, and one... And when I save the nation,
I shall not sit upon the throne, my friends,
Nor near it, nor beneath it. Like incense,
I shall be all consumed at the oblation,
With nothing to remain after cremation
But a mere echo, and an empty space,
A great vacuum, and where there should be praise,
There will be nothing but oblivion!
Nothing! No name! Except, perhaps, for "He,"
With which some exasperated royal nanny
Will fill her naughty charges with fright,
So that they'll bawl and dream of me at night —
The nameless spirit, that knocks sceptres down...
For you: life, liberty; for you the crown,
Just place yourself into my hands! In place
Of sceptre, I wish to wield my race!
And thus I'll set, among the chaplet-bands
Of God, a pearl! — Place yourselves in my hands! —
The pearl of a nation resurrected!
Give yourself into my hands! I shall be checked
By no pride or dream bestial; till I succeed
In winning for you ages of liberty,
Let these two eyes of mine never close in sleep.
Are you afraid? Come, nail me to the cross,
Cut off my eyelids, just like Regulus,
Let me behold, in endless agony,
Never to rest, my nation. Then, carry
This badge before you: the cross of suffering.
It shall not lead you to your undoing;
I swear to you, on my forefathers' wraiths,
And on Christ's Passion, that the holy faith
Speaks to you: "You are the land of conscience.
Rebel! And toss from you all the Tsar's sins!"
I give my oath to you, and sincerely:
As I desire salvation, and believe
In it — Place yourselves into my hands!

PRESIDENT
My voice freezes
In my throat... I cannot speak...
*He sits and covers his face with his cloak.*

CADET
Old man! Does my enthusiasm outfly
Your halting steps? ... I conquer the Tsar, or I die!
This is our first victory!
                    Tsar! You stole
Our Polish homeland? Death! You had to know
When you were stealing her, such was the barter —
Your death! You murdered her, and then you quartered
And nailed her martyred flesh, that we hallow,
To three thrones, as if to three gallows!
Tsar! Had you two lives, I'd slaughter you again,
And haul you twice before the throne of God!

*Murmurs in the crowd... People rise from the benches... hold their stilettos aloft.*

PRESIDENT
*Takes the cloak from his face, stands, and makes a gesture as if he were washing his hands. Then, slowly and solemnly:*
I wash my hands of this... Do what you want.

CADET
*To the conspirators.*
And you?

*A long pause.*

SENTRY
*At the entrance.*
Who goes there? Password?

*Silence.*

CONSPIRATORS
                    We are lost! Betrayed!

CADET
Hush...

*The sound of a falling body is heard.*

SENTRY
          He didn't know the password...

FIRST CONSPIRATOR
                                       A corpse
Falls down the stairs.

CADET
*To President.*
                        Why tremble with remorse?
You've washed your hands of blood — Be not afraid!
*Brings a lantern near the corpse.*
Give me some light... a dagger in his hand,
And on his breast, a paper, wrinkled, torn...
It's a report — he was a spy, this man.
Dig him a grave, there, in that dark corner.

*Two Conspirators carry the body into the corner. They light two lanterns and start to dig the grave.*

PRESIDENT
Let us disperse. This meeting's at an end.
And I shall call no other.

CADET
                      Wait, old man!
You take advantage of fate's lightning-flare
To slink away? But I will not despair —
Come, let each here serve as jury-man
To pardon the Tsar-criminal, or to damn;
Let's put it to a vote, this crucial matter,
And see what wins — To stand firm? Or to scatter?

PRESIDENT
All right, so let it be. I have no doubt
But ancient Polish virtue will win out.
What shall we use to cast our ballots?

PRIEST
Who says the Tsar should die, will place a bullet
Upon the table; who says he should live,

A coin. Someone get the poor box. We'll give
Our mercy to the poor. Thus... the man of God.

*He tosses a coin on the table, after which the President does the same, and then each of the Conspirators tosses either a coin or a bullet. We hear the clatter of metal as they fall.*

FIRST OF THE CONSPIRATORS
As did our chief — my coin's for the poor box.

ANOTHER
I haven't got a penny to my name,
And so — a bullet. Long live liberty!

ANOTHER
I'm not as poor as you, but as for me,
I wouldn't give a farthing for the life
Of the Tsar!
I do the same.

ANOTHER
                    With our coins, do we betray
Our country? Let the chief reckon the sum
Of our collection, for the time will come.

FIRST OF CONSPIRATORS
*To those digging the grave.*
Hey, you gravediggers! Come on over here
And cast your votes: a bullet or a penny.

GRAVEDIGGERS
We heard! This one is deaf, but we haven't any
Problems with our ears. We hear you loud and clear.

FIRST OF THE CONSPIRATORS
They tossed in coins. I guess they want to save
Themselves the toil of digging royal graves.
All right, let's see which way the wind blows.*

---

\*    In the original Polish: *Obaczymyż, z którego wiatr powieje miechu / I pogra na organach?* "Shall we see from which bellows the wind blows / And plays on the organ?"

*All have now voted; the President counts.*

PRESIDENT
I need some more light. Bring your torches close...
Only five votes "to die," the Lord be praised!

CADET
And so, the Tsar dies...

PRESIDENT
                        Boy, you only raised
Five votes. One hundred fifty voted down the crime!

CADET
How pale life seems now to these eyes of mine!
I risked my life on one cast of the die
And... nothing. Midgets I espy
Around me, whom for giants I mistook —
Dwarves fallen from stilts! Come, men, let's look
Into these tombs. Let's search through every one;
I fear we'll find that this here skeleton
*Points at the President.*
Has rattled out amongst us living men!
*To President.*
Old man, I look into your mouldy brain
And see there: You come from ages long forgot.
Why wear that mask? Modern man knows you not!

PRESIDENT
I didn't pull a mask over my grey hair.

CADET
The same old song, set to the same old air!
You're like a schoolmarm drilling kids by rote
To rise at the entrance of any grey old goat.
Remember — there are those with flaming souls
And beating hearts whose hair has silvered white
Over the space of just one sleepless night,
Touched by misfortune! On your feet before these,
You aged child!
*To the Conspirators.*

As for you, you sheep,
Oh, please!
See that close to your shepherd's heels you keep:
Follow the lantern of that bobbing white
Head into the unending servile night!
All of the hopes I've had have disappeared.
Among the piles of human chaff, you appeared
The greatest seeds — and now you are so small...
Away with you! For I despise you all!
Perhaps those, who couldn't bring themselves to dare
Great things, might now turn traitor? I don't care!
And as a sign of my contempt, I cast
My mask at your feet... and my forgiveness...
*Tears the mask from his face.*

CONSPIRATORS
It's Kordian! Kordian! Kordian's here!
You don't know us, Kordian! Look us in the face —
There's not a single traitor in the place!

*Everyone takes their masks off. Kordian glances around, deep in thought, then, he lifts his head and speaks, slowly.*

KORDIAN
Among the nobles, Kordian conquers.
You show your face; he bears his heart and mind.
Kordian's on duty at the castle, tonight... Do you hear?
Kordian's on duty at the castle tonight...

*He nears the table, writes some words on a scrap of paper, then tosses it in the direction of the Conspirators.*

FIRST OF THE CONSPIRATORS
*Reads.*
"To the Nation, I leave all that I can give:
My blood, and my life, which is all that I own...
And for their best disposal, an empty throne."

KORDIAN
*Leans against the altar and looks around, frenzied, at the silent Conspirators. Then he waves his hand and says:*
Away, subversives!

*Everyone departs in silence. Kordian remains, leaning at the altar, sunk in thought... The two Gravediggers finish burying the body. Leaving their lit lanterns on the grave, they too go off. Only the President remains — he kneels down at the altar, behind Kordian, standing.*

PRESIDENT
Kordian!

KORDIAN
*Turns, in a rising frenzy.*
              Who wakes me? My hour — does it sound?
Wait a bit... Lanterns... Graves all around...
Are you a sexton, looking for your pay?
Here — two ducats with the Virgin, which, one day,
My mother gave me with her blessing, when
I went away... You too must have children?
Listen, I beg you: have your family
Sigh now and then to God in prayer for me...

PRESIDENT
I have no children!

KORDIAN
              No? Your head is grey —
It shines like silver. How will you repay
The Lord for the debt of life He's given you?

PRESIDENT
Kordian!
I kneel here at the altar with bowed head,
But not before God do I kneel; instead
I bow the knee before you. It was I
That lit in you this will to fight, and die —
And now, you see the uncertainty that rends
My heart; my judgement's conquered by my conscience...

KORDIAN
Old man! You're adding sin to sin, I fear,
Kneeling before a criminal. Come here —
Let's search the pages of the past, and then
We'll spread the word throughout the entire earth,
That Poland, all of Poland, isn't worth
My turning criminal...

PRESIDENT
                    For God's sake, Kordian!
You're fevered! Your eyes glow with a strange light...

KORDIAN
It's nothing... My hair hurts... It's turning white...
Each hair hurts... I feel each hair sickening to death...
It's nothing... Listen, on my grave, please: set
Two poplar saplings, and a rose or two,
And when like thick tears falls the morning dew
My hair will come alive... Have you a pen?
I'd like to write down the names of all my kin,
And all who'll weep me... Father — in the tomb;
Mother — dead, and all my relatives, too...
And She — might as well be dead.... and so you see!
Everyone I love is dead. Just like me.
My monument will be the gallows tree...

PRESIDENT
Kordian! Burn this scrap that you just now
Showed to the plotters. Here! Be free of your vow!

KORDIAN
One, two, shoulder arms! Guard the palace gate!
Vigilance... How stupid the words they prate!
Shall I strut on command? Old man, you're a bore
And your immobile mug bores me the more...
I can't forget that I'll never be old...
If ever you see me, where children roll
Laughing at my feet... spit on my grey head!

*The clock tower strikes eleven.*

The clock strikes eleven,
Thus beckons heaven.

*He runs out. The President stretches his arms after him.*

PRESIDENT
Kordian, wait!
For God's sake...
Kordian!


### Scene 5
*The so-called Concert Chamber in the Royal Palace, lit with one lamp. Round about are marble columns; the walls are covered with painted arabesques. Through the wide open doors a long tract of dark rooms may be seen. At the far end there shines the faint light of the Tsar's bedroom. Kordian rests upon the bayonet stock of his carbine.*
*Various Phantoms.*

KORDIAN
*Moving forward with his carbine*
Let me go! Let me go! I'm the murderer of Tsars;
I go to kill... Who restrains me, by a hair?

IMAGINATION
Listen! I can see what's there!

FEAR
Listen! My voice — the beating of your heart!

KORDIAN
No one is there;
I hear some gibbering.

IMAGINATION
Don't look at me — look where I'm fingering!

KORDIAN
I cannot see your finger, but my sight falls
There, where you're pointing. I can see faces,
Arabesques, painted on the walls.

FEAR
Look closer! see? Those are the traces
Of reptiles! See them scurry? Disgusting!
Each snake has a sting of fire...
Look at them squirm in rings, twisting
On the walls —
The columns' capitals,
— Look higher! —
 Are sphinxes, with snakes instead of hair.
They crawl
From the marble along the wall;
The sphinxes cry like children; the snakes twine,
Hissing like the wind...
Look! And mind
Your step — they slither and shine...

IMAGINATION
A trembling butterfly, awhirl
Flits from the wall. No, it's a girl;
Perhaps it is some charmed princess,
Spell-bound? Or a sorceress?
Think! Is she not known to you?
Think! Like someone you once knew!
        Think, and remember!
The one you knew is sad, and her
        Gaze more modest;
        She was dressed
In stars, stars flashed
Upon her sapphire dress;
An astral shepherdess
She was, with flowers placed
Above her angel's face.

FEAR
But her eyes! Dead, hollow —
Wherever you turn, they follow!

IMAGINATION
Can you smell her braids, their scent?

FEAR
Watch out! you've trod
Upon a snake — it's burst apart.

KORDIAN
O, my God!!!
*He rubs his eyes.*
The nightmare's past — Onward!
To sink my bayonet into the Tsar's heart!

*He enters the next chamber. It is completely dark. To the left, open doors give on to a conference room. This chamber, in the shape of a gilded egg, is completely illuminated by the moon. In the centre stands a tripod artfully fashioned of gold, on which rests the Tsar's crown.*

BOTH
Stop!

KORDIAN
Let me go! I'm bent
Beneath the burden of divine punishment!

BOTH
Listen! The dead silence hums
Like a wind that whistling comes
  Through the throat of these rooms;
  Like the rustle of dry grain
  Like a hard rain
Thundering on the palace roof up there;

It thunders — beneath the glare
  Of the moon!

KORDIAN
*Glancing in the conference room.*
It fills the chamber with a silver glow.
A golden tripod's there, on which to lay
The crown — it is the crown of Tsars today,
  But at the break of dawn
Only... to God will it belong,
  Tomorrow...

Let us be gone!
From that crown I can't tear my eyes away!

IMAGINATION
Keep looking! See? Blood now drips from it
And there, beneath it, bows
A man as black as tar
    Busy at work, busy...

FEAR
Two horns sprout from his brow
    No eyelid
Covers his smouldering eye...
What's he at? Who is he?

KORDIAN
What man is that, there? And why?

SPECTRE
This crown is the Tsars'.
Piotr's blood and Ivan's blood
Flow from it, as from a broken jar.
I use the blood to wash the wood
Of this Polish floor —
Smeared with the gore
Of Tsars, and their blood.
I'll wash it good,
But I'll leave the spoor
For another century!

KORDIAN
If water from Polish rivers won't be
Enough to cleanse it, I'll bring more blood tonight;
We'll scour it until it's as white
As a corpse's skin.
*Pause.*
One more chamber, and I'm in.
*He enters the throne room.*
No stars — it's black... the sky is dead; dark panes...
The path leads me on — like a pillar of fire —
One lamp guards Caesar, lighting up his bed

And on the glassy floors
It pours
Its light;
Like the moon on a calm lake's skin at night;
It leads my skiff to the blazing shores...
I'm dizzy; who'll give me the spur I require?

IMAGINATION
Your bayonet flashed... And bayonets of flame
Swarm through the air to light upon your blade,
    Like tiny fish
    As if a pinch
Of food tossed in the water ripples splayed;
    They school about the steel
    And there they burn.
    Stab at the air, and feel
How the atmosphere sparks to storm!
Just wait until the fiery hive should swarm...

FEAR
Don't look behind you! There loom two forms...

IMAGINATION
Two malachite vases, in which grow
    Whether scorch or snow
    Outside, two trees
With blossom-like eyes, that see
Everything... Look! And here:
Leaves like attentive human ears!
The seeds they cast are just like tongues
But the Tsar stifles them, rips the young
    Shoots out
    As soon as they sprout,
And so, like mute sentries do they stand
    One on each hand
    At the chamber sill;
They gaze with blooms for eyes;
With leaves they hear their fill;
They drink in all they hear and see
In silence like a cemetery's,
The while their trunks expand in size...

KORDIAN
They see! And hear! Trees...

FEAR
Don't glance out the window into the dark streets!

*Kordian glances through the window.*

IMAGINATION
From church to castle, a procession comes,
    A long procession of the dead
    With yellow tapers in their hands
    So many corpses — one, two...
    One thousand thousands!
The smoke of their tapers billows blue...
Sceptres in hand, crowns on their heads,
    Their faces are like skeletons.
And each corpse has a casket — There!
    They pile them at the wall,
And like a hayrick, the pile grows tall —
    They're building stairs!
    Over the caskets they crawl;
Beneath their weight, the wood is crushed,
    Yet they'll get in — they must!

KORDIAN
In where?

IMAGINATION
    In here.

KORDIAN
        To kill the Tsar?
To smother him with caskets?

IMAGINATION
        Ah!
Hush! Look there! What a fright!
Some red-faced spirit's come out
Of the Tsar's bedroom! With so light
A step, it seems, his foot

Makes no sound,
Yet at each bound
Of his disgusting hoof, the floor
Tiles splinter beneath his tread...
Ugh! He gives me the creeps!

FEAR
I smell blood! It's coming through that door...
From the room where the Tsar's asleep
In his white bed;
The room from which that red man slid...

IMAGINATION
You saw...

KORDIAN
I did?

FEAR
What was he doing there?

KORDIAN
What was he doing there?

DEVIL
I was about to kill the Tsar, to smother
Him, yet, in sleep he looked so like my father,

I had to spare
Him.

IMAGINATION
Hear the bells toll, far and wide?
A mournful sound, from every side?
All through the city... Hear the knell!

KORDIAN
*Terrified.*
I hear — bells —

IMAGINATION
A flash in the window pane:
A corpse stands in the window there —
He's climbed the coffin-stairs,
And his taper glares
On the glass with its blue flame;
And now a sudden wind has spread
Open his cloak — see the worms!
In each fibre, like a white thread:
A maggot in each rag of muscle churns!
This is the hangman of the dead.
It is his task to carry
Out the decrees of the remains
You see chattering below.
Now, with one blow,
He's shattered the window pane!

KORDIAN
Jesus and Mary!

IMAGINATION
And now, he's vanished...
Everything, gone in a lightning-flash.

FEAR
This is the devil's house! Be gone!

KONRAD
Despite the devil, I'll go on!
I'm hot and fevered? Well and good!
I'll cool myself off in some blood.
But now the road is blocked — a train
Of figures, like great fields of grain
Uprise before me — Tread them down?
I cannot knock them to the ground —
Spectres silent, spectres pale,
So many eyes! A peacock's tail
Of witnesses look through the door
Between me and the sleeping Tsar.
Is it they're curious to see
What colour the Tsar's blood might be?

Go on, speak up! He shall not wake;
A hundred thousand voices wouldn't slake
My need to hear!
It's like the grave! How very...
Silent...

*A bell rings for matins.*

          Oh, oh!
Someone pushes a stiletto
Into my brain, through my ear!
Jesus and Mary!

*While speaking these last words, Kordian faints and falls to the floor, crosswise, on his bayonet,\* right at the threshold of the Tsar's bedroom. The Tsar, night light in hand, comes in.*

TSAR
I heard a noise, and, as if a storm had broke,
I was awakened from my sleep;
I felt as if my throat were being choked;
I felt, just like my father once did... but more...
Must dreams always be like frightful winds
That set atremble the strings of conscience?
Let's go... But I don't know this place just yet,
I may get lost...
*He moves to go, and trips over Kordian's body.*
                    What is this here on the floor?
A Polish uniform... a bayonet...
By his insignias, he's a cadet.
A sentry? Or, was he plotting my death?
And yet my brother guaranteed their faith...
Still, at my very threshold here, he fell...
O, Constantine! — No! Tempter, back to Hell!
You paint his face on every enemy —

---

\*    *Pada bez czucia krzyżem na bagnecie.* We assume that this means that he falls on his weapon, which is lying prone beneath him, not that he falls upon its point. Kordian's dramatic death here, if the latter case was correct, would be in line with the shifting border between death and life in *Kordian*'s prototype, *Forefathers' Eve,* but there is no other evidence that would suggest this.

Each plot, my brother's! No! It cannot be!
O, if he'd only wake, and speak to me...
He's warm... Hey! Wake up! Can you hear?
Speak! Or with my sword, I'll slit you ear to ear!
Did my brother send you?

*He jabs Kordian in the hand with his sabre. Kordian opens his eyes.*

KORDIAN
*In a frenzy*
                                        At the window-pane,
A corpse and taper...

TSAR
                         What? Say that again —
Say: brother? Come on, is it him? Repeat
What you just said. Brother?

KORDIAN
                                        White as a sheet,
The Tsar is sleeping... It's nearly dawn... O, God!

TSAR
I won't learn anything from him, nor thought
Nor word, nor gesture... O, brother mine!
*Calls*
                                        Guard!
*Soldiers run in. The Tsar points at Kordian.*

If he's not mad, take him out to be shot.

## Scene 6
*HOSPITAL FOR THE INSANE.*
*Cages can be seen, in which the mentally ill are sitting, chained, although some are walking about unrestrained. Kordian is lying abed in a fever. The Hospital Caretaker, and an unknown Doctor.*

CARETAKER
And so you'd like to inspect the mental ward?

DOCTOR
*Bribes him with a ducat.*
Here is my permit.

CARETAKER
                    Right this way, my lord!
Feel free to wander anywhere you've a mind to.
This is the men's wing, the women's is behind you.
Just like a watch, I'll take the place apart
And show you how it works. You are, I guess
A practitioner of the Asclepian art?

DOCTOR
Yes.

CARETAKER
What therapy do you judge best of all?

DOCTOR
Massaging the scalp.

CARETAKER
            Ah! The regimen of Gall...

DOCTOR
Quite.

CARETAKER
And can you tell — pardon, I'm curious —
By a mere touch, which head is... the most nuts?

DOCTOR
I use the system of Lavatière —
By looking at their faces. O! Say — there...
*Pointing at Kordian.*

CARETAKER
Doctor, you've missed your mark there, I'm afraid.
The Tsar had him committed, for he thought
That he must be insane. But no, he's not.
That young man's intellect's sharp as a blade!

He has a fever, but a healthy reason —
He's saner than you, doctor. Or me, even.

DOCTOR
Than you, even?

CARETAKER
          Ha! I've insulted you,
Gallic masseur — You'd like to pay me back,
And prove to me that fevered fellow lacks
A full deck, and thereby, that I'm cuckoo?

DOCTOR
Who knows, dear sir? Ah — do you think I might
Smoke a cigar?

CARETAKER
          I haven't got a light.
*He suddenly drops the money he had been holding.*
What the...?! That coin's as hot as Hell!

*The Doctor picks up the coin, lights his cigar with it, and then hands it back to the Caretaker.*

DOCTOR
                            Here. Thanks.

CARETAKER
Dear God above! These are Satanic pranks!

DOCTOR
Hardly, my dear sane man. It's in your head.
The coin's ice-cold. It burns, because it's red.

CARETAKER
All in my head? Am I not quite all there?
Most Holy Virgin, keep me in your care!

DOCTOR
The eye of reason cannot deal with pure
Elements such as money...

CARETAKER
                    That's for sure!
I'm out of here, while I've still got a brain!
*He exits.*

DOCTOR
I've chased him out. Shortly, he'll go insane
Racking his noggin over that hot coin...
And now, to have a chat with that mad boy.
*He sits down on Kordian's bed.*

KORDIAN
Who are you? My brother?

DOCTOR
                    An enthusiast.*

KORDIAN
And everyone was saying I'm the last
Man alive. So you were born yesterday...

DOCTOR
Well, you — they know. But me they do not know.
I was sitting quiet in your stiletto.

KORDIAN
I'm fevered. Water. I hear what you say,
But I can't understand...

DOCTOR
                    Then, concentrate
On what I say. It's easy to explain,
But you must focus better. Come now, strain!

KORDIAN
I'm straining, hard... I know you...

---

\*         In Polish, the word is *zapaleniec*. With *zapalić,* "to set aflame," at its base, the word is a humorous pun on both the "Doctor's" identity, and the comic scene with the coin just past.

DOCTOR
                    At midnight,
When I left the Tsar's bedroom, you caught sight
Of me.

KORDIAN
         What were you doing there?

DOCTOR
                              Nothing.
Watering
The flowers.

KORDIAN
            What? Those ear-trees, without tongues...

DOCTOR
Yes. Those are maples... Others put forth leaves
Crossed, like Maltese nails. Others are like reeds:
Full knees and empty ones
And the Tsar's sons
Learn to play the bones
On the hollow knees.

KORDIAN
Why do the words you speak hum and buzz like bees?
Speak more softly, please.
Do you not know any prayer?

DOCTOR
I know one, that pushes people where
The fighting is...

KORDIAN
             That one's not for me.
It's loud, I bet, and impious, maybe?

DOCTOR
It is a Turkish prayer — a two-horned moon.
The death of enemies rests on one side,
And on the other point, there's suicide.

KORDIAN
But enemies must be slain, is that not true?

DOCTOR
They must indeed.
And nations too must perish, for people like to read,
And bards must have subjects for verse, you know —
Nothing's created ex nihilo...
They strike a little spark among the Folk
And, presto! An angel is dug up; awoke,
He sings to the skies.
See how highly I prize
The bardic tribes?

KORDIAN
No, not like that... but otherwise:
From heaven, descend to earth.

DOCTOR
I get it. From angel's hymns come bardic births.
The nation perishes, because the bard sings.

KORDIAN
How stupid you are! Tell me something
From the Old Testament.

DOCTOR
All right. One day, mighty Pharaoh was sent
A prophetic dream.
In it, he seemed
To see seven bulls, fat and sleek
Eat seven others, thin and weak.

KORDIAN
No! That's not how it goes!

DOCTOR
Of course it is! Just ask those
Descended from the Mongols.

KORDIAN
Speak of something else.
I've been slain by the Holy Script.
Are you, perhaps, a botanist?

DOCTOR
I am. But first you've got to swear
Yourself to secrecy. I have a rare
New herb discovered. It's found
On my sill, sprouting from the crown
Of an upturned helmet, filled with the dust
Scraped from a hundred ruined towns.
I reckon that it soon shall sprout
Buds countless — like a million thoughts,
And then a gorgeous blossom, red
As human blood. Then it shall shed
Seeds packed tight in massive pods,
Which, when they bust,
They will give out
A roar like millions of cannons... Why,
I think I've touched you. Did I not just spy
A flash of delight in your poetic eye?

KORDIAN
Your plant, is it blooming? Giving forth seed?

DOCTOR
It's sprouting.

KORDIAN
        Only sprouting?

DOCTOR
                Yes indeed —
It was troubled by a sudden frost,
And so I cover it with kitchen pots.

KORDIAN
You torture me — bore me — break me — bite — I'm sleepy...
Enough about plants.

DOCTOR
There are three elements
That make up reason — three
Dashes of thought,
That can even suss out the mystery
Of the Holy Trinity.
From unity is born plurality;
From endlessness definitiveness forms;
And what holds these two in union
Is comparison.
Without the image of number, unity goes
Off, endlessness is lost without definition,
So, one equals the other, like Father – Son,
The Holy Ghost arising from the relativity
That runs between 'em;
And all together form a Trinity of ideas — reason.

KORDIAN
You fill my ears like the ocean's roar —
I'm fevered... What the hell
Are you going on about, man?

DOCTOR
I'm here to make you well.
So let me tell you how the world began,
Or, rather, how God made all the tribes of man.
The world shall disappear before
Mankind; the world's a nut that's placed
Within a shell of clouds and sky.
God laboured at the nations for six days —
That praying nation He created first,
The Jews, which is to say, the earth,
From which the nations have sprung;
Then on the second day He flung
The waters of the nations of the east;
On the third day, the Greeks sprouted like trees,
And on the fourth — the sun of Socrates.
The fifth day was marked by the signs
Of Roman eagles — birds now, mind —
As the fifth sun sank out of sight
The long mediaeval night came on;

On the sixth day, God made... Napoléon.
Today we have the seventh day. God sets
One arm across the other, and He Rests,
Creating no one.

KORDIAN
You lie, you wretch! Each man who dedicates
Himself to freedom is a new creation
Of God — a new man.

DOCTOR
      Ha ha! You're right.
Who spins the potter's wheel of freedom might
Make something new — clay plates.

KORDIAN
That potter's wheel will bring forth people!

DOCTOR
You see? The flames of fever now begin to cool.
You're starting to speak sense.

KORDIAN
        Listen, tell me true:
Have you never seen angel, or man, bring
In sacrifice, a load of suffering
On his brothers' behalf, raising his eyes
To accept the bolt that falls from the skies,
And like his Saviour hung upon the tree,
On their behalf...

DOCTOR
     I've brought some here with me.
Let me go get them.

*He calls two insane men. One of them holds his arms stretched crosswise, the other holds one hand stiffly aloft.*

Here are two, suffering for the people's sake.
Their sacrifice? Just listen, and you will rate
Them for yourself.

*To the one with his arms spread crosswise.*
                    Brother, you're some great
Person, surely.

FIRST INSANE MAN
                    I'm no person. Long ago
I was transformed into a cross of wood.
          I was the Cross of pain and woe
          On which Christ was nailed;
But nails were unneeded — these hands held
          Onto His own, like those of a child
Weeping uncomforted. I am the Cross! Should
The Pope display some chip or peg
And say "Here is a piece of the true Cross,"
          Don't believe him! Look — arms, legs —
          I'm whole! Nothing's been lost.
Here, take your finger, count my limbs...
*Going off, sadly:*
Lord, may this bitter chalice pass me by!

DOCTOR
*To Kordian.*
How's that for a sacrifice?

KORDIAN
                    He's insane!

DOCTOR
*To the one holding his hand aloft.*
Why do you hold your hand like that, so high?

SECOND INSANE MAN
          Not so loud! I'm holding up the sky!
And in this way, I'm protecting all the world.
          If I let go, the sky,
          The sun, the moon of white,
          Quite every one
Of the stars and planets will be hurled
          Upon the people's heads!
          But I stand here, instead,
Bored and suffering, never sleeping,

>            My harsh vigil ever keeping,
>                    You ought to say
>            Your prayers to me, an everyday
>            Saviour who shields you from the fell
>                    Deluge of planets. People,
>            Good night! May you sleep well!

*Goes off.*

DOCTOR
Well, how about his self-sacrifice?
Ever seen anyone as great as him?

KORDIAN
His mind's diseased...!

DOCTOR
Hush! You utter blasphemies!

KORDIAN
They're crazy, both! And you've sprained your own brain.

DOCTOR
How do you know that you're not just as insane
As those two? Well, you yourself wished
To kill a phantom — sacrificing
Yourself, for what? For nothing!
You're in a crystal bowl, tiny goldfish —
Beating your head against walls you can't see —
A crystal bowl of air —
That's all that's there.
That's all that ever shall be.
The whole world but a vain and empty sea.

KORDIAN
I think.

DOCTOR
And so the whole world is your thought.

KORDIAN
I suffer.

DOCTOR
Then, think not.

KORDIAN
I can't...

DOCTOR
You can —
Think up a plan
All thinking to negate.
Go nuts. You'll be a Turkish potentate.

KORDIAN
Satan! You've come to kill the soul of my soul!
This is the one last wealth of mine you'd tear away —
My convictions, my last ray
You snuff!

DOCTOR
I crush divine clay.

KORDIAN
Deliver me, merciful Lord
From his jaws!

GRAND PRINCE CONSTANTINE
*Enters, with soldiers.*
Take him. I have in store for him some pain!
A painful death!

KORDIAN
          A human voice! God, Thou hast deigned
To save me from that man, through death...
*Pointing to the spot, where the Doctor, who has now disappeared, had been standing.*
Where is he?

GRAND PRINCE
          Dress him in his uniform again
And lead him out at once to Saski Square.

KORDIAN
Where is he gone? Where?

SOLDIER
Let's go. The Prince is waiting.

### Scene 7

*Saski Square. The Polish army, not yet formed up in ranks. On one side of the square is a group of generals, among them the Tsar. Grand Prince Constantine is walking about nervously. Further back, the people of Warsaw, all around the Square.*

CHORUS
A thousand men, a thousand bayonets;
Untrembling blades, limply hang the pennants;
Everything's silent — like the Judgement Day.

GRAND PRINCE
*Commanding.*
Join ranks! Even space...!

CHORUS
The infantry forms up in a straight line.
If you set up the Tsar there at one end
And had him puff his chest out by an inch,
While from the other, Wilhelm Tell should send
An arrow speeding down the ranks — it would find
Its mark in the Tsar, sparing all the rest,
Although its fletching tickled every breast —
As long as no one in the ranks should flinch.

GRAND PRINCE
Music!

CHORUS
Janissary music plays —
Then stops. The Tsar speaks. Let's hear what he says.

**TSAR**
*To the soldiers.*
You're well, my children?

**SOLDIERS**
                By the grace of God!

**CHORUS**
But what they shouted, God alone may know.
Lost like a prayer, when seas roar and winds blow.

*Six soldiers lead forth Kordian, pale. They stand him in front of the Tsar. The Grand Prince runs up in a fury.*

**GRAND PRINCE**
*To Kordian, foaming at the mouth.*
Ha! You Polish dog! You're here! Why are you pale?
You have an inkling of what's coming? Well?
Assassin! Rebel! What's this? Epaulettes?
Away with them! I'll crush them here like pests!
And you I'll toss beneath a caisson's wheels!
Or knock you on the sand here at my heels,
And carve *vor*\* on your forehead, with my spurs!
The Tsar gave you to me — so much the worse
For you! That's not a pardon, that's the grave!
From the Grand Prince's grip, no one can save
You — not even the devil!

**TSAR**
*Aside.*
                Does he think
He's fooling me?

**GRAND PRINCE**
                You, soldiers! Quick time! Bring
Four horses over here! You dog! You're hot
With fever, are you? Well then, but you've got
A healthy body — Ah, but we'll tie him
To each horse's tail, and tear him limb from limb!

---

\*    In Russian, *vor* means "thief." Today, it has a special application to the mafia.

My horse — the strongest — will pull off his head!
You won't speak? I'll go mad! This dog won't beg.

*He punches Kordian in the chest.*

I'm hungry as a wolf to tear your flesh!
I'd bite you now!
*Grinds his teeth.*
                  Ha ha ha! Your Highness,
Do you like tricks with horses? In that case,
We'll set up here a little steeplechase.
Soldiers — stack your carbines in pyramids —
Fastened together, with fixed bayonets.

*The soldiers do so.*

Now, dog — mount up! And ride your steed to Hell!
You're silent... At the sight, you feel unwell?
This isn't mercy — I will lose a horse
To send you packing. What are you waiting for?
Let's go! Let's go! Let's go! Mount up and ride!
If I could lift you up and jam your hide
Down on those blades, just like a pachyderm
With his strong trunk, I would!
*Cooling down.*
                        Look, Pole, I burn
With shame here — I've boasted before the Tsar
Of how insanely brave the Polish are:
Ready to leap into the river from
The topmost castle tower! Come!
*With fury.*
Jump, damn you! Or off to the Carmelites,
Where I'll have you walled up instead
Inside the crypt this very night
And starve you dead!
*In a pleading tone.*
Come on, Pole, listen! If you clear the knives
You have my word, you'll be preserved alive.

**KORDIAN**
Thank you, Your Highness, for revealing all.

If just a tiny wiggle of this small
Finger of mine would keep me safe and sound,
I wouldn't budge it.

GRAND PRINCE
          He's scared, the scoundrel!

TSAR
If that's what's going on, hear me: I swear
That even if you sail safe through the air,
Clearing the bayonets
As a bird a high forest,
You'll still be shot... Grand Prince, he's afraid!

GRAND PRINCE
You see! The Tsar himself says that you're dead!
Soldiers — Who'll make the jump? Whoever can
Will be awarded the Cross of St Anne —
And St Stanisław — And if he's injured,
A pension of a thousand, no, more:
Two thousand złoty... Not two thousand, four!

O, you dogs! No, you're not dogs, you're hares!
Polacks!

KORDIAN
         Give me the horse...

*He sits astride the horse and rides off to the far end of the square.*

GRAND PRINCE
                    Kuruta! Look there!
O, if he makes it...!

KURUTA
         He'll deserve the knout.

GRAND PRINCE
O, let him make it! I want him to win out!
The Tsar will recognise by what great heights
My soldiers overtop his Muscovites!

Look! Here he comes — he stops... He turns his glance
Upon the people... who wait in silence,
Black, muddy...
*Frowns like a tiger.*
      O, I do not like this folk —
They toss their hats and hankies... Any hope,
Kuruta?

KURUTA
  If you say so, Your Excellency.

GRAND PRINCE
*Violently.*
Look! What a cloud of dust he kicks up! Ah —
I can't see... Come on, boy! He made it!

SOLDIERS
          Hurrah!

PEOPLE
*From afar.*
He lives!
*The soldiers lead up Kordian, who comes on trembling legs. The Grand Prince embraces him.*

GRAND PRINCE
How's that, my friend! Now there's a bold youth! Well, well!
And my steed? Jumps like a devil straight from Hell!
I bet you didn't even feel him leap...
*To the Tsar.*
          Did you see,
Your Royal Highness?
*To the Soldiers*
       Take my horse, and lead
Him out to pasture — let him stretch those legs.
*To Kordian.*
You've won your life. Now go. You're ill? To bed!
To bed with you!
*To the Soldiers.*
     Go, let him get some sleep.

*The Soldiers exit with Kordian.*

TSAR
*To his generals, in a whisper, so that the Grand Prince shouldn't hear.*
Set up a court marital, today.
He tried to kill me... Firing squad!

GRAND PRINCE
*Gaily.*
Trumpeters! I want to hear you play
"Dąbrowski's Mazurka!"\* The Grand Prince wants to leap
A bit himself, by God!

## Scene 8

*A cell in a monastery made over into a prison. Barred windows, a table and cot of wood. Kordian, sentenced to death, is conversing with a Priest. Grzegorz, his old servant, is pacing the room with tears in his eyes.*

GRZEGORZ
*To himself.*
For an hour he's nagging my master, that priest!
Enough! He's facing death! Leave him in peace!
What sort of God locks children in a cell?
There is no God! I switch my allegiance to Hell!

KORDIAN
Grzegorz, pray for me.

*Like a chastened child, Grzegorz drops to his knees and prays... Kordian kneels before the Priest, and receives his blessing.*

PRIEST
*Raising Kordian to his feet.*
                    Stand up now, my son.
And go to God, forgiving all the world.

---

\*         A patriotic song, on a traditional tune, with words by Józef Wybicki (circa 1797). Also known as the "Hymn of the Polish Legions in Italy," its use is rather ironic here, in that it was sung by revolutionary Polish troops, fighting against the partitioning powers, including, of course (primarily) Russia. To day, it is Poland's national anthem.

God plucks you from the lion's jaws, this dungeon,
In which, like a flower, you'd sicken, curled,
Starved of light and air. But now, my son,
Have you any words to pass to anyone?

KORDIAN
No.

PRIEST
There's no one in the world you'd like to send
A word to?

KORDIAN
    No.

PRIEST
    Had you no single friend?

KORDIAN
No.

PRIEST
    There is a sin that you've not confessed!
Have mercy on his errant soul, dear Lord!

KORDIAN
Before my body in the grave will rest,
I hear a yearning echo in my soul...
A trace remains... a single deathless word...

PRIEST
That's sinful too, my son! You young ones would,
Parting the world "leave some trace" if you could —
A trace burnt here by thought, or some red stain
Made by a bloody sword — and what would you gain?
Prayer for the soul mumbled by those who pass
By, are worth more than a hundred epitaphs...
"Traces!" Even the soil balks at such fare
Of desiccated leaves — lets them lie there
Where they've fallen... Forgive me.
I've made you gloomy. I'm old; I can't see

What you do, as a child of spring, maybe...
Listen — There's a garden in the monastery,
Dark, with paths meandering through the close;
Among the pines I'll plant a monthly rose
And give it your name... That it should splay
Its petals in the gloom...

KORDIAN
                        May God repay
Your kindness... You'll give it my name, Father?
Perhaps it will not wither...

*Exit Priest.*

O, all you dreams that flit throughout the sky,
Gather together in one cloud of thought
And be with me! Heaven! Pour down your light
Of sun and moon and stars; for I am not
To see them shortly. Out there, even hung
Upon a gallows, I can hold my tongue,
Conquering pain, enclosing suffering
Within my heart, so none should ever know
My torments... But here, my tears must flow —
My pride can't hold them back; O, if I knew
That I was to bid farewell to it all,
My eyes would look upon the world with new
Hunger in those moments before the fall
Into the blackness — lingering, and who knows?
Perhaps with tears... For nearby, there grows
A beautiful flower in some garden plot —
I'll know it's there, although I'll know it not!
Perhaps a string touched, will give off a note
I've never heard — and now I never will —
Something's not right... I don't want to know people,
But I would like to get to know the earth,
The people's foster-mother... what sort of nurse
Were you to me, O earth, since I was born?
*Pause, then with contempt.*
O let the vicious tribes of people swarm,
And let them spit upon their mother's corpse.
I shall not be among them! Let the herds

Of people spawn only monsters henceforth;
Let vice be virtue, and serenity, fear,
Until the world, reflected in a mirror
Backwards, return to the bosom of God
Like something contrary to His first thought!
And let that petty multitude of pests,
As small as pismires! let that mob confess
Themselves men — the crown of all creation!
I shall not be among them! Let the nation
Be circumscribed in these four letters: TSAR.
Letters omnipotent let them be — so far
As to be synonyms for love and faith;
Let them contain the sum, the height, the depth
Of all these human creatures would express;
I shall not be among them! Let a press
Of gallows-poles rise in the city parks
Like posts upon the paths for Sunday walks —
For people hating tears; folk ever gay;
Let nannies watch their charges as they play
Beneath the leafless branches of gibbet-trees;
And let them dig the sand, upon their knees,
Sand rusty with the blood of martyred souls —
I shall not be among them! O, dead Poles,
I'm on my way to join you! I am he,
That harvest-hand whom Christ granted his fee
Although he started late, yet still he stayed
For recompense — a dark grave; so were you paid...

GRZEGORZ
Young master, I can't finish my prayer.
I keep getting hung up there, where
It says "forgive us, as we forgive..."
By God I won't, as long as I live!
May God send them plagues, here and now!
My lord, why did you point it at your brow,
That pistol? I can still remember it all:
The night, the full moon — I heard someone call
My name as I wandered among the forest trees...
So dark — I went, and what did I see
By my child on the heather lying —
Blood-drops like rubies — my child, dying!

KORDIAN
Don't remind me of that...

GRZEGORZ
Your own hand stamped in red
A seal satanic on your own forehead —
And now you're paying for that pact.
A man loves himself more than any other —
God cursed Cain, when he killed his brother;
So anyone who'll gun or poison use
Against himself, the light of life to smother...
*Pause, with despair.*
I foresaw you misfortune, but a hangman's noose!?!
O comfort me, young master! Say some words
Of comfort to old Grzegorz! I'll have a scribe
Write them down, and while I be alive
I'll keep them near my heart; and when it bursts,
I'll have them buried with me in the earth...
I'll tell my children I would be interred
With these words next to me in the tomb.
A child's words are an old man's best-loved blooms...

KORDIAN
Have you children?

GRZEGORZ
        A son.

KORDIAN
        A married man?

*Grzegorz nods.*

So, if your son has a son of his own,
Then christen him with my name, Kordian.

GRZEGORZ
And every time I'd call him, I would moan!

KORDIAN
You're right. My name would be harmful. Name him not
Kordian.

GRZEGORZ
   Young master, take not now away
The gift you've just now given me.
For I've already grown used to the thought...
The little boy, though he won't have a lot, he
Shall be named Kordian. And if he's naughty,
Why, I won't punish him — let him grow wild
Like a cornflower! Kordian! My child!
*He laughs, with tears in his eyes.*
O master! And you'll never see him! Why?

KORDIAN
Thou shalt not punish children, Lord on high,
For what they're called? Nor shall the fate that I
Must meet, be passed on with my name?
I'm like a shipwrecked man, drowning — how strange...
I grasp at every little straw in hope
Of outliving myself!
*Deep in thought.*
      And thus I cope
With present death... When I am dead and gone,
And the old man, too! Some boy, laughing on
A meadow, will hear his mother's voice
Call, "Kordian! Kordian!" at which he will
Respond with laughter from the flower-thick rill...
And by some dark wall in a quiet cloister,
My rose will bloom. Over it, with soft voice
A priest will pray... And so, a rose, a boy...

*Enter Officer with Priest, who had been weeping.*

PRIEST
My son...!

KORDIAN
   How shall I die?

OFFICER
                    By firing squad.

*Grzegorz falls to his knees. Kordian takes his grey head in both hands, kisses him warmly, and says, with breaking voice:*

KORDIAN
Be well — my faithful — father...

GRZEGORZ
*Stretching forth his arms.*
                    Lord! Lord! Lord!

*He falls to the ground, then gets up quickly and goes out in haste, after Kordian.*


## Scene 9
*A room in the Royal Castle.*

TSAR
*Solus.*
I'm bored. I shouldn't have got rid of him,
That little, diverting court chamberlain
Who skipped before me... "Jump, boy! Jump! Now, beg!"
Just like a pug dancing on his hind legs —
I'd like to get Mahmoud the Sultan yet
To skip before me like a little pet!
I'd feed him black powder and sulphur smoke,
Until I made the little fellow choke...
*Looking at the wall.*
What's this? Are there smudges on the walls?
There in the corner, a spider spins her web...
Dust... dust... I like it. Proves these halls
Unused... These cobwebs are like weeds that spread
Upon an enemy's grave. Poland's gone cold.
She's dead, for all time. As a compass shows
True north, evermore she looks to the snows
Siberian... From far away, her corpse
Looked sinister: all conquest forbidding,
Unwelcome, inimical... and worse;

I came, the corpse stirred, and began to sing!
I saw no tears, but smiles. Windows festooned...
So, on we go, westward. Europe, I'll soon
Slice you like an apple, with a poisoned knife.
All you crowned heads! Your fealty or your life!
Ha ha! Am I great, or is this world small?
Is the world daft, and I cleverest of all?
The shah, though grand, gave me a hefty parcel
Of his immense land; in a crucible
I had a handful of it put to flame
And then, out of the melting pot, there came
A bed of crystal, where he, grateful, rests...
Are you not cold on the Tsar's crystal mattress,
Great son of the sun? Brother of the moon?
There to the west a mighty hydra looms —
A hundred heads, but for them too I'll soon
Have a crystal bed made, for the western folk;
I'll use Muscovites measured for bespoke
Carpentry; if the mattress doesn't fit
Their length, I won't stretch the crystal a bit!
I'll shorten the tall peoples by a head...
O Europe! I'll send you a crystal bed!
Who's here...? My brother! Hello, Kostusiu!

GRAND PRINCE
*Runs in breathlessly.*
Your Majesty... please... I beg...

TSAR
       What's wrong with you?
You can't catch your breath? Why are you racing so?
Surely it's some good news you're bringing me?

GRAND PRINCE
Ha — Your Highness... had...

TSAR
       ...What? I'm listening to you...

GRAND PRINCE
...Him... firing squad...!

TSAR
                    Yes, because I wanted to,
My brother...

GRAND PRINCE
                    Call it back, Your Highness, deign
Recall the death sentence!

TSAR
                    What does this mean?

GRAND PRINCE
Your Highness, let him live! We still have time...
A moment... I have the pardon here. Just sign
Right here... Use my pen...

TSAR
                    Brother, I used mine
To write the death sentence, and it shall stand.

GRAND PRINCE
Your Highness, just a flourish of your hand,
And he is saved! O, damn it all! Just jot
Your name here — make a little blot...

TSAR
Brother, let's talk this over, man to man.
You'd save Kordian?

GRAND PRINCE
                    Yes, yes!

TSAR
                            And though I can,
For that reason I won't. Kordian shall die.

GRAND PRINCE
What? What?

TSAR
                    Brother, let's quit this quarrel. I'm
Sleepy...

*The Grand Prince paces the room. His fury is evident. He takes a piece of porcelain from the mantel and crushes it in his hand.*

GRAND PRINCE
You won't grant me this one thing, alone?
One little mercy? I gave you a throne!

TSAR
Brother, restrain your fury!

GRAND PRINCE
                    Sire, forgive
My passion, but please — Let that man live!

TSAR
If he's not the assassin, then, it's clear —
You are. Retire now, my brother dear.
Let's not sift through the dry-rot in your heart.
I'd rather pry two month old graves apart.

GRAND PRINCE
What? I don't understand...

TSAR
                    Go now, and don't worry...

GRAND PRINCE
Listen, brother, with me don't start a war!
Don't poke a tiger! That throne you sit upon,
I gave you! At its feet I lie, a lion
Of bronze. But what if I begin to roar?
What if the people hear me? And what's more,
Remember that it's me should wear the crown,
And you — barking commands on the parade ground!

TSAR
Prince! I see you've overfilled your cup with wine.
You gave me this throne? I took what was mine!
Who was born in the purple chamber? You!
Over whose golden cradle cannon boomed,
A hundred, in salute? Who bears the name
Of the Greek Caesar of immortal fame?
But later, mother, wife of Paul the Tsar,
Grew sick of you, with your nose of a Tatar,
And when she suckled you, you bit her full
Upon the breast... You grew; she said, "You're dull!
Too stupid to be Tsar," and her words were right!
She said, "Give him the throne." You said, "Let him buy it,"
And so, your abdication was purchased.
Why did you sell it? You might have gripped it fast.
But could you look your mother in the eye
With the glance of a Tsar? And bear her sly
Smiles and "you're stupids," and sip, brother,
At the cup poured you by your wrinkled mother...?

GRAND PRINCE
What's all this talk of cups? Your venom reserve
For later. O, I know you, hangman bold
And proud! Mother taught you to kill with words!
There were two clever ones in our happy fold
As well — with them, one day, a plot was hatched:
"We'll kill your father — strangle him with a sash."
And they replied, "Agreed." They went and choked
Him — Remember the words Beningsen spoke?
"We've strangled Paul the Tsar." They said "Amen."
They killed father! But there's a punishment
For sashes — Tossed out like some used up things
Far from Moscow, into the neighbouring
States; they gave Europe a nest of yellow
Snakes, and father's sacred corpse they tossed below
Into the crypt, so fast, the funeral
Was one priest's hurried prayer. And that was all.
You wouldn't bear him on a golden bier
Before his subjects' eyes, and that out of fear
They'd mark each murderous bruise, each wound, each trace...
Like to a leopard's was his mottled face!

But the nation cried out, "Sons! You've stolen
A comedy from us: your princely tears,
The pleasant sight of kings so lowly fallen;
Carry the Tsar out on his royal bier —
Come, kiss his hands in public! We would see
How criminals can slip the law, scot-free!"
Remember how, choking on incense-clouds,
You kissed that hand, and the funeral shroud?
And then you went and washed your kisser so,
The Neva barely had water left to flow!
How similar you are to our dead father!
Come, wash again his likeness from your face...
For I can't bear to look at you! The trace
Of him you murdered, wash it now, dear brother,
Or I will curse so loud that God, this time,
Will hear my words!

TSAR                     This is a royal crime.

GRAND PRINCE
Is there a difference? Those you send each day
To Siberia might cry out and say
As their armed transports rumble through the dust,
"Your Royal Highness! Come and ride with us!
You killed your father, come and join us now,
And let the hangman's brand caress your brow!"
You keep your subjects stupid and unschooled —
But there's a couple guardsmen won't be fooled...
So, off to fight the Turks with them! "Mikhail,
Lead them!" Mikhail just drools and smiles;
"You idiot!" you screamed, "Just light a fire
Beneath the ranks and blow them all sky high!"
Our brother Mikhail made a wordless bow
And left. He got your message, though, and how!
A month later, saltpetre sunk below
The guardsmen's barracks happened to explode!
With Russian blood the thirsty soil was slaked;
The Tsar just laughed and said, "It's a mistake!"
You know what, Tsar? Too great these royal crimes
For knout, Siberian exile, or the mines!

TSAR
Brother, a hired assassin would be shy
To house a heart like yours beneath his skin.
Let me remind you of another sin...

GRAND PRINCE
What are you getting at?

TSAR
                  ... and I won't lie...

*The Tsar whispers a few words in the Grand Prince's ear.*

GRAND PRINCE
Your Highness! Quiet! No!

TSAR
                  No, you must hear
My knout-like words until you break! until I sear
My brand unto your very innermost thoughts.

GRAND PRINCE
Quiet! I'll go mad!

TSAR
              Quiet? I'm not
The prince's conscience, or his paid toady.

GRAND PRINCE
Sire, I beg you — by all that's holy...!

TSAR
Tell me, where is that pretty English girl?
Blue eyes... O, how gaily she danced, you know!
Only sixteen, a child! As white as snow,
Unused to feelings, or the adult world,
She could fall mad in love with a white rose,
And before the flower's glance, the curtains close
To shield her modest bed...

*The Grand Prince sits down, his eyes fixed on the wall.*

                    God poured largesse
Of shining diamonds, the adamantine fires
Of stars into her crystal form... Alas,
Crystal won't bend; it shatters beneath the press
Of unwelcome desires...

GRAND PRINCE
Her... I see her...

TSAR
                    Well then — A certain day
A court fiacre drove up to the house
In which our English rose was wont to stay...
The lackeys bade her to the Princess' ball.
The innocent girl, suspecting nothing at all,
As careless as a butterfly, got in,
Drove to the palace, skipped up the stairs, and then —
Where's the ball? The lights? The music? The blooms?
All's silent as the grave. Into a room
They led her — You know where? You haven't scoured
Off the spittle yet, she shot at your broad brow...
O, you were angry! "Guards!" and the whole force
Ran in, eager at your command, of course...

GRAND PRINCE
Go on, go on, your tongue is nearly dried!

TSAR
Sit there and listen what was to betide!
The lady's lover thought up a nice jest —
Where to hide the body? In some ice?
For it was summer, and it would be best
To hide it from the Tsar's — and the ambassador's — eyes
(For it was from a foreign folk he stole her);
But then the prince's friend showed up to shoulder
The burden — He dyed his hair and dressed
Up in rich clothing, titled like a graf
This new Pylades — it's hard not to laugh!
Crosses and medals! — Soon he found a nest
To rent under a false name, paying the rent
A year in advance. Among the things he sent

As furniture was a great, heavy chest...
What was in it? I really cannot say,
But the concierge's daughters thought it looked
Like a young lady's wardrobe. Tucked away
The furniture, Pylades clicked the lock,
And slipped away, never more to be seen.
A week passed, two; whispers and strange rumours...
The concierge put eye to keyhole... No one there,
But then something got to him; now, quite scared
He screamed "A plague! a plague!" burst down the doors...
Pried ope the wardrobe... all his senses were attacked
At once: a corpse was hanging on the rack,
Rotting and melting — of a girl once fair —
And on her hand, a diamond ring did glare,
Incised thereon, two names — both hers... and yours.

GRAND PRINCE
*Awakens from a deep musing, tears himself from his chair, and speaks with barely suppressed violence.*
You know who murdered her? Because you know it,
I have to choke your words back down your throat!
You swallow mysteries you can't digest?
My sword will help — I'll tear them from you breast!
Or is your brain sick with them? If that's all,
I'll smash them from your skull against this wall!
Know this — Should my sword at the window shine,
Forty thousand bayonets would rush here — mine!
But why? I can choke you with a sash!
And once I've got your carrion safely stashed
Within a royal wardrobe, I'll go out,
And mix in gaily with the Varsovian rout,
"Ha, ha!" they'll ask, "Where's your brother the Tsar?"
"Safe in a cupboard like a pickle jar!"
I'll bury my sabre in your rotting meat
Just like a hangman slides his in a sheath
All gory; let the rust consume it there!
And let the people nose you out upstairs!
So what, my brother? Do you quake with fear?
It's you and I — Nobody else is here —
I'm as strong as a tiger — that's no lie!
It's me and you. Well? Look me in the eye!

*The Tsar looks his brother in the eye. They stare at each other a long time, each trying to make the other blink. Constantine drops his eyes first and moves away. He paces the room. The Tsar carefully follows each of his movements, and speaks to himself:*

TSAR
All right... I'm all right... that Muscovite snake
Raised a rebellious thought — and is crushed beneath its weight.
I would be dead, if he'd wielded his sword
Instead of stabbing with word after word...
*He's lost in thought; he beats his furrowed pate —*
I've got to cut this short... Constantine, wait!

GRAND PRINCE
*Takes off his sword and hands it to his brother.*
I render my sabre unto Your Highness...

TSAR
A brother begs a brother's forgiveness...

*Constantine stands there in silence, with bowed head. The Tsar takes his sabre, then signs Kordian's reprieve. Sticking it on the point of the sabre, he hands both to the Grand Prince, saying:*

Take this, with the sword.

*The Grand Prince bows, takes the sword, rings violently. Enter Adjutant... The Grand Prince hands him the pardon.*

GRAND PRINCE
Quick! To the Place de Mars! Don't spare the spurs —
Take my horse — Gallop! And outfly the birds!
Woe to you if from Kordian's head one sole
Hair should fall...

*Exit Adjutant.*

TSAR
*Wringing hands firmly.*\*
                    My brother — is a Pole!


**FINAL SCENE**
*The Place de Mars. To the rear, Kordian stands facing a platoon of soldiers.*
*To the front of the stage, people, talking.*

FIRST OF THE PEOPLE
The hangman's broken a sword over his head.

SECOND OF THE PEOPLE
Who cried out? Was it him?

FIRST OF THE PEOPLE
                    No, his lips are white.
It was some old man; he fell down as if dead.
But Kordian's said nothing. That old chap, might
He be his servant?

SECOND OF THE PEOPLE
                    And so they've deprived
Him of his noble rank.

THIRD OF THE PEOPLE
                    So the decree lied:
He, as a peasant, never at plough shall toil;
It's him they're ploughing underneath the soil!

FIRST OF THE PEOPLE
They'd offered... and he's refused a blindfold...

---

\*    In Polish: ściskając dłoń wściekle. "Pressing the palm furiously." It is unsure from the text whether the Tsar is shaking the Grand Prince's hand firmly (ściskanie dłoni is a handshake), in a congratulatory manner, or whether he is wringing his own hands in surprise and worry. Słowacki runs two contrastive ideas together — a handshake and fury — perhaps intending to make the situation equivocal.

SECOND OF THE PEOPLE
The officer now turns from him, retreats
To where the squad waits... O, how my heart beats!
They've taken aim...

CRY IN THE CROWD
                      Wait! Here comes the Adjutant!

FIRST OF THE PEOPLE
The officer can't see... He's raised his arm...

                    END OF PART I

# BALLADYNA

*a tragedy in five acts*

**My Dear Poet of the Ruins!**[*]

Permit me to begin my letter to you with a parable that was told me on the shores of Salamis Bay.

An old, blind harpist from the Island of Skiathos once wandered to the shores of the Aegean. Hearing the waves pummelling the beach with a loud roar, he imagined that the sound was coming from a great crowd of people who had come to listen to his heroic songs. And so, leaning upon his harp, he began to sing to the empty shore. When he finished, he was surprised to hear no human voice, no sigh — no applause. So he flung his harp far away from his side, and those waves, which the singer had taken to be a crowd of people, lifted up the golden instrument of song and laid it at his feet. But the sad Greek walked away from his harp, never realising that his most beautiful rhapsody had sunk, not into the hearts of men, but into the depths of the Aegean waves.

My dear Irydion! Let this parable of the harpist and the waves take the place of an introduction to *Balladyna*. Balladyna comes into the world with a smile of Ariosto on her lips, gifted with the inner power to outrageously abuse the human species, its systems and the orders by which everything in the world comes about; and with unexpected fruits of the type given by trees grafted by the human hand. Let Kirkor, the mender of all lawlessness, fall victim to his own pure intentions; let old Rake cherish Kirkor's kitchen; let the aethereal Goplana fall in love with the ruddy boy, and let sentimental Filon purposely seek out the torments of love, and his dead lover; let thousands of anachronisms terrify historians and chroniclers sleeping in their graves — and if all of this possesses and inner, vital force; if it was created in the poet's mind according to the laws of God; if his inspiration was no mere fever, but the result of that strange mastery, which whispers to the ear words never heard before, and displays to the eyes beings never before seen, not even in

---

[*] Zygmunt Krasiński (1812–1859), poet, author of *Irydion* (1836), a monumental drama set in Rome.

dreams; if his poetic instinct had the better of his reason, which now and then condemned this or that; then, against all prudence and history, Balladyna shall become Queen of Poland, and the lightning bolt, which fell upon her temporary reign, shall flash again and reconstitute the mist of events long past.

Now smile, Irydion! For in imitation of the French poets, I will tell you that *Balladyna* is but one episode of a vast poem in the manner of Ariosto, which is to be constituted of six linked tragedies, or dramatic chronicles. Various spectres of people who never were have now emerged from the mists of pre-creation* and surround me in a chattering throng; all that is needed is for them to form up in distinct groups, so that their actions might arrange themselves in the pyramid-like figures of events. Then, one after the other, I will toss them out into the world by handfuls, and the dreams of my childhood may perhaps come true. For however many times I would gaze up at the old castle, the ruins of which crown the hill in my hometown, I would dream of someday spilling spectres, spirits, knights into its jagged wreath of battlements; that I would reconstruct the grand halls and illuminate them with the fire of a night filled with lightning, and that I would make the vaults ring with the echoes of ancient Sophocles' "Alas!" And for this I hoped that my name would be heard in the rushing of the stream that flows at the foot of the castle hill; and that a rainbow of sorts, made up of my thoughts, would float above the castle ruins. — O! Don't tell me that the pealing of bells in the fields is a greater ornament for the ruins than this garland of thought, which the poet weaves for them! Because even though the roses growing on the ruins of Nero's palace have brightened that rubble beauteously, they are lit up for me still more brightly by Irydion's spirit, which you placed beneath the cross in the Colosseum, covering him with the golden wings of an angel.

And so, as you fill the old, statuesque forms of Romans with the volcanic soul of our age, so I am creating a fantastic legend from the antiquity of Poland, drawing forth prophetic choirs from the silence of the ages — and leading forth bright, rainbow-hued Ariostan clouds to greet your black, thunderous, Dantean stormhead, sure that our meeting in the upper regions will not result in combat, but rather be a play of colour and shadow, all the same ending sadly for me in that your cloud, sped on by a greater wind and fuller of the fire of the heavens, can muscle aside and even consume my breezy and varicoloured mist.

I have been told by the Sylphs that you have wandered afar to visit red Aetna. As soon as I heard this, I sent my Skierka before you to open all the flowers at your feet, and light up all the stars above your head. In gratitude, I ask this of you: When you stand upon the summit of the volcano, gaze out upon the broad blue of the seas and think, that not too long ago, my ship

---

\*      In the manner of Krasiński, Słowacki coins a word here: *przedstworzenie.*

was travelling over that watery mirror, its white sails spread like the wings of a swan. Tell me — can you not make out some trace upon those waves, some vestige of the wake left by my ephemeral ship? At the time, the priests were intoning a hymn to the Blessed Virgin, and I stood on the deck, my eyes fixed upon the fires of Aetna, sad that the waves were bearing me back to Europe. Train your ear intently upon the quiet air. Do you not hear the echo of that hymn, which brought peace to my heart? Does it not tremble still in the crystal atmosphere? Search for my traces in the air and in the waves, and if you hear nothing of me from either, find me then in your heart; let me be with you for at least the space of one hour. For it is one of God's gifts that we are able to visit one another on the wings of thought.

Well, I have written on and on, while all that I intended to write was:

TO THE AUTHOR
OF *IRYDION*,
AS A SOUVENIR,

*Juliusz Słowacki*

PRESENTS
*BALLADYNA.*

Paris, 9 July 1839

## PERSONS

Hermit, *Popiel III, in exile.*
Kirkor, *Lord of the castle.*
Mother, *a widow.*
Balladyna
  and Alina, *her daughters.*
Filon, *a shepherd.*
Rake, *the sacristan's son.*
Fon Kostryn, *head of the guards at Kirkor's castle.*
Gralon, *a knight of Kirkor's.*
Chancellor
Wawel, *a chronicler.*
Page
An Envoy from the Capital Gniezno
Prosecutor
Royal Physician
Lords — Knights — Castle servants — Villagers — Children

## FANTASTIC PERSONS
Goplana, *a nymph, queen of Lake Gopło.*
Chochlik
Skierka

*The action of the play is set in the days of fable, in the environs of Lake Gopło.*

## ACT I

### Scene 1

*A wood near Lake Gopło. The cottage of the Hermit, festooned with flowers and ivy. Enter Kirkor, dressed in Karacena armour.\* He is richly dressed, and adorned with eagle's wings...*

**KIRKOR**
*Solus.*
Worthwhile, to seek advice of such a man

---

\*     A rich, fish-scale armour with a leather under-layer. It was very popular in early modern Poland.

Who hides himself in wooded solitude;
A pious oldster, yet his mind is crazed
Somewhat — just speak to him of kings,
And castles, courtiers at court,
And off he goes, spinning away from reason,
Thundering curses, foaming at the mouth —
He must have, in his day, been served much evil
By kings; since then, he is the commons' friend.
*Knocks at the cottage door.*
Knock, knock!

VOICE FROM WITHIN
>Who's there?

KIRKOR
>Kirkor.

HERMIT
*Emerging from his cell.*
>Welcome, my son!
What do you seek?

KIRKOR
>Advice.

HERMIT
>Become a monk.

KIRKOR
If I had reached my tenth decade already,
Perhaps I might retire to an oaken glade,
But I am young — the lord of four tall towers.
Today I'm pondering how best to marry.
Advise me, old man.

HERMIT
>It's now twenty years
I live here in the desert...

KIRKOR
>So?

HERMIT

                        And so,
I am unable to evaluate
Men, or tell you, which maid you should marry.

KIRKOR
Those, who were buttons on the bush when you
Were in the world, have blossomed now as maids:
Red buds become red roses, white to white
Blossoms; think back — the most beautiful sprite
Among them, white, as in an angel's hand
A lily, fairest child of all the land,
Whose voice the nightingale is jealous of;
Whose faithfulness outdoes the turtledove...
Where can I find a girl like that, old man?
Advise me! People say that princesses
Have just such graces?

HERMIT

                      Ah! A viper's clan!
In crime, the wife a rival to her man,
The daughter to her sire, son to his dam,
A writhing pit of reptiles! Lord of flame,
Send you down lightning bolt...!

KIRKOR

                      Curse not!

HERMIT

                            Young man,
Curse you along with me! It's just deserts.
Would that they came to know hunger and plague,
To fall at last within earth's gaping jaws,
With dust for a surcoat, a viper for a crown,
Great God! I've torn my strength with cursing bandits,
Teased rabid as a mastiff on a chain.
For once I too was lord above all lords,
Beloved of a numerous folk — tens of thousands.
I who now go in rags, once wore the purple,
And so I must curse! I once had three children —
One night, my brother's toughs entered their chamber,

And snipped those roses there, still in the bud!
My little girls — their throats cut, in their cradle!
My angels... All my children...

KIRKOR
                          Who are you,
Old man?

HERMIT
      Me?... I am King Popiel the Third.

KIRKOR
*Drops to a knee.*
My sovereign!

HERMIT
               Who sees other than a wretch?

KIRKOR
I'll arm my peasants, and fly to Gniezno
To wreak revenge for you...

HERMIT
                      Prudence, young man!

KIRKOR
This is injustice worse than Moses' plagues!
It fouls the earth and spreads like quick disease;
The king, splashed with the blood of innocents,
Unworthy is to lead a crowd of knights.
And so, let come what ought to come, by God,
He, looking on this poor and befouled land.

HERMIT
Are you an angel, stooped on golden wings
From Heaven above?

KIRKOR
                    These wings came from the back
Of eagles; on a knight's broad shoulders now,
Will they be any less use to the people

Than when borne by the bird? What can reptiles,
When faced with a knight stretching eagle's wings?

HERMIT
O man of iron! You are one of those
Who topple thrones!

KIRKOR
                    You know full well yourself
How thick our poor land is with harlotry —
The king's! The man who bears your name is bloody,
And spends his time inventing cruelties.
I have seen whole ponds tinted crimson
In which the king feeds carp on slave's remains.
Sometimes, he picks the tenth man from the lines
And dices him in pieces for the chum
He tosses his pet fish. What they won't eat,
He sweeps outside and fattens furrows ruby
With offal. Those states neighbouring this butcher's
Call it, in jest, Red Rus. There was a time
When those who lived beneath the crown of Lech
Were wanting nothing; unseen, valleys clustered
With grain provided by the hand of God.
Now it is blight and famine that He rains
In largesse on our prone, dumbfounded realm.
The soil is parched in summer, cracks in seams;
The fleece of spring turns golden ere the seed
Bows gravid to the earth, and reapers gather
But tufts empty of wheat. And this is Poland,
Once opulent in corn, once warlike and strong;
Her knights are pale today, and battle now
Fierce hunger, and the phantoms of the plague.

HERMIT
Ah, me accurst! Accurst and thricely damned!
I am the pustule spread the leprosy
Throughout the body of my wretched people!

KIRKOR
Why, how are you to blame?

HERMIT

                The realm of Lech
Was once a far-famed miracle of bread;
Herein the people's happiness; herein
The strength of the land lay... But I, exiled,
Deprived the people of their crown.

KIRKOR

                                      Old man...?

HERMIT
My brother's crown is false and made of tin.
The real crown, I secreted 'neath rotten stumps
Here in the forest... I had planned to wear it
To my grave.

KIRKOR

                Has that crown some wondrous strength?

HERMIT
Ages ago, three holy kings: a Scythian,
And two magi, were returning to their homes
From Bethlehem. That northern king got lost
Among our cornfields as if in a forest,
For wheat, in Lech's time, grew as tall as oaks.
Losing his way, the king cried out, "Dear Lord,
Lead me to safety!" Then, at once, the thatch
Of our king's cottage rose before his ken
— For Lech dwelt in a simple peasant's cottage —
The Scythian approached his door, and called,
"Greetings, my brother! I ride from Bethlehem...
The cornflowers of your fields lead me to you."
And Lech replied, "Come in, reside with me;
This land of mine is happy and of brave heart.
I'll share this heritage of mine with you,
If you desire so." "I'll stay," said the king,
"But I don't want your land. A realm divided
Borders on blood, and women's and children's grief."
And they remained together... O, but the tale
Is long to tell...

KIRKOR
                    But speak on!

HERMIT
                                'Twas a custom
Amongst the ancient kings to exchange
Their rings. Thus did Lech. Ah, but the Scythian,
Who loved him from the bottom of his heart,
Gave him the crown... Our crown, of which I spoke.
Our Saviour, as a Babe, stretched forth his hands
Toward that crown once... Crawling from the lap
Of His astonished Mother, he pursed his lips
— Like rosebuds peeking forth from their green nests —
And cried out, "Pretty!" Taking it in hand,
Joyed with the rubies and the other stones,
He kissed a white gem, leaving pearls thereon,
When brushed by his pink lips.

KIRKOR
                                O, you poor blossom!
Was it for this you bloomed to be affixed
To the rough wood of a cross of torture?
Why was I not there then, on Mount Golgotha,
On my black charger, leading my armed train!

I would have saved the Saviour; that, or hacked
His butchers all to pieces in revenge!

HERMIT
My son, the Lord accepts your pure intention
For act accomplished. In our own day and age,
When banished by my brother, I bore forth
The holy crown into these forests deep.

KIRKOR
It shall return! It shall! I swear to you!
And yet...

HERMIT
          What is it you would say?

KIRKOR
>Before Kirkor
Hurls himself into the fell abyss
Of vengeance — I, I'd like to question you...
To what slim sapling should I graft the tree
Of the Kirkors, so that it someday bear
Harvest of knightly arms to shield your throne?
Whom might I lead across my castle threshold
With a wife's name?

HERMIT
>Many men have raced
After the ghost of greatness with a ring,
And almost all have won — not their lost rib,
But merely a bone of contention. You,
Do otherwise. You are noble and young;
Let the first swallow lead you to the beam
Beneath which she's plaited her nest, and there,
Beneath a thatched roof, where a maiden's face
Flashes by window-sill — Hesitate not!
She is your loved predestined. Take her poor;
Marry simplicity, and then be happy
And better off, than had you wed a queen...

KIRKOR
This is your counsel?

HERMIT
>Go, my son — trust me —
To a poor cottage; choose a humble wife,
Pleasant and innocent...

KIRKOR
>Hey now, black swallow!
Now, harbinger, where is it you shall lead me?

HERMIT
Heed me, my son.

KIRKOR
                I shall; you counsel well!
Lead me, O swallow, swallow!
*Exit.*

HERMIT
*Solus.*
                        Ah, young men!
They part from us with loud cries: "Comrades, come!
We go in search of fortune!" We old men,
Who've tramped the roads of this sad land, far, and wide,
Never encountered her, that fickle bride
Good Fortune. Perhaps we searched wrongly? Well —
Come, come old man! Go search out your cell…

*He makes to go inside, then halts at the threshold. Enter Filon, a shepherd… deep in thought, dressed fantastically in ribbons and flowers.*

FILON
*Exaltedly.*
O golden sun! O my beloved trees!
O! Stream that winds and purls about the pebbles,
Urging your glossy ripples with low sobs!
Roses of spring! Enamoured of the moan
Of nightingales! With you Filon shall die!
For Filon dreamt he shares Endymion's fate;
He dreamt that once, a white goddess stooped down,
In roses garlanded, stooped down, I say,
From the high sapphire heavens, on a ray
Of moonlight, trembling; then, her forehead she dips
And with her mouth of coral, she sets afire my lips!
Ah! So I dreamed! And yet upon the earth
There's no Diana. Lonely I shall wither
Just like a violet, or a bloom in winter.

HERMIT
What's with these peevish moans, you mad young man?
Where's common sense? You overturn the frame
Of order by the Hand divine arranged;
Like leery Actaeon panting at bath-side,
You wait upon the advent of a god

Here on the earth! This is the cause
So many old maids mope about unwed!
Search out an earthly lover!

FILON
                                            All throughout
The earth I've searched in vain, examining
The tribe of mortal maidens. Now my glance
Was held, in hunger, by the sunburnt face
Of harvest-girl beneath a cap of straw;
Red cheeks like poppy blooms amidst the corn.
Sometimes, I'd stand enchanted at white linen
Stretched on the green to blanch in the sun;
My heart was so aswarm with love, they seemed
Foam of the seas, from which would shortly spring
The alabaster shape of the goddess of love...
Ah, so deranged I lived here in the world
As 'twas a desert, never slaked, never calm,
Always crackling in thought. I've been at courts;
I have seen princesses as bright as stars — hers,
Venus', that in the evening sapphire twinkles
With its pale sheen, though it put forth no ray;
Heartless they are, and yet these empty breasts
Are priced as only gems in coronets.

HERMIT
You idiot, who'd barter for the stars!
Begone, you prowler of the keeps of queens!
Away, you sterile blossom — as useless as
A broken jar at wellside; the hot sun
In fallow autumn...! Just as soon as I
Ascend my throne again, I'll fetter you
In madhouse — or banish you to school bench!

FILON
Sit you down, father! God have mercy, good man!
You must be ill, you speak so waywardly...

HERMIT
All of the madmen congregate around me!
And all are daydreaming of royal courts;

They dream of kings and hide in hedges, moaning,
Moaning like blind owls!

FILON
                          Dunk your head, old man,
There in the crystal stream. You're overheated.

HERMIT
Water won't wash away the crimson furrow
Stamped on my brow with wearing of the crown!
Two decades of inhabiting these woods
Have not smoothed out the ditch; I am marked there;
Another trench is carved upon my heart...
*Points to his chest.*
And this was dug there by the blades of them
That slaughtered my poor children... O! I am orphaned!
Unnatural! 'Twas the father left behind...!

FILON
The ancient bores me. Addled in the head
By shades incorporeal. Far too long alone,
Far too much fasting.

HERMIT
                    Painful memories
Sting like nettles. But reality,
That wounds and kills like iron.

FILON
                            Well, we'll speak
Another time. I hope then to convince you
That heartache...

HERMIT
                Heal it with a muddy grave,
You puke-inducer! Let this nothing be killed
By nothing, with nothing its epitaph!

FILON
My darling!
*He puts his hand on his heart.*

                    Undiscovered yet, your image,
But here it lives! And undiscovered is worse
Than found but to be lost! — I see you, love,
Before me — I shall go into the woods
Where I shall be alone — shall be with you...
Blessed art thou, wonder of fantasy!
Thou shalt preserve me!
*Exit, to the woods.*

HERMIT
            People are insane!


Scene 2
*Another part of the forest. Enter Skierka and Chochlik.*

SKIERKA
Where is our queen, Goplana?

CHOCHLIK
                    Still asleep,
Deep in Lake Gopło.

SKIERKA
                    Neither scent of pine,
Nor spring's perfumes have yet awakened her?
Can she not hear how, with a thousand wings,
Black swallows beat the surface of the lake,
Staining its mirror with a thousand ripples?

CHOCHLIK
Too soon you'll find the old hag will awaken
To set us drudging: "Fill the empty acorn
With butterfly eggs! Go and aid the ants
To build their capitals! Go and sweep the streets
To clear safe passage for the formic trains!
Help with the harness of the grasshoppers;
Unwind their winter sheaths, that they may fly!"
Or else we'll traipse from hive to hive and read
Their constitutions to the bees, take their oaths,
Or call the yearling swallows to the reeds

And teach them how to build their first homesteads;
Or else she'll have us set off all the traps
That lurk upon the feet of birds unwary,
Or lecture pies against the vice of theiving,
Or flatter sparrows so, with lovely voice
They'll trill in thatched roofs all the summer long...
O, what a life it is! We sweat and strain
Like pagan horses all the summer long,
And in the winter — rest! behind some foul
Stove bench, among pots and cauldrons, pinched between
A toothless sour old hag and a bawling brat!

SKIERKA
Chochlik, you are a lazy drone.
*Looks toward the lake.*
Look there! On that sunbeam of gold
Goplana rises from the lake;
An airy leaf of lacy brake
That lightly by the breeze is rolled,
Just like a swan, with wings spread wide,
Topsails and jib of woven snows
She rocks, and bobs, then stately goes!
See how, how graceful in her pride!
Out of the lake she blithely flips,
And from the braids of forget-me-nots
She clings by her slim fingertips,
Then, with her toes, she lightly hops,
With each skip raising sparks of flame.
Ah, who can guess? Treads she the hoop
Of ripples? Or flies she again?
Or hangs she from that bloom that droops?

CHOCHLIK
Around her brows, what is that lush
Garland? Of flowers? or of rush?

SKIERKA
O no... upon her ivory forehead those
You see are slumbering swallows
Who once, their tiny legs fast tied
Fell in the river's depths, and died...

By current borne to riverside,
They form a wreath now, ebony,
For the blond locks of the Goplan queen.

CHOCHLIK
I warrant you, my Skierka, let's be off!
The witch even now is framing schemes to set
Us labouring — to spin the heavy millwheel
For the poor miller down by the spent creek,
Or flog the lazy hornet to confession
Before Acedia carts him off to Hell
For theft of others' honey — or paint eyes
On peacock tails...

SKIERKA
                         So then, be off!
I'm having too much fun here in the sun,
Whose rays are shining through the wet
Wings of the swallows, black as jet —
Their lungs swell, and again they live!
They shudder, blink, and fly away
Like clouds of startled sparrow chicks.
And there she stands, our queen, amazed,
Eyes wide and bending startled ear —
To bind again her loosened hair
She's not the skill, nor does she dare...
But how came it, the garland sear
Came back to life, and flew away?
Goplana, ho! Goplana, hey!

GOPLANA
Pluck me some roses, Chochlik, for my wreath
Is flown away.

CHOCHLIK
                   Thus we begin to drudge!
*Exit, grumbling.*

GOPLANA
Is it still morning?

SKIERKA
                    One o'clock
In the springtime.

GOPLANA
                Ah, where's my lover?

SKIERKA
What is it you command, my queen?
To weave some rainbow beams, or cover
Palace roofs with ivy green?
To set the flowers' foundations well
On mallow column and bluebell?

GOPLANA
No!

SKIERKA
Shall I fix you a new throne
From the weeping clouds of heaven?
Would you like a string of pearls
Of the fashion that are grown
To mix up bird-lime? Those with swirls
Of liquid light, Calcutta drupes,
Hey? Let me fly off to the bog
And snatch the will-o'-wisp that swoops
Above the marshes through the fog;
I'll take a lily-cup and fashion
A cresset for its pulsing light;
I'll satisfy your slightest yen,
My lady — Command me! And I'm in flight.
Whatever's found under the sun,
Whatever charm of flower, tree,
Above the earth, beneath its dun
Bosom — what no eyes ever see,
Or common things — lightbeams, the dew,
Sounds, echoes — all I'll fetch for you.
Every desire of yours I'll slake,
What you dreamt up deep in the lake.

GOPLANA
I'm in love, Skierka my dear.

SKIERKA
With what? This thornless rosebush here?
With the viburnum, or the clover?
Or the bloom called "The Peace God Grants,"
Which flower a stepmother plants
On the lonely sods that cover
Her husband's children? Ah, for sure
It is the gauzy gossamer
That floats upon the summer breeze?
Perhaps it is the black eyed Susan
That brought the loveless girl to ruin
When, plucking petals in despair
She heard it "loves you not" declare?
Whichever one it be of these,
Send forth your Skierka, and he'll bring
Your lover near to cuddle and kiss,
And bind into the flowery ring
That winds your brow! You'll live in bliss
With him until the planets swing
Us round to the next age — next spring.

GOPLANA
Ah, I'm in love — I'm in love with a man!

SKIERKA
Black magic!

GOPLANA
While I was resting in my winter sleep,
Deep in the lake, upon my crystal bed,
I was awakened, suddenly, by fire —
A bright red glow shining right through the ice;
Then came a pounding, grinding... fishermen,
Boring a hole to snatch the cozened fish...
Then came a shout — a man fell through the ice!
He fell right on my bed! Was it the light
That penetrated through the fishers' hole,
Or were his rosy cheeks, fainting in death,

So bright and comely? Ah, so beautiful,
So beautiful was he! I would have clipt
Him in these icy arms of mine forever!
To bind him in their soft chains and fetter him
With links of kisses... He began to fade,
And I — I had to give him up, alas!
If only I might have borne him ashore
In these two arms, my lips pressing his lips,
Cloven to him, pouring into his cold breast
Warm life! But you know how our nature's ruled —
We share the springtime glory of the blooms,
But when the winter comes, our colour fades,
Our freshness withers. We fade and grow sere,
Grey as the stones that cobble the lake floor.
Such was I then, and such I might not show
Myself to the thin winter sun; half dead,
I raised him to the hole with trembling hand
And tossed him through the fissure; I returned
In agony, in heartbreak to my bed;
The happy cries of fishermen doubling
The pain I felt, as they greeted the foundling
I bade farewell to. How I longed for spring!
And now, it's here! At last! I reawaken,
My heart brimming with love... Flowers are nought
Beside his blushing cheeks... The stars grow dim
Beside his flashing eyes... I love, I love!

SKIERKA
Someone's approaching through the woods.

GOPLANA
                                    It's him!
My love! It's him! Skierka, be gone!

*Exit Skierka. Enter Rake — a ruddy-cheeked fellow dressed like a villager.*

RAKE
What sort of lass is this? She has a nose,
Two legs, a stomach, but she seems of glass.
A beast of mist and jelly? There are men

With a taste for such women, but I, pah!
She smells somewhat of fish!

GOPLANA
                                    What is your name,
You handsome fellow?

RAKE
                            Nothing to speak of...

GOPLANA
O, darling Nothing-to-Speak-of!

RAKE
                                    Ha, ha!
You silly girl! "Nothing to speak of" means
There's nothing you might name in the whole world
That might find aught amiss in my beauty.
My name is Rake.

GOPLANA
                         Rake, Rake... O what angel
Leads you into these woods?

RAKE
                             Well, by my troth!
What a nosy thing, this slender pork chop!

GOPLANA
Pardon me, Mr Rake?
RAKE
                           O, drop the Mister;
You have my permission — Just call me Rake.

GOPLANA
What might you be?

RAKE
                         You ask me who I am?
It's a long story but... your humble servant...
There in our village church a great organ stands;

My dad played on the bagpipes — wonderfully
When soused, but false when he was sober;
Besides that, he was the village barber —
He shaved and squeezed. That is, on Saturday,
He shaved the village beards; on Sunday, squeezed
The bellows. O, he was a man of virtue:
He never shaved when drunk, but when he played,
The blowstick always smelt of liquor. Thus,
He lived a peaceful life. Then Cupid struck,
And Dad took Mum to wife. Mum had a beard,
Which Dad would shave, but — well, who would have guessed?
Mum too was musical: the bag she squeezed
Was Dad. She played on him, and played so hard
He popped his chanter reed in apoplexy
And went the way of all sheep's bladders. I,
Posthumous melody of the old piper,
Am spitting image of my Da, they say —
I like old mead and vodka young or old,
And hide from Mother.

GOPLANA
      Ah, his words breathe forth
Springlike aroma to my greedy ears...
O, darling, how I love you!

RAKE
      What a girl!
That's rather forward. Then again, what wonder?
Whenever I pass down the high street, hearts
Thunder to the ground like overripe plums.
All the girls cry out "Rake! O, Mr Rake!
Remember, Rake, tomorrow I'm raking hay;
Come, Rake, and help me rake!" They'd die for me...
Or let me kiss them underneath the ricks...

GOPLANA
Do you love me, my sweetheart?

RAKE
      I'm not sure...
Let's have a taste...

GOPLANA
                    Hold on! Kisses are vows
For maidens pure — at each peck drops a petal
Wilted from her garland. Gripped with remorse,
At but one petal peeled back from the heart,
More than one maiden grows so shy to love,
She bids farewell, forever, to the world
And slips in the cold covers of the grave
Unloved.

RAKE
          You sermonise just like a nun.

GOPLNA
You kiss me once, and I am yours forever.
And you are mine.

RAKE
                         Ha! Kisses lay at inches,
And that "mine" is miles away...
*He kisses her.*

GOPLANA
                    O, my love!

RAKE
Pah! Pah! I kissed a fragrant rose, or so
I thought... Pah! She is rosy to the eye,
But that rose stinks like week-old rotten roe!

GOPLANA
My darling! Now! at nightfall you must come
To meet me in the wooded meadows here,
Where we shall walk about beneath the moonshine,
With nightingales a-chirping at the lake,
Beneath the wide-spread branches of the larch.
Here we shall dream our fill beneath the moon...

RAKE
*Aside.*
I don't know about that... What can I say
To this minx?

GOPLANA
              Are you sad? Are you speechless?

RAKE
We shall, we shall, but not this evening... darling...
And not so near the lake.

GOPLANA
              Whyever not?

RAKE
I hate the watery element, like rabid dogs.

GOPLANA
Well then, I'll gather raspberries for you,
Wild strawberries...

RAKE
              Alas, they give me hives;
When I see young girls balancing berry-jars
Atop their heads, I knock them over... not
For the berries' sake...

GOPLANA
              But ah, my lover, you
Must like flowers... Come here, every evening,
Where I shall gather —

RAKE
              This is overmuch!
I won't be coming here ever again!

GOPLANA
Why not?

RAKE
>Because another waits for me —
The other side of this brake, every evening.

GOPLANA
A girl?

RAKE
>Of course, a girl!

GOPLANA
>A pretty girl?

RAKE
What's that to you? Her name is Balladyna.

GOPLANA
Alina's sister? The widow's daughter?
She has an evil heart...

RAKE
>You must be mad.
I don't believe in old maids' superstitions.
All girls who have such tiny feet as hers
Have lovely hearts as well... and lips... and... legs...
And she has very pretty little feet!

GOPLANA
*Growing angry.*
Ha! May the sun be doused to a sputtering coal
Before anyone tears you from my arms!
For you are mine! And mine forever more!
Though in your wedding band the moon was set,
I'd pulverise that planet, snuff its glow,
That lit the path you tread to her embrace —
Be you true to me! I beg you! I implore!
I swear an oath upon your own good fortune!
For you shall perish... No, we both shall die —
For as you die, so I come to my grave,
And with my death, so you perish as well!
I do not wish to die — so you may live!

At least this one evening — don't go to her!
At least tonight, go not! So I command!

RAKE
Command? And who are you then, to "command?"

GOPLANA
A queen! Goplana! The Lady of the Lake!

RAKE
Oo-hoo! Come legs, away! Jesus and Mary!
That's all I need, to cuddle Satan's wife!

*He runs off.*

GOPLANA
*Sola.*
So let the sun be doused! Stars, come unlatched
And tumble erring through the trackless sky!
Roses, wilt! Die, sun! Die, flowers and stars!
I'll lose this universe before I lose
That man — and I have might not of their earth,
Over this earth, and I shall bend it to
The conquest of that heart! Skierka! Chochlik!

*Enter Skierka at a run.*

Skierka, were you eavesdropping on our talk,
My conversation with that lovely angel?

SKIERKA
Punish me not — I was so curious —
My heart is full of penitence... I was.
I snipped a lupin, raised the stem to ear,
And listened in...

GOPLANA
       Where's Chochlik?

SKIERKA
                                Lazing somewhere.
He's long about that garland...

*Enter Chochlik with a garland.*

GOPLANA
                                Shame on you!
You've wound a wreath of weed and nettles —
Wormwood and clover and grass!

SKIERKA
                                Allow me, ma'am,
To thrash him for that garland —

CHOCHLIK
                                Eh! Just try!
I'll spell you fast amongst these stinging nettles —

GOPLANA
Hush now and listen to me, little imps!
Chochlik — fly after my departing lover.
Go by his side, before him and behind him,
Just like the Friar's Lanterns, lead him wide
Across the bogs and marshes all night long,
And far away from every cottage door,
Especially that, which opens on two maids,
Two gorgeous blossoms — the widow's daughters —
You understand? And then, at dawn, lead him
Here to me.

CHOCHLIK
                    Deep in the slops and puddles,
The sucking mud and clay, ha ha! he'll wallow!
*Exit.*

GOPLANA
And you, my Skierka, fly off to the bridge,
There where the ghost of him is said to walk,
Who took his life with his own hand.
Secrete yourself where the reeds thickly stand;

Within the hour a wealthy man,
Decked out in gold and fine array,
As if it were his wedding day,
Will ride that way toward the strand.
With gold his carriage will shine bright;
Five horses will be harnessed to it:
Four stallions strong, and black as soot,
And one mare, mincing, milky-white.
Her hooves are prancing; sparks they flick;
The wood is rotten, the planks are slick...
Understand...?

SKIERKA
    They, slip, they fall...

GOPLANA
          Of course.
But see that no harm comes to horse,
Or man.

SKIERKA
   And then?

GOPLANA
    The man in gold,
Lead him with tender melodies
To that cottage among the trees
Where live the two girls with their old
Poor widowed mother — Knead his heart
So that he chooses him a wife
To draw off in his shining cart.
Fly now, my Skierka!

SKIERKA
       'Pon my life,
The girl will be a bride before
The moon thrice rests beyond the shore.
*Flies off.*

GOPLANA
*Sola.*
And so I send abroad my sylphs; they strain
On my behalf, this time, not so the spring
Might bloom with flowers vying in their pride,
Neither to guard the tender seed, nor plait
The seven strands of rainbow, nor to teach
The nightingale her tune, the swallow dips
And whirls and rolls above the glassy lake —
I love! I die! Ah, if he not love me?
I shall disperse entirely in the mists
And fall upon the wildflowers like tears
Of dew, with them to wither in the swelter.
*She melts away in the air.*


### Scene 3
*The widow's cottage. The widow enters with her daughters Balladyna and Alina. They all carry sickles.*

WIDOW
And so the day is done. Balladyna,
Your little hands will melt away like ice
Beneath the sun! Tomorrow morning I
And Alina alone will scythe the rest;
And you, my child, will rest here in the shade...

ALINA
No, no! Tomorrow it's you who shall rest,
Mother. Sister and I will bring it in.
The sun is much too fond of your grey head
And flies to it like an insistent wasp
To a sweet flower, with no leaves to shoo
It from your brows. And God sends nary a wisp
Of cloud to shade you, O, my poor, poor mother!

WIDOW
My good girls — even poverty is pleasant
By your side! Now, who sows for God, reaps well.
And so I always think, God shall repay you
With wealthy husbands. Who knows? Maybe you're known

At court, even? Think: here we be a-toiling
Beneath the sun, and then, out of the thickets
Some princeling comes — Ah, let him be a cook
Or even stablehand! — comes riding up,
And says to me, "My honest dame, I beg
Thee for the hand of one of thy daughters."
"My Lord," I make replay, "Take Balladyna.
As pretty as the velvet plant." You too
Alina, will take a knight to husband. But the eldest
Ought to be married first. The rushing stream
Sends current after current, the first flow
Is chased by those thereafter. "Balladyna,
Take Balladyna, your Royal Highness."

BALLADYNA
What have you done now with my comb, Alina?
Come on, stop dreaming there along with Ma!

ALINA
I like when she day-dreams aloud like this.
Look how her face glows, Balladyna...

WIDOW
*To Balladyna.*
You're right, my girl. The hut in disarray,
And here I stand mooning, like God knows what...
But God must be a dreamer too, I'm sure —
If only he'd dream up a son-in-law,
A gold one, for this widow...

BALLADYNA
                        O, look there!
You hear that rumbling there, along the road?
Five horses... golden cart... Who might that be?
A prince, with royal train... Along the road
He goes, all golden, how beautiful! Flashing
Between the trees! My God! What's happened now?
Here, on our bridge, he's stopped... The horses rear...
He cannot pass...

WIDOW
>He's watering his horses.

BALLADYNA
Along the road, just like that? Well, maybe —
A lord, watering horses...

WIDOW
>If they're thirsty!

ALINA
The sun is going down. It's time to light
The pine-torch.

BALLADYNA
*Running from the window.*
>Light the lamp! Quick! Light the lamp!
O, where's my comb!

*A knock at the door.*

WIDOW
>What's that? Somebody knocks...
Open the door, Balladyna...

BALLADYNA
>Alina,
You do it!

WIDOW
>Open it! Somebody's knocking!

ALINA
O, I'm afraid!

WIDOW
>All spirits praise the Lord!
I'll open it myself...
*Peeks through the keyhole.*
>What shining clothes!

*Opens.*
You come in the name of God?

KIRKOR
*Enters.*
                                            Yes, in God's name.
I beg your pardon — there upon the bridge
That spans the stream, a rotten plank broke off
Beneath my wheel... I need somewhere to rest.

WIDOW
Please, please, come in, your highness, sit you down!
It's a poor cottage, ours, but clean — You say
The bridge has grabbed your wheel? Ah, what bad luck...
Girls! Girls! These are my two daughters, your grace —
I can't remember whenever such a thing
Happened before — last spring, perhaps it was,
The miller's cart broke down...

BALLADYNA
                              Mother, enough —
Let the young man speak...

*Enter Skierka, invisible to the others.*

KIRKOR
                                  Somewhere near your house
I heard the sound of lutes. Was that your daughters
Strumming the strings?

WIDOW
                      I'm sorry sir. Afraid not,
... Your highness...

SKIERKA
                          From my cloud invisible,
I'll sprinkle flowery charm upon both girls,
Since Goplana, my queen, did not specify
Which of the two he must fall for... If he
Likes music, the air will ring with lovely song,

And flowers such delicious scent expand
As will make his heart to faint, and fall in love...
One heart shall fall in love with two...
*He sets garlands of flowers on the heads of both girls. Music.*

WIDOW

                                                                  Perhaps
The prince would like to rest?

KIRKOR
*With wonder and unease.*

                                              Who would retire
With such fair maids to keep one company?
And that... that music... Girls, are these your songs
I hear? I hear some singing...

ALINA

                                                Do you... dream?
Here in the cottage all is quiet.

KIRKOR

                                            Ah!
How noisome seems my empty castle now!

SKIERKA
*Aside.*
The spell begins to work...

KIRKOR

                                          What incense wafts
Such sweet aroma through the air? For sure
It is the garlands in your hair, bedecked
With evening's tears?

BALLADYNA

                                        Garlands? But we have none...

*Enter Kirkor's Servant, also richly dressed.*

SERVANT
The wheel's been fixed...

KIRKOR
            Unharness the horses.
I shall remain here.

*Exit Servant.*

WIDOW
            What? Is this a dream?
Kings in the cottage! On what sort of bed
Shall I spread sheets for him? They scatter him
Rose petals, surely...

KIRKOR
            Hermit, you were right!
Where roses blush on simple window sills,
Beneath a thatched roof...

SKIERKA
*To himself.*
            The charms are at an end.

KIRKOR
*To Widow.*
Listen here, mother. I've travelled the world
In search of a poor and virtuous wife;
I'll go no farther, for here I have found
Such wonderful goddesses... Had I two thrones,
Or rather, let me say, had I two hearts...
And yet it seems I have, and each one bids
A daughter for itself! But God allows
Each man one wife alone to take for his.
So I must choose... Why have the waves of fate
Shipwrecked my heart against two rocks? O, why
Did not my eyes light upon one at first,
And lead my love in tow? I cannot choose,
Today...

WIDOW
            My lord, I cannot comprehend you...

KIRKOR
I'm asking for the hand of one of your girls.
Perhaps word of Count Kirkor's met your ears?
He has a castle, large, with four towers,
A golden carriage, horses, men at arms,
All at his service? That Kirkor... am I...
And it is he that seeks your daughter's hand...

WIDOW
My daughter's hand? I've two. But Balladyna...

KIRKOR
She is the elder?

WIDOW
                    Yes, Alina is
The younger — Like an angel too...

KIRKOR
*Aside.*
                                        Tough choice!
The elder, white as snow, such wondrous braids...
As if she were adorned in sprigs of birch;
An alabaster girl... the other, pink —
With coal-black eyes beneath her long eyelashes,
Like violets... An angel at golden dawn,
The other, like the night, whitening to morning —
The one shall be my wife, the other... mistress...
So, love both, marry one of them? But which?
Which shall I love, and which I'll merely... like...?
Well, let their rosy lips confess, at least
Which of them loves me?
*To the girls.*
                    My lissom does,
Do you love me?

BALLADYNA
                    I shall not tell you "no,"
And yet I dare not say "I do, my lord."

Why don't you guess, while I remain silent?
Guess, sir knight.

KIRKOR
*To Alina.*
                  And as for you, my white rose?

ALINA
*Flinging herself upon her mother's bosom.*
I love...

KIRKOR
    Both of them love.

WIDOW
                  Why, certainly!
Why should they not? Now, that would be a story,
Should they not love a knight, who might well take
A princess for a bride, gorgeous and bold!

KIRKOR
But which one of you girls will love me more,
After the wedding? And how will you love me?
Will you like what I like? How will you still
The angry swells of my stormy discontent?

BALLADYNA
My lord, if there are dungeons in your castle,
Abysses roaring flame, and you command
Me jump therein, I'll jump. If at confession
The priest refuse you absolution, I
Shall take upon myself your stains of sin.
Should I see an arrow speeding at your breast,
I'll leap before you, and receive its point
In my own bosom. I shall die for you.
What more might you ask?

WIDOW
                  Take her! Balladyna!

As pure as gold!

**KIRKOR**
*To Alina.*
                    And you, the younger daughter?
What do you swear?

**ALINA**
                    To love you; to be faithful.

**KIRKOR**
And still I do not know which one to take
By the left hand, as a sister-in-law,
And which to offer my one wedding band.
O, if I only could be led by it,
The star that led the kings unto the Manger!
I have but one heart, and it longs for both.
Which must I wive, and which one spurn aside?
They both love me, and so the one must suffer
Injustice at my hands, her rival chosen.
In both there shines simplicity, tenderness...
In both love, and the self-same virtue... which?

**ALINA**
If you choose me, noble sir, you must swear
To take my sister and my mother too
Along with me, to your castle. For who
Will warm my mother's pottage, tend her health?
She cannot stay alone in this poor cottage,
While I will live in castles. See how grey
She is, like a white rose! You see, my lord?
You must take her with me...

**KIRKOR**
                    Ah, what a strange
Delight now fills my heart... O, my darling...
**WIDOW**
But Balladyna said the selfsame things,
In thought, and in the depths of her heart, sir,
Believe me. Balladyna loves her old
Mother as well...

KIRKOR
                I had already chosen,
And once again I feel my two hearts thump...

BALLADYNA
I'd be a fiend unworthy of your hand,
And fit for Hell, were I to disown her,
My mother dear — Save her and my sweet sister,
I give you all that I possess...

KIRKOR
                        Perhaps
The blind hand of fate will point out my wife...

SKIERKA
*Sings into the Widow's ear.*
There are berries in the wood;
Send your girls to the lakeside.
She who gathers the most, should
Become Count Kirkor's chosen bride.

WIDOW
I've an old head, but it's worth something still...
My prince, I know how you might solve your problem,
If you permit me, humbly to advise.
So then, my charming lad, send forth the girls
Into the woods at dawn, each with a jar
Of black clay — let them seek out raspberries.
The first to bring her jar back full of fruit
Will be the one that you shall take to wife.

KIRKOR
Splendid advice! O, golden simplicity!
Thus shall you give me joy unsullied,
Days of delight, enwoven with virtue.
Yes, Mother! When at dawn the new sun rises,
Your daughters shall head to the woods with jars.
We shall remain here in the linden's shade,
And she who first returns will be my countess.
Great God, Thou shalt resolve this quandary.

WIDOW
My prince, you'll find a bed here in the cottage
Fragrant with straw and dressed in clean linen.
No toad shall nestle in the straw, believe me.
I'll lead you to the alcove. Follow me.

KIRKOR
*Claps his hands. Enter Servant.*
Bring here the crystal goblet from the carriage,
Wine and cold bison roast...

*Exit Servant.*

I bid you good night, my pretty fiancées.
*Kirkor follows the Widow out, to the alcove.*

ALINA
Sister! What luck! What strange and joyful things!

BALLADYNA
You haven't snatched it yet, my sister.
Perhaps that joy and luck are not for you...

ALINA
Ah, sister... After all, in the high heavens,
If not the sun, I've the stars overhead;
If I shall not be Countess Kirkor, why
I shall be sister to the countess! But,
Ready yourself for a sharp contest tomorrow —
You know I'm always first in filling jars
With plucked raspberries — how my pot fills first
I do not know — do the raspberries leap
Into the jar themselves, or is it that you
Lag behind somehow, with... a lover, maybe...

BALLADYNA
Quiet!

ALINA
    Ha, sister, I know why it takes
You so long to return home from the forest...

BALLADYNA
What's that to you?

ALINA
Nothing at all, except
I know that I would not abandon my love
Even for knight, even for king. For if I loved,
And was beloved in return, whether farmer
Or shepherd, no Kirkor would turn my head.

BALLADYNA
I don't ask stupid girls for their advice.

*A coughing is heard outside. Balladyna lights a candle and, concealing it in her palms, exits.*

ALINA
Ha! A coughing from the wood, and out she goes,
Candle in hand... O great Lord God in Heaven —
What will he say, Mr Rake, of this betrayal?
'Cos sister wants to marry Kirkor, too...
While I once saw them, in the fallow fields
Among the flowers — Ah! among our aspens!
A hundred kisses... Ah, forgive me, Christ
For passing judgement on a love not mine,
A love I've not experienced myself...
*Kneels down.*
You know, my God, that I have a pure heart,
And when I vow, I never break my vow...
Lord! Little birds dare to approach Thy throne
To beg of Thee black cherries... Thou dost fill
The beaks of swallows with their feed of flies...
Dearest my only Lord, if Thou but wish,
Thou mayst... set raspberries... wherever I turn...
*She sits down on the bench and falls asleep.*

SKIERKA
*Sings.*
May gold dreams of fortune fair
Now descend, and close her eyes
While Skierka to Goplana flies...

*Exit*

ALINA
*Dreaming.*
Berries! Berries everywhere...

[END OF ACT I]

# ACT II

## Scene 1

*A forest near Lake Gopło. Sunrise. Chochlik and Rake, the latter all caked in red mud and quite drunk.*

RAKE
Not one step farther.

CHOCHLIK
                    But you are so close
To your own hearthside!

RAKE
                    Ah, my big black dog,
I don't believe you... You lead me astray
In mud up to my ears, and wag your tail!
Ah no, you black cat — I wanted to pet you
And blue flames crackled from your fur... I'm tired.
I want to go to bed.

CHOCHLIK
                    Have some tobacco.

RAKE
*Embracing an oak.*
Just look — the oak hugs me. And no wonder there —
The oak and the rake are made for each other.\*
Believe me, oak, I look up to you, oak...
So tall... Straight from the heart, the words I spoke.

CHOCHLIK
Come on, let's go.

---

\*    *Dąb przyjaciel grabiny.*

RAKE
                    I'll stay here with my friend.
Not a step farther, not even to see
The heavens where the Lord God shoots at sparrows...
I will not leave this oak — look how he sways...
He needs my support, or he'll faint dead away.
Here dog! And bring a light! Where'd the oak go?
He ran off... ha! Didn't recognise me:
Sitting so long in the mud, I've grown weedy.

CHOCHLIK
Come one, we'll go to the tavern.

RAKE
                            Now you're talking!
Easy peasy lemon squeezy, no no —
It's not right. If the tavern girl's in love with me,
Like I love her, well, she'll come here herself!
It's stupid to go mooning after girls...
Where'd you get that snuff?

CHOCHLIK
                    From Mr Lucifer.

RAKE
O, right. Heard that one before. Listen, dog,
Go flush a rabbit, and I'll plunk him one.

CHOCHLIK
With what?

RAKE
                A lightning bolt! Listen, my friend.
Because I love you, yes! I'll say I'm sorry —
Apologise, I led you in the mud,
Where we sat down and sunk and sneezed, and sneezed,
Nose to nose, shall we say, just like mud brothers.

CHOCHLIK
Remember what the reed told us?

RAKE
                    The dear!
She came to help us...

CHOCHLIK
                    She saved the bagpipe.

RAKE
And here I always called her a hollow thing.
*Lies down.*

CHOCHLIK
Come on! Get up!

RAKE
                  I want to go to sleep.

CHOCHLIK
It's better if you climbed up in the oak.

RAKE
O the oak, the oak
The bullfrogs croak,
The ducks swim on the pondie;
O be a dear,
These trousers here,
Come, take 'em to the laundry...

CHOCHLIK
What's this? You'll sleep without a nightcap?

RAKE
You don't wanna? Then go to Hell, you witch-cat.

CHOCHLIK
Good night.

RAKE
            Good night, good night, you pleasant pup.
I'd go to the inn, but I just can't get up.

Good night...
*Falls asleep.*

CHOCHLIK
    What stupid creatures these men be!
Three sheets to the wind, and all beshat with mud,
He snores. Just let Goplana see him now!

*Enter Goplana and Skierka.*

GOPLANA
Where is he? Ah, he's sleeping! Let the sun
Caress his face first with her rosy fingers;
But let the dawn arrive a little sad,
To wet his cheeks with dew, and thus protect him
From the harsh rays that would pry at his eyelids...
Here, Chochlik, from my willing hand
Receive your just reward...

CHOCHLIK
*Taking it.*
A wormy nutshell of mouldy tobacco.
Thank you, my queen. Now I can treat the peasants
To Spanish flu for two days straight.

GOPLANA
*To Skierka.*
        And so,
Which girl has fallen in love with Kirkor?

SKIERKA
Both of them...

GOPLANA
    O, you mad little fool, you!

SKIERKA
Tomorrow they both go into the woods
To fill their jars with berries — I told you...

GOPLANA
But what am I to do?

SKIERKA
                        Fall on the elder —
On Balladyna — she has a black heart.
I saw a tiny speck of jealousy
Therein — no, something more than jealousy...

GOPLANA
And tonight? What are they doing?

SKIERKA
                        Alina
Fell fast asleep, begging the aid of God,
Dreaming of raspberries. But Balladyna
Lit up a candle, and hurried outside,
'Cos someone coughed a signal from the woods.
I flew after her to suss out the secret
Of this nocturnal promenade... She went
Over the lawns just like a misty spectre,
Trembling and silent, while the candle glowed
Through the pink cracks between her ivory fingers —
Her palm looked like the cup of a pale rose.
The flame grew, and expired, blew high, and died down;
She roused a bird from sleep in the dark thickets,
But so still was her breezy tread, it soon
Fell back asleep... so silent was her passing...
A wreath of golden moths flew round her head,
And where the maiden trod, the garland whirled.
She stopped, I bent my ear... her whispered words
Mixed in with the rustle of trembling aspen leaves...
Someone made answer...

GOPLANA
                      'Twas some friend, perhaps?

SKIERKA
Ah no, my queen...

GOPLANA
>	Then who?

SKIERKA
>	You wish to know?

GOPLANA
*Pointing at the sleeping Rake.*
Him?

SKIERKA
>	Yes.

GOPLANA
*To Chochlik.*
>	Chochlik! I ordered you
To prevent that!

CHOCHLIK
>	Even the devil can't
Prevent lovers from meeting…

GOPLANA
>	Skierka!
Shut Chochlik up inside a dried toad skin
And toss him out into the lake, just like
A blind cat in a bag!

CHOCHLIK
>	O no, my lady!
Anything but that! Murder me instead!

GOPLANA
I cannot kill, but I may punish you.

SKIERKA
Let's go, Sir Chochlik — we'll find you a boat…

*Making faces like an unruly child, Chochlik goes off with Skierka.*

GOPLANA
*Sola.*
And so he saw her... and saw her at night;
Damnation! Yesterday he saw her midst
The alders. Let the stars of heaven blacken
That cast their light before their feet! The moon,
Let the moon shrivel, the Milky Way disperse
In clouds of powder! He was there? How horrid!
If only that slut sold me one brief glance
For all the diamonds of the world! And him?
How shall I punish him? I'll be transformed
Into a creeping vine and wind him round,
I'll choke him blue as me with flowery fetters...
Ah, no, from such a noose, the lover escapes
Unscathed, the while his flaming mistress faints
Away in love; how shall I punish him?
Let him be changed into a willow, wrapped
In bark; let each leaf he grows droop, sobbing
In eternal penitence... but O, my darling —
If I should see you so, I'd weep as well,
Because the willow sobs.

*Enter Skierka.*

SKIERKA
Trapped in a dead frog's husk, he slips downstream,
And makes for the lake, the moody amphibian.

GOPLANA
Cut me a lash of rushes.

*Skierka does, and gives it to her.*
*She pokes Rake.*

Hello! Darling! Wake up, my sweet!
Why are you sleeping?

RAKE
                    Because I'm drunk! I wanna...

GOPLANA
Inebriated? With what? The evening song,
Like to the loving nightingale?

RAKE
*Half asleep.*
Hand me that cow-spunk for a pillow, hey?
No? Off to the lake, then, mackerel! Baboon!

GOPLANA
What? You'll come to know the might of Goplana!
Feet — sink in soil moist and dark!
Flesh — be wrapped round in rough, dun bark!
Head — spread out twigs than hang and sweep
With lazy leaves — now, willow, weep!

*Rake sinks into the earth; a willow grows up from the spot where he disappears.*

Rise, weeping willow, bob and bow;
Complain of birds that weigh you down,
Making your branches sag, and keen
When you are dragged along the stream!
Sob in autumn, when each breeze
Strips you and blows away your leaves.
Skierka! Call forth the nightingale and have her perch
Here in this tree, every night to sing
Her songs of love, until the willow learns
To love and weep for love. But let no raven
Dare sadly croak a tune of death above him,
He is not dead.

SKIERKA
Ah, look! Such pretty leaves now fan
The heavens, nodding to bloom and star;
The willow grows from what was man —
The tree more beauteous by far!

GOPLANA
Now he can wait for his love patiently.
Let him with knotted eye behold his girl,
Balladyna, from beneath lids of bark.

SKIERKA
Look!
Here come two girls — upon their heads they bear
Vessels of clay — searching for raspberries.

GOPLANA
Come, let's hide in the thicket.

ALINA
Raspberries, everywhere! Just look how ruddy!
And on them, crystal pearls of morning dew;
The lips of Kirkor are of this same colour.
Ah, my fresh violets, you sigh in vain —
I have no time to pluck you; look! My sister
Fills her jar, and soon will rush from the wood
To win a husband, while I shall remain
An old maid amongst the violets! Even if
You had been roses of pure gold, I'd still
Prefer the raspberries today...
*Plucking berries, she sings.*
Sweet my love,
       My love is merry
I've found a trove
          Of sweet raspberries
That I shall pluck for my golden man,
For such, last night, was his command.
Berries he wants, berries are worth
Today, more than the entire earth.
*Exits right.*

*Enter Balladyna, with a jar on her head.*

BALLADYNA
Raspberries, nowhere! Just a few — as red
As blood. How few! Where shall I go to find
More? I don't know — And... how red is the sky!

As red as blood. Why, sun, do you rise bloody?
I prefer dark night to such a sanguine dawn.
Where is my sister? ... She must have gone right.
I bet her jar is overfull with berries,
And here I wander in the thickets stripped,
Lost in despair. My tears increase the dew.

ALINA
*From the depths of the woods.*
Sister, my sister! Where are you, my dear?

BALLADYNA
What laughter in her voice! Her jar is filled
For sure...

ALINA
*Enters.*
   Ah, Balladyna! Well?

BALLADYNA
         Well, what?

ALINA
Your jar — is it filled?

BALLADYNA
       No...

ALINA
         Bladyna,* what's wrong?
What were you doing?

BALLADYNA
        Nothing...

---

\*   Thus here, and in other places, Balladyna's sister or mother will call her "Bladyna" or "Bladina." These forms may be diminutives of the name invented Słowacki; more than the full name Balladyna they emphasise "paleness" (*Blada* = pale).

ALINA

                                         That's bad, sweet...
My jar is almost filled. I need one more.

BALLADYNA
Take it from my jar...

ALINA

                               My darling sister!
But tell me — where have you been all this morning?
We left together; you had time enough;
I didn't steal the whole forest from you...
Why are you so pale now, your lips, drawn tight?

BALLADYNA
Your raspberries slither forth from your jar
Like snakes to bite me with venomous reproaches.
Go, and be wived! Your sister shall be harnessed
Unto a plough like an ox; she'll press oil
From bitter seeds and black poppies.

ALINA

                                  For shame!
I beg you, Balladyna! Don't grow bitter
At my good fortune.

BALLADYNA
        Ha, ha!

ALINA

                             What does that mean,
This horrid laugh of yours? Sister, you're ill?
If you're in such a great despair, just tell me...
Do you love Kirkor? Very much? Speak truly!
For there are other knights throughout the world —
When I become his lady, I'll find you one!

BALLADYNA
His lady — you?
*She pulls out a knife.*

ALINA
                    Balladyna! A knife?
Why?

BALLADYNA
          With this knife I'll slay the viper curled
Among the raspberries...

ALINA
                    Sister! You're pale!
Your lips have gone quite blue, my sweet wild rose!
What's wrong with you? What's wrong? Why are you pale?
O, how horrid this is! Speak at least one word!
Come, lets both sit down and talk to one another,
Openly, and prudently, like sisters.

*They sit down on the grass.*

I am in love with Kirkor not because
He's rich, a knight, lord of a mighty manor,
And not because he has a golden carriage,
Clothes of gold, and yet ... I will admit it ...
I like how he goes about dressed in gold;
I like that he has servants, a shiny sword;
He's like a knight straight from a fairy tale,
Son of a great king, who in the forest finds
A charmed princess.

BALLADYNA
*Rises, confused.*
                              O!

ALINA
*Gets up.*
                              What, my sister dear?
What's wrong with you?

BALLADYNA
*Even more deranged.*
                    And if I... killed you, sister?

ALINA
What did you say?

BALLADYNA
    Give me those raspberries!

ALINA
Who knows, my sister? If you asked me kindly;
If you kissed your Alina on the lips,
Maybe I'd give them to you? Come, Balladyna... try!

BALLADYNA
Am I to... beg?

ALINA
    Yes. Otherwise, farewell.

BALLADYNA
*Drawing closer.*
What?

ALINA
    You see, my sister, this jar holds my future —
My happiness, my husband, my lover,
My golden dreams and my wedding garland,
And all my...

BALLADYNA
*With an ugly fury.*
    Give that jar here!

ALINA
    Balladyna?

BALLADYNA
Give it here, or...

ALINA
*Teasing, like a child.*
    Give it there, or what?
Or what? You have no raspberries — go pick

Some dry acorns, or... weeping willow leaves!
And anyway, I can run faster than you —
I'll beat you home!

BALLADYNA
        You will?

ALINA
                    Of course I will —
Even if I gave you a nice head start.

BALLADYNA
        You!

ALINA
O, don't come near me with your eyes like that!
I don't know why... but I'm afraid of you!

BALLADYNA
*Comes close and takes her by the hand.*
And I'm afraid too... lie down on the ground...
Lie down! ... Ha!
*Stabs her.*

ALINA
        Let me go! You've... stabbed me...
*Falls.*

BALLADYNA
What have my hands done? O...!

VOICE FROM THE WILLOW
                    Jesus and Mary!

BALLADYNA
*Terrified.*
Who's that? I heard a voice? Was that my voice?
Did my lips form a prayer? O, the viper!
Woman, sister — no sister... Stains of blood
Here, here, and here...
*She stains her forehead with her bloody hand.*

and here. Who kills a sister
Over a jar of berries? If someone asks,
I'll answer: Balladyna. I can't lie —
I'll say it straight. I did it. What's that? I?
Just yesterday I would have sworn it off,
Impossible, and now... Into the woods!
The woods! Off on your road! Yesterday's heart
Will pray for you — And I forgot to pray
Last night! That's bad! No time for prayer today...
God's in His heaven — Well, I'll forget that —
I'll live as if there were no God at all.

*She runs off into the woods.*
*Enter Goplana and Skierka.*
*Alina lies there, dead.*

GOPLANA
How horrible, what people do with knives!
I don't get it — where is the prudence here,
In such an act? We spirits mayn't know
The herbs that heal wounds... But she is warm...
Perhaps she's still alive? The hermit gathers
Simples in the forest; maybe he,
If he had care of her, might bring her back
To life? O Skierka, darling, go and bring
The hermit here.

*Skierka goes off.*

Hawthorn and nettle,
Wherever she settle,
Or fall upon a knee,
The killer,
I will her
To suffer. Painfully!
Let the wind haste her!
The streamlet face her
With fears in its mournful running;
Let it ever be drumming
Her sister's tears
In her guilty ears!

*She makes to go into the woods.*

I see that shepherd there, who's ever erring,
"Exiled from realms of joy," or so he says —
Searching for love throughout the whole wide world,
In vain... today a flower is his idol,
Or stars, or the sun... let him see the girl's corpse.

*She goes off into the woods. Enter Filon, gazing skyward.*

FILON
Why dost thou shine to me, bedmate of Titan,
Thy face paling from rose to milky white?
Why dost thou shine upon me, thou, Phoebus,
Who sighed the night away on Tethys' bosom,
And now thou givest thy stallions free rein,
Whilst from thy robes dost flick around the dew
Upon thy rising from her couch Oceanic?
O happy, happy Phoebus — pale Diana,
Gazing upon thy gold encircled brow
Secretes her visage in the azure from
Endymion's view, wounded unto her heart
By the sunbeams — Ah, love, O, love is light,
Is heaven, is life! And I have never loved!
O woe is me! Woe!
*He notices Alina's body.*
                    What goddess is this?
As pale as marble... Dead? Dear God! So like
The goddesses immortal, and yet — dead...
Ah, how the weeping willow sobs for her!
And yet my soul, so tender unto dreams
Has not a single tear for her? Solitude
Has clogged the wellsprings of my eyes. O look!
How beautiful she is! And yesterday,
How tender she must have been! Wedding sprays
Would suit her brow — O, how she might have loved!
And now, death, that hypocrite, has torn away
Her life, while leaving her posthumous grace
To slay me with? O, angel mine! You sweet
Lover of death! O look how lovingly
Your white hand caresses your black clay vessel,

From which raspberries spill — while from your breast
Of alabaster spurts another stream,
More beautiful in hue than those berries —
Your murderer will be hounded by two
Sins on his conscience for these two red streams...
No, some beast of the woods it was that killed you —
No man could ever raise his hand against...
But, God! A rusty blade lies here beside you!
It was a man! O fly, my love, to Heaven!
Hide there from all such people — there are many!
Sleep, sleep my love... This kiss will not awaken
You — how I wish that it could bring me death...

*He kisses the lips of the dead girl and lifts the knife. The Hermit rushes in.*

HERMIT
Stop! Killer, stop! He would hide the blade
In his own bosom...

FILON
    Father, look at her!
I've found my love ... too late, for she lives not.

HERMIT
Whose blade could it be that should wound such blossoms?
Who stains the wilderness with living blood?
Has King Popiel arrived here, to dye forest
Lilies crimson?

FILON
    I'll wash clean her wound
With tears...

HERMIT
    For shame.

FILON
      But she is dead... Just look!
Here! Here! This dark blue blossom on her breast
Of ivory, the sign, the star of death...

HERMIT
Come on, you're young and hale — lift up the girl
And bear her on your shoulders. She's not heavy —
I'll help you. In my cell I have some herbs...

FILON
Your words of hope refresh my fainting spirit!
Lending your aid to an unfortunate soul
That was but now to recline in the grave
Of sadness and remorse. Permit me but
To break a sprig of willow, underneath
The which she fell, my love, murdered. Here it was
I first laid eyes on her, and first I loved,
And lost her, first, before I loved... alas!
My happiness was lost in dusky dawn —
I found a treasure, and lost all I had
And ever shall have...
*Pulls off a twig of willow.*

VOICE FROM THE WILLOW
                        Stop jostling, I'm drunk...

FILON
That willow talks!

HERMIT
               There's devils in these woods —
I know them well. Sometimes they come and rap
The windows of my cell...

FILON
                    And there are angels
In these woods, but they're dead.

HERMIT
                        Come on.
Take up your angel there, and follow me.

*Filon takes Alina's body on his shoulders and follows the Hermit out. Goplana and Skierka emerge from the thickets.*

GOPLANA
*Pointing at the willow.*
Damned people! How dare they break off a twig
From this tree? That must have caused him pain...

SKIERKA
Ah, something bitter flies forth from the wound...
It tastes like the water that they mix with wheat
And torment with fire. The people drink it.

GOPLANA
A lost tear... O, I so regret each tear
That doesn't fall for me from your sad eyes...
You shall be free tomorrow, my lover;
Tomorrow you shall blame the cruel woman
Who tortured you from one dawn to the next...
Hush! Skierka, hide! Look there — It's Balladyna —
Livid, and wandering lost amongst the trees —
How pale she is — her tangled hair is loose...
I'll hide my face and sit beneath the willow,
And speak to her with the voice of her sister,
And bite the girl deranged — I'll bite her!

*Exit Skierka.*

BALLADYNA
*Runs on stage, wildly.*
The wind keeps chasing me, and asking, asking
About my sister: "Dead!" I scream, "Killed, killed!"
The trees all cry to me, "Where is your sister?"
I wanted to wash off the blood, but there,
From the blue spring a pale and silent face
Stared back at me — O, where now have I come?
This weeping willow... the same willing willow...
The same where I... My sister! You're alive!

GOPLANA
Sister...

BALLADYNA
How can you call me by so foul a name?
A corpse... a corpse... a corpse waves its white hand
At me — each hair of mine is thickly stained
With conscience — and rears stiffly back, and pulls...
But I can't follow; my feet are rooted fast...

GOPLANA
And sorrow, sister, does it not advert
You to the fact that you've done evilly?
But if your sister were alive...

BALLADYNA
                        Alive?

GOPLANA
Perhaps you'd kill her a second time?

BALLADYNA
*Searches around herself, frantically.*
I've lost my knife...

GOPLANA
                    That knife wasn't long enough,
O sister...

BALLADYNA
      That's not my fault!

GOPLANA
                   Balladyna!
And what if Alina were to forgive you?
Forget it all, and say to you, "O, sister —
I had a dream... Last night, before you left
Our cottage with your candle for the glade
Of aspens, came a knight — a phantom knight,
Who fell in love with both of us, and sent
Us to the woods in search of raspberries...
I dreamt that, when we'd reached the deepest woods,
My sister took a knife... Then I awoke.

Come, let's go to the wise woman. We'll ask
Her to explain my dream.

BALLADYNA
*Musing.*
                                        It was a dream…
Ah, truly… so it seems to me, it was
Merely a dream, my sister…

GOPLANA
                                        Meaning nothing.

BALLADYNA
A dream…

GOPLANA
              And Mama will just scold us both
For playing all the day long in the woods.

BALLADYNA
And so the knight…

GOPLANA
                            Has vanished. Like a dream.

BALLADYNA
But that can't be! Ha! The knight vanishes
Just like a dream? That's awful!

GOPLANA
                                But, I live…

BALLADYNA
Would you were dead! A nightmare… just a dream…
Yes? But my mind had gotten used to it,
Your death; as soon as I wiped from my hand
The blood that stains it… I would be so happy…

GOPLANA
*Uncovers her face.*
And be so, Satan! Your sister is dead.

BALLADYNA
Great God! What sort of spectre might this be?

GOPLANA
A crystal bubble, which the breezes raise
From the blue ripples, and the dawning suns
Paint with a rainbow's colours — be at peace.
I won't reveal your secret to the world.
I leave you to your fate: You shall unite
The hand of crime with that of chivalry,
And that hand — stained with blood — will lead to crime
Again. Now shrivel with the ageless burden
Of keeping secret what your conscience keeps
Forever before your eyes — for every berry
Might well betray you, and this willow here
Was witness to your crime. Its bark has tongues.
Beware the tree!
Beware the blossom!
And every lily, every white rose
There at the altar, and after your wedding,
Will be stained with scarlet;
Each petal dyed with red.
Go... take that jar... I shall not turn you in.
But nature, foully ravished by your act
Will be revenged. Go! Back to your cottage.

*Balladyna takes Alina's jar in hand from Goplana and exits, silent.*

She's gone to wash her garments clean of blood,
But on her brow, that bloodstain shall endure.
I told her not — 'twould be in vain to warn her —
That smudge will never be wiped from her front.
Now I return me to the crystal waves.
I'll sink this dark image of crime beneath
The bright ripples of mirror-like Lake Gopło.
When the moon's up again, I shall return
To hear the mournful soughing of the willow.
*Exit.*

## Scene 2

*A porch before the Widow's cottage, shaded by a linden tree. The Widow and Kirkor sit upon a bench.*

KIRKOR
I do not see your daughters...

WIDOW
                    They'll be back!
They'll come like two white geese: one after the other.
Ah, I can't help it, as the Saviour lives,
The tears spring to my old eyes by themselves
When I catch sight of them...

KIRKOR
                    Who will be first?
Balladyna?

WIDOW
        O, Balladyna, sure.
She's always first in church, first everywhere —
Starts up the hymn right when the organ groans...
But Alina's quick too.

KIRKOR
                    So, Alina
Might get here first?

WIDOW
                Alina —
Perhaps! Ha! Only God in Heaven knows...

KIRKOR
You know what, my old woman? I'm a bit
Uneasy for your daughters...

WIDOW
                        As am I.
Bad thoughts, like nightmares, nag about my head;
Who can remember a spring without raspberries?
What's taking them? And if it so turned out

That there were no raspberries in the woods?
I had a dream like that last night, I did...
Before I woke ... What if amongst the thickets
There were no raspberries? But then I thought,
"Stupid old woman! Even the mangered horse,
When there's no oats, will chomp on hay instead!
If the girls find no raspberries to pluck,
They'll fill their jars with wild strawberries!"
Ah, kings! There in your castles, maybe you don't know
The difference between a chokecherry,
Chalk and cheese and wild strawberries,
What is a beehive, what a rabbit hutch;
'Cos all you care about is gold, gold, gold,
About which you care overmuch, I ween...

KIRKOR
Ah, don't believe it! Ofttimes bitterness
And worries gnaw away at peace and calm
Within a castle's walls. There too, old mother,
A man can live in wretched misery.
One hundred times more, I value this life,
Here on a village porch, waiting my wife,
A simple village girl... O, that breeze
In the bright morning, how it soothes my heart!
And you, you are so good, though you be clothed
In coarsest homespun!

WIDOW
                      What? Coarsest... what?!
These are my Sunday clothes!
Chintz cloth! I only get dressed up like this
On holidays! ...O, here comes Balladyna...

KIRKOR
Where?

WIDOW
       O, you can't see her yet... My mother's heart
Knows without looking. There, sir, look! That little
Blue swallow sitting tight beneath the thatch...
If it was Alina on her way home,

You'd hear a chirping and a fluttering
There in the beams; one swallow after another,
*Pyrr, pyrr...* They fly out of their nests
At her approach, and wheel about her head
Like a constellation of little black stars
Around a white sun...

KIRKOR
                    Why is it that the birds
Flock so to the cadet?

WIDOW
                    Who knows, my lord?
O, Balladyna's coming. Can you see?

KIRKOR
How pretty — how that earthen jar becomes her,
Perched on her head...

*Balladyna enters with head bowed.*

Maiden! Give me the jar, and in exchange
Accept this wedding ring...

*He takes the jar; Balladyna turns away. Kirkor slips the ring on her finger.*

WIDOW
                    How the gems flash!

KIRKOR
May our lives be a sweet new paradise!
Go to your chamber. As the custom is,
Have your maids braid your hair, twining in flowers,
And in an hour's time, trembling, but crowned,
I'll take you from your mother's hands, and you
Shall be my wife. My horses have been harnessed;
I'll go and get the priest.
*Exit.*

BALLADYNA
                    O!

WIDOW
                        Why do you moan?
And why have you gone pale, your lips drawn tight?

BALLADYNA
Mother, my mother... I don't know how to tell you...

WIDOW
What, darling child? Is it... the bed you fear,
And would escape from, like a timid doe?

BALLADYNA
I'm burdened with evil tidings.

WIDOW
                        What?

BALLADYNA
                            Mother,
You won't believe me, but... Alina, O!
My younger sister, dear... O, tragedy!

WIDOW
What is it?

BALLADYNA
            It's your fault, after all!
You spoilt her, and now...

WIDOW
                    Tell me! I'm dying...

BALLADYNA
I fear to speak, for your blind mother's love
Will beat back all conviction... Who'd believe —
The young doe would escape, once in the woods...

WIDOW
Daughter... Alina?

BALLADYNA
She's run off...

WIDOW
But where?
How? Why? With whom? Dear God! Disowning me,
Her mother!

BALLADYNA
Well, I've long expected this.
I've seen this ragamuffin sniffing round
Alina, everywhere, and whispering
Into her ear... I scolded her, I did!
But you know how she listens to my words,
Sermons from her older sister, and now,
This very day... she's run away with him...

WIDOW
Unnatural child! May she follow him to Hell!
You gave no thought to these old eyes of mine,
That they'd beweep you! All right, so they won't!
They will not shed a tear! This mother has
A dragon's whelp now in place of a heart —
A heart can be broken, and cut to pieces,
But try that with this creature in my breast!
The sinews will but knot together again,
A reptile's membrane, weaving warp and woof
In one whole canvas — O, had I her here,
How I would thrash her, curse her, torture her!
These eyes of mine, these eyes of mine, you know,
Would pierce her bosom like a thirsty knife —
A dry knife! No tears rusting its sharp edge...
Did she imagine me frantic? No, no!
What good are tears...
*She bursts out sobbing.*

BALLADYNA
                    My God, to plunge you in
Such sadness!

WIDOW
            O, such sadness twists me raw!

BALLADYNA
To plunge one's old mother into such sadness...?

WIDOW
O God! And how old... But she may return...
Who knows? Is it not true, she may return?
Some night, when she sits lonely in the light
Of distant stars, and thinks, "Where is my mother?"
For she'd have no heart, were she not to think
Ever of her mother again...

BALLADYNA
                    The bridesmaids come...

*Wedding music.*

WIDOW
How gay the sound of this music — and how sad...
You are my only treasure now... bend down
Your brow that I may kiss you... What is this?
A stain — as red as blood!

BALLADYNA
*With terror.*
                            Blood?

WIDOW
                                It must be
From the berries. Here. I'll rub it clean...

BALLADYNA
*Rubbing at it.*
I'll rub it clean myself.

WIDOW
    It's still there.

BALLADYNA
*Rubbing her brow.*
                            Now?
WIDOW
Yes, it's still there — red, as red as the ruby
That shines so prettily upon your ring.

BALLADYNA
*Again tries to rub it off.*
And now...?

WIDOW
        It's still there. Like a wee red leaf
Against the whitewashed barn.

BALLADYNA
                How horrible!

WIDOW
Bend your brow down here — I'll rub it away
Before the wedding. Maybe it's a wound?
*Stands on tiptoe.*

BALLADYNA
Mother! No! Don't touch it!

WIDOW
                Does it hurt?

BALLADYNA
It doesn't hurt, no...

WIDOW
        I'll bring you some water
From underneath the poplar, where the sparrows
Drink...
*She goes out.*

BALLADYNA
    Blood, stain, be out!

*Enter the wedding trains and bridesmaids, festively dressed, with music. They near Balladyna, and she turns away her face.*

YOUTHS*
*Sing.*
Don't hide your pretty face
    O maiden shy.
Your husband would embrace
    You, he draws nigh;
Don't hide your pretty face...

MAIDENS
*Sing.*
They boys, they wish to steal away
    The bride —
    Come lass, hide
Among the white blooms of your bridal spray!

YOUTHS
*Sing.*
Rush to hide, and rush to cover!
    Blooms can't defend
You from your friend,
    Your lover!

*The maidens hand Balladyna baskets of flowers.*

BALLADYNA
Take them away! Take them away! Since when
Do white roses grow with red stains on their petals?
Take out these baskets!
*She runs into the cottage.*

---

\*    Słowacki has *swaty* here, which depending on the context, can mean [parents] in-law or matchmakers. Since both of these options don't quite fit the situation with Kirkor and Balladyna's wedding, we take *swaty* to signify the male portion of the bridal train, which is to lead Balladyna to the altar.

FIRST MAIDEN
She refused the flowers that I bought her,
And I'm an old friend!

FIRST YOUTH
                          Look — a cloud of dust —
The golden carriage flashes. It's Kirkor
Bringing the priest.

SECOND YOUTH
                          Compared to that golden cart
The sun's as dull as brass...

[END OF ACT II]

## ACT III

### Scene 1
*Outside the smoking ruins of the Widow's cottage. A handful of villagers are grouped around the cooling ashes.*

FIRST WOMAN
Well, here you see the luck the devil brings you.
The wretched old widow with her pretty peacock
Rides along on her carriage all of gold,
Splashing us poor folk... Well, the hens have come
Home to roost!

SECOND WOMAN
     True enough — it's bitterness
What falls to our lot from the joy of others.

OLD MAN
I tell you no. The old woman's a good
Woman. Had our ancient father Adam
Taken her to wife in place of Eve,
He'd've been better off.

FIRST WOMAN
     She has no teeth —
No apple would've tempted her, for sure...!

OLD MAN
Don't you forget — she took care of the sick!
You know yourself, my lady, you who snipe
At her now — it's not all that long ago
That Satan would've received you in his glory
If not for that old woman.

SECOND WOMAN
     That's the truth —
And my little Stasik owes her his life, too.

So I'm not jealous of her better fortune —
One day I'll line my wagon with fresh straw
And pay her a visit there in her castle.

GIRL
It'd be nice to see good old Balladyna!
I'll go along too, Mother.

SECOND WOMAN
      If you please,
My child. You'll pluck some wild roses
And cornflowers to wind 'er a pretty wreath.

OLD MAN
No! Don't do, woman! Don't you see this mess?

SECOND WOMAN
What do you mean? Some tamped-down straw took fire...
So what?

OLD MAN
  So what? It means that they're ashamed of thatch
And straw, and cornflowers, and us.

FIRST WOMAN
See? It's what I said. They mock us poor peasants.

OLD MAN
Leave'm alone already.

GIRL
     And the bride?
She went about with her nose in the air!
Did you see that black band she wore on her brow
Instead of flowers? Everything, just to
Stand out, be different... And how about the bouquet?
Not white roses, yellow ones! But her face,
Pale as a ghost's! And such a haughty grin —
Even when she laughed, she didn't show her teeth.

SECOND WOMAN
Come on, girl. Let's be off to Kirkor's castle
Before the sun gets hot...

SECOND GIRL
                Don't go! Don't go!

GIRL
I'm not going.

SECOND WOMAN
Old as I am, I'll spread the straw myself
And go... How should a soul address them now?

OLD MAN
Politely.

SECOND WOMAN
      I'm going.

GIRL
              That's just what they need:
They'll have a crust of bread flung out to you
Down in the courtyard waiting, and you'll bow
And bow just like the lid of some old crate,
While from above Milady spits at you!
Ha! Look, your Grace, I've brought you some fresh eggs —
You know, she was once destined for the hoe...
She was supposed to marry Rake the drunk...
You know that, right? For God's sake, it's no secret!
As thick as thieves they were — I wonder where
He is now? He wasn't at the wedding...

FIRST WOMAN
Maybe he drowned himself out of despair.

GIRL
Who's destined to be hanged, don't easily drown...

FIRST WOMAN
Look — here he comes! Running in from the woods!
As usual, the village kids all round him,
Like sparrows chasing off a sparrow-hawk.

*Rake tumbles onto the stage, chased by a cloud of children.*

GIRL
Go — speak to him. If he knows nothing yet,
Don't tell him. I'll go wind a sweet-pea garland.
*Exit.*

CHILDREN
Rake! Rake! Rake! Let's dance with Rake! Rake! Rake!

RAKE
Be off, you bastards!

OLD MAN
      Where have you been, Rake?
And why so gloomy?

RAKE
      What? Where have I been?

GIRL
What were you doing?

RAKE
      Growing.

GIRL
Groaning? What does that mean?

RAKE
      Growing, I was!

CHILDREN
Did you hear Rake? He was groaning like an ass!

RAKE
Shut your traps, damned brats! For it seems
My leaves are still sighing in the wind... If only
I had as many twigs as yesterday,
I'd wind a fine switch, and make you all bray!

CHILDREN
He's talking nonsense! Hee-haw, hee-haw!

RAKE
*To Old Man.*
Tell me, old man, can it be, such a thing?
I still feel my bark — how it itches and stings!
Can a fellow become a willow?

OLD MAN
Only a willow can become a willow —
A dry rake pole can't push forth any shoot.

RAKE
But I was ... a willow!

OLD MAN
      What's that you say?

RAKE
I said what I said! Ah! May the devil turn
You all into willow saplings, and then send
The goats of Hell to nibble at your leaves!
You don't believe me! I have been a willow!

OLD MAN
That means that you've been in the tavern,
Right?

RAKE
  Before I was a willow, yes, I was.
I was at the inn.

OLD MAN
     And you drank, didn't you?

RAKE
I did.

OLD MAN
*Laughing.*
So it's a nightmare, Rake, your weeping willow!

RAKE
*Points at the smoking ruins.*
Where is the cottage?

GIRL
                                  What cottage?

RAKE
                                                The one
Where the old widow lives, with her two daughters.

GIRL
Right here...

RAKE
                   Where?

GIRL
                            Are you drunk?

RAKE
                                       Where?

GIRL
                                                It's right here!

RAKE
O may the devil's brew turn your heads too,
As it did mine, if there's a cottage here...

GIRL
Just as you were transformed, the cottage changed
Was, into your red nose!

RAKE
                    May a tonsured stockfish
Marry you to Satan! Where is she?

GIRL
Who?

RAKE
    Balladyna!

*Enter the Second Girl with the sweet pea chaplet.*

SECOND GIRL
                    Changed into this wreath.
*She tosses the wreath onto Rake's head.*

CHILDREN
Ha, ha! The sweet-pea grows upon the willow,
Forsaking the pear! O Rake, where have you been?
And hear the nightingale to his lover sing,
On behalf of her husband...

GIRL
Rake was a willow!

CHILDREN
                    Rake grew in the woods!

GIRL
And the wife in a golden chariot rode
Away, ha, ha!

CHILDREN
                    But you shall be a groom —
Rake, take to wife a witch's broom!
Ha, ha, ha!

OLD MAN
*Takes Rake by the hand.*
Le's go to the tavern. Over a cup of mead

I'll tell you everything you need to know.
*Exit, with Rake.*

CHILDREN
Shrike, bullfinch and sparrow
      Sat on a rake
And sang, "I'm a willow!"
      While a knight came to take
His beloved away!
Let the bagpipes play!
      Ha, ha, ha!
Willow brake,
Fellow take, willow, willow!

*The children and the crowd exit, following Rake.*


## Scene 2
*A proudly decorated hall in Kirkor's castle. Enter Balladyna, richly dressed, deep in thought, with a black band over her brow.*

BALLADYNA
*Sola.*
And so now I have everything... everything...
And now I've got to use it... Learn to smile
The way great people do... and be like them,
The great, upon whom fortune fell
From heaven... After all, many they are
More sinful, more steeped in blood than I —
And they live! In the morning, nags the conscience;
And in the evening it torments, terrifies,
While in the nights, I'm waked with ferocious dreams...
O! If only... Silence! The wall responds
"O! If only...!"

KIRKOR
      Well now, my sweet young wife,
How do you feel in my castle?

BALLADYNA

        I'm calm.

*Enter Fon Kostryn.*

KOSTRYN
The armed knights await you down below.

BALLADYNA
Count! Why so early, and why are they armed?

KIRKOR
My dear, I must leave you now.

BALLADYNA

        Why?

KIRKOR

        My dear!
I've made a sacred oath to keep that secret.

BALLADYNA
You're leaving me? O, me, how miserable!

KIRKOR
For God's sake, weep not, darling, for the voice
That bids farewell to you will crack unmanly...
Nor seek to hold me back with enticing smiles,
For then my eye, blinded by their sunflashes,
Will fail to see the road I must traverse.
Let no loving sign escape the bosom swelling
Beneath your crinoline; hang down those
Arms at your sides like withered ivy.

BALLADYNA
*Throwing her arms around his neck.*
Where are you off to? I won't let you go!
Why are you going? To whom have you vowed?

KIRKOR
To my own honour.

BALLADYNA
                May God fling the fire
Of heaven at the forefeet of your steed,
That, frighted by the thunder, he may speed
Like lightning back here to the courtyard!
For how long do you wish to abandon me?

KIRKOR
I'll be back in three days.

BALLADYNA
                    Have you summed up
How many hours there be in just one day?
How many moments in those many hours?

KIRKOR
All a man needs to know is this: God's lent him
But a short space of life, which he must fill
With actions owed to God.

BALLADYNA
                And to your wife?
You owe her to remain here by her side...

KIRKOR
Nothing will hold me — I must be away.
Give me your white forehead to kiss.
*He does.*
Under the eyes of men, you know, all true
Kisses are exchanged by the eyes, and lips,
Poor lips like startled swallows must, in flight,
Snag the sweet fly that flits from white flower
To white flower... Be well, my wife. And where
Is our old mother? Is she still asleep?
Perhaps; if so, bid her farewell for me.
I can no longer wait.
*He leads her aside.*
                    In the strongbox
There's money. Waste it, and be merry. Now,
Give me your white forehead once more to kiss...
My wife! I do not like this black ribbon.

Your brow belongs to me — quite all of it.
Untie this band...

BALLADYNA
          I too have made a vow.

KIRKOR
On your sister's account — I understand.
But when I am returned, walk with your God,
But break that vow for me...

BALLADYNA
                I shall...

KIRKOR
                      If not,
We'll quarrel, lover, and quite fiercely, too.
Farewell... Lads, saddle up! And let the watch
Keep safe the castle...
*To Balladyna.*
                Think of me sometimes.

*Exeunt all except Balladyna.*

BALLADYNA
*Sola.*
Husband! He's gone. Why? Where? Conscience, you snake,
You say "Your husband's gone to find Alina!"
She's in the grave. She is? And if he finds it,
Her grave? He smiled oddly at me,
As if he wished to say, "I'll bring her here,
And you'll unbind that ribbon when I do!"

*Enter Fon Kostryn.*

KOSTRYN
My lady, the Count commands that, from the window,
You send your smile to him...

*Balladyna stands at the window and smiles.*

**KOSTRYN**
*Aside.*
                              Men, bidden farewell
By smiling wives, themselves melt away in tears.

**BALLADYNA**
*Moving from the window.*
He's gone...
*To Kostryn.*
                    And you, Sir Knight, are...?

**KOSTRYN**
                                        The commander
Of the castle watch.

**BALLADYNA**
                    Watch well and be faithful,
And your reward from me will be generous.

**KOSTRYN**
Who serves by knightly troth needs no goad
His duty to fulfil to you, Madame.
No one abroad knows that the lord is hence;
We guard in secret, both of us: I guard
An angel, you, the angel, must watch over me.

**BALLADYNA**
What is your name?

**KOSTRYN**
          Fon Kostryn.

**BALLADYNA**
                    Not a Lechite?

**KOSTRYN**
I am descended from German princes.

**BALLADYNA**
Exiled from there?

KOSTRYN
                    Just as a little bird
Is exiled when the thatch above its nest
Takes fire — thus I began my flight from home.
Today I am unknown in my own homeland,
A stranger, servant in a foreign land;
May this not lead me to damnation!
But you've been exiled, too.

BALLADYNA
                            How so?

KOSTRYN
                                From Heaven.
*Exit.*

BALLADYNA
How quickly I have caught the spark that shines
In that foreigner's eye — I owe him nothing —
I sought amongst the crowd a frightened eye,
Believing that there must be here some soul
Fraternal, like my soul, for my soul, how
Must I begin? A glance, and should that glance
Be understood... It's strange how people fear
Each other, as they fear God — even more
Than they fear God... I shall be bold with people...

*Enter Widow, dressed as she was in Act II — in her Sunday best.*

WIDOW
Daughter dear!
What's happened? Has the prince then gone away?

BALLADYNA
What if he has?

WIDOW
                    One day after the wedding?
To leave his bride like that? You angered him?
O, that would be something, that! How did you sleep?
My pigeon, people say you can't forget

Your first dream in a new bed; as for me,
I dreamt Alina came to me — from Heaven,
Like, in this sea of clouds floating... she said...

BALLADYNA
A rosary, Mother. You'd be better off
If you stuck to your rosary.

WIDOW
                    What? You want
To place a muzzle on your mother's face
As if she were a dog?

BALLADYNA
                    My mother dear —
A castle's not a cottage — there's so much
To do here, I just don't have time for dreams...

SERVANT
*Enters.*
My lady, there's a village woman waiting
Outside before the gate. Bold and loud,
She demands to be let in. The pikemen stand
With staves crossed at the closed portcullis, but
The old peasant won't budge with her hayrack,
And she keeps calling to the men, "My doves,
Somebody go tell Balladyna's mother,
Kirkor's wife, that her old chum's here —
Barbara, come to pay a social visit."

WIDOW
That's my old gossip! I wonder what's new?

BALLADYNA
Send her away with her hayrack and all.

WIDOW
Balladyna...?

BALLADYNA
    What, mother? Have you grown tired
Of castle life already? So, farewell!
You can drive off with your old gossip too!

WIDOW
What? On a hayrack, pulled by an old nag?
For God's sake, daughter — Did you mean what you said?

BALLADYNA
Mother, I'm only joking. Listen — you
Command the men — Send the hayrack away.

WIDOW
*With a sigh.*
Send her away. Tell her that I'm asleep.

BALLADYNA
*To servant.*
If she'll be stubborn, we've a palace guard...
You understand...

WIDOW
*To servant.*
But no fleering at wretchedness...! She's old.

*Exit Servant.*

You're right, my honey. If we let her in,
There'd be a swarm of simple country folk
To see us. Let them love us — from afar,
Right? O, my daughters, they ain't lacking in
Common sense — O, you're no thick-polled damsel!
When you start flapping with that tongue of yours,
You'd even make the priest's head spin, my daughter!
You'll have the seamstress make me a new frock,
Won't you? This chintz one has such pale flowers —
And here, it doesn't fit for one to dress
In homespun, like some rabbit in the field —
Eh, my daughter? My life?

BALLADYNA

                        Remind me tomorrow.
And, Mother, it would be fitter for you,
An old woman, to stay in your warm room.

WIDOW
But it's so tiresome there! I'm all alone...
Like sitting in the grave. You wouldn't forbid
Your mama access to the castle?

BALLADYNA

                        No...

WIDOW
Balladyna, you do love me, right?
How about that raspberry smudge on your brow?
Show me — is it still there? And does it hurt you?
You'd never even whimper if it did —
Does it? Hurt you?

BALLADYNA
Enough of that, mother.

WIDOW
Even water from beneath the poplar tree
Couldn't wash it clean. O, my dear daughter —
It's some horrid, mysterious wound;
You blanch at its very mention.

BALLADYNA

                      So, why mention it,
Mother?

WIDOW
      Because I love you. I'm concerned.

BALLADYNA
I know! I know! I know! But, Mother, now
Go back to your warm chamber in the tower.

WIDOW
Back to the clink!

BALLADYNA
They'll bring you food
And drink there.

WIDOW
Just like a bird in a cage.

BALLADYNA
Mother, go!

WIDOW
All right. I'll braid and unbraid
My grey hair. Just make sure to tell the lackey
To bring my dinner. Don't forget...
*Exit.*

BALLADYNA
O, Hell!
I get confused, I pale... I shall betray
My secret to my mother, my husband...
Everything's charmed to work my ruin.
People, like starlings taught to speak man's speech,
By some horrible spirit of justice
Talk to me as if, by oblique ways
They'd penetrate the bowels of my heart.
They aim not, yet they hit the very mark
Like judges, questioning, "Are you guilty, woman?"
By winding paths... Mother, and husband, both...
Both husband and mother — She's a simple woman...
And I must love her. She's my mother...

KOSTRYN
*Enters.*
I've had
Them hang the halls, ma'am, thick with asphodels.
Today your vassals come: lords, many knights,
To celebrate your wedding...

BALLADYNA
                        Have them lock the door
That leads to the tower-chamber of my...nurse...*
She's ill, and needs her rest.

KOSTRYN
                              Impossible!
That monster wet your lips divine with milk?
Oh no! It was some heavenly goddess, rather!
The one that spurted wide the Milky Way,
Whose every drop engemmed the firmament
With a new star, that shines to us today.
'Twas such a nurse lulled you on her white bosom...

BALLADYNA
Well you, Sir Knight, have got a silver tongue.

KOSTRYN
And you, a heart of diamond. I've had
Them fire hogsheads of tar along the shore
Of Lake Gopło, to lead the wedding guests
Here to the feast. Do you approve, Madame?

BALLADYNA
Do as you see fit.

KOSTRYN
                  All the towers are lit
With torches, and only some chosen ones
Shall be admitted to the castle keep.
Even today some crazy simpleton
Found his way in; I chased him off with dogs
Beyond the gate; O, he was a bold one!
He barked back at the dogs, over and over
Repeating that he knew you! Blasphemies
Of that sort — and in so foul a mouth!

---

\* The Polish word for wet-nurse is *mamka* — a diminutive of *mama*; thus the hesitation and final decision to use the word by Balladyna, in Polish, is very effective.

BALLADYNA
Who might that have been?

KOSTRYN
Ah, one of those
Who'll panhandle a count at noble windows...
Tramps wrapped in rags, all patched and stitched
With threads unravelled from the cloaks of betters,
When those allow them too close an approach...
Rough throats gone horse with too much barking...
How could you know him? Your lips cannot twist
To form the phonemes of a name like his...
Some boor named Rake...

BALLADYNA
What? Rake? That crowd of yokels
Is worse than locusts.

KOSTRYN
Pardon them, my lady.
In vain the queen of blossoms holds a grudge
Against the drones that swarm and buzz around her...
Blame rather many-hued Iris, who clothes
The air about you unseen. That, or suffer
Our hungry eyes with patience.

BALLADYNA
Princely soul!
Why do you mix yourself with these who scrabble
In clods of dirt? Out of thousands of men
You might be first, if only you knew how
To keep a secret.

*Kostryn kneels and kisses the hem of her skirt.*

Come to the treasury.
We'll take some gold, to greet the guests arriving
In worthy fashion.

KOSTRYN
                      I'll carry the torch.
*Exeunt, Balladyna following Kostryn.*

## Scene 3

*The woods, before the cottage of the Hermit. Kirkor, armed, Hermit with crown in hand.*

HERMIT
Here is the golden crown we spoke of, Kirkor.
Perhaps, with your aid, one day it shall return
To Gniezno, there to shine before the people
Unstained with blood.

KIRKOR
                      See how it shines just now,
Flashing in sunlight; a fortunate omen!

HERMIT
Dear Lord, deign Thou to bless our undertaking!
Kirkor... you've take a young maid to wife?

KIRKOR
I have, a simple girl. I leave untroubled.

HERMIT
I have but one thing to suggest to you.
A woman should be fully trusted when,
And only when, she's proved free of the taint
That stained our mother Eve. Put her to test.
Send her a casket sealed up tight, with words
Of admonition, threatening angry
Consequences, should she break its seal,
Her husband's.

*Brings forth an iron chest.*

KIRKOR
                Good. Let it be as you say.
Here is my seal: Two golden acorns gripped

In a boar's maw. Take it to her yourself,
My faithful servant.
*Enter servant, takes casket.*

                        Place it in her hands
And say, however long I'll be away,
She must not open it. This I command.

*Exit Servant.*

But she is so sincere! You taught me well
The path that leads to happiness, and so,
I can but pay you back with deeds. Farewell,
Old man. Soon I shall greet you as my king.

HERMIT
Upon your forehead I read victory.

KIRKOR
To horse, my knights!

*Kirkor exits. The sound of horses moving off.*

HERMIT
Why was that knight not born two decades ago?
When I was on the throne, the land entire
Bore only freaks misshapen in its womb;
Like some inept stonemason, who attempts
To bring forth human faces from the rock,
And but succeeds in shaping men of stone,
Without a soul… Is it that Nature dreams
Long of creation, before she creates,
And toys at plaster casts, bringing forth dwarves
Before creating men like Kirkor?

*Enter Filon in fantastic garb.*

FILON
                         Ah!
Old man, where is my love?

HERMIT
                    She's not revived.
FILON
Then show me where you've placed her in the grave...
What tomb contains my heart as well? I would
See what blooms from the hopes there sown —
They must be pale...

HERMIT
                    O, you eternal weeper!
Why do you wander, uselessly, these thickets?
Run after Kirkor! Cover up your curls
With a steel helmet, and toss upon the dishes
That balance human destiny on earth
The poppyseed of your past life, and see —
Perhaps that mite shall tip the scale of fate!

FILON
Where does she lie? O where?

HERMIT
                        There, where dull clay
Has swallowed her bosom, and where vermin crawl
Upon her face...

FILON
              O no! There, in the earth,
Like a nymph of the rivers, she leans upon
An urn of clay, from which spill galaxies
Of berry-coloured stars! In rosy garlands,
Her milk-white body, charmed, rests near the rill;
She cannot wake until forget-me-nots
Grow from her grave mound, and, in the ruby dawn,
Behold the hillock with eyes like azure stars.
They twinkle in the grave now...

HERMIT
                    In the grave
There's as much light as there is between your ears.

FILON
Sometimes her shade, her pale shade, wanders there,
Where birches sadly stoop among the stones;
Like lutes set trembling by the nightingale,
They weep and moan with strings of tender leaves.
Sometimes the silver wormwood winds her round;
Sometimes the blooming cornflower pauses there;
Sometimes, a furry blossom of chicory
Stands there and sighs, like a lonely, wandering child.
Her body rests beneath a cold granite slab —
Her soul floats about on the moon-rays,
Plucking from time to time those timid blossoms,
Whose petals count the fleet moments of youth.
O tell me, old man... those in the grave
Thus dream of happiness?

HERMIT
       Die, and find out.
And if you ever resurrect, you'll speak
Of such dreams to the consciences of killers.
Perhaps then they'll be able to sleep at night.

FILON
I'll go now... Where the forest crossroads meet,
I'll stand and watch. If a quick green lizard
Runs to the right, then one dreams in the grave;
If to the left... then man is nothing. When he dies
He dreams not...
*Exit.*

HERMIT
     How many such wretches are there
In this poor world? Earth is the mad mother
Of lunatics! Who comes now?

*Enter Balladyna, quickly.*
         Who are you?

BALLADYNA
I am the lady of the nearby castle.

HERMIT
What do you seek here?

BALLADYNA
                       I've heard that you concoct
Wound-healing brews from simples... medicines...

HERMIT
You look quite hale to me. Show me the wound.

BALLADYNA
Old man!

HERMIT
      A doctor must inspect the blessure
Before he tries to heal it.

BALLADYNA
But do you swear to heal it?

HERMIT
                    Show the wound!

BALLADYNA
It's on my forehead... Ha! Well?

HERMIT
                    Like the moon,
Afloat in bloody mists... this wound of yours,
So red, and livid. Tell me now, what sin
Is at its root?

BALLADYNA
      None!

HERMIT
            A doctor must know all
Before he moves to healing.

BALLADYNA

         A red berry
Set the stain there.


HERMIT
    When did this happen? Come,
You must tell me.

BALLADYNA
   Yesterday.

HERMIT
        In the morning?

BALLADYNA
Yes.

HERMIT
Give me your hand, that I might feel the pulse
Of your heart. Tell me, do raspberries grow
Beneath the weeping willow? Come, speak boldly.
Speak to me as if I were your confessor.
Was that raspberry ever white of hue?
Was it this hand of yours that made it red?
Set to your heart the fruit that wounded you...
*He pushes her away violently.*
You wretch! Your heart betrays you...!

BALLADYNA
         What? Old man...!

HERMIT
You killed your sister!

BALLADYNA
       No, no — here, I've gold —
Take this — I'll bring you more — a treble portion...

HERMIT
Why? What are you paying for?

BALLADYNA
> I know not...

HERMIT
That wound burns you, like an ember from Hell,
Am I not right?

BALLADYNA
> You are, it burns!

HERMIT
> And yet
You slept last night.

BALLADYNA
> I did.

HERMIT
> With such a wound?

BALLADYNA
Old man, I have confessed nothing to you!

HERMIT
Nothing! You prize of Satan! Tell me then,
What would you pay for?

BALLADYNA
> For your medicines.

HERMIT
God grant the wound will fester putridly
Until your face is overrun entire
By the shades of death! My simples shan't
Steal one drop of your torment from the devil...

BALLADYNA
Woe to you, old man!

HERMIT
*With irony.*
                              What? You threaten me,
When I'm at work concocting medicine
To wipe that stain clean from your countenance?
If you so wish it, I shall go and wake
Your sister.

BALLADYNA
           You can wake her?

HERMIT
                             Let sister
Call to sister. The dead shall rise and wipe
Away that stain. Is that what you would like?

BALLADYNA
No! If I had three faces, and each one pale,
And on each face three stains more horrible
Than this, I'd rather wear them all until
I came to God's own bench, than...

HERMIT
                          Silence, killer!
Now we have come to know each other, clean
Unto the inner chambers of the heart!
From the leprous wound that riots upon your brow,
May hungry worms spawn, to feed on your brain;
May your conscience become a nest of snakes
Forever snapping until you're consumed
Within, becoming one unwholesome wound
Of rot, although you'll seem to be alive —
Alive like the undead — a living corpse!
Away! Begone! Now you must wait upon
The righteousness of God, Who shall determine
What shall become of you; and even now
God has predestined you to something horrid —
Which even tomorrow may be fulfilled.
Perhaps He'll sweep away your daily bread;
Perhaps those shining locks of yours will tangle
In rotten mats; perhaps He'll end your life

Swiftly, and without warning, you unshriven,
Struck with the fire of Heaven! Wretch! Tomorrow
You shall behold the finger of God Almighty
Upon your castle walls! You carrion
Infecting the pure air! Upon your heart
You bear a worse wound than that on your brow!
What... are you dead, now?... Hey! Woman! Wake up!
Wake up and listen!

BALLADYNA
*As if sleeping.*
                            What's that? Did you say
My sister shall awake? I'd rather die...
Why did you fall into a frenzy, old man?
Woe is you! Woe!
*She runs off.*

HERMIT
*Solus.*
                    In the sad stillnesses
Of forests, crimes resound like woodpeckers
Drumming dry branches, and the slitting knife
Echoes like the poll-axe of the hangman
Biting through flesh to thud into the block.
God hears it all, and all these sounds are crammed
Into the horrid trumpet that one day
Shall call to final judgement all the damned.

*Laughter in the woods is heard.*

All spirits praise the Lord! The devils laugh
Here in the woods — the Goplan witch leads forth
Her train of imps to laugh at the gloomy oaks
And mock the sobbing birches...

*The echoes of a hunt, baying dogs, are heard.*

                            A dead huntsman
Chivvies the auroch blinded by the flash
Of windy lightning, with his dogs of mist...
I'll go... and chase away the damned hunter

That he may perish for all time... but is it wise
To risk open war with my devil-neighbours?

*Underground bells are heard.*

What's that? The ancient city sunk beneath
The waters of Gopło — crying out to God
For mercy, from a flooded steeple? Perhaps
Some cross still high upon a tower of Sodom
Now peeks above the waves among the lilies?
I'll go — I can't bear not to — and I'll pray,
Blessing the city damned; perhaps the prayers
Of an old man will bring it peaceful rest
There in its flooded grave, as litanies
Whispered by children might bring some relief
To a damned soul.

## Scene 4

*The wood, as before.*

CHOCHLIK
He flaps away, the clown,
Like a startled crow.

SKIERKA
*Picks up the crown that had been left behind.*
Behold, the old man's crown.
Now let it glow
Upon the forehead of our queen,
With the pale sheen
Of the moon;
Like wreathed fata morgana,
Let it adorn Goplana
The fair;
Binding her golden hair.

CHOCHLIK
Look there —
Here comes our lady.

*Enter Goplana and Rake.*

RAKE
My sweetest hag, my maiden of the rain,
The lakebed is your... bed, the clouds your skirt.
When through the woods you walk, each flower and tree
Ought to cry out to you: "Come, maid of downpours!"
The ploughman prefers you to the dried-up tilth —
And if I were a flower, mustard, or nettle —
Or rosemary! — I'd vow unending troth
To you, and take your hand in marriage.
But I, alas, am neither bloom nor herb;
I am a man of flesh, my maiden sweet;
These bones of mine would wear through the thinned membranes
Of my skin, were I but to nourish them
With mist and starlight; so... your humble servant...

GOPLANA
O wretched me!
Today my rose was blighted on the stalk;
Some fisherman poisoned my golden smelt,
My favourite, and some peasant slaughtered
The little bird that, on his hoary bough,
Sang to me all night long down at the lakeside —
As with his axe, he felled the silver birch...

RAKE
Well, your trees took it out on me today.
Lashed I was with sharp whips of willow boughs
Today at Kirkor's castle — my back still smarts.
But if they beat poor fellows at the castle,
They feed the help well! Streams of sparkling vodka
Course day and night from open barrel taps;
And so the fates decree: Betimes I shall
Enter the service at Kirkor's kitchen!

GOPLANA
Always to her! Always to her! You saw
That woman's evil heart just yesterday!
My dear, what do you long for? Power? Wealth?
Strength? ... A different face? ... Ask for the stone

That wonders works, that makes invisible
A man before his fellows' eyes, as in a dream
Vanishing; ask, it shall be yours!
How sad it makes me to bid for your heart
With spells! Would you prefer a flying carpet
Which carries you wherever your thought leads?
O, darling, tell me! Would you like to look
Just like that knight who suddenly appeared
To the Polish ranks, upon the clouds, in gold
And blue from tip to toe?

RAKE
                    It would be nice
To look just like the king of diamonds: crown,
Apple in left, and sceptre in right hand...
*Aside.*
Let's see the witch measure with that demand!
*Aloud.*
So let me have a sceptre and an orb,
A crown, a robe, gold slippers on my feet,
O, cap-à-pie, just like the king our liege...

GOPLANA
Imps!
Rush to the dawn and get
A snatch of her violet;
Ask pearls of the rose
And sapphire of the clouds;
Beg some indigos
Of the blue sky; when proud
The sun rises, borrow gold,
And the threads that hold
The rainbow in the sky;
Unravel its pied wool,
Pull, pull, and pull!
Go, little thieves,
Snatch, and weave!

*Chochlik and Skierka exit.*

*To Rake:*

Whatever though might trace
Within this ring of charms,
See thy Goplana haste
To thrust it in thy arms...

RAKE
The king of diamonds — I've squandered all my cards.

GOPLANA
*Draws a circle.*
Stand silently within the ring;
Hear how the wilds about you sing,
How through the tufts of pine and hazel
There hops and chatters, flits and plays all
Type of songbird — nightingale
And finch and oriole; they sail
Down here among us, chirping loud.
But soon the heavens overcloud;
Through trembling leaf and mist, the moon
All golden rises, followed soon
By pale stars, like heavy air
With thunder, lightning!

*Skierka and Chochlik bring in robes and the crown.*

SKIERKA
      All's prepared.

RAKE
*Yawns.*
I am so sleepy...

GOPLANA
     Bow your head
And slumber. Soon you shall awake
In royal robes, by spirits clad,
As measure of your dreams they take.

RAKE
*Falling asleep.*
Wonders... Good night then, Mr Rake... we'll see

You next upon the throne, organist's son...
Matthew Mark, and Dick and Tom,
Bless this bed I...
*Yawns.*
                                      wonders!... Ah!
*Falls asleep.*

GOPLANA
Watch over the sleeper, while I go to buy
A spell or two from old Grimalkin.

*It grows dark. Red clouds sail by, and spectres surround Goplana, whose back is to the audience.*

SKIERKA
Wrap him round in cloth of gold
And slip these shoes upon his feet.

*It grows entirely dark. A half-moon rests upon Goplana's head.*

Sprinkle him with pearls of dew —
Gather them from the lawns cold,
And sew them here upon his sleeve.

CHOCHLIK
O, how he snores, his majesty!
And turns upon his other flank.

SKIERKA
Goplana, let the moon shine down —
Your lover has now been transformed.

*Goplana makes a sign; the moon disappears from her brow, and light returns.*

GOPLANA
*Pointing at the sleeper.*
What a strange character he's dreamed up.

*Rake gets up from the ground dressed like the king of diamonds.*

RAKE
*Yawning.*
Ahhhh... Good morning — ahh — fine weather, this...
What's this? Whiskers? Devil take it! A grey beard!
What's going on? What have those devils done?
Transformed me — again! What sort of robe is this?
And these here arabesques... I dreamed, I dreamed...
As God's my witness, what'd I dream about?
A tavern, an a barrel full of beer,
An open spigot, and a flood! Of beer!
And I swam in that flood just like a fish!
The devil take it! They've made me a whale!
Leviathan in cloth of gold, with a grey beard!
Hey! Come to me, my witch, my glassy freak —
Tell me, who decorated me like this:
Red robe and gold, and this grey beard? Tell me —
What has become of me?

GOPLANA
                Now you're a king.

RAKE
*Raises his hand to his head, feels the crown there.*
Well then, what's done cannot now be undone...
I went to scratch my noggin, and found a crown!
Wonders...

GOPLANA
                You wear the authentic crown of the Poles.
The crown of Popiel...

RAKE
                So this is a crown?
Serves the same purpose as a toque. Covers
The ears. And this?
*Shows his wooden sceptre.*

GOPLANA
                That is your sceptre. Well,
Let it be as you wish, my eel. I'll dream
It a sceptre... Let the eye aid the old skull

And think it regal. Where'd you get the stick,
My brimstone imps?

CHOCHLIK
                          Every rake needs a handle.
RAKE
*With contempt.*
Speak to us not of Rakes! Ha! Churlish rakes?

CHOCHLIK
When yesterday your majesty was but
A common forest citizen — a tree —
Filon broke off that twig of yours.

RAKE
                    Aha —
And my left hand scabbed over with some bark —
The same that sheathes this sceptre... ha! It's rough!
I'll rasp it smooth across the peasants' backs.
Ah, too bad my Dad the barber's passed away
To trim St Peter — he'd've whisked this beard
Away like dandelion puffs. Hey, witch,
Who walk upon the waters like some saint,
Could you perhaps kindly get rid of this,
These whiskers on my chin? No? Well then, basta;
Some other barber will have the renown
Of mowing this king's chin... It'd be good
To have an orb yet in my other hand,
And then I'd walk about the world a twin
To the king of diamonds — his reflection.

SKIERKA
For an orb, I took the trouble
Of filching you a bright soap bubble
From the village boys. I flew
Beneath the hot sun and the blue
Heavens on that bubble, when
I spotted a blue stream, and then
I set him down, my orb of gold
And on the waves I gaily rolled
Until a grasshopper — naughty thing —

Saw me within, calmly asleep,
At which he took his gauzy wing
And punctured it! Then with a leap
He hopped away. Rudely awakened, I fought

My way to a forget-me-not
On the bankside...

RAKE
                    Thickwitted Señor Imp!
An apple! Even a royal orb's an apple,
And not the sugarplums that dance through dreams!

*Chochlik gives him an apple.*

RAKE
I thank you, noble sir. It's not a crab?
*Bites into it.*
And so I'm all tricked out as might befit
A king... Aha! But where my loyal swine?
My knaves and villains over whom I reign?

GOPLANA
All that upon the earth obeys my rule
Is subject now to you: the birds, the trees,
The dews, the rainbows — every flower, yours...

RAKE
And so it's time that we imposed new taxes.
Oyez, oyez, give hear and memorise
The codex of the king — eternise it
Within the rotting bark of some old willow.
From now on, we shall draft into our ranks
Bison and rabbit, boar and all the elk,
Who proudly bear their halberds on their brows.
Henceforth, should flowers wish to dip their leaves
Into the dew, let them pay per the ounce;
The Jews are hereby granted letters patent
Over the usufruct of dew. Starlings
Are hereby strictly forbidden to think
While they are chattering. We too forbid

The swallow senate free association
To discuss politics among the reeds.
The House of Sparrows is henceforth abolished.
Judgement and hanging and the distribution
Of favour shall be centred in our hands.
The swallows are forbidden to leave our borders
Without a passport, such as which includes
A nice description of beak, claw, and wing,
As well as tail and characteristic marks.
No bird shall dare henceforth enrol his chicks
In German institutions, where parrots
Are headmaster and beadle — we except
From this law magpies, who enrich thereby
Our native tongue. All foreigners, that is,
Canaries... must be watched. Tariffs upon
All foreign goods shall be enacted. Thus,
An ell of rainbow woven in the land
Of sun or moon, be it white, red, or purple,
As long as it be silk, are tariffed at
A rate of three gold pieces. As for fabric
Of white Bavarian cobweb...

GOPLANA
                              My dear man,
What are you going on about, like that?

RAKE
What? This is what you call being a king!
Making the coffers healthy, repairing
The royal budget... Roses are to pay
By bud — the same holds true for viburnum.
The hazel tree shall be taxed by the nut,
Whether the shell be meaty, or void.
Poppies shall pay by seed, not by seed-head.
Speaking of heads — mine's not just for parade...

GOPLANA
I leave you Chochlik and Skierka. Put them
To work. Let them pluck flowers, and with fans
Of rose waft you asleep. Farewell, till night.
I shall await you at the lakeside, weeping,

To coax the nightingale near with my sobs.
*Exit.*

RAKE
Uff! That's better! The jellyfish is gone!
Hey! Subject peoples!
*To Chochlik.*
                      You're my prime minister,
Because you're stupid.
*To Skierka.*
                      And you, the other devil,
With the quick eye — you'll be my jester.
Make me laugh, churl, till my sides split.
Prime Minister, where's my carriage?

CHOCHLIK
                                    Your majesty,
Four stallions black, who rear their hooves of moon,
And Mephistopheles' own cart, await.
But say nothing to Goplana...

RAKE
                                      Why not?

CHOCHLIK
                                      Because
She doesn't much like borrowing from Hell.

RAKE
That's crazy! When the devil himself is lending,
You take the loan! Who ride, preserve their soles.
*To Skierka.*
Up on the box seat, you! Prime Minister,
Out on the outrider. Up! It's time to go.

SKIERKA
Where are you going, Sire?

RAKE

                                    To the wedding
Banquet at Kirkor's.
*Exeunt.*

## Scene 5
*A hall in Kirkor's castle.*

KOSTRYN
*Solus.*
Hidden amongst the trees that shade the cell
Of the old hermit, I heard the confession
Of that woman. What good fortune! For now,
I am the lord of her golden secret,
Which I might scream abroad from palace roof,
Or to my lord and master reveal it,
Or sift its contents, grain by grain, like sand
Through hourglass into her own shy ear,
Until I see the castle coffers as bald
As the brow of Ararat... Ah, she returns.
I might have her, and treasure, both! Happy hour!
*Stands to the side.*

BALLADYNA
*Enters, deep in thought.*
That old man knows it all...! He'll tell the trees,
And they will talk it over in the nights
Until the horrid news puts down sure roots
And grows, and spreads... O you poor skittish thoughts!
Like stupid children terrified of shadows.
Let the old man knit together what I've said,
Fit them this, that way, pile them one by one...
He'll scratch his head: "It can't be, that young woman
Killed no one." Yet, what if he knows, is sure?
But who could such a thing ever believe,
As in the Credo? But what if he does?
What if he tells some stranger wandering
The woods by chance, about the lady's crime?
Before he blurts my name out, he'll take fright,
Fright at the vengeance of the lord, my husband.

And yet — perhaps he has a kindly heart,
And so shall find his tongue weighed down at last
By mercy — why cause people needless pain?
Perhaps by now he's forgotten it all,
And it's but I, who needlessly rehearse
These thoughts which no more through his mind revolve?
For who am I that others should regard,
And spy upon, and seek to ruin? Hell!
Why can't the pressure of one thousand words
Squeeze out the life of these mere two: "He knows?"
What drove me to his cell to speak with him?
What Satan took me by the hand and led
Me there to speak with the hermit of the woods?
If I am ruined, 'tis I that ruined me;
And just think — if not for that sick visit,
He'd be no different from the million souls
Throughout the world whom I have never met!
To think, this present hour so full of fright
Would have been like the calm of yesterday,
And even calmer, maybe... Hours pass,
And with each hour more of this my secret
Is rubbed by silence, till it's near erased —
And now the scab is torn from off the wound
Which shows itself more horrid, for having been
So close to healing! How I envy her,
The she that I was just this morning past!

*Kostryn draws near her.*

KOSTRYN
Madame, a courier has come with gifts
Sent by my lord the Graf for you. He waits
Upon your command.

BALLADYNA
                    Gifts from my husband?
Call the fellow here. Let them be lain
Here at my feet. Wait... that ancient beggar
Who lives deep in the woods — do you know him?

KOSTRYN
The hermit?

BALLADYNA
I don't know what made me think
Of him... Where is that courier with the gifts?
They must be handsome ones...?

KOSTRYN
The Graf is famed
For generosity — just like the sun
Who spreads his light all over, far and wide...

BALLADYNA
I wonder at his new largesse. Call him...
Call him here now.

*Kostryn exits.*
O, to receive presents
When one's mind is not paralysed with fear!
Why did I ask Kostryn about the hermit?

*Enter Kostryn and Gralon.*

GRALON
Through Gralon, Kirkor sends his heartfelt greeting.

BALLADYNA
My lord is well?

GRALON
Ripe as a raspberry!

BALLADYNA
And did my lord the count also teach you
Such sugary responses?

GRALON
My lord bade
Me take this casket stamped with his red seal
Here to the castle, and commands that you,

His wife, leave the seal unbroken, the lid
Unopened, till he should return.

BALLADYNA
                          Strike me dead
If I should say I comprehend a thing
This man says! Once more, from the top!

GRALON
                          Count Kirkor...

BALLADYNA
I know! But why should he send me as gift
A casket locked and sealed? And command
I keep it locked until the Judgement Day?

GRALON
Your husband said, "Because I so command..."
No more...

BALLADNA
                  You fool! Who wear your narrow poll
Upon your neck encased in a tin shell,
Where sparrows, as in an old, punctured pot,
Might make their nests! This chest must remain closed?
Ha, ha! Kirkor sends an odd token of love —
Distrust, not faithfulness! You churlish villain —
Although long years of friendship bound you fast
To your lord, still you'd lack the courage, certainly,
To open a locked chest. Of course! For you'd
Already feel the swinges raining down
Upon your bowed back. But I am his wife!
If I but wish... If a fly whispered close,
Ha! If the quiet swallow mouthed, "Undo it!"
While Satan himself barred me the way, fanning
His fiery wings... Know this, you cringing slave —
That my free will —

KOSTRYN
                  Your grace...

BALLADYNA

                              And you, perhaps,
Wish to remind me of my husband's rights?
Let him assert them! What care I? My God,
If only I were nosy, like some others,
I'd... But you know me not! I swear to you!
I am so skittish, even in the garden,
Should from a tree an apple fall, I'd not
Bend down to pick it up! If it's his wish,
I'll live on bread and water, ever gay,
Just like a crow perched on a stranger's fence.
I'm in no passion, now... Here then, old man,
*To Gralon.*
A guilder for your pains. Go, drink it up,
Or lose it at the dice. And run on, run on,
Back to your master: Say that I await him
Impatiently; say that I drown in tears,
Embroidering with gold a scarf for him.
Where did you leave him, Gralon?

GRALON

                                In the woods
Close by Lake Gopło.

BALLADYNA

                            Did he pause his march
As he passed through the forest?

GRALON

                                  At the hermit's.

BALLADYNA
What? At the hermit's? O dear God, speak on,
And I'll reward you — a handful of gold
For every word — but speak! I want to know
It all! You understand? I shall reward you
Splendidly — come now, speak freely, man,
Even if what you say is horrid — speak!

GRALON
Well then, through the dark overgrown wooded paths
My lord rode, first, upon his leopard charger,
And we, like geese, behind him, single file.
Then, suddenly, his horse reared as if he'd
Just met a flaming devil, while the Graf
Declared, "The forest smells of carrion..."

BALLADYNA
*Horrified.*
"And he dismounted?"

GRALON
                    Calling, "With me, friends!"
And then, on foot, he leapt beneath a willow,
Sword in hand. A corpse was lying there
Upon the moss — a wreathe of iron vermin
Roiling its bosom...

BALLADYNA
            O!

GRALON
                    "We've come across
An omen," the Graf said, "Here lies before us
The corpse of a slain auroch."

BALLADYNA
*Sighs.*
            Ah!

GRALON
                    "This is
A favourable omen for bold knights."
Thus Kirkor, and the rest of us: "Hurrah!"
Again we took to horse.

KOSTRYN
            Gralon, you say
The carrion lay beneath a willow tree?
With iron reptiles upon its white breast?

GRALON
Yes — that of the auroch.

KOSTRYN
                    Ah, the poor, poor doe...

GRALON
It was an auroch. And a male.

KOSTRYN
                              Beneath
The weeping willow? Where raspberries grow?
Is that it?

GRALON
        Yes, your grace.

KOSTRYN
                    Not far from where
The hermit lives?

GRALON
            Yes...

KOSTRYN
                    An auroch, you say,
Lay split beneath the willow?

GRALON
                        Yes.

KOSTRYN
                                Then swear!

GRALON
Why should I swear?

KOSTRYN
            For I will swear in turn
Upon the horns of Satan, that the corpse

Was no auroch of all... but... With this sword
I'll cut out all your lies!

*To Balladyna, unsheathing his sword.*

       This man must die.

BALLADYNA
*Confusedly.*
He must.

KOSTRYN
*Rushing at him.*
   Defend yourself!

GRALON
*Doing so.*
       What does this mean?

*They fight. Balladyna takes a sword down from the wall and, approaching Gralon from the rear, kills him.*

BALLADYNA
Just this!

GRALON
   O heavens above! Murder!!
*He expires.*

KOSTRYN
Madame, together we attacked
The old man. Do you know what this means?

BALLADYNA
         Yes.
O, my God!

KOSTRYN
   I accept half your fear,
Your secret, your despair.

BALLADYNA
                O Kostryn, what
Must we do now?

KOSTRYN
         Well, we must keep our heads.

        [END OF ACT III]

# ACT IV

## Scene 1

*A hall in Kirkor's castle. A feast. Through the windows, lightning flashes. Rake, dressed as a king, sits in the place of honour. Balladyna, Kostryn, Nobles, Castle Servants; Chochlik and Skierka stand behind Rake's chair.*

ONE OF THE NOBLES
To his majesty's health!

RAKE
*To Chochlik.*
      Thank him, minister.

CHOCHLIK
*With a comic gesture.*
The king thanks you.

RAKE
      Now, jester, go and bid
The kitchen-masters serve up some new fare.

SKIERKA
The cook tells me there's nothing left to eat
Except a half-baked calf's head, and, alas,
That rests upon your majesty's neck, still.

RAKE
We saw two peacocks strutting in the courtyard —
Have them prepared and baked. We shall be patient.

KOSTRYN
Servants! Now, as a final course, fill up
His majesty's bowl with guilders.

RAKE
*Taking some from the tray, he presents them to Chochlik and Skierka,
after which he fills his own pockets.*
                                    Minister,
Here is your annual salary, fully paid
In advance; now, grumble no more as do
The common rabble. Now, my jester sweet —
A guilder for your thousand japes. Come now,
Dissolve us in tears of jolly laughter!
And now, ourselves we shall reward the pain
Of rule... the rest, we'll keep, cold cates for breakfast...

BALLADYNA
Your majesty, you do me a great honour
That you have deigned to grace my home, my table.
Drink up, my lords!
*Quietly, to Kostryn, who has given her hand a squeeze.*
                    Be not so forward, boy!
For God's sake, look — We'll be betrayed, and die!
*To the others.*
Drink up, my lords! My lord of Jemioła,
Drink up! Why do you sit so silently?
Come, Graf, it is gay banter we desire.

FIRST NOBLE
We speak of coats of arms.

RAKE
                    We have a coat,
And golden slippers, too. A crown, a head...

FIRST NOBLE
I have two sticks of kindling.

SECOND NOBLE
                        Half a hive
On mine.

FIRST NOBLE
And you, Countess?

**BALLADYNA**
                      I?

**KOSTRYN**
                             My lady was princess
Of mighty Trebizond.

**RAKE**
                      Well, whaddaya say?
Most Holy Virgin! How many princes
Hast thou created on this tiny planet.
Had you, madame, two cents to rub together?

**BALLADYNA**
What? I? O, what harsh memories flood back —
An uncle merciless deprived me of my state,
Laid waste my holdings, snipped our royal line
By murdering my brothers...

**RAKE**
                          You don't say!
Who would believe it possible?

**BALLADYNA**
                            You find
My story unbelievable, my lord?
I ask no commiseration, better off
I am for having thus preserved my life.
But my poor mother! Ah, my mother, lords,
Was walled alive into a window frame.

**RAKE**
The poor old girl!

**BALLADYNA**
                    But I'm trying your patience
With tales of my sorrows. Drink, my lords!
Please! Where are the carvers? Where is the steward?
Let them bring wine! Come, fill your goblet full,
Rejoice!

SERVANT'S VOICE
*Offstage.*
                        Stop, mother!

WIDOW'S VOICE
*Offstage.*
                        Let me go, I say!

BALLADYNA
Where can I crawl and hide?

WIDOW
*Pushes her way through the servant and falls in; standing amidst the guests, she curtsies uncertainly.*
Greetings, Sir knightly fellows — Daughter, hey!
It's not right to ignore your mother, girl!

BALLADYNA
What is that crazy hag babbling about?
Does anyone know this old woman here?

WIDOW
You youngsters are enjoying yourselves? Good.
But mothers ought not to be forgotten, either.
Just think — they kept me locked up in a cage!
An old woman waiting, waiting, waiting,
And not even a crumb of bread they send!
Starvation, daughter! At least a drop of milk,
All right? No manna drops to oldsters from the skies.

BALLADYNA
What does this mean? This old woman is crazed.

WIDOW
Here, daughter — Hand me one of them gold cups.
Your mama's thirsty.

BALLADYNA
                        Why was she let in,
The old hag...?

KOSTRYN
                    Take her out! Now, go with God,
Be off! Your majesty, her mind, it wanders...

WIDOW
*To Balladyna.*
No! Call me Mama, girl! I'm not just some old hag!
"Old woman?" I'm your mother!

BALLADYNA
                              Out with her!

RAKE
Ha, ha, ha! This is some village scarecrow!
Let her be, people! Set a place for her
Amongst yourselves!

WIDOW
                    Now there's a good man, see?
Make room there on that bench and I'll squeeze in.
Yes, yes, that's the way, Sir Knight, you'll teach her
To honour her old mother! As for this —
What'm I to do? Spin a pretty Sunday frock
From cobwebs? This is Balladyna's fault,
My daughter there — that ducky there, tricked out,
While me, in rags — whether I will or no.
Let none of you smart set here be surprised
That, O —
*Points to herself.*
                    it's not gold cloth I wear, but rags
Falling to pieces on my ancient bones.
But no, forgive my daughter, please...

BALLADYNA
                              O, Hell!
Who let this mad old beggar woman in!
Tell me, you — how'd you make your way side
This golden chamber? For I know you not!

WIDOW
O, holy angels! You do not know me?
Your very mother? You do not know me?

RAKE
Ha, ha! Our ears are tickled by this sport!
A comedy fit for kings!

BALLADYNA
            Do you know her,
My lords? Tell me, who knows this frenzied witch?

WIDOW
O stars, you be my witnesses! And you,
If any of you present is a father...
You are a witch! O horrid, horrid daughter!
I don't know you!

BALLADYNA
*To Kostryn.*
            Have someone take the bitch
And fling her past the gates! She barks too loud.

WIDOW
I gave birth to my coffin, O dear God!

*At a sign from Kostryn, the Servants take the widow by her hands.*

WIDOW
No, let me go! Daughter! Come to your senses!
Daughter! Just look! It's dark outside, and raining —
The lightning lies in wait for my grey head...
Look through the window! Ah, the storm itself
Will not believe it, seeing me thrust out,
That I'm a mother, not some murderer
Who slinks through the dark night...

*At an angry sign from Balladyna, they drag her out.*

                I'll tell the clouds —
I'll beg them toss their fires upon this castle!

Stop dragging me! I'll go myself. The world
Is one big wilderness for old mothers.

BALLADYNA
Give her a heel of bread.

WIDOW
       Eat it yourself —
And may it choke you! May it throttle you!
Stop pulling! My dress is in tatters
Already — the harsh wind will have a toy —
An ancient mother's telltales... O, you! Devil
You are, not daughter! Not mine! None of mine!

*Exit, led by Servant.*

BALLADYNA
*After a long silence.*
Why are you sad? When feasts are winding down,
Guests often chatter whatever comes to mind,
And you are quiet, still, as if it were
A bandit's castle?

*A horse is heard.*
      Who's that riding up?

SERVANT
A courier from my lord the Graf.

BALLADYNA
      Let him enter.

BALLADYNA
What news do you bring me from my husband?

COURIER
I bring his greetings.

BALLADYNA
      When shall he return?

COURIER
The storm surprised him in the woods nearby.
Skittish from thunder, all our coursers slogged
Through bog and muddy paths, the while the wind
Bent tall pines low as if they were but reeds —
Some shattered with a terrifying boom.
The sheets of rain hid the castle from our sight;
The Count is waiting out the storm within
The Hermit's hut.

BALLADYNA
              What news of your campaign?

COURIER
It was successful; hardly entered in
The streets of Gniezno, we met with a troop
Of armed knights, just near the crimson gate;
Popiel was at their head, horsed; his steed
Cried proudly, pummelling the empty air
With iron-shod fore-hooves, just above the heads
Of all the people humbly kneeling there.
Then Kirkor — who would have thought it? — grabbed the reins
Of the king's charger, crying out: "Tyrant!
Who climbed to your usurped throw over three
Corpses! Off to Hell with you!" Thus saying,
He sliced through the coronet-ringed helmet,
And, grabbing Popiel's torso, shook the corpse
And showed the people. These stood dumb with shock,
And then made the heavens shake with one great shout —
One couldn't tell — praise was this? or reproach?
Then, suddenly, they flooded us three there
Like a great sounding billow — a moment more,
And we would have been crushed like three small ants
Beneath a giant's foot. With his one hand
Kirkor held Popiel's corpse, while with the other
His bloodied sword. We two, at his command,
Unsheathed not our weapons. Then the crowd,
As if knocked over by a sudden wind,
Fell to their knees before the giant figure
Of Count Kirkor. They cried aloud "Vivat!
Long live Count Kirkor! The people's avenger!"

BALLADYNA
What do you say? Is Kirkor now the king?

COURIER
Permit me to bring my story to an end.
The crowd acclaimed him king, while Kirkor cleaned
His sword against the tunic of the corpse.
One saw that he was deep in thought, struggling
For words, unable yet to form them.
At last he cried: "Lech's people! I am but
A knight unsung; it cannot fall to me
To lead a famous nation. What I've done
I did not for my own ascendancy,
But for the people's happiness. I'm fit
For country peace and calm simplicity —
The title of a Graf sits on my shoulder
A heavy fardel, none too comfortable,
And even that I've taken down a notch,
Taking as wife, not princess, but a common
Peasant girl. She, instead of coats of arms,
Has quartered mine with a clay berry-jar;
Unlike a queen, the lords of our country
Will rankle at submitting their children
To kneel before a peasant!"

BALLADYNA
                    Lies, all lies!
He's lying!

COURIER
        Kirkor continued to speak:
"Announce an interregnum in the land —
Then, he who wearing the authentic crown
Of Popiel's race, shall appear at my castle
— The crown on which the viper's-eye gem flashes
Between two rubies, resting on three pearls —
He shall be chosen king." At once the crowd
Shouted assent in wild acclamation,
And now they wait upon the king's advent,
The true inheritor of the true crown.

RAKE
*As all eyes are on him.*
What are you staring at, like a murder of crows?

NOBLES
We bend our knee before your majesty...
Behold our king!

RAKE
                What? You call me a king?
If not that I was soused, I would be drunk
With joy! How's that for crazy destiny?
I'd leap out of my skin if it were not
Unseemly, as it now is royal hide...

NOBLE
Long live your majesty! One hundred years!

RAKE
A hundred years? I'll live a hundred years!
Now that I've got new skin, just like the snake...
And, look here, gentlemen — the viper's eye!
I'd cut a jig around the hall with you,
My countess, were it not beneath my state,
Am I not right? Which says "Sit still now, king!"
Ha! I shall grow so into this my throne
That no amount of men will tear me hence!
Ha! What a miracle!

BALLADYNA
*To Kostryn.*
                    Can you hear the storm?
The gutters ring like bells... In the storm winds
I hear voices, sobbing...

KOSTRYN
                      That's just the watch —
Challenge and password.

BALLADYNA
>No, I hear voices
Other than theirs — a moan emerging from
The realm of the dead... Here, pour me some wine!
Events entwine themselves into a noose!

RAKE
Now, dinner's over, so it's time to play!
Have them bring in the bears that, in the kitchen,
Make the spit spin. I'd like to see them dance.

FIRST SERVANT
They're clumsy — since the count first shot them.

RAKE
>So,

*To Chochlik.*
You, Prime Minister — take my sceptre
Of willow-wood and pipe a tune, as if
It were a bagpipe. Come — finger the holes,
And make the people happy with whatever
Sails through your tuneful nut. Now, silence, all!
Play!

CHOCHLIK
>What shall I play, my lord?

RAKE
>Stop the holes
With your fingers — my sceptre knows my taste;
She'll do the rest — just blow your breath upon her.

SKIERKA
Come, play.
I'll conjure forth the echo from the wood
Which saw what it saw!

*Chochlik plays a sombre village tune on this flute, while airy voices, confused at first, begin to sing.*

SONG
A handsome squire
Whom both desire —
Into the woods they hied;
Whichever fills
Her jar, he wills
To take her for his bride!
    Ha! ... Ha! ...
*The song dies away among the echoes.*

BALLADYNA
What does this mean? Who said that? And who ended
A song like that with laughter?

KOSTRYN
                Hush, my lady —
You're hearing things!

BALLADYNA
                I heard a song...
*To Chochlik.*
                        Play on.
*To Kostryn, aside.*
And you, Kostryn, study the faces here
And, should you see a singer, let me know —
Then I'll decide what fate shall meet the singer...
*To Chochlik.*
Play, piper, a rustic ballad, and wake
The echoes hanging there above my head
In the copula. Torches! Light it up!

*Chochlik plays.*

SONG OF THE SPIRITS
O bride to be,
'Twas Satan, he
The knife in your hand thrust,
While sister rushed
From bush to bush,
Plucking the berries ruddy.
Alas, what's made

Your livid blade
Stain angry red, and bloody?
  O...! O...!
*The song dies away with echoed moans.*

**KOSTRYNA**
Stop now! The countess faints.

**BALLADYNA**
         No, I'm all right...
Sing... yet... Torches! Light!

*Chochlik plays.*

**SONG OF THE SPIRITS**
A drop of red
On your forehead:
I wonder how it got there?
A berry stain?
Or then again,
Perhaps... ha!
*The song fades in echoes.*

**BALLADYNA**
*Making a sign with her hand.*
More...

**NOBLEMAN**
Why are the countess' eyes so wide and wild?
A simple harvest song that peasants sing,
And whistle on rude pipes — oppresses her?

**BALLADYNA**
More!

**NOBLEMAN**
She's in a trance, poor thing — come, someone, rouse her!
She sleeps with eyes wide open...

KOSTRYN
*To Balladyna, who is unmoving.*
                                        My lady!

NOBLEMAN
Call in the servants — have them carry her
To a warm bed — she's cold and stiff as wood!

*A loud thunderclap, and Balladyna awakes.*

BALLADYNA
What happened to me? I am terrified
With horrid dreams...
*To Kostryn.*
                    Listen, for sure I spoke
While sleeping — Did I say anything?

KOSTRYN
No...

BALLADYNA
Thanks be to God. But while I was asleep,
For sure you must have talked about something
Quite terrible, aloud?
*To guests.*
                        Drink up! I see
I ought to sit down to embroidery
Rather than wine.

RAKE
*Waking.*
                    Our apologies, lords.

GUESTS
For what?

RAKE
        We tender our apologies, ashamed
For having drowsed.
*Drinks.*

>                Health to the lord
> Of this castle!
>
> GUESTS
>                Health to Count Kirkor!
> RAKE
> An honest lord! An honest lord and merry!
> Instead of rule, he prefers to eat raspberry!
> Go! Send some forester into the woods
> To pluck some raspberries for these his guests.
>
> BALLADYNA
> Such an odd hankering...
>
> RAKE
>                    In the woods nearby
> There must be raspberries, large ones and sweet,
> And tasty, since Count Kirkor values them
> More than slippers of parrot and royal cloak...
> Here — have the steward offer to the guests
> A taste of raspberries...
>
> BALLADYNA
>                Courage, now!
> Nothing worse may betide me — I have heard
> Echoes emerging from the ruptured tombs —
> Now let me see if they can anything
> Cast forth but words! Hey! Raspberries! Bring them!
>
> *The white ghost of Alina appears, with a jar of raspberries, balanced on her head.*
>
> I've sensed you in the air for some time now,
> And now I see you. How your eyes shine — white!
> I'm not afraid — you see — but don't you dare
> Come close to me...
>
> FIRST NOBLE
>                What is she saying, now?

BALLADYNA
Stay there — speak to me across the table.
A man's hand — please — I'm frightened.

FIRST NOBLE
                                    Can you hear
How her teeth chatter from fright?

BALLADYNA
                        Go, damned one!
Back where you filled that jar with something... moving...
Like vermin of the grave. Is this a shade
Cast by a corpse hanged sometime long ago
In the high tower — standing here, breathless?
Away, white shade of her, who was cut down...

*The ghost vanishes.*

FIRST NOBLE
Smell that? An aroma of raspberries!

SECOND NOBLE
The air is filled with it — raspberry scent...

BALLADYNA
I die!

KOSTRYN
Water! Hey, water! I'll loosen her bodice —
Pour it full on her bosom! Servants, here!

*Women enter.*

Take out the countess...

*They carry Balladyna out.*

                        Deign rise from the table now;
The torches die. This table's fully stained
With scraps of bread and beef — revolting!
Do you want to toss the gnawed bones at one another,

As do the Danes? Please, come into the hall...
You — clear the tables. You — bring torches near
To light the king's way to where his bed's prepared
In the side tower — a goose-feather bed.
Enough for one day. Tomorrow the castle
Will be as jolly and lively as tonight,
But now is time for sleep. My lords, please, come —
Leave now the benches and the chalices...
How hard it is to budge a Pole from food
And drink! They cling to cups just like leeches,
And hiccup drunk at music, and at speeches.

*The tables are cleared and taken out while he is speaking. Rake is led out by servants with torches, and after him, everyone follows. Kostryn exits last.*


### Scene 2
*The woods near the Hermit's cell. The storm continues.*

KIRKOR
Come in out of the rain, old man. This storm
Will steal the grey hair from your head. Events
As well as people can be thieves; a man
May steal a cloak, and misery — one's shirt.
It needs an armed hand to resist, always
On guard — but you are gloomy far too rashly,
I swear to you — I'll win back the filched crown
Or die in the attempt. So near I am
To home! Although I might within the hour
Receive one thousand kisses from the lips
Of my wife, drinking pearls of dew from out
That rosy cup, just like a thirsty bird,
I'd rather set aside for now delights,
Race back to Gniezno on this very night
And gather up the people, to declare
To all the nations: this man is the heir
Authentic to the throne, who has but lost
His rights by shameless theft. Then, trumpeters
Throughout country and town would spread the word
That he who should show up to claim Lech's throne,

His brows encircled with the crown of Popiel,
I do deny, tossing into his teeth
His falsehood, and inscribing on his brow
The word USURPER. Pray with me, old man,
So that the living God grant victory
To me on the tilt-yard — and wait for me.

HERMIT
God bless you.

KIRKOR
*Claps. Enter soldiers.*
                    Now, to horse! Away, with speed,
To Gniezno!
*Makes to exit.*

HERMIT
                    Listen — here is my advice:
Return home to your castle. Think it through,
And you shall see what your next move must be.

KIRKOR
Like to a lazy peasant, my corvée
I'd work off in a day, so as to hence
Live happily, untroubled, with my wife.
I'll rest the burden of the fatherland
Upon your shoulders. When it's settled there,
I'll lay me down warm-nestled in the peace
Of my hearthside, busy with nothing more
Than my fruit trees, or with an infant son
To rock asleep in these arms. Thus I pray...
I'll wait upon a letter from your throne
Each year. Once in a twelvemonth may a pigeon
Drop from the clouds, bearing beneath his wings
Some news of grand events to raise a smile
As I rest 'neath my lindens and drowse off
To a sweet sleep ... you'll grow jealous of me,
Sire, of my wife and children, of my lime trees,
Of shade and naps beneath them, of my honey...
Bid me farewell! Before the morning dawns
I'll be in the capital. Let's go, my boys!

*Exit Kirkor. Horses are heard galloping away.*

**HERMIT**
*Solus.*
Great God! He prefers to return to Gniezno
Then press that bloody wife to his noble bosom...
O, God forbid that you should ever learn
What sort of mother bears you children, Kirkor...
Should God deprive you of her, before she
Might bear your progeny, that would indeed
Be a reward, not punishment.

**WIDOW**
*Offstage.*
                    Woe, ah, woe is me!

**HERMIT**
What cry is this, so heavy-fraught with tears?

**WIDOW**
*Offstage.*
Wretchedness, misery!
*Enter the Widow, as if blind, feeling her way with her hands.*

**HERMIT**
                Some ragged woman,
Alone and blind, on such a horrid night!
Where are you tending, mother?

**WIDOW**
                          Mother, O!
Call me not mother, you unworthy girl!
Mother? Bitch, rather!

**HERMIT**
                     Whence come you, poor thing?

**WIDOW**
I am not poor. But I am grey. Grey, grey —
Grey as a pigeon. Know you not what's chanced?
The countess — my daughter, so grand a dame —

And I, uncovered, weathering the storm,
Calling the lightning down, "Come now! Strike here!"
But it won't listen. Up there in the castle
They drink and raise their drunken toasts, and she,
My daughter, drinks among them, the grand dame!
D'you understand? She has castle and towers,
The countess...

HERMIT
                What's her name?

WIDOW
                      She was called daughter,
But call her Blind — she has no eyes in her head,
For eyeballs weep sometimes... in such a bluster,
Amidst such crackling bolts, to cast me out!
Her mother! Teats that gave her suck now withered
With age, head crowned with white hair, like a halo...

HERMIT
Come here beneath my roof, old mother! See,
How you shiver with cold! Come!

WIDOW
                      The whole castle
Belongs to her — as big as half the world...
You know?... The countess?!

HERMIT
                Come.

WIDOW
                      No, I'll wait here.
My daughter — does she know where your hut stands?
Who knows? Perhaps a dog will bark at some old rags
And she'll recall her mother, and go out

In search of her, the world over. Perhaps!
God, after all, is merciful!

**HERMIT**
                    Come in!
You'll weep away this stormy night inside,
And when the dawn breaks, I'll lead you unto
A great king, at whose feet you'll cast you down,
To beg his mercy and...

**WIDOW**
                    ...And I'll tell —him:
"I am a poor mother who grovels here...
*Kneels.*
Sire! Golden majesty, command my daughter
Who has gold enough herself, to love me!"
*Gets up.*
And from his throne the king will rise and lead me
Back to my daughter's heart. O! O! O!
*Sobs.*
You know, I looped my scapular around
A creaky pine, to hang myself; alas,
The tree branch broke... Stupid old woman!
For the branch was dead.
A branch — the daughter of the tree — you asp!
You had no mercy on your widowed mother?
And all I asked was a mere crust of bread
From all your palace stores! Ah, may your hand
That sprinkles fists of seed there on your lawn
To fatten doves not shoo away your mother,
Who bends among them to assuage her hunger!
Banished into the storm! Into the woods!
A mother, chased out! I fell in a puddle,
And lightning flashed red to eat out my eyes
From underneath my lids — eat to the bone...

**HERMIT**
You're blinded?

**WIDOW**
                    There's a darkness in my head —
A horrid darkness. Just this afternoon
I had enough light, so much, I might tell

The white sun past the forest from the moon.
But now...

HERMIT
     How is it? You can't even see
The lightning flash?

WIDOW
     The hand of God will strike
Whether you see it on its way, or not.
What need I now with eyes? You know something?
I now believe what I did not believe
Before: Each year, before they cross the seas,
The swallows stifle all their old grey mothers.
They throttle 'em. Yes, yes, yes — truth must be told.
And I must tell 'em. Begging on my way,
I'll write a song worth three pennies at least —
Of the black swallows what stifle their mums...
Ha! Little birds, and yet so merciless!
Thrust out your mother, hungry, in the night
Where hurricanoes tear at her thin hair.

HERMIT
Thousands of honest folk throughout the world
Fall victim to bad people. If I should
Call you to witness my misfortune...

WIDOW
     What?
Are you a mother too? Ah no, I shan't
Go with you; we'd soon fall to quarrelling,
Whose daughter is the lovelier... It's mine...
Ah, when I'm in my grave, I'll resurrect
At the mere sound of her name: "Bladina."
I go now to search out a stream to drink
Just like the sparrows, cocking up my head
In the Lord God's direction, thanking Him
For water.
*Mumbles sleepily.*
Old lady had a cow
A cottage and a garden,

Two daughters...
*Exit to the woods.*

HERMIT
I'll have that woman sought out everywhere
And pass a harsh verdict upon her child!
*Enters his cell.*

## Scene 3
*Night — lightning — a dark hall in Kirkor's castle. Skierka and Chochlik exit through the doors, through which they had earlier led Rake to his bed.*

SKIERKA
Our lord's abed in the tower,
Nestled in the folds
Of dream. While yet the power
Of the storm lasts,
I'm off now, fast,
To ride the lightning bolts.

CHOCHLIK
I'm off to do some mischief in the stables,
Where no pie has been pinned above the gates.
D'you know a one-eyed owl lives in the tower?
I've been invited to a feast — she'll look
Askance at me if I don't accept
A haunch of field mouse.

SKIERKA
I'm off to feed an old grey
Stork who doesn't hear
In her right ear.
She's blind, too. Yesterday
I pulled her from the path
Of the brutal swath
Made by the peasant's scythe —
I can't wait any longer.
The storm is getting stronger,
Poor frightened thing — she's only half alive!

CHOCHLIK
What was that sound?

SKIERKA
The stormwind slammed a gate.

CHOCHLIK
Hush! Someone's coming — wait...

SKIERKA
A ghost in white!
I'll take to flight
Here through the window...
*Exits through the window.*

CHOCHLIK
And I follow!
The horses manes to flounce.
*Exits.*

## Scene 4

*The same.*

BALLADYNA
*Enters in her nightgown, knife in hand.*
I couldn't sleep... the knife was at my side...
I took it... In my nightshirt! Ah, for shame!
Should someone see me thus, and knife in hand?
How dark it is here!
*Approaches the tower.*
        What's that noise? The wind
Puts out my candle — that's an omen, sure...
So silent... all the castle is asleep.
But if he's not? If he's just lying there, staring,
With open eye? Then what? Then what? If I
Don't do it now, tomorrow I'll be sorry —
Ah! The wind closed the door behind me now —
Like some black spirit barring my return.
I daren't turn around for fear I'd see

Something too frightful...
*Turns.*
                            Ha! There's nothing there.
You see? Dark emptiness — and fog at most;
There is no ghost.
*Lightning.*
Every spirit praise the Lord on high!
How red that lightning flashed! All the white walls
Were lit up like the day — Hush! There's no sound...
Get on your way! But if a sudden flash
Should light me up when I bend over him
With knife in hand? Well, what of that? The flame
Will show me where to strike, O, lightning bolt!
Make me a bloody daylight in the womb
Of night! Be sun to my night's reaping. Now, I go.
*She enters the tower.*


## Scene 5

*The same.*

KOSTRYN
*Enters armed with a sword.*
The door is open. Fortune, fail me not!
Lead me onward unto that golden calf
As you once led the argonaut unto
The golden fleece. And thus I promise you —
This son of a hanged man shall one day sit
Upon the throne like a pure-blooded princeling!
Today I'm servant to much baser folk;
Tomorrow I shall rule my betters. Hush!
It's just an owl hooting in the tower.
Come, here's a ladder. All's in readiness —
I've all the castle keys here in this clutch;
I'll muffle my steed's hooves with cloth, and thus
I'll disappear with the charmed coronet
Into the black night, like a sable ghost...

And then, adulterous wife, farewell forever!
O Satan, guide my steps!

*He makes to ascend the ladder, but meets Balladyna at the door, returning.*

                        Ah! Who is this!

*He retreats a step in fright.*

BALLADYNA
It's me.

KOSTRYN
         Alone? In the deep darkness? Why?
I heard a moan, and hastened near to help.

BALLADYNA
Light — bring me light — and let the light behold
How red I must be stained with his blood.
It is finished. Who was it you would save?
It seems to me the storm has run its course.
The lightning flashes no more... So you heard
That horrid groan? It was heard even here?!
That's odd... For when he stopped breathing, he sighed,
Just once... Light! Go and bring me light,
Kostryn! Go down for light!

*Kostryn exits.*
                        How strongly I smell
Of blood... It's happened now... It's happened...
Now it were vain to regret what is passed.
It happened... and it all shall pass away.
All of us will lie dead like that some day —
Light! Candles! Come! Illuminate my castle!

*Kostryn enters without light.*

KOSTRYN
All is asleep in this our brick fortress.
Even the cressets on the castle gates
Have seen their torches slumber. Shall I call
Your servants?

BALLADYNA
                No, wake no one. Ah, my arms
Must drip with red from past my elbows! Odd,
How odd they smell.

KOSTRYN
                But did you take the crown?

BALLADYNA
No... wait. I'll go back now and get it.
I'm not afraid. I know where the bed stands.

*Balladyna enters the tower.*

KOSTRYN
Such a bold woman! I might thank Thee, God,
That she has stolen that horrid sin from me!
I'd like to see her face now, and discover
To what colour a lioness grows, when she pales.

*Balladyna returns without the crown.*

BALLADYNA
It was too dark. In vain I sought by touch
To find the crown — and O, that table-top —
It had the features of a man's cold face...
Perhaps it was no table after all...

KOSTRYN
Wait here. Keep watch. I'll go and look for it...

BALLADYNA
Wait! ... No, go on. I do not fear myself —
Nor am I even sorry...

*Kostryn enters the tower.*

                But I know
That mourning oft infects the dreams of Poles,
Making them restless in their beds... Perhaps
The bloody corpse even now appears before

The sleepers' eyes, and they, in sleep,
Do bless themselves, shooing the silent ghost.
He's coming down — Ah, how those ancient rungs
Creak so and crack...

*To Kostryn, entering with the crown*
                                You found it? In your hand
You're bearing something?

KOSTRYN
*Gloomily.*
                                  Yes.

BALLADYNA
                                  Here! Give it here!
No, don't come near me... I'll cry out for help...
Stay there.

KOSTRYN
                    What do you mean? Your words are mad.

BALLADYNA
Stay there, or I will scream! I'll wake them up,
The whole castle — stay there! Until the thought
I smell here in the air passes away...
Your thought, O Kostryn — You had it in mind
To kill me — O, how loudly beat your heart —
As loud as mine does, when I'm cutting flesh.

KOSTRYN
If I did think that, I damn now for all time
The matrix of my mind that could give birth
To such a crazy child.

BALLADYNA
                          Come now, with me...
Back to the room where we can plan in silence
Tomorrow's duties...
*It grows brighter.*

KOSTRYN
                    The watch sent me word
That Kirkor went back to Gniezno last night —
With sword unsheathed against the usurper
Who should appear, pretending, with the crown.
BALLADYNA
That's nothing. I have swords and people too.
On my side there shall stand a host of men
Who grew stout on the castle fare. How can
Kirkor tame a thunderstorm of gold?
Hush!

KIRKOR
        No, that's only sparrows in the yard.

BALLADYNA
What? Is it day already? O, my God —
What a bright light — it makes me sick! I'm ill!

KOSTRYN
Go, rest. Sleep through the grey hour of the dawn
I'll come and wake you when the sun is high —
A ring of armed knights will encircle you.
It shall work out. We'll cobble up some troops.
Give me the treasury keys. I'll sift the gold
Onto persuasive dishes.

BALLADYNA
                    The old man —
The hermit in the woods — have done with him
As well. Then only two of us shall know of this.

KOSTRYN
Three. You're with child.

BALLADYNA
                    How can that be? The child
Here in my womb shall know my secrets too?
Go! — Ah, in a poor unborn creature, such
A secret! Are you mocking me with this?
If it were true, what you say, I'd give birth

To a mad thing! Impossible! But no —
It shall be born alive — and know nothing.

KOSTRYN
Then go, my lioness. And lay you down
To sleep. When you awaken, you'll be fresh
And strong for further action, armed cap-à-pie.
*Exeunt.*

[END OF ACT IV]

# ACT V

## Scene 1
*Morning, a wooded meadow.*

SKIERKA
The morning's so fresh
After the storm
I return from the nest
Of mother stork.

CHOCHLIK
I kept myself warm
At the owl's feast
In the castle tower
But where is our
Lady, Goplana?

SKIERKA
I'll take another scan of
Meadow and wood and track;
I'll set all the bent blossoms back
On their green feet, and comb
The long locks of the rye;
Then over Lake Gopło I'll fly
And "Swan, here! Come cob, come pen!"
I'll cry
Above the glassy lake, and when
They fly up from their cosy reeds
I'll spill a grip of golden seeds
To fill their snowy bellies, and
Again I'll swoop to the wooded strand
To tend the bushes;
To make sure there blushes
A rainbow above their scruffy polls n,
And above those
I'll paint the sky rose.

All this before I even come a cropper,
Steeplechasing on my steed-grasshopper.

*A swirl of morning mist, lit up in rainbow colours, blows in; from beneath it, Goplana steps.*

GOPLANA
Come, little angels, kiss goodbye
Goplana — never more your eye
Shall light on her... My weepy violets!
My roses! Fare you well! Now, let's
Part, embracing one last time.

SKIERKA
What's that you're singing?

GOPLANA
      Doleful rhymes
Of parting songs...

SKIERKA
But it's still very long
Till autumn... look: the reeds
Unburdened yet with swallows; still the meads
Breathe the first breaths of spring!

GOPLANA
I'm travelling
To a sad land of pine and snow,
Where the sun sputters like a coal
About to die, and where the moon
Pales like a ghost fording the gloom
Of cemeteries.
Look how the penal angel harries
Me forth: screaming through my soul:
"Remember the raspberry wold,
The land of roses!" Ah, farewell —
I've tangled so the acts of men
That God must now undo the spell
With vengeful fire, once again —
In payment for their guilty acts.

SKIERKA
Goplana, no! We want you back!
We will not let you go, dear lady!

GOPLANA
But go I must, and I am ready
For my exile... from time to time
A bird, come from some foreign clime
Will light upon a weeping tree
And sing, and you'll remember me —
Farewell! no one is to blame but I
That banished to the North I fly...

CHOCHLIK
I'll race before you for a while,
Your herald, lighting your first mile.

GOPLANA
Today the broad keys of the geese
Are flying north; I'll hitch on one of these
And float more quickly through the air —
As when a maid takes from her hair
A harvest garland, which she'll throw
Upon the stream...

SKIERKA
    O misery! O, woe!

GOPLANA
In vain you weep; vain are your tears.
*Points to the woods.*
Hark! A key of migrating cranes nears —
Soon they'll alight on the meadow
For a short rest. And when they go,
I'll hitch myself upon the last
And thus into the azure, fast
I'll soar, pale as the moon burnt by the sun,
Light as a leaf when summer's done.
When we fly over Gniezno's walls,
I'll sing my farewell to you all.

*Exit. Skierka and Chochlik follow her, quickly.*


SCENE 2
*At the walls of Gniezno. Kirkor, sword unsheathed, with eagle's wings at his back, enters, at the head of his troops. Banners are unfurled, trumpets blare.*

KIRKOR
*To knights.*
Whoever it is unjustly claims Lech's sceptre
Refuses to enter the lists with me.
Like some vile snake, he hides, waiting his chance
To strike with all the men he's gathered — Ah!
What am I saying? All the men he's bribed
With gold! This knight of unknown ancestry
Seeks to usurp the throne by waging war —
My grave is to be his first ladder-rung
To rule. And many of our knights (may God
Preserve us from such blindness and frenzy!)
Many of our knights have flocked to the tents
Of this deceiver. Yet God is on high,
And He sees clearly through the hearts of men!
We need no venal traitors in our ranks!
As soon as King Popiel arrives here, whom
I've sent three knights into the woods to fetch,
We'll rush upon the camp of the usurper
Like screaming eagles.
*To the knights standing on the walls.*
                          Now, make fast the gates,
Spike every crenellation with the throats
Of cannon — Should I lose the day, these walls
Can still hold out a long time. The grey heads
Among you will remember — the south wall
Is weakest; there men's chests must spackle up
The cracks. God is good, may He favour us,
So that tomorrow's dawn see you awaken,
Safe in a city free of cads and villains.

KNIGHTS
Kirkor shall be victorious!

KIRKOR
                If God wills.
Ah, when shall I set helm aside at last?
When shall I return to my wife? And when
Shall I see the end of banditry,
The bloody matters of the kingdom?

FIRST KNIGHT
                Look —
An envoy.

*Enter Envoy, covered in dust.*

KIRKOR
    I sent three into the woods;
Where are the other two, and where is Popiel?

ENVOY
Ah, horror! Horror!

KIRKOR
        What? Did you not find
The old man in his cottage? Speak! A war
Awaits you.

ENVOY
      There was no one in the cottage,
But on a creaking bough before the porch
His corpse was hanging from a thick-wound noose;
The wind was playing with his snowy hair
And torn tunic, while he swayed back and forth
Like an old wet-nurse.

KIRKOR
           Sound the battle cry
Throughout the camp! Such is relentless fate —
Adding to the misfortunes of his life
Death by an unknown hand. My heart is weakened
By your narration — make the difference up
With bravery on the field. Hanged, you say?

ENVOY
Hanged in his hermit's robes before his hut.
And on the wretched tree, a raven croaked.

KIRKOR
Onward! Set pennons dancing on the wind!
Close ranks! Our hope is in our manliness...!
The archers will begin this war with a volley.
*Exits with army.*


## Scene 3

*Balladyna's tent. Kostryn and Balladyna in armour; they enter with beavers lowered over their faces.*

KOSTRYN
Stay in the tent. Don't venture on to the field —
For I've a feeling that soon Kirkor's men
Will start the battle. But they're down below —
Our camp is set high like an eagle's aerie.

BALLADYNA
Soon many souls will stand before God's bench.

KOSTRYN
Where wheat is threshed, there flies the chaff as well
Toward the heavens. Stay at the barn-porch
And set not on the wheel of your conscience
What has been bound and buried long ago.

*Enter Soldier.*

SOLDIER
The ranks of Kirkor have begun their rush,
Bellowing fiercely.

KOSTRYN
          Princess, and my princeling,
Fare you well!

BALLADYNA
>We'll be victorious?

KOSTRYN
Stay, madame, in the tent. Let vanity
Not lead you, golden, out into the light
Where arrow-stings fall thickly as sunbeams.
By God, sit quietly at warp and shuttle,
Weaving a royal robe — or a winding sheet.
It's certain that you'll stand in need of one
Or the other. Ha, ha! See crossbows let fly
Their lead — see how they bristle — Squire! My lance
And buckler!
*Takes these from the Squire's hands and exits.*

BALLADYNA
*Sola.*
>If he is victorious,
What shall be his reward? The earth's womb
Bears no such ore to sate that German gullet.
But should he lose? If he loses, I've lost —
Quite everything; in one horrible moment
It shall be finished, everything resolved,
As in an awful story of some witch:
She loses, and she plunges a sharp blade
Into her own breast — O, a blade envenomed
With viper's poison. Where is that old woman?
In the forest I saw an ancient hag
Who looked just like an oak shattered by storms...
It's her I sent among the hungry crows
Beyond the camp to cull the deadly liquor...

*An Old Woman, dressed in rags, lifts the tent flaps and enters.*

And so?

OLD WOMAN
>I've brought a horn brimful of bane.

BALLADYNA
Give it here... Now, off to the woods with you!
Begone, I say, you ancient sorceress...
Once I have tested this poison on someone,
I'll pay you for it... Go! Before my men
Seize you and split you open with a sword.

*Old Woman exits hastily.*

Abhorrent hag! ... Her hair a nest of snakes
Writhing in tethers, and her bloodshot eyes
As red as wolves' fangs tearing at some carrion...
Should I fall alive into my husband's hands
This poisoned blade will tear my breast and bite
Into my heart like the sting of a wasp.
See how the side I've smeared with venom dulls
To a black sheen — and now breeds rust — the obverse,
Untouched with viper's spittle is as bright
As axe-blade freshly whetted on the wheel...

*Enter Soldier.*

What news?

SOLDIER
          Madame, it is a bloody blizzard
Above the field —such is the mist of death
That nothing can be seen.

BALLADYNA
          But are we losing?

SOLDIER
Atop the battlement, there on the hill
Where beeches grow about the spring, I saw
Count Kirkor, walled about with corpses, thickly —
But he fights on, swinging a deadly axe.

BALLADYNA
And so, why have you been sent to me?

SOLDIER
I've come to tell you, madame, that two hundred
Of those you ... purchased yesterday, have crossed
From Kirkor's ranks, to ours. If but the flank
Of archers to his left, whom you have bribed,
Dissolve, the field is ours.

BALLADYNA
      But they have not!
Ah, lazy treachery is worse than troth!
Go take yourself unto the cauldron, boiling
With bloody greed; should you fish out
Some noble's head therefrom with iron spoon,
You'll be a lord. You understand? One might
Approach with ease beyond the hillock, there,
And pounce upon some villain's back, hacking
With pickaxe through his thin helmet —
Go — Go and kill!

*Enter Second Envoy.*

SECOND ENVOY
The left flank of the archers starts to thin,
Sprinting to Gniezno — soon the moil will end;
Ours is the victory!

BALLADYNA
     For such good news, receive
Fitting reward...
*Gives him coin.*
    Is our foe's leader taken?

SECOND ENVOY
I saw Count Kirkor's pennon fixed fast
Upon the hillock where the birches grow;
A battlement of corpses was there raised,
With more thereunto added, as if masons
Were hard at work with bricks of flesh — It froze
The blood to see it, seeing Kirkor not,
Or any passage through this wall of death.

BALLADYNA
IF you have manhood in you; if you wish
To see your pockets overflow with silver,
Climb on those battlements — let dead men's ribs
Be ladder rungs unto your feet, and hair
Your pulley-ropes — Be off with you, and kill!
*Cries are heard.*
What's that?

*Kostryn enters, his arm stained with blood.*

    And Kirkor?

KOSTRYN
      Dead.

BALLADYNA
*Putting away the knife poisoned on one side.*
         And I had readied
My blade... I owe my life to you. Go, have
The hangman chop off the heads of his leaders.
Go — give the command.

*Kostryn exits.*

VOICES OUTSIDE THE TENT
      Long live our leader,
Fon Kostryn!

BALLADYNA
      Long live your leader, Fon Kostryn...
Thus I repeat their words, like a senseless pie.
I'l toss my arms around the German, and smother
Him with thick fetters of kisses.

*Enter Kostryn with an embassy from the city — One of the citizens approaches Balladyna with a golden tray upon which bread and salt are resting.*

KOSTRYN
Here is an embassy from Gneizno, fallen.

BALLADYNA
You've started hanging men?

KOSTRYN
             The first rebels
Are grouped beneath the pear-tree of contention,
Which is delighted that she will bear fruit
Twice in one year.

BALLADYNA
*To embassy.*
             What is your desire?

MUNICIPAL ENVOY
                    Good knight,
The hearts of your orphaned nation are raised
To you, as to an angel from on high —
Begging you, be the ruler of our land.
All of the capital waits on bended knee
With gates spread wide — enter them, we beg you!
Our hearts, our treasury, everything we own
Shall flow before your feet in flooding rivers,
For you have earned your people's gratitude
By casting down the bandits who oppressed us,
Kept us imprisoned within by force of arms,
Maltreated us with torture, martial law,
Starvation, while our hearts cried out for you —
Believe us, that among us you will find
No perjurer to move your ire, no one
Deserving stripes; Long live our Sovereign!
Come and enjoy our treasure, and receive
Your subjects who await on bended knee
Down in the humble dust, seeking your hand
To raise us from abasement. Bread and salt
We here present to you in humble greeting,
Your faithful subjects and your servants true.

BALLADYNA
*To Kostryn.*
Did any of this mob bear arms against us?

KOSTRYN
Two used their tongues as weapons, from the walls
Urging the people to fight on.

BALLADYNA
                Where are they?

KOSTRYN
*Pointing.*
The burgher Courier there, and alderman Scribbler.

BALLADYNA
They fought with tongues, so hang them from the tongues
Of the castle bells.

FIRST AMBASSADOR
                Ah, victor, in your breast
A heart of stone is fixed.

BALLADYNA
                To prove you wrong,
I shall be moved your sentence to commute:
Knock out their teeth and break their jaws, that they
Will fight no more.

FIRST AMBASSADOR
                And so there is no way
To beg your mercy with our tears and groans,
O iron master?

BALLADYNA
                Master? I'm a woman.
*Seeing that they recoil in terror:*
What's this? They shrink away as if the plague
Were standing here before them, and again
Like rye-stalks in the wind, they bow and beat
Their brows before me?

FIRST AMBASSADOR
                We await your orders,
Madame — rule with your folk's consent.

**BALLADYNA**
With or without it... Bring that bread and salt.
Good sirs, I trust the yeast that made this rise...
Come, Kostryn, I owe you so much,
That half the town, and half this loaf of bread
Belong to you by right...

*She takes out the knife poisoned on one side, and cuts the loaf in two.*

I share it all,
Except my heart, which you shall have entire.

**KOSTRYN**
*Kneeling.*
My queen!

**BALLADYNA**
*Tasting the bread, she watches as Kostryn eats the half she gave him.*
Do as I do. I fear no treachery
Baked in the loaf my subjects offer me.
If here instead of rye a reptile's scales
Were milled for flour, still the cake would taste
Sweet in your mouth, for being won with iron.
Eat, please — one needs to place one's trust in men.
But now, let trumpets sound our victory.
Go now, my warriors; let's inspect the city
Whose gates we unlocked with our iron blades.

*Leaning on Kostryn, she exits, and after them, the Ambassadors and the rest.*

## Scene 4

*A hall in the castle in Gniezno. To the rear, a throne. At its foot, the Chancellor stands. Lords of the land. The chronicler Wawel. Page, Count, Judges.*

**CHANCELLOR**
All is made ready for the lord's arrival.
Come, take your seats now, at the appointed benches —
The leaders and the judges near the throne;

The ministers of grain, the cupbearers —
Now, all together, let's greet our new king.

*Enter Envoy.*

ENVOY
Your graces, I come with important news.
Our king, our new lord — is a woman.

CHANCELLOR
                              A woman!

ALL
A woman king!

CHANCELLOR
            Well, let her be a brave one,
As Wanda was... and let her be so good,
But happier...

*Enter Second Envoy.*

SECOND ENVOY
                Your grace, lord officers,
The queen is now within the city gates.

CHANCELLOR
Have all the bells in all the towers rung,
All through the day, as do her people's hearts.

FIRST NOBLE
No seer might explain the miracle
Revealed unto the nation on this day.
The people are unsettled.

CHANCELLOR
                    Why? What's happened?

FIRST NOBLE
It's beyond words. But if you wish, I'll try
To tell the tale — and let our noble scribe
Indite my words into his chronicle.

CHANCELLOR
Wise Wawel, have you seen this wonder too?

WAWEL
What many have seen, this I might describe
As an eyewitness. Today, at dawning,
The sky was dark on both sides of the heavens,
Which brightened towards the east. And as I saw —
Or heard — from one end of the sky, Orion's
Quarter, came flying a long key of cranes,
And, in the rear, holding on with white arms,
A misty woman flew along with them.

CHANCELLOR
You saw all this with your own eyes, sage Wawel?

WAWEL
I didn't see it myself, but many did,
And on their guarantee I do affirm it.

PAGE
I saw the girl who flew behind the cranes
From the direction of Lake Gopło.
She fell upon the last bird in the key,
Her arms around its neck, her yellow curls
Spilling towards the earth, shining like gold
In the new sunlight. Thus, prone, she flew on.

CHANCELLOR
It needs a child's eye to paint such wonders,
Upon the cloudy canvas of the sky.

*It grows dark, as before a storm.*

FIRST NOBLE
What's this? A gloomy darkness falls upon
The throne, and on our faces — like an eclipse...
Pale, in the greenish light, we'll greet our queen.

SEVERAL
An eerie darkness.

*Enter the Tower Guard.*

GUARD
                    O'er the copper roof
Of the royal palace, where the gilded spire
Shoots heavenward, an angry cloud is hanging,
Surrounded by a black garland of mists —
And ever thicker does it grow, and lower
About the porch, where the musicians wait.
But all the sky elsewhere is blue and clear —
It's like all of the clouds were gathered here
That might be found through the expanse of heaven.

CHANCELLOR
Have the bells ring.

GUARD
            Its bosom is dark purple,
Livid, fiery.

CHANCELLOR
            We need rain; let it come.

GUARD
And then a pale hag in a sable wagon
Drawn by a team of hellish cranes, harnessed
With snakes did cleave the air to rise within
The cloud above the castle, while those cranes
Sounded a fearful moaning — can you hear?

*Moans from the tower.*

CHANCELLOR
Indeed, I hear an unfamiliar moan!

NOBLES
*Rising quickly from their benches.*
How frightful!

CHANCELLOR
No! Rise not! Resume your seats!
And you, guard, must be drunk. A witch, you say?

GUARD
I saw it, as did the surrounding people,
The folk of Gniezno...

CRIES
*Offstage.*
Long live the queen!

*Enter Balladyna in royal robes, crowned. Kostryn, in armour, follows, as do the People.*

CHANCELLOR
Madame, the brow that bears the crown of Popiel,
Returning it to us, must be anointed!
Greetings! Rule thou in wisdom, generous,
Leading thy people with God's aid unto
The greatest deeds. Wrap thou around thy hips
The robe of purity, and raise thy brow
Unto the heavens; be thou merciful
And deign to rule thy people in righteousness.

BALLADYNA
*From the throne.*
What must I do now?

CHANCELLOR
Such is our custom
From ancient times, such our zeal for the law,
That, before the king sit down to his first meal
Or rest his tired head upon a pillow

(So great the crown's weight that he bears by day),
He must seat himself at the judgement bench
And hear the criminal cases.

BALLADYNA
                Let it be
According to your custom.

*Kostryn totters and falls.*

FIRST NOBLE
                What is this?
The leader pales, and falls?

BALLADYNA
*Approaching Kostryn on the ground.*
                What does this mean?
You're ill?

KOSTRYN
    I'm dying.

BALLADYNA
            O, my dear! My God!

KOSTRYN
No! Begone, you witch! You poisoner!
Keep her from your throne! I am the first
To broach the iron doors of the tomb
Where many thousands soon shall follow me,
Her subjects in misfortune...

BALLADYNA
                He's raving...
Carry him out! Out! His body grows cold —
Call a physician! He who shaves him shall
Take half my kingdom as his fee —

DOCTOR
                He's dead.

*Kostryn is borne out, the Doctor following.*

CHANCELLOR
Madame, be patient at this heavy loss.
It's God that warns you, as you mount your throne:
Death stands attendance here, invisible.
The same waits on us all.

BALLADYNA
*Aside.*
                                  What's past is passed,
Buried, entombed... the secret now is mine
Alone!
*Aloud.*
           Now let those taken in the wars
Be freed — Strike off their fetters, and bedeck
The streets and squares with tables piled with cheer,
That Gniezno's beggars too may eat their full.

CHANCELLOR
A grateful people thank your majesty.
Glory to you!

BALLADYNA
                It's not glory I seek,
Though I am raised above the common law,
I shall be now as I would have been, had
I been conceived beneath another star.
A life that's filled with labour has been split
In two halves by the crown. My past age falls
Away as viper's venom from a blade
Half smeared therewith — when it divides an apple,
One half remains whole, healthy, while the other
Blackens and rots. None of you knew me such
As I have been — let not my people seek
To delve into my history. You know
What I have told you. For the rest, the priest
Who shall absolve me of my sins shall hear,
And no one else. Aha, there's one more thing.
Go search among the dead Count Kirkor's body.
He lies upon that hillock where white birches

Slashed by his axe-strokes stand — Go, take a bier
Covered in silk, and bring to me the corpse
Of Kirkor slumbering. And let the thousands
Weep at the bier of him, my enemy,
Who was at one time very dear to me;
Who was my husband. Yes, in verity,
I am the widowed countess. All the same,
I'll have no poems written, no songs sung
Among the simple folk upon this theme —
What the queen was to reveal, so she has;
The rest is but for my confessor's ear.
Now, chancellor, summon near your criminals.
I take my seat upon the judge's bench.
If I should render verdict false, may I
Become a nest of vermin yet in life!
Let fire consume me! I shall not be swayed
By smile or threat, nor shall I be led false
By people or by demons. Thus I swear
Myself, here in the eyes of God. I shall
Deal righteously.

CHANCELLOR
          Bailiff!

BAILIFF
                Hear ye, hear ye.
The court is now in session, her majesty
The queen presiding.

CHANCELLOR
                Behold the book of law —
Behold our Saviour stretched upon the Cross.
Kiss book and Crucifix.

BAILIFF
                Who brings a charge?

*The royal Doctor rises.*

CHANCELLOR
You are?

DOCTOR
 I am the royal physician.

CHANCELLOR
What charge bring you?

DOCTOR
    A case of poisoning.

CHANCELLOR
Who is the victim?

DOCTOR
    Kostryn, the leader
Of your armed hosts, O queen most merciful.
Kostryn died murdered, murdered by poison —
A great knight foully felled by crafty venom.
His skin took on an iron colour, mottled
With myriad stains — and all this points to poison.

CHANCELLOR
Whom do you suspect?

DOCTOR
    It is not my place
To search out suspects; that's the task of courts.

BALLADYNA
An unknown criminal? Let's set aside
This matter for a later time. We'll give
The poisoner some time for penitence.

CHANCELLOR
The custom of the land, your royal highness,
Is to announce a verdict, even when
The criminal's unknown. The sentence then
Is held in abeyance until such time
As said criminal is apprehended,
And offers up his throat.

BALLADYNA
                    And yet there be
Such criminals as can't be judged by laws
Made for the common people — the anointed,
For one example, are untouchable.

CHANCELLOR
Such God Himself will punish. All the same,
An earthly sentence must be passed on them,
In accordance with our conscience.

BALLADYNA
And the law? What provision does it make?

CHANCELLOR
Should knight or nobleman deprive of life
A person of rank equal to his own,
By bitter poison, he shall have his head
Struck off by the hangman. If whom he killed
Be base-born...

BALLADYNA
                    Yes! Enough!

CHANCELLOR
                    Your verdict, Ma'am?
And may the dictate of your conscience weigh
More than the letter of the law.

BALLADYNA
                    Enough!
The poisoner must lose his head!

CHANCELLOR
                    Bailiff,
Have the queen's verdict sounded far and wide.
And what the vengeful executioner's
Unable to perform, we leave to God!

*Trumpets.*

And now let him approach who has a charge
To be decided at this court of law.

*Enter Filon, dressed in flowers, bearing a knife and a jar of raspberries.*

You are?

FILON
      A shadow of the man I was.
O, sadness!
Sorrow bereaves me of my memory
By keeping my eyes fixed upon the past.
Like blossoms flounced upon a streamlet's waves
They find their happiness in bobbing over
The azure waves — So I, wave-beaten too
By currents strong of sorrow, but in tears
And sleeplessness find I any relief.

CHANCELLOR
Such charges are not covered by the law.
Speak plainly!

FILON
      Then behold this berry-jar
And this sharp knife. I found the raspberries
Beneath the head of a murdered girl;
The knife was in her bosom. Let this jar
With new tears of Eurotas overflow,
To bear the sorrowing lover on its stream
To where his best beloved lies entombed —
And I shall tell him: "O, you wandering stream,
You have my everlasting gratitude
For dredging both of us a common grave
Where we shall taste of rest and calm, deep seas...
Forgive, Apollo! Thou radiant god!
That I have come to shed these tears in public
And break my sorrow with men, as if bread.
I come to sing to people's ears a song
Of sadness, as Orpheus in Erebus,
To beg of Pluto a fair wife's return."
Listen you all — she was my wife indeed,

Wife of my soul; today a lonely grave
Covers her snowy limbs made bloody by
This knife — behold! Here on this jar
I found her dead, one fine morning in spring,
Killed with this knife!

CHANCELLOR
                     I smell a crime
In all this doggerel.

BALLADYNA
                Chancellor, disdain
Is all I feel for such a lunatic speech.

CHANCELLOR
Your majesty, the law must follow through
On its examinations to the end.
We mustn't hold this sad man in contempt,
As if he were a stray dog howling; So,
Shepherd, you say your wife was murdered?
You found her body, stabbed with this knife? When?

FILON
Three times the moon hath paled, three times the stars
Did fade before Apollo.

CHANCELLOR
                  Have you any
That you suspect of this bloody murder?

FILON
Ah, ah, the Parcae! Yes, hard-hearted fates —
'Twas they snipped clean the silver thread in twain
That was her lifeline; it might also be
Some golden star in Heaven grown envious
Of how my lover shone, her eyes, her eyes...
And had their flames extinguished forever.

CHANCELLOR
Where did you find her?

FILON
                    In the dreamy woods,
Beneath a weeping willow tree's cool shade;
'Twas there she fell into this iron sleep.

CHANCELLOR
A complicated case... Your majesty,
Pronounce the verdict on the unknown killer —
Be ruled by your conscience.

BALLADYNA
                    What says the law?

CHANCELLOR
Death calls for death.

BALLADYNA
                    And hears no answer back.
We have the victims, but no murderers...

CHANCELLOR
And yet the verdict must be passed!

BALLADYNA
                    Death, then!
To death she must be sentenced.

CHANCELLOR
                    She, your highness?
You reckon that the murderer is a woman?

BALLADYNA
I reckon what I reckon.

CHANCELLOR
                    Bailiff —
Have the queen's verdict sounded far and wide,
And what the vengeful executioner's
Unable to perform, we leave to God!

*Trumpets.*

And now let him approach who has a charge
To be decided at this court of law.

*Enter the blind Widow, Balladyna's mother.*

You are?

WIDOW
    A widow.

CHANCELLOR
              And you bring a charge
Against whom?

WIDOW
              Against my children, Excellencies.
I'm told the queen's as pretty as an angel —
So let her judge as heaven's angel would.
I had two daughters, I a poor old widow;
I nourished both into their maidenhoods.
How often errs the man who seeks his joy
Upon the earth! The younger of the two
Ran off one day from her old mother's cottage,
The bad girl! But the other, O dear Lord!
My queen, you, pretty as an angel,
Judge you my case! The second was the wife
Of a grand Count — strike me dead if I lie!
A count took her to wife! Your majesty,
God grant the crown entrusted to your brows
Cover a head He shall preserve in wisdom
For all times! Judge my case! This other girl
Had reason as a poppy, poppyseed.
The count, he loved her dearly, but her mother,
Her mother — me — loved her as mothers love!
But in her castle, all her servants sneered
At poor old me, ah, but I suffered it;
In patience did I suffer. Near the grave,
I bore it ... Then one night, this daughter — tfu!
Denied me to my face, in front of guests!
Saying I'm not her mother! "Daughter mine,"
I cried, "have mercy on your mother! Old,

So near the grave..." It was a horrid night —
Thunder and lightning, rain a-pouring down;
And what did she do, but throw me outside,
Her old mother! Into the wind and rain,
The night and lightning strikes, the storm... and hungry!
Starving I was, and she chucked me outside,
May the lord forgive her — hungry and cold!
Into the woods! The wind tore at my rags,
The lightning burnt my eyes out. O, my king,
My darling golden sire, have mercy, lord!

CHANCELLOR
Madame, you're silent? Such a great injustice
Must be avenged, and strictly, by our law.

BALLADYNA
But not by death?

CHANCELLOR
              The Polish law allows
Such penalty for ungrateful children.
Let the book of laws enlighten you.
Read it... and read what your conscience decrees.
And you, old woman, name that wicked child,
Unnatural, and our hangman will see
Her punished, even if she be the first
Countess in all the land by virtue of
Her marriage to her count. Such was her fate
To rise so high; her fate is now to fall.
What is the count's name? And that of your daughter?
The law will pierce even their castle walls.

WIDOW
What? Death to my daughter? Sir, have you gone mad?
Farewell, queen. I return now to my woods
To live on dew...

CHANCELLOR
              According to the law,
He who advances a charge in public court
May not withdraw it. Come, what are their names?

WIDOW
No! No!

CHANCELLOR
Take her to the dungeon,
And have her joints bound fast in iron pincers.
Well then, old mother? Come, tell us their names.

WIDOW
I won't, sir.

CHANCELLOR
One more time I ask the name
Of your unnatural daughter.

WIDOW
No... she's innocent.

CHANCELLOR
Put her to torture.

WIDOW
*Pushing past the guard.*
Please, your majesty!
Have mercy on an old woman! I might
Be your own mother! God! You say nothing?
Nothing? That's not a queen upon that throne,
A ghost, rather! All right, I'll lay me down
Upon that iron bed, and there I'll die.
May God in Heaven forgive you all.

CHANCELLOR
You'll speak,
When it begins to hurt.

WIDOW
Your excellency!
You too have a hard heart!

*Goes off, with guards.*

CHANCELLOR
>Such is the law,
And thus I follow it, to the very letter.
The Lord Himself will judge me right, or wrong.
But you, dread monarch, know — I have a heart
Brimming with tears and bitterness, and horror.

*Moans.*

What is that?

SOLDIER
>The old woman cries in pain.

CHANCELLOR
And she said nothing?

SOLDIER
>Nothing.

CHANCELLOR
>Let us wait.

BALLADYNA
It is my very heart the hangman pulls
And stretches on the rack... Give me some water!

*They do, she drinks.*

SOLDIER
She's taken from the rack.

BALLADYNA
>So soon? Did she
Say anything?

SOLDIER
>She's dead.

BALLADYNA
>She's dead, you say?

SOLDIER
When she was laid out on the bed of torture,
Hands and feet shackled to the iron pincers,
She opened wide her eyes... To look at her,
One might grow pious, for indeed she seemed
A tortured Christ, expired.
Each bone, withered and dry when stretched
Upon the rack, seemed through her tightened skin
To beg for mercy of its own accord.

CHANCELLOR
        And yet
She said nothing?

SOLDIER
     She died without a word.
But on her desiccated face, within the sockets
Of her skeletal eyes, there were two tears.
That's all she gave up.

BALLADYNA
        Since the morning
I've sat in judgement. Never toiled a slave
As long and noisomely as I. My lords,
The night has fallen.

CHANCELLOR
      No ma'am, that's a cloud
That's hung over the palace for some time.
Search out your conscience, say: what is she worth
Who so torments the dam that gave her birth?

BALLADYNA
Judge her yourselves.

CHANCELLOR
       Endow your shining crown
With splendours new by speaking righteously:
She should be sentenced to a stake of fire
To be transformed into a coal from Hell
While yet alive. Your verdict?

ALL
                        Judge her, ma'am!

CHANCELLOR
By the immortal God above us, she,
If anyone, deserves a verdict!

ALL
                        Death!
Draw her, and quarter her!

CHANCELLOR
                        Madame, you judge her.
Search your conscience.

BALLADYNA
*After a long silence.*
                        She is
Condemned to death.

*A bolt of lightning falls and kills the queen. Everyone is terrified.*

CHANCELLOR
The woman-king was shot through by God's fire —
The bells will peal not for coronation,
They'll toll now for a royal funeral!

THE END

## EPILOGUE

PUBLIC
*Calling.*
Wawel! Hey, where's the chronicler! Hey, Wawel!

WAWEL
My gracious public — here you have the notes
I've drawn up to be fleshed out on the pages
Of the royal chronicle. Now please, my friends,
You've interrupted me...

PUBLIC
      Whose side you on?

WAWEL
I am both judge impartial, and eyewitness.

PUBLIC
But how will you describe the lightning strike?
Tell us! We saw the whole thing, start to finish.

WAWEL
A grain of sand contains whole galaxies;
The humblest things narrate great mysteries.
The queen ruled wisely, like King Solomon,
She was wise; there is virtue in wisdom.

PUBLIC
Wawel, your summation's a risky thing;
What would you say had you watched from the wings?

WAWEL
I was tasked with composing threnodies
For Popiel's funeral.

PUBLIC
                But what of the queen?
Where did she come from?

WAWEL
              I'm a historian;
From my perspective, she is of that clan
Who eat no flesh. Their name: the Abodrites.
One noted scholar — but he's far from right —
Called her an Amazon, but, people, hear me:
I've otherwhere extirpated his theory;
He lies now in his tomb, and lie he will,
Fixed fast, his heart shot quite through by my quill.

PUBLIC
What of that lightning bolt?

WAWEL
                    When there's a storm,
You ought to have all the city bells sound;
And laurel wreaths are better far than crowns.
Around the laurel, lightning doesn't swarm.

PUBLIC
You're sure of this?

WAWEL
              He, who struts laureate
(The author of this play) will plainly state
That since he's worn laurel instead of hat, or
Coronet, he fears no lightning bolt.

PUBLIC
O Wawel, sage Wawel, how you cringe and flatter
Both kings and poets! Off the stage, you dolt!

                END OF EPILOGUE

# HORSZTYŃSKI

*a play in five acts*[*]

PERSONS:

Ksawery Horsztyński, *former Confederacy of Bar conspirator*
Salomea Horsztyńska, *Horsztyński's wife*
Świętosz, *a servant in the Horsztyński household*
Father Procopius, *a Capuchin*
Szymon Kossakowski, *Hetman of Lithuania*
Felix Kossakowski, *Szymon's son*
Michał Kossakowski, *Szymon's son*
Amelia Kossakowska, *Szymon's daughter*
Ksiński, *Nobleman at Kossakowski's court*
Dwarf, *Clown at Kossakowski's court*
Sforka, *Old servant at Kossakowski's court*
Małgorzata, *Sforka's wife*
Servant
Hajduk (Peasant infantryman)
Stranger
Skowicz
Garnosz, *Trumpeter*

*The action is set in Lithuania, in the year 1794.*

---

[*]  *Horsztyński* was left unfinished by Słowacki, and printed in its inchoate form by Eugeniusz Sawrymowicz in his edition of the *Selected Works*. Our translation is based on that received text. However, to aid the narrative flow, we have translated the additional scenes included by Juliusz Mien for production in Kraków toward the end of the nineteenth century, and printed there in 1883. These additions are indicated by [[double brackets]]. I believe that, given the generally graceful and intuitive (if sometimes overpious) nature of Mien's work, the reading experience of the play as drama has been enhanced. The reader who prefers to read only Słowacki's words may do so by omitting all text in double brackets. In scene 1 of act III, [single brackets] indicate lacunae in the manuscript, and were placed there by Sawrymowicz.

424 JULIUSZ SŁOWACKI

# ACT I

### Scene 1
*The Hetman's palace, in the countryside.*

FELIX
The songs of this world begin out of tune — and end with a violent tearing of the strings, the smashing of the harp...

AMELIA
You're melancholic... you've become strange...

FELIX
I'm bored...

AMELIA
So seek diversions...

FELIX
Oh... one needn't look too far... My father's rustled me up ten revolutionary harlequins, surrounding me with mercenary jokers... and sometimes, it's true, I laugh so childishly hard that I think my sides will split, having looped a single string around the limbs of these cardboard figures so that, when it's pulled, it sets the whole pack of freeloading dogs twitching and leaping...

AMELIA
Father is unable to comprehend the sudden change in your character, and for this reason he's trying everything he can to arouse you from torpidity; to tear you from it and set you in an elevated position amongst men...

FELIX
Father has an elevated sense of fatherly respect for me...

AMELIA
What do you mean?...

FELIX
He values me as a Dutchman does a rare sort of tulip... He respects me as that rare person whom he does not pay — but who must love him anyway.

AMELIA
By that reasoning I should be a still dearer person to father, for he does not love me, and I pay him back with love. It seems that this my love of father is the sum of all my feelings... Is it not true, Felix, that he is a good man, a great man?...

FELIX
Yes... a hetman... a great one, as a hetman...

AMELIA
Just think, my brother — he is the one support of the crumbling throne of Stanisław August...

FELIX
Yes, he supports Stanisław's throne...

AMELIA
How strange, the echo in your mouth...

FELIX
Three times only it repeats your praise, but at the praise and adoration of strangers, it responds not...

AMELIA
Why?

FELIX
It's funny when a son praises his father.... Once when I praised father in public, he immediately paid me back... with a Turkish steed...

AMELIA
What was it you said to the people about father?

FELIX
What?... I said this, that he is better than his brother — our uncle, the bishop... for he does not dress in violet cloth —

AMELIA
Stop it, stop! ... You're bitter — and you're insulting the pure, virgin faith of your sister... And so the poor man is that unfortunate, that he can find no true feeling of love, no equitable judgement in the heart of his son? ... Look at the grey heads of the old men who bow before him — look at the orders of merit that shine on his chest... and then have a glance at your loneliness — your passivity...

FELIX
I am nothing...

AMELIA
Why don't you try to be useful?

FELIX
I can't — I can't... I don't want to...

AMELIA
You're keeping something secret... perhaps it's love...

FELIX
Perhaps it's love...

AMELIA
Confide in me, dear brother — Tell me everything! ... Ah, how happy she must be, the girl that you love... I bet you never answer her with bitter irony... With her, you must be elevated, beautiful. I know your soul; I know its deepest feelings and secrets... If I were not your sister, I would needs become your intended... or ... a nun.

FELIX
What were you saying? ... I'm so distracted, I didn't hear a single word... It's late now... The blue bindweeds of your chaplet are opening to the moonlight... Go, sister, and read the Bible, you devoted soul, you...*

---

\* Słowacki uses the word świętoszka here, which also has the meaning of "hypocrite." This meaning is either not intended, or Amelia does not take offence at it, as can be seen from her reply.

AMELIA
Good night, then! ... But first call here little Michał, your brother. I have to dress him for bed, and help him say his prayers. Don't I deserve a kiss for teaching your little brother to pray for you?...

FELIX
You do well to send your prayers aloft through the lips of a child. Blessed are the little ones...

AMELIA
So you won't give me a kiss, brother?

FELIX
No.

AMELIA
Good night!
*She exits, sadly.*

FELIX
How brightly lit, the right wing of the palace — Father is feasting his toadies. He pays them for laughter and jokes, for jokes and laughter have become rare commodities in Poland. O sadness! Sadness! From time to time a lightning bolt will reveal to me the nothingness of everything, sometimes even the nothingness of the thought that dreams of nothingness... Sometimes it seems that an apish grovelling grin is a small price to pay for the world...

MICHAŁ
*Runs in.*
Ha, ha, ha! Brother!

FELIX
What are you laughing at, boy?

MICHAŁ
I had a look inside the banquet hall through the keyhole... Daddy is sitting there with a feather of diamonds, as beautiful as the Lord God in the missal...

FELIX
What happened to your nurse?

MICHAŁ
She's in the kitchen, and I am as free as a bird...

FELIX
Amelka is waiting for you. Go say your prayers.

MICHAŁ
But listen first, brother, to what I saw... Our papa filled up a great glass snifter and cried out: "Here's to our Kasia!" Now, when he cried out "Here's to our Kasia,"* everybody jumped to their feet as stiff as candles, while one old man, as white as a dove, who was sitting at the end of the table, didn't get up... Daddy went over and gave him a wallop... Pow!... and the old man tumbled over like a wooden doll...

FELIX
The horror! The horror!
*He starts, as if to run out of the room.*
Michasiu!... If your mother were alive, she'd shed hot tears for you... and give you a wallop herself...

MICHAŁ
For what?

FELIX
Get to your sister, boy, now! What you saw through the keyhole was... a picture, just like...

MICHAŁ
So why were the people moving?

FELIX
I tell you, Daddy is asleep... that was a picture... Go and don't say anything to Amelka, because she'll laugh at you for being fooled by a painting. Give her a kiss on her forehead...
*He pushes him towards Amelia's room.*
Oh, these walls — a real Sodom! To strike an old man for not drinking

---

\* Catherine the Great, Empress of Russia.

the health of a northern whore... And if I were to mark my father with a sign... Hush!... First of all, that old man needs help...

KSIŃSKI
*Enters.*
Your father wants you at the feast.

FELIX
And the old man? What happened to the old man? Ksiński, go, tell the old man my father insulted to come see me here. I'll give him a sabre*... and revenge.

KSIŃSKI
Revenge... against your father?

FELIX
The son will stand in for the father. Tell him: I will make myself as old as he... my hand will shake with an old man's palsy... tell him that... Go, tell him that if he has children, he need not worry about them...

KSIŃSKI
Give me your hand...

FELIX
What? Do you think I'm playacting?

KSIŃSKI
No! Be at peace as far as that old man is concerned. As soon as your father struck him, he fell beneath the table — and then suddenly jumped to his feet and, with a red face...

FELIX
What? ... Hacked...? Cut him down, my...

KSIŃSKI
No! No! Bowed low to him, and said: "I humbly thank my illustrious lord, the Hetman, for waking me from my drowse."

---

\*    *Karabela.* A curved, scimitar-like sword popular in the Polish-Lithuanian Commonwealth.

FELIX
Ha! He said that? ... Did they all laugh?

KSIŃSKI
They laughed like lunatics...

FELIX
And you?

KSIŃSKI
I figured that he had been reading the Gospel... and falling asleep, dreamt that he was St. Peter...

FELIX
Return to the feast... and drink for both of us...

KSIŃSKI
So you won't come? What am I to tell your father?

FELIX
Nothing — Tell him... that you didn't find me.

KSIŃSKI
Felix! Think this over. Why is the wakening of that old man such a big deal to you?

FELIX
For God's sake, Ksiński, stop reminding me of that! Tell my father whatever you wish. You're right, after all — the old man was asleep — I swear to you that he was asleep, as we all of us are asleep... Good night, Ksiński.
*Exits.*

KSIŃSKI
He mocks me to my face. How did he find out about that incident? Nobody was here before me... That young fellow is like a white raven in this house. I thought for a moment that he wanted to raise his sword against his father...
*Falls to musing.*

DWARF
*Peeking in through the door, curiously.*
MrKsiński!!

KSIŃSKI
Ah, it's you! What do you want, buffoon?

DWARF
How come so glum? Sick with philosophising?

KSIŃSKI
And if I am?

DWARF
Well, what do you know! Ksiński turns philosopher! That's all we needed. So, what are you dreaming about there, you lover of wisdom?

KSIŃSKI
That's none of your concern, pint-barrel...

DWARF
At least for once in my life I'd like to believe that you were able to think, Mr Ksiński!

KSIŃSKI
Ah! Such a long tongue for such a little chap!

DWARF
So, cover your Midas ears and be well!

KSIŃSKI
A little respect there!

DWARF
Tell me, Mr Ksiński, where have you been so long? I mean, you only arrived yesterday, and the rumours have been flying. Some say that you were in Italy, others, that you were up north, to observe the stars... As for me, I think that they put you out to pasture...

KSIŃSKI
Clown, I'll whip you!

DWARF
Whip away, but listen. Take my advice, and if you do what I tell you, a star will appear on your uniform lapel, or maybe even a chamberlain's keys will rattle in your pocket. You're returning from Milan, Mr Ksiński... Listen... You shall be a deputy from Milan...

KSIŃSKI
What sort of crazy idea — Who are you playing a joke on this time?

DWARF
Be calm, be calm, Mr Ksiński. It's not on you. You know Sforka?

KSIŃSKI
The Hetman's steward?

DWARF
The very one, Mr Ksiński. *He takes a paper out of his pocket.* Like many people... *He glances knowingly at Ksiński.* ...Sforka's just dying to clamber his way to nobility. Somebody's put it into his head that he's not a Sforka at all, but a Sfortia.

KSIŃSKI
So what?

DWARF
Just wait. Not long ago, a letter came to him announcing the arrival of a dignitary from Italy...

KSIŃSKI
Enough of your nonsense already!

DWARF
I've sense enough if you'd the sense to see it! The letter was forged, of course...

KSIŃSKI
And...?

DWARF
Don't interrupt! This dignitary is supposed to bring him some important papers, in which the future fortune of Sforka is contained.

KSIŃSKI
And the deputy...?

DWARF
*Handing him the papers.*
Is you, Mr Ksiński. You will be the deputy... It's not a bad role at all. But don't worry, I'll rehearse you well...

KSIŃSKI
Forget it, clown!

DWARF
You don't want to? Well then, farewell, Mr Ksiński. You're the one losing out. More than you imagine.
*He pretends to go out.*

KSIŃSKI
*Shrugs.*
You're talking rubbish, pint-barrel. It's an awkward joke. Sforka would recognise me from the start. But I have something more important to speak with you about.

DWARF
There'll time for that later!
We'll trick you out like a zebra, Mr. Ksiński... He'll swallow the devil himself before he discovers that you're Ksiński. He never saw you in galloons, and always took you for Christ's own mule...

KSIŃSKI
I'll give you such a swat, you dog!

DWARF
I shall be swatted, then, and you, Mr Ksiński, will be the deputy from Milan. But, listen — if Mr Sforka invites you to dinner, eat nothing but salad. Because Mr Sforka is convinced that Italians eat nothing but leaves...

KSIŃSKI
Tell me what you've learnt about Felix's behaviour, dwarf, and maybe you'll be better rewarded for your tongue.

DWARF
I've learnt that Master Felix is in love...

KSIŃSKI
With whom?

DWARF
Well, since returning from Warsaw, Master Felix's taken to spending whole days in a boat, floating around the pond, gaping up at the sky. Now, once day, a couple of white swans chanced to land at the pond — Mr Sforka... confiscated them, as belonging to Mr Horsztyński, from the neighbouring village, with whom the Hetman is at odds, financially speaking... But then Madame Horsztyńska drove up in a buggy, and at her mere request Master Felix handed the swans over to her. And they talked and talked about swans so, that... that...

KSIŃSKI
Who is this Horsztyński?

DWARF
An old conspirator — of the Bar Confederation. He fell into Drevitsch's hands and the Muscovites took him to church...

KSIŃSKI
To church?

DWARF
...Where they held him down on his back, crosswise, and dropped molten wax from burning candles on his eyes. He doesn't need his glasses anymore...

KSIŃSKI
And on top of that, Master Felix's fixed him the sort of horns that even sighted husbands can't see in the mirror? Is that how it is? Horsztyński has a young wife? She must be...

DWARF
She was a girl from a poor family, raised by nuns. Her mother lost her mind — they found her one day, drowned in a muddy ditch... It was a doctor foretold that Miss Salomea — that's her name — inherited a genetic disposition to melancholy, and that's why — she being a

young maiden with a time-bomb of insanity ticking away inside her for a dowry — she couldn't expect a young husband. Or a rich one, either. Mr. Horsztyński, neither young nor rich, made his proposal... And today... maybe he's sorrier for having slipped that ring on her finger than he is for the wax they dripped on his eyes... But I reckon he doesn't know anything about what his wife is up to, because Master Felix's a discreet fellow in such matters.

KSIŃSKI
So tell me, my little barrel of Dutch herring, what possible concern is it to the Hetman, that his son has sent spinning the head of a blind man's wife?

DWARF
First, Mr Ksiński, kindly acknowledge the fact that I've got more brains than you.

KSIŃSKI
Such a "fact" has hardly ever been proven!

DWARF
And yet you are not completely devoid of common sense... You will admit at the very least that you seek out reason, wherever it might be found?

KSIŃSKI
And you've arrived at that conclusion...?

DWARF
At dinner yesterday. For when the ortolans were served, I saw you take particular care to sop up the cervelles...

KSIŃSKI
As God is my witness, the dwarf is mocking me!

DWARF
Shame, Mr. Ksiński! How dare you even suppose such a thing!

KSIŃSKI
Remember who you are dealing with!

DWARF
I do, and I quake — For when you stretch yourself so to your full height, you look just like the jack of clubs!

KSIŃSKI
You dwarf!... You midget!... You little ball of...

*The dwarf runs off, as does Ksiński, giving chase.*

### Scene 2
*An unostentatious, but nobly appointed room in Horsztyński's house.*

HORSTYŃSKI
And so you say that my plot of young fruit trees is maturing nicely?

FR PROCOPIUS
The rennet apples and grey butter pears are already in bloom.

HORSTYŃSKI
When the autumn comes round, Father, we'll share some red apples.

FR PROCOPIUS
If God grant us life.

HORSTYŃSKI
Right. If only God grant us to live that long! — Did you by any chance see my Salusia?

FR PROCOPIUS
I did see your wife, walking alone along the alley of lindens.

HORSTYŃSKI
Father, I haven't seen her angelic face since I lost my eyes. Is she still as beautiful as I remember her?

FR PROCOPIUS
So she seems to me — always beautiful.

HORSTYŃSKI
But not as gay as she once was...

FR PROCOPIUS
More or less, she's always gay enough... Would you like me to read you a chapter of the *Janissary's Memoirs*, Mr Horsztyński?

HORSTYŃSKI
No, thank you, Father. It's late now. Listen... It seems to me that my wife is not as carefree as she once was...

*Long moment of silence.*

FR PROCOPIUS
They say that there's a good deal of unease among the people of Vilnius. The pot's about to boil over again.

HORSTYŃSKI
I don't want to hear anything about that, Father...

FR PROCOPIUS
But if Vilnius rebelled, as well?

HORSTYŃSKI
Then they'll burn their eyes out with hot wax, too!

FR PROCOPIUS
But maybe they'd pull it off this time, after all...

HORSTYŃSKI
Father — you, who don't expect pears and apples from my nursery trees in the fall, are looking for fruit on rotten branches... Listen — is that someone riding up on horseback I hear?

FR PROCOPIUS
It's the young count.

HORSTYŃSKI
Good. We'll have a nice chat, then.

FR PROCOPIUS
You like that young man...

**HORSTYŃSKI**
His voice reminds me of... I'll tell you later, Father, why I like the sound of Felix's voice... I want to receive Communion tomorrow...

**FR PROCOPIUS**
That youngster is a great, but as yet still unfinished, work of Providence.

**FELIX**
*Enters.*
Greetings, Mr Horsztyński! And how are you, Father Procopius?

**HORSTYŃSKI**
Take a seat, my Eulenspiegel... Well, what news do you bring me today?

**FELIX**
News? I have none...

**HORSTYŃSKI**
Tell me, how is it possible to live in this world knowing nothing about anything?

**FELIX**
That's just as if I asked you how is it possible to live in this world without seeing anything.

**FR PROCOPIUS**
Young man, it's not right to remind a man of his disability.

**FELIX**
I do so only through envy.

**HORSTYŃSKI**
See, Father? At least someone in this world still envies me...

**FELIX**
He, who had his eyes burnt out by candles — eyes the size of reason, the eyes of hope... He stumbles about the region of thought like a blind man... You must have beautiful memories, lit up by the sunlight, Mr Horsztyński.

HORSTYŃSKI
Yes. I have pleasant memories... Once, in the area around Bar — on a great open plain there — we drew up against the troops of Drevitsch. Oh, it was a beautiful morning, so still... No sound but the larks singing... To our right was a birch wood, and behind us...

*Salomea enters and stands there noiselessly. Felix is listening to the old man, with his hands covering his eyes.*

HORSTYŃSKI
...My dear sirs, behind us was a village, with copper spires... I commanded the entire cavalry... "Forward! Forward!" And at that moment it crossed my mind, "I wonder what my wife is doing, just now?" I glanced at the hour, for I still had my eyesight. My watch said five o'clock. Ha! She's still sleeping, my wife, as sweetly as a child, and she has no idea that here, her old husband, just like a young boy, his hair spread to the wind and his sabre upraised in his hand, is crying out "Forward! Forward!..." I thought I'd die that day, and that my wife would be sleeping on through the hour of my death, sweetly, at the hour of my death... It was both a sad thought, and a sweet one... Ha, ha! And moreover, at that moment, I had the strangest desire: I wished that I had one of the white pigeons from my village there with me... No, that's not right... This was after the victorious battle, while I was resting in the birch wood; it was then that it came upon me, that strange desire, for a pigeon, so that I could scrawl a message in pencil and send it to my wife by that pigeon, a note with just "Your lips, my Sally!..." Ah, my dear sirs, that morning, we'd beat two whole *bataillons carrés* to a pulp!

FELIX
I must bid you farewell now, Mr Horsztyński. For I just remembered that there are two *bataillons carrés* of friends awaiting me at home with champagne.

*Felix rises and sees Salomea.*
FELIX
Ha!... Madame...

HORSTYŃSKI
What? My wife? Was she listening all this while? How silently you entered, my Salusia... You've probably had a good laugh at your big mouthed husband, with that talk of sending you a pigeon...

FR PROCOPIUS
How pale she's gone...

SALOMEA
You never told me about that, my... husband...

HORSTYŃSKI
When? When could I... Listen, because these memories can't remain locked in my heart forever, either... When they took me prisoner... in the evening, it was evening... two Muscovites led me to the chapel. The chapel, I remember, was in a cemetery, and the cemetery was all shaded with lindens... In the cemetery... Ah, horrible!... Twenty of my men, buried up to their necks, and the Muscovites — hacked at their heads with scythes! Now and then, when a head was lopped off, it would roll to my feet... One of them gazed up at me — I swear it — the eyes, looking me right in the face...! And then by a huge linden tree I caught sight of a fellow in white, bound... naked, old — on his naked shoulders they'd carved epaulettes — on his flesh! They carved a hussar's epaulettes! He looked at me and said, "Bid me farewell, sir, Mr Horsztyński..." I made him no answer... May God punish me at the hour of my death for not responding to that man in the hour of his agony...! But what was I to do? Weep like a child...? That was Grzegorz, an old fisherman from the village nearby... You must have known him, Felix. He was a peasant on your land.

FELIX
A fisherman... Grzegorz...

FR PROCOPIUS
What's wrong, young man?

HORSTYŃSKI
Be good to his children, will you? ... If he has children...
FELIX
A fisherman... Grzegorz...

HORSTYŃSKI
You must know — His cottage stands opposite your manor, on the other side of the Wilia. You must know... if he has children...

FELIX
He has... a daughter...

HORSTYŃSKI
Is she pretty? Marry her off! I'll give a hundred złoty to set them up with a cow...

FELIX
Tell me, Mr Horsztyński, what sort of feeling was it, when they blackened your eyes with the candles?

HORSTYŃSKI
There was a great pain at first... then, something like the pricking of needles... But when they scraped away the shell of cold wax from my lashes in order to... Is my wife still in the room?

FR PROCOPIUS
Let the woman suffer in the hearing of what others have suffered in the flesh... Speak on, Mr Horsztyński.

HORSTYŃSKI
You priests always want people to suffer for no reason... It's enough for them to know how to suffer when suffer they must. Sally! As God is my witness, I thought of you at that moment... It came to me that I'd never again see you with my eyes — that your voice would now be like the song of a lark, somewhere in the sky, unseen...

SALOMEA
O, angels of God! Why did you not stand in his defence!

HORSTYŃSKI
What do you think, Salusia, that this world is like a Muscovite icon in church, where Abraham takes aim at his son Isaac with his musket, while from the clouds an angel pours water onto the pan so that it should not fire?

FELIX
God doesn't mix Himself up in the affairs of this world... Listen, when I served as a page to King Stanisław, once I committed a dreadful sin... In the aviary of Princess Sapieha in Bielany, I started to massacre the peacocks and parrots. I was as drunk as a lord... As God's my witness, no angel with palm frond stood to the defence of those poor little birds. It was a horrible slaughter. On the next day, I was as famous in Warsaw as Prince Józef himself! Ha, ha, ha! Don't laugh... I wanted to show you all what a great man I am... For didn't you, Father, think of me as a great man? Weren't you puffed up in pride on my account? So I wanted to let you know, today, Father, that I am... What I am... Believe me! A certain Frenchman included the story of my deed in a book he wrote about his travels in Poland... I will live for ever and ever, amen! Ha, ha! What's more, he added to this that I owned a phaeton just like Prince Józef Poniatowski's. The Frenchman included a description of it in his book as well...

SALOMEA
You laugh at us, sir, sadly.

FELIX
I swear to God... It's all true... I'll show you the book, Madame... and you will be good enough to read to your husband some pages of it concerning my deeds...

SALOMEA
You were a child then, Count.

FELIX
I was wiser then, than many adults... Fame is a beautiful thing... worth striving for! The nation basks in the glory of the deeds of her citizens!

HORSTYŃSKI
I understand you, young fellow. You place a laurel wreath upon my grey head...

FELIX
I? I? I?... I tell you in all honesty, that if I were not me, I'd like to be you, Mr Horsztyński. — God created people so strangely, that they always attach such importance to that word "I." Except for women,

who sometimes feel the same way about the word "my." But they're wrong, so very wrong to do so...

FR PROCOPIUS
Salomea, go and fix your husband some blood soup.

SALOMEA
In a moment... O! not now...

FELIX
Women mistake us for angels and then, with so much effort, we must sweat away at our comedic role, keeping our balance on one leg on that high pedestal, where they set us... We must weigh each word carefully, but all the same, in the end, exhausted, we topple off the column and into the muck below. We must put an end to this *amour propre* once and for all and be what we are... ourselves... in other words, nothing...

HORSTYŃSKI
What is the point of all this irony of yours?

FELIX
But no! In the place of a woman's words, I'll set those of a priest. — Reverend Father Procopius, I've spent many a sleepless night thinking about what you once said to me... You said, "I see a great man in you." Immediately, I set off on the path leading to that greatness, until at last I grew exhausted with the strain and nervous tension of my natural forces — so ungainly — constantly striving to transform nothingness into the greatness of a giant. For God's sake, tell me at least that you've changed your opinion of me, so that I might finally get a good night's sleep... I'm tired of trying to think the way people think I think... I'm suffocating under the mask they've set upon my face. People bind us with the tiny threads of praise and then we miss the turning in the road that would lead to our destiny, because we dare not burst apart the weak knots with which we're bound. Mr Horsztyński was telling us about great suffering; and all the while I was listening to the beating of my heart... And I swear to God, what I felt in my heart, I don't dare reveal. Something horrible was born in the depths of my mind... an insane pride...

HORSTYŃSKI
Turn it to a good end!

FELIX
For that, first you need a good character, Mr Horstzyński... First you've got to teach people not to be jealous, and sometimes I'm jealous of the herdboy warming his hands at a campfire in the depths of the woods... and sometimes I'm jealous of King Stanisław sitting dressed in his theatrical robes on the throne in the Chamber of Deputies. — Show me the end to aim at, which should satisfy both those two strange envies! ... You'd need to be an actor in a low comedy, full of gags, and a tragedy, at one and the same time...

SALOMEA
You're like my poor harp today, my lord. The musician from Vilnius who was to tune it for me didn't arrive... I wanted to play a gay song for my husband, but there emerged such discordant tones from the untuned harp, that I couldn't go on...

FELIX
And perhaps you wept, Madame, because the harp sounded so wildly discordant...

HORSTYŃSKI
See how well Count Felix knows you, Sally...

FELIX
Woe to women, who listen too long to the wind moaning through the weeping birchwoods, or the song of the nightingales... These latter days offer us a strange antidote to the venom of sadness — poetry...

SALOMEA
I'd like to know those nightingales of ours.

FELIX
Cold water... warm water... rhymed! I'll bring you the *Fables* of Krasicki with the strophe:
    "O sacred love of the dear fatherland,
        Only they know you, who..."
But pardon me, Mr Horsztyński. I forgot that you've no taste for verse, no feeling for its graces...

HORSTYŃSKI
I do like the hymn "Holy God, Mighty God..."

FELIX
No rhymes... no rhymes! I'd rather listen to the rhyming of my horse's hooves as he goes off at a gallop than to poetry that doesn't rhyme... Farewell, neighbours...

SALOMEA
Please — You'll take a bouquet of our flowers for your sister...

FELIX
My sister only likes belles-de-miche. Because they've got a French name.

SALOMEA
*Pulling one from her braid.*
So take her this flower. One of these days I'd like to see my cloister-friend...˙

FELIX
She's rather busy these days... Embroidering my father's history on canvas with red silk, and teaching my little brother his prayers... I bid you all good night...
*Exits.*

HORSTYŃSKI
Father, what will you say about that young fellow?

FR PROCOPIUS
I see that there's a horrid battle being waged in his heart.

HORSTYŃSKI
Do you think that his father's egging him on to something criminal — something that goes against his conscience, and his good name?

---

\*     *Klasztorna przyjaciółka.* There is probably a double entendre here. It can mean that both the girls were at the same convent school, but also — that they're locked up here, in their home, as if they were cloistered.

FR PROCOPIUS
I've heard that the Hetman is gathering a strong force together. His house is full of mercenary bands...

HORSTYŃSKI
Father, it's time to make use of those papers...

FR PROCOPIUS
Tomorrow, I'll go to Vilnius myself...

HORSTYŃSKI
Come, Salomea. Lead me to my room.

SALOMEA
Father, here is your lantern, lit and ready... Come, husband! — Good night, Father!
*Exits, with Horsztyński.*

FR PROCOPIUS
That woman... is lost.
*Exits.*

### Scene 3
*A hall in the Hetman's manor.*
*Enter Hetman, Ksiński*

HETMAN
So it's certain, what you've told me about my son?

KSIŃSKI
Unfortunately.

HETMAN
And you, sir, are not married yourself, by any chance?

KSIŃSKI
No, my lord, I'm not.

HETMAN
Ha! Because it seems to me that you feel quite sorry for the husband! — I won't forget you, Mr Ksiński. Call here my dwarf, or Sforka. I have some matters to conclude with them.

KSIŃSKI
Can't I be of any further service to you, Count?

HETMAN
Indeed you can — Call my people here.

*Ksiński exits.*

HETMAN
Ha, Horsztyński! Now, I've one more weapon in my quiver! ... Where is that old heart of yours, Horsztyński? I'll teach you suffering. — Get in here!

*Enter Sforka.*

Sforka — you've sent the people into town?

SFORKA
They're at their snooping, my lord.

HETMAN
We've got to the get the shoemakers and tailors of Vilnius in our pay. Bring two hundred of those drunks here, and have them stitch some new livery for the people in the castle.

SFORKA
Tomorrow, I'll send five wagons to fetch that mob.

HETMAN
Choose the boldest and rowdiest from among them.

SFORKA
The powder's been laid in.

HETMAN
How much?

SFORKA
Nine barrels, and two Russian caissons.

HETMAN
Where have you placed them?

SFORKA
In that tower.

HETMAN
Who's mustering my legions?

SFORKA
Mr Horda, sir.

HETMAN
Tell him to always lock the gates at the rear of the yard where the muster is taking place. Don't let anybody peep into that yard. Can I trust you to keep on your toes?

SFORKA
I have been, sir, ever since you shot dead that cook who, out of curiosity, poked his head out of the side loophole...

HETMAN
I thought it was a cat.

SFORKA
A reasonable mistake, my lord... The deceased cook used to go about in a fur cap of rather poor quality... Permit me, sir, to take up my old refrain. I'd very much like it if my lord could see his way to clear the forest of Goszczenice... and settle there a colony of the Moravian brethren. They're honest folk... and ground rent for one hundred cottages would bring in an annual income of twenty thousand Polish złoty... And then the timber sold...

HETMAN
We'll talk about that later. Can you not see, Mr Sforka, that I've got more important things on my hands?

SFORKA
Politics, your Grace! I myself know a little bit about politics. I'd like to bid my lord —

HETMAN
A good night? What?

SFORKA
No. There's something in the castle, something important, that might offend her Grace the Tsaritsa, should she learn of it.

HETMAN
In my castle? What could it be?

SFORKA
Well, my lord — as you know, the clock in the tower is fashioned in such a way that, when twelve o'clock strikes, noon or midnight, a figure of the Lithuanian knight jumps out and strikes the Russian eagle on the head with his sword. It's that which, I believe, might offend the great lady.

HETMAN
Ha, ha, ha! You old diplomat, you! Thank you very much for opening the path to greatness before me... Really, you are a sensible and circumspect fellow.

SFORKA
So, I'll have the clock pulled out of the wall and...

HETMAN
Don't even dare, stupid... I loved that clock when I was a child. Mind the hens, Mr Sforka. You yourself, old man, entertained me when I was a child — that's why you're still sitting on this side of the wall beneath that clock.

SFORKA
Well then, since the Hetman deigns still to treat me so kindly, I'd like to pass on one more bit of news to him. It seems I've come into a small fortune...

HETMAN
How? At your age? What sort of ancient greybeard tottered on past you to leave you a testament?

SFORKA
It's as if it fell from the heavens, actually...

HETMAN
Congratulations... Off to bed with you.

SFORKA
Have you ever given any thought to my last name, my lord?

HETMAN
It's rather graceful...

SFORKA
But have you ever really considered it, this last name of mine — as one of my learned friends puts it — from an estimological point of view?

HETMAN
I esteem it, for sure.

SFORKA
My lord is so kind as to hear me out so far, that my tongue can't keep still. It seems that my last name is derived...

HETMAN
From — from...?

SFORKA
From Sforza.*

HETMAN
You stupid old man! Your father, or your grandfather, kept kennel for my father, or my grandfather. And that's the "estimological" history of your name. From *sfora*, pack of dogs. That's where it comes from...

---

\*   The Sforzas were a noble family of Milan. Bona Sforza (1494–1557) was Queen of Poland (the second wife of Zygmunt Stary (1467–1548); her progeny subsequently ruled as kings and queens of Poland, Hungary, Sweden, and Duchess of Brunswick.

Now, be off with you. You're starting to bore me. And have the dwarf come to my bedroom to recite the litany with me.

SFORKA
At once, my lord.
*Exits.*

HETMAN
A few days more and all will be decided... If only my son will agree to stand at the head... Why are those dogs howling so mournfully in my courtyard? They're chivvying me to my palace in Vilnius, those dogs. Great deeds always have a gloomy colouration, and elicit sad thoughts... Here, dwarf!

*Enter Dwarf.*

DWARF
Shall I make you laugh, sir? Or just sit here and count the teeth in my head...

HETMAN
Let's recite the litany.

*They exit.*

### Scene 4
*Night. A garden near the Wilia. Above, a large white manor is seen; on the other bank of the Wilia, a fisherman's cottage.*

FELIX
*Solus.*
I look up at the stars, and my soul strains to the heavens. If only the breadth and elevation of the thoughts which flash through my soul at this moment like lightning bolts were the natural state of man — not to disappear at the rising of the sun — that man would be a great hero... Or at the very least he would be happy with an inner sense of greatness and pride...

VOICE FROM AFAR
O-ho!

FELIX
*Whistles.*
That's him. Right on time. Not even a quarter of an hour late.

*A boat floats up. The Stranger gets out onto the bank, wearing a long cloak.*

STRANGER
Have you been waiting long for me?

FELIX
Not at all.

STRANGER
Have you given it any thought, then?

FELIX
Both deep — and shallow.

STRANGER
So, can we count on you?

FELIX
No…

STRANGER
But I assure you — it's a sure thing…

FELIX
If that's the case, then I'm unnecessary.

STRANGER
The unnecessary ones are those ranged against us.

FELIX
And yet the unnecessary ones must live, despite the fact that they don't know how to be in the world without taking up two feet of earth… As long as he's alive, a man needs only two, but when he dies, he needs six…. Show me where the Eldorado of unnecessary people lies, and I'll be grateful to you… I'd apply for citizenship in the land of the unnecessary…

STRANGER
I don't know what to think of you, friend.

FELIX
Think of me as I think of myself — that I'm too great a man to perish on the cobbles amidst struggling mobs, cutting short a life predestined to great deeds with an insignificant death... And then that I'm petty — so small... that I'm not even fit for cannon fodder...

STRANGER
Devote yourself to a great cause, and you'll grow along with the course of events.

FELIX
Here's the misfortunate rub: At times, these events seem to be so great, that it's like I don't dare stand next to the statue of a giant, fearing lest people take me for a dwarf... And then again those events of yours seem so small, that I fear to set my foot down and crush people beneath my careless heel...

STRANGER
Farewell. I feel sorry for you...

FELIX
Were I to start something, I'd finish it... The wretched thing is that I cannot begin... Were I a Roman, I'd begin with a deed of horror... Last night I dreamt of it... and all the while my eyes were open...

STRANGER
Right now, you have the face of a killer.

FELIX
It's worse than that — I'm dreaming again... Farewell... Be well... I have a lover's rendezvous hereabout...

STRANGER
I'm sorry for you, Felix...

FELIX
Don't be... Don't be... I'm making use of life.

STRANGER
So you don't want to be with us?

FELIX
I don't... I can't...

STRANGER
My friends will think you a coward.

FELIX
That will make my father very sad.

STRANGER
Well, I reckon that we'll meet again... You still have time until tomorrow. Be well.
*Exits.*

FELIX
This is what — you might call a decision... Today I cast away from me all spectres, all illusions... You, little blue flower, withered in Sally's tresses... I cast you away too, into the current... This is what you call a decision... How those little fish splash happily about the blue waters of the river! ... Maryna!

*A light comes on in the fisherman's cottage. A voice is heard.*

VOICE
I swim...

FELIX
... Like a Nereid...

[END OF ACT I]

# ACT II

## Scene 1

*A room in Horsztyński's house.*
*Horsztyński, and his old servant Świętosz*

HORSZTYŃSKI
Where is my wife?

ŚWIĘTOSZ
At daybreak, Madame went to Fr. Procopius' cell. To Holy Communion, I'm certain.

HORSZTYŃSKI
Load my shotgun.

ŚWIĘTOSZ
You always did like to shoot at birds…

HORSZTYŃSKI
How do you picture me doing that now, old man, blind as I am? It's not for birds I want it. Load it with bullets, not shot.

ŚWIĘTOSZ
What do you have in mind?

HORSZTYŃSKI
The Hetman is about to pay me a visit.

ŚWIĘTOSZ
What? His grace Hetman Kossakowski in our home? So put on your golden sash…

HORSZTYŃSKI
No need, no need. Listen — load the shotgun and stand there just past the wall in the dark alcove. If you hear me whistle an old confederation melody, shoot!

ŚWIĘTOSZ
Jesus Mary and Joseph!

HORSZTYŃSKI
Shoot him right in the head, both barrels!

ŚWIĘTOSZ
If you whistle an old confederation melody?

HORSZTYŃSKI
Right.

ŚWIĘTOSZ
Maybe it's not an unchristian thing you're devising, after all... People say the rich old boy's been sniffing around the Muscovites...

HORSZTYŃSKI
Go — Go! I think I hear the rumble of his wagon outside... Shh! — And don't show yourself... In the name of the Father, and the Son, and the Holy Ghost... We must do our duty...
Świętosz exits.

HORSZTYŃSKI
Death will stand between your anger and me, Hetman! I haven't sunk so low just yet, that I will be shamed in my own home...

*Enter Hetman, richly dressed.*

HETMAN
Praised be the Lord Jesus Christ!

HORSZTYŃSKI
Now and forever, Amen.

HETMAN
Just as you demanded, I've come here to you alone, Sir, ready to extend my hand...

HORSZTYŃSKI
I'm a blind man — I don't know if I'm to stretch out my hand to the east, or to the north, in order to meet with yours.

HETMAN
And so you judge, my Horsztyński, that I always hold with the north...

HORSZTYŃSKI
It is for God alone to judge you, Hetman.

HETMAN
I know, Horsztyński, that you have in your possession some circumstantial evidence...

HORSZTYŃSKI
Evidence on paper, sir.

HETMAN
Exactly! In taking that Muscovite camp, among the trash you collected there you found a document, written perhaps with that very thing in mind — to slander my name amongst my fellow countrymen! Perhaps the Muscovites even allowed their material to be seized, purposefully, so that this document too would fall into Polish hands.

HORSZTYŃSKI
I lost twelve men, my noble Hetman, in order to take that purposefully abandoned camp...

HETMAN
That may be... that may be... But all the same, I swear to you, Horsztyński, that I knew nothing of that roguish scrap of paper. They wanted to ruin me! Just think — knowing that such a paper was in the hands of my enemy, they figured that I would have to cast myself into the abyss, for my purest intentions — my most immaculate deeds, would all be for naught, as long as one old grey-headed man, not completely in possession of his senses, might threaten to topple me with that defamatory weapon...

HORSZTYŃSKI
A little more gently with that enemy of yours, if you don't mind, Hetman. You know that he's not completely in possession of his senses, after all...

HETMAN
Horsztyński, let's make a pact to cast our old quarrels into oblivion! You, after all, were first to injure me...

HORSZTYŃSKI
You tore her from my side!

HETMAN
And even when torn away, her love remained with you! Listen, the shame of my wife lives yet in my house. Under the name of "daughter!"

HORSZTYŃSKI
Hetman, I'm ready to fall to my knees before you, to beg you not to cast curses upon her grave... Hers was a horrible death...

HETMAN
Ha! Horrible! You see that our two hearts are united in a horrible secret! Hand over those papers — Give them here — Let my hands busy themselves with shredding and mauling them, for when I look at you, I see...

HORSZTYŃSKI
Speak more softly, for God's sake!

HETMAN
I won't come back to you tomorrow, old man. I'm here today.

HORSZTYŃSKI
Even should you die, your shade will kneel at the threshold of my house at midnight, begging me for the evidence of that horrible... horrible... treachery...

HETMAN
That's what you think? There are mountains so lofty that, when a man stands on their summit, no missile cast by anyone's hand might reach him.

HORSZTYŃSKI
That's what you think, Hetman?

HETMAN
Mr Horsztyński, I say to you one last time — Hand over those papers. I will burn them here at your hearth and henceforth I will sleep soundly in my castle...

HORSZTYŃSKI
But I would no longer sleep soundly in my hovel. Those papers are the eyes I see you with, my gracious lord — and I am at peace, for, it seems that thus I hold you pent, like a snake a bird, by its stare.

HETMAN
You nobleman! Ha! Villainous lordling, rather!*

HORSZTYŃSKI
What?!... You are in my home, sir!

HETMAN
I am, as my son also visits your home. And for what reason?

HORSZTYŃSKI
Because... Because his voice reminds me of that of your wife, sir!

HETMAN
*Unsheathes his sword.*
Ha! Repeat that...

---

\*   Słowacki has the Hetman call Horsztyński *podły szlachciuro*. The term comprises both an acknowledgement of Horsztyński's noble descent, as well as contempt for his unwillingness to compromise his ideals. The Hetman both outranks Horsztyński in an aristocratic sense, and in a practical sense, as he seems to acknowledge his nation's dependence on the Russian Empire, whereas Horsztyński is unbending in his opposition to the Tsarist status quo. It must be remembered that Poland had one of the largest percentages of recognised noble families in Europe — over 10% of the entire population, many of whom had fallen on hard times, and were practically indistinguishable from the lower classes. The Hetman is contemptuous of Horsztyński, both as a magnate, and a pragmatic Pole in step with the times, as it were.

HORSZTYŃSKI
Put up your sword, Hetman, before I whistle it from your hand!

*The Hetman smashes a mirror with his sword.*

HORSZTYŃSKI
What was that noise?

HETMAN
I slew your treachery, Horsztyński... That mirror!

HORSZTYŃSKI
I don't understand.

HETMAN
In that mirror I saw a man standing, with a shotgun...

HORSZTYŃSKI
O, my God!

HETMAN
*To Świętosz.*
Get in here, now! Stand there behind your master's chair, so that he should not be afraid...

*Świętosz enters, at a martial pace.*

HETMAN
People such as I walk boldly into the very cave of treason, fearing nothing... O, shame! The word of a nobleman is not to be trusted! I don't want those documents of yours, Horsztyński. Maybe you forged them yourself! People will learn what they should think of you, Mr Horsztyński. Tomorrow... I shall seize your home and your possessions. For you were in debt to the Jews to the tune of five thousand ducats, and I bought that debt from them at half price. Why? Because nobody honours your promissory notes any more. Not by half, Horsztyński! And the verdict of the land courts already lies on the jurist's desk... And when Hetman Kossakowski executes the eviction, you and your wife shall take those documents of yours to the threshold of some old confederate, and try to sell them for a couple pennies — and with these you'll purchase your last mouthfuls

of bread, bought, not begged — for you shortly shall turn beggar, Mr Horsztyński!

HORSZTYŃSKI
My wife...!

HETMAN
Your wife? O, my son will keep your wife in money, Horsztyński!

HORSZTYŃSKI
Your son? Why your son?

HETMAN
The old fellow's as thick as a boot sole! Have your fellow there shoot me in the back!
*Exits.*

ŚWIĘTOSZ
My Lord...

HORSZTYŃSKI
Leave me alone!... Has he gone?

ŚWIĘTOSZ
Yes.

HORSZTYŃSKI
Go then, Świętosz. Leave me alone with my shame. What was that old man saying about my wife? What on earth? Rack my brains as I might... Sometimes, by staring at a certain place, I could gather my thoughts and think something through... Now I have no eyes to help me... I see only darkness... I don't understand. God, I can't understand...

*Pause, then, violently:*

The adulteress!

*He gets up, then falls back into his chair.*

I'll go insane! Why did I not give him the papers? Then I'd have known nothing. But that's even worse, not to know, and to kiss her on the forehead all the while... Brr! How cold I feel of a sudden! And the priest — even the priest — even the priest!... He has eyes, after all... If indeed he know anything, my old friend!... Ha! Now I've regained my sight; a sight that sees into the future — where I see horrid things... they swindle the old man and make sport of him... just waiting for him to die... No, I can't ask my wife — shyness, a shyness clamps tight my lips... And if she should say "No," I still won't be able to believe her... And she can't say anything except "No, no!... I'm innocent!" and her face, which I won't be able to see anyway, might turn away from me with an expression of... O! My God! God! Let the earth gape beneath my feet to swallow me!

Sally! Sally!... You were so wretched and unhappy when I led you to the altar... The words your raving mother bellowed at my ear: "Who takes my Sally takes a crazy woman, for Sally... is me!" And the poor girl wept, and I swore to lead her along the flowering paths of life — that I would be a father to her. And... so I was... a father...

Consider, old man, what you are leaving her as an inheritance: bitterness, regret and beggary! The poor girl! The wretched girl! ... I must do as Jesus Christ commanded — What do I care for this pitiful world? Let us leave these people in peace... let them groan... and laugh... let them rave and skip about — Let them seek their happiness in the misfortune of others — But let them not curse the dead! ... And I am dead... Peace! peace, peace...

I have a strange vision of human destiny... peace...

SALOMEA
*Enters, wearing a straw hat.*
Asleep? Shh... I'll close the shutters. The sun is beating down on his grey head.

HORSZTYŃSKI
Grey head... ha...

SALOMEA
I thought you were asleep. Let me go and fix you your breakfast outside, beneath the lindens. I'll draw the fresh cream myself — I've gathered the wild strawberries myself.

HORSZTYŃSKI
Where have you been, Sally?

SALOMEA
At Father Procopius'.

HORSZTYŃSKI
Did you gather those wild strawberries for me among the graves of the little churchyard?

SALOMEA
No, my Ksawery. I gathered them on the road home, as I went through the woods.

HORSZTYŃSKI
Have you been to confession today?

SALOMEA
I went there with that intention, because I was sad... But the priest wasn't at home. Maybe he was in the village at old Grzegorz's place.* They say the old man is very ill. I sat there in his cell, waiting for him, and I grew bored. But how quiet is that cell, and lit up by the rising sun, how beautiful, how pleasant! — And the pine woods there at his window, swaying and sighing — the orioles were singing sadly — And I fell to thinking, and then, wishing to entertain myself while I waited, I began to look through the books on the dusty shelves there. It's obvious that our dear little priest doesn't often turn his attention to them, so dusty they are! And how strange are the pictures in those books. In one of them I saw some sainted lady batting a lion on the nose with a lily! And in another I found an illustration of Hell. There was this black devil smoking a black pipe, as it were, but in the bowl, instead of tobacco, there were poor little souls frying and giving off smoke...

HORSZTYŃSKI
But did you confess?

---

\*    Słowacki likes this name; he gives it to a character in *Kordian* as well. Is this another Grzegorz — not Maryna's father, who was tortured to death by the Russians? Or is this more evidence of the unfinished nature of the play — a mistake on the poet's part, which he would have caught and cleared up, had he returned to it?

SALOMEA
No, I didn't. Because the illustrations made me laugh, in a childish sort of way...

HORSZTYŃSKI
Why didn't you confess!

SALOMEA
I told you — the pictures put me off the mood... How irritated you are today, my Ksawery! Was someone here?

HORSZTYŃSKI
Wife! Tell me...

SALOMEA
What, husband?

HORSZTYŃSKI
Now, beating your bosom, tell me...

SALOMEA
Beating my bosom?

HORSZTYŃSKI
Tell me!... But I've quite forgotten what I wanted to ask you... What an old man I am!

SALOMEA
Maybe I can remind you, husband.

HORSZTYŃSKI
No, no, no!... You can't know what's in my mind! Go and get some paper and a pen. You'll write a letter for me. Only a few words...

SALOMEA
*Sitting down.*
Go ahead.

HORSZTYŃSKI
Most noble and kind Benefactor, Sir...

SALOMEA
Benefactor...

HORSZTYŃSKI
That's a rather funny word, actually...

SALOMEA
What's next?

HORSZTYŃSKI
Hold on. Let me think... Write: "If, sir, you be a man of honour, I shall await you tonight, at my house."

SALOMEA
Who are you writing to?

HORSZTYŃSKI
Give it here. I'll sign it.

SALOMEA
But for God's sake, who is it for?

HORSZTYŃSKI
What's that to you, woman!

SALOMEA
You speak so harshly to me...

HORSZTYŃSKI
Sally! Because you nag me like a child! Give me the paper here. Where shall I sign it?

SALOMEA
Here.

HORSZTYŃSKI
Go now. Get my breakfast ready, and tell Świętosz I want to see him.

SALOMEA
All right. But kiss my forehead first, and apologise for that "woman!"

HORSZTYŃSKI
All right. I'll kiss you, if your strawberries will be tasty.

SALOMEA
*Drops the bowl, it smashes.*
Husband, I've smashed the bowl.

HORSZTYŃSKI
On purpose?

SALOMEA
On purpose. So that your kiss would not depend on strawberries.

HORSZTYŃSKI
You've done wrong, Sally... Świętosz!

ŚWIĘTOSZ
*Enters.*
Yes, sir?

HORSZTYŃSKI
After breakfast, you'll take me to my room. I have an important errand for you. *To Salomea.* Your hand, wife! Lead me beneath the lindens...

*They exit.*


### Scene 2
*Felix and Maryna*
*She is dressed in a long homespun shirt, belted at the waist. She has a garland of cornflowers in her hair.*

FELIX
Where were you going, Maryna?

MARYNA
I was picking cornflowers in the rye, to dress myself up for you, my lord. Do I look pretty?

FELIX
More or less...

MARYNA
Yesterday you said I was.

FELIX
Yesterday, when you glided up out of the Wilia onto the garden bank, to the jasmine bower, the nightingales were singing, the moon was shining... yesterday you were pretty.

MARYNA
But today?... So a person needn't take you at your word.

FELIX
As you like...

MARYNA
You were better once. You came to my cottage, taught me to read, just like a schoolmaster; you laughed and joked...

FELIX
What are you reading now?

MARYNA
The book you gave me.

FELIX
It seems that your father died...

MARYNA
The Muscovites killed him.

FELIX
Do you pray for his soul?

MARYNA
When I think of him, I pray for him... When I don't, I don't.

FELIX
If he had lived, Maryna, maybe you'd make him sad, your father.

MARYNA
Why?

FELIX
You yourself know that I won't marry you.

MARYNA
You think I can't find a boy by myself?

FELIX
So, you intend to marry... an honest man, Maryna?

MARYNA
An honest and a handsome one.

FELIX
So you don't love me?

MARYNA
What more can you want of me, my lord?

FELIX
That's true! I'm crazy... You're a good girl. What's all that noise? Go see who's coming this way.

MARYNA
*Exits.*

FELIX
How strange the human heart. My senses had been in such a ferment that I'd never noticed until today that it's made of stone... She once seemed to me a Nereid of the Wilia. Our hearts once beat in time. Our lips, aflame... This old bower seemed a kind of mythological temple of love — nightingales, moon... they were all a part of that woman... I must grow up, grow old, already...

MARYNA
*Runs in.*
My lord! There are some men coming here in a hurry!

FELIX
Why? Are they after you?

MARYNA
What do you take me for?

KSIŃSKI, WYRWIK, SKOWICZ
*Enter hastily.*

KSIŃSKI
Ha! As God's my witness, Count Felix... with a pretty girl!

FELIX
You like the looks of her, Mr Ksiński?

KSIŃSKI
As I live and breathe, she's pretty.

MARYNA
Stand up for me, my lord. They're mocking me!

WYRWIK
Who would dare to mock so fair and rare a pair? That's fairly daring!

FELIX
Are you drunk, sir?

KSIŃSKI
You've got to excuse poor Wyrwik. He used to stammer, and this is how he keeps his tongue loose. He's the Demosthenes of our party these days...

WYRWIK
Allow me, your grace, to praise the face, with a kiss for the miss, in a trice, to sacrifice to those eyes...

SKOWICZ
Stop it! Can't you see how the count glowers at you?

WYRWIK
A glower has no power at such a late hour — Whatever his intents, it causes no offence, among friends...

KSIŃSKI
Count Felix, can it be true that this country slut holds your heart in her hands?

FELIX
To show you that it's not so, I'm bestowing a dowry of a thousand ducats upon her. Let one of you take her to wife.

KSIŃSKI
Skowicz...

SKOWICZ
A peasant girl!

FELIX
And thus farewell, Republicans...
*Exit.*

KSIŃSKI
Is Count Felix in love with you, girl?

MARYNA
What's that to you?

KSIŃSKI
You know, gentlemen, this girl can be of service to us. We need to work on Felix's imagination in order to get him in the saddle, where the Hetman wants him got. Listen, girl — what's your name?

MARYNA
Maryna.

KSIŃSKI
Maryna, my beauty, can you ride a horse?

MARYNA
I lack the courage...

KSIŃSKI
Listen: this evening we'll dress you up in a beautiful lancer's uniform. We'll teach you what to say, and you'll come off to the castle with us...

MARYNA
Oh, no! I'm afraid of the Hetman. He's a frightful one, and red... He shoots at people.

KSIŃSKI
Don't be afraid. The hetman will give you a splendid dowry if you do what we ask of you.

MARYNA
But will Count Felix be angry with me if I do?

KSIŃSKI
Don't worry... Don't worry... Count Felix will fall in love with you in your pretty lancer's uniform.

MARYNA
I'll think about it.

KSIŃSKI
Gentlemen, I give you — born of the head of Ksiński — the Joan of Arc of the Targowica party... Champagne, my friends! And your speech, Wyrwik Demosthenes!

ALL
Bravo! Bravo!

KSIŃSKI.
*To Maryna*
Until we meet again, this evening.

MARYNA
I'll think it over.

KSIŃSKI
There's no time to think!

MARYNA
I need to understand what it's all about...

KSIŃSKI
See! You agree already. Let's go, let's go...!

*He exits.*

MARYNA
What is it that you want of me? They're joking... Let's see where they're off to...
*Exits.*


### Scene 3.
*Hetman's office. The dwarf, arranging papers.*

DWARF
What is greatness? People enter this office bent double. Sometimes I see their eyes grow wide with terror when they see me dare to lay a finger upon a sealed letter, or the hetman's dressing gown... Idiots... I've seen the Jew set leeches to the hetman's hide — fine noblewomen they were, tossing bloody puddles from behind his ear, pumping blood from his red nose!... From which time I've become a philosopher — and begun laughing at dwarves.

SFORKA
*Drawing apart the curtains.*
The hetman's not back yet?

DWARF
And what might you be after, Steward? *To himself.* He keeps his tongue behind his teeth. Mad at me ever since I called him an overseer.

SFORKA
What's open to the dwarf is closed to Sforka.
*He enters and sits down.*

DWARF
It's come to my attention, Mr Sforka, that lately you've been visited by a rather important person.

SFORKA
What? You know about that, Stynko?

DWARF
I recognised the gentleman by his uniform.

SFORKA
If you only knew how hard it is to hold a conversation with an Italian!

DWARF
Especially for someone who knows nothing of geography.

SFORKA
I know my geography!

DWARF
And yet you quarrelled with me about Emperor Vesuvius.

SFORKA
You lie like a dog, whitefish! Vesuvius is a mountain! I always said it was a mountain!

DWARF
And I tell you it's a lava fountain!

SFORKA
Volcano! From "Vulcan!"

DWARF
Vulcan is a mythological figure.

SFORKA
I know that!

DWARF
Then why do you call him a mountain?

SFORKA
I wanted to tease you, clown.

DWARF
When you've become a great man, you'll have your own clowns to tease.

SFORKA
How do you know that I will become a great man?

DWARF
The world is a game of chances, Sforka. Even idiots win great sums at the lottery.

SFORKA
I'm not an idiot!

DWARF
Of course you're not. But if idiots win the lottery often, Mr Sforka, a smart man like you ought to win even more frequently.

SFORKA
So, you think I'm about to fall into a large fortune?

DWARF
No, that can't happen. That's clear enough.

SFORKA
It just might happen, Mr Dwarf. I have something here in my pocket, a few words — I just need to add a few words in answer — and ten questions multiplied by B, plus ten answers — algebraically and arithmetically, we arrive at...

DWARF
X.

SFORKA
And you know what X means?

DWARF
When written in front of a name, X marks the spot of a princely title.

SFORKA
As God is my witness, the dwarf's not stupid. I hadn't even thought of that myself.

*Enter Hetman. Dwarf and Sforka rise immediately.*

HETMAN
What are you two bums doing here in my office — with your heads covered?

SFORKA
We were waiting on you, Excellency, my Lord...

HETMAN
You could at least have doffed your hat to my chair — even as a synonym of the throne.

SFORKA
What does that mean, dwarf — "synonym of the throne?"

DWARF
It means that it's a sin on'm, there's no throne for his son.

SFORKA
O, my Lord's son will soon seat himself on the throne, if we are successful...

HETMAN
Listen — tomorrow, at the break of dawn, I'm off to Vilnius...

SFORKA
Alone, my lord?

HETMAN
Alone... Things have changed. It's time to act. My son will stay here in the castle and, in the evening, he'll lead my legions to me.

SFORKA
Has Count Felix agreed to this plan?

HETMAN
Has he agreed? Ten freeloaders will pay with their heads if he doesn't. After all, they were always telling me how improbable it would be for him not to want this. "Leave it to us, my Lord Hetman..." So let them cross all their Ts and dot all their Is tonight, or, by God! I'll hang them all in the chimney like smoked meats! If my son compromised himself but once, he will no longer be of use to me. These days, the people look at him as a hook from which to hang his father. Did you know that Jasiński himself met with him the other night, but didn't win him over?

SFORKA
Jasiński? That carrion!

HETMAN
Ksiński saw him in the garden last night. If he'd only had a few men with him, he'd have snared him like a bird... They say he's hiding out somewhere near Ponary.

SFORKA
He could fall on Vilnius from there.

HETMAN
You heard I'm off to Vilnius?

SFORKA
Of course, Hetman, your Excellency...

DWARF
And the Most Holy Virgin of Ostra Brama...

SFORKA
And the Most Holy Virgin of Ostra Brama... will not permit...

HETMAN
You have a list of the nobles who are to gather tonight?

SFORKA
Here it is.
*Hands him a paper.*

HETMAN
My glasses... *Puts them on.* Let's see what news is here.... *Reads*
Easy the tasks,
But the questions it asks
Are tough to solve...

SFORKA
*Falls to his knees.*
My Lord! That's the wrong paper!

HETMAN
*Kicks him in the chest.*
You dog!

*Sforka faints.*

HETMAN
What — Is he dead? Dwarf, come see.

DWARF
He's breathing...

HETMAN
The old fool doesn't know that each beat of my heart is a bolt of lightning, locked in my breast... Call the soldiers here! The old man's head made a horrid sound when it hit the pavement. Sforka! Sforka! Sforka!

*Dwarf enters with soldiers.*

HETMAN
Carry him out and call the doctor. You, brother, have a free hand. Take this midget *Points at the dwarf.* And give him ten lashes.

DWARF
My lord!

HETMAN
Twenty lashes.

DWARF
For what?

HETMAN
Thirty lashes.

*They carry out Sforka and the Dwarf.*

HETMAN
Will my son agree? They ask me about my son's heart... What's that noise? Hey!

*Soldier enters.*

HETMAN
What's going on?

SOLDIER
They let the dogs out at the bear we keep.

HETMAN
Call the dwarf here — I made a bet with him that the bear would flay that black magpie... Hey! Call the dwarf here!
*Exits.*

### Scene 4

*A room in the castle.*
*Ksiński solus.*

KSIŃSKI
The hour of action approaches — I swore to the hetman that I would set his son astride a horse, but up until now I have been unable to pry one word of truth from the lips of that youngster... It's time for him to declare himself. If only I were the Hetman's son! Ha, ha! Mother Nature has no idea what she's up to. As stupid as a fool who would pour champagne into a porter bottle. Now, Mother Nature has given me a long neck, legs and arms... and set me amongst the cringing sort! The genuflectors! It's still not been settled whether it's easier for a short man, or a tall one, to bend double. No. Mother Nature is a witty old lady. Instead of a fat stomach, she's given me a waist like the parchment hinges of a cardboard box. A stomach, my lord, like an empty satchel; wrinkled, concave and creaking when I'm made to bow...

*Enter Felix, with a book.*

KSIŃSKI
Greetings, my lord.

FELIX
How are you, friend?

KSIŃSKI
I see my lord is entertaining himself with a book.

FELIX
Yes.

KSIŃSKI
Such is the pastime of the great...

FELIX
Do you read often?

KSIŃSKI
Me, my lord? Since I left school...

FELIX
I understand... Why are you not at the bear baiting?

KSIŃSKI
I'm wholly occupied with a matter of great civic import. My lord, today is an important day for our cause. All of Poland awaits the rising of a new sun on the political horizon.

FELIX
Have you made ready your smoked-lenses glasses?

KSIŃSKI
I beg your pardon, Count?

FELIX
Otherwise you could go blind, staring at the sun with naked eye.

KSIŃSKI
Your friends will shade you like clouds, Felix...

FELIX
Ha! Am I to be that sun of yours?
*Reads.*

KSIŃSKI
I'm certain that you don't wish to sadden your father with shameful hesitation. Literature is a good thing, Count Felix — in calm times. But when the time of action rolls around, what good is the distillation of printed words into the essence of thought?

FELIX
Have you ever read Plato's dialogue on the immortality of the soul?

KSIŃSKI
I believe I have...

FELIX
What is your opinion of it?

KSIŃSKI
My opinion, Count, is that the time has come to decide.

FELIX
Decide what?

KSIŃSKI
You will admit, my lord, that our country is in the need of resilient aid... otherwise, otherwise... What is the immortality of the soul to me?... If Plato were living in these days of ours, he would be a Republican, like me.

FELIX
Death is not death...

KSIŃSKI
But if a nation should die?

FELIX
The soul is immortal, Mr Ksiński. Listen! It is a matter of great importance — you see, even the most insignificant fragment of a great matter cannot die. Here, after the passage of two thousand years, on this 25th of June, 1794, I know that Socrates and Phaedon conversed on beauty, just as I am speaking with you now. Well, maybe not exactly, because neither of them were wearing shoes...

KSIŃSKI
Trifles!

FELIX
But there's something to these trifles, in comparison with the great causes of our day and age! Socrates said to Phaedon — "It's hot today... If you like, we'll go down to the blue stream and talk there, dipping our legs into the cool water."And so they went... I see them... They sat down on a slightly sloping bank covered with thick grass... The living current stroked their naked legs; a wide-spreading plane-tree provided them with a pleasant shade. You could hear the chirping of the crickets that hid themselves in the long grass, from the afternoon heat.

KSIŃSKI
Tell me, Count, where do you find greatness in all that?

FELIX
Nowhere...

KSIŃSKI
So what does it teach us?

FELIX
To go down to the stream, both of us, because it's hot. If you are Plato, you, or somebody round here — even my father's dwarf — then after the passage of two thousand years, people will know that we lay together on the grass beside the Wilia.

KSIŃSKI
Metaphysics. Not my bag.

FELIX
Speaking of beauty, Socrates compared the nature of man to a cart hitched to two horses. One is black, and he rears and foams. The other, as white as milk, resists the mettle of his partner. The coachman controls the opposed tendencies of both with reins of gold... The black horse represents the senses, and the white, the soul. The coachman is reason...

KSIŃSKI
I don't get it, you know? I don't, really.

FELIX
You know how to drive a wagon?

KSIŃSKI
I do...

FELIX
But someone else's cart, with unfamiliar horses?

KSIŃSKI
As I live and breathe, I do.

FELIX
So, push off the coachman, and drive yourself.
*Moves to leave, then stands.*

KSIŃSKI
For God's sake, my lord! If someone heard you, they'd reckon —

FELIX
What?

KSIŃSKI
That you've lost your mind!

FELIX
Spread that rumour, will you?
*Goes off.*

KSIŃSKI
And there he goes! Is he stupid, or am I? Is he babbling nonsense? He must be, for he speaks, and says nothing...

*Enter Amelia.*

AMELIA
I heard my brother's voice.

KSIŃSKI
My lady... I tender you my deepest respect...

AMELIA
I heard my brother's voice, and I'd like to have a word with him.

KSIŃSKI
O, may your rosy lips prompt him to action, my lady... He's constantly mumbling trifles...

AMELIA
As a matter of fact, my father asked the same thing of me — That I should encourage him to a more active life.

KSIŃSKI
Then please, my lady, convince him to be present at the banquet this evening. We'll exalt him there, with speeches and champagne...

AMELIA
With champagne? Shame, Mr Ksiński! You want to bend a great soul to great deeds through deceit? O, I'm starting to lose faith in the purity of your intentions, if you would use such flimsy and base means to arrive at your goal... I will rather defend my brother from your blandishments. Now, will you be so kind as to search him out in the garden and send him here to me?

KSIŃSKI
My lady...
*He goes off.*

AMELIA
How different my brother is from these people! More than once I've wondered why Felix seems so beautiful and lofty to me — especially when he's calm... Because when he flies off into the aether in thought, I can't keep up with him and my thoughts get lost in the clouds... O, how I'd like to see him on the active stage of the world — elevated above others...

FELIX
*Enters.*
Good day, sister.

AMELIA
Felix, Father has asked me to have a word with you.

FELIX
That works. I'd rather talk with you than with him.

AMELIA
And so I'll speak straight from the heart. You've always been so good to your sister. I remember when we were children, running about together on the meadows around the Wilia, chasing the butterflies of spring, or walking about the footpaths deep in dead leaves, musing... How we enjoyed that! I haven't changed since then, Felix, but you have. Quite a bit.

FELIX
And did you reckon I'd never grow up?

AMELIA
Do you think me such a trivial creature as to be unworthy of even one sad word from your soul?

FELIX
I'm speaking to you in great sadness...

AMELIA
I see that I've lost your trust.

FELIX
Did Ksiński tell you that I've gone crazy?

AMELIA
Leave those people be, Felix, and speak with me as you would speak with a friend, just this once... For fifteen minutes only. Tell me why it is that you do not wish to do the will of your father? He can't ask anything vile of you — Do you think he's working for your destruction? Tell me, brother, what is it you see in father's intentions that makes you not want to further his plans?

FELIX
I see nothing. That's just it.

AMELIA
What? Why?

FELIX
I'm blind...

AMELIA
I once read something à propos concerning John Lackland. Blind, he had himself bound between two bold soldiers and thus, with sword unsheathed, he fell upon his enemies and died... Be you bound between your father and your sister. Let us lead you to the field of glory...

FELIX
You've certainly read a lot.
*Paces about the room in thought.*

AMELIA
I can see, my dearest brother, my beloved brother, that your sister's words are starting to turn you... I can read an elevated thought in the furrows of your brow.

FELIX
An elevated thought? A childish one, rather!

AMELIA
O, enough irony!

FELIX
As God is my witness, my thought was a childish one. Look — You've got a white daisy there in your nosegay. Tear it apart, petal by petal saying "yes, no..." with each petal plucked. If the last one is "yes," I'll do my father's will.

AMELIA
How can you decide such an important matter in such a silly way? Blind fortune is to command you, when your sister can't?

FELIX
Yes. Blind fortune can command me in an indifferent matter. For really, all this is quite indifferent to me now... And I'll even confess

to you that I've so snarled myself in the tangled webs of this world that I will be happy if the daisy says "yes." It will forestall the pangs of conscience, loosing me from the hateful knots that bind me...

AMELIA
What's eating at your conscience? My dear brother, sometimes when I look at your thought-wracked brow, I can't find anything to compare it to other than a drooping, white, and immaculate lily... It is true that your soul is pure...

FELIX
The daisy...

AMELIA
*Plucking it.*
Yes, no... Yes, no...

FELIX
I watch those petals fall and am terrified, horribly... O! The vanity of human intentions!

AMELIA
Yes.

FELIX
Hell! And so it's "yes!"... Go, tell my father that I am with him from age upon age — forever! ...And I will be with him, until in the next life he is made to answer for the blood he spills, the groans he elicits!

AMELIA
O God, O God!

FELIX
Pray to God on my behalf. For I tell you, far better had it been for me had I died in my mother's womb. For now I should be sleeping, resting, and thus... thus...What will become of me?

AMELIA
Brother, forgive me...

FELIX
Forgive you? What for? I'm the only one I can't forgive, having desired in the depths of my heart... O, greatness! Glory! But on the living God I swear, it was not this sort of glory I desired — not this sort of greatness... But so it has come to pass.

AMELIA
Brother, I lied to you. The last petal remains — *no!*

FELIX
Now you are lying, Amelia. The last petal was *yes*. I know that fate has chosen to set me on this path... I hesitated only a hair, and now the hair has snapped, and all of the mountains that had hung therefrom shall come crashing down upon my head.

*Enter Servant.*

SERVANT
A letter for your lordship.

FELIX
From whom?

SERVANT
Some old grey haired gentleman... wearing an old frock...

FELIX
But there's no address...

SERVANT
The man who brought it said it was from a blind man.

FELIX
Ha!
*Breaks the seal, reads.*

AMELIA
Felix, what an expression on your face — It must be bad news...

FELIX
What? — No, it's very good news! I begin now, to become who I am. People will now see me for who I am... Go and tell him that I am on my way... O, if one could only go back in time, by one year, only! I would not go to meet with such an hour. Amelia! ... Amelia! ... Amelia!

AMELIA
How you groan!

FELIX
No... Sit down... It's true that I'm not an evil-hearted man — You believe in me, right, Amelia?

AMELIA
Brother, what unknown misfortune have I called down upon your head by what I took to be a white lie? I swear to you on the soul of my mother that the last petal said *no!*

FELIX
O, my Amelia — Now, the future is no longer my concern. Or the past. I'd like to tell you everything, but I can't. There is a horrid secret that would kill us both. And yet, without revealing it, I cannot justify the slightest event in my entire life... Amelia, I beg you in the name of your mother, don't judge me as others will. Keep one long memory of me in your heart — only such sad and unequivocal memories lift the human heart to God...

AMELIA
You're preparing yourself for something terrible.

FELIX
I've always loved you very much, more than...
*Gets up all of a sudden.*
Be well! I loved you like a brother. Listen — someday you'll have a husband and children, but there will be times when their love will not be enough for you... and you will compare their love with that of your brother... and something will be lacking, and you will weep. O! We were such happy children, once!

AMELIA
What's with you, brother?

FELIX
I have great debts to pay.

AMELIA
Debts? But my father... He'll pay them all for you, I swear to you here and now!

FELIX
Yes, my father will also pay... But I... You can't understand, sister, the convoluted events of this world... Worse than the most horrid prophecies of St John... There are hearts drawn and quartered, torn apart like the paper on which was written the stupid poem of a wise man... Be well! Take my advice, and enter a nunnery.

AMELIA
A nunnery?

FELIX
You're not married yet. You've no husband, or even a lover — I wouldn't want you to be deceived by anyone. Ha! But what will you tell my father from me? Wait... You'll say that... that I went to settle my debts, but that maybe I'll be back in the evening. If I return, I'll be nothing but a rag from which no flag for any party might be fashioned. So let him do with me what he will.
*Exits.*

AMELIA
I understand... My God! Now I understand! Felix! Felix!
*Exits.*

[END OF ACT II]

# ACT III

## Scene 1[*]

*A room in Horsztyński's house, as it was in Act I.*
*Horsztyński and Felix*

HORSZTYŃSKI
Are we alone, count?

FELIX
There's no one else in the room.

HORSZTYŃSKI
This was my father's favourite chamber... There, to the right, his portrait must still be hanging. That old man had a quiet and peaceful expression. His hair was as white as snow, and just as immaculate. And above the door must still be hanging the crucifix — of ebony, with a corpus of ivory.

FELIX
Yes.

HORSZTYŃSKI
And beneath the crucifix hang a brace of pistols.

FELIX
*Taking them down.*
Here they are.

HORSZTYŃSKI
Unloaded... On the table there to the right is a powder horn, and bullets.

---

[*] Our translation of this scene follows the, longer manuscript version adopted by Sawrymowicz for the *Dzieła wybrane*, rather than that of Juliusz Mien.

FELIX
*Taking them from the table.*
I've found them.

HORSZTYŃSKI
So you know that one of the pistols must be loaded — I suppose you know how... One of the pistols has a hilt of sandalwood, the other, apple... Load one of them, sir. I can smell the aroma of the lindens in bloom beneath the windows. I had thought that I would enjoy a quiet old age... Is the pistol loaded?

FELIX
Choose which one you want.

HORSZTYŃSKI
I'm blind! Give me both.

FELIX
Here they are.

HORSZTYŃSKI
Please, you choose.

FELIX
But I know which one is loaded.

HORSZTYŃSKI
Choose, please.

FELIX
*Takes one.*
I have.

HORSZTYŃSKI
Sit down and give me your left hand.

FELIX
Let's shoot, then.

HORSZTYŃSKI
If I die, you will truly be your father's son. If you die, it will be suicide.

FELIX
I know. Let's shoot.

HORSZTYŃSKI
Young man, sometimes, a point of honour, pride, is so strong in a man that, given the choice between life and death, he will be ashamed to choose life, thinking that the choice will sully him. And so he chooses self-sacrifice. Count, I have sacrificed my life to my country, and now I recognise the emptiness of that sacrifice. If you are innocent, come to your senses and don't rush to your grave with such indifference. Let the words of an old man remind you that it was not in vain that God poured the fear of death into the heart of man — Death is something horrible, so horrible. After I went blind — having nothing else to do — I spent entire days thinking about the mystery of the grave, and, really —death is an indescribable horror... The shadow of all thought, the spring of all hesitation. If you are innocent, come to your senses. Do not burden my grey head with crime — Let us lay aside the pistols. Choose again.

FELIX
I'd like to get this scene over with as quickly as possible.

HORSZTYŃSKI
But you know, I still can't believe that you're guilty. I respected you, trusted you, and even if you should give up your life, now, still I will despise you. I swear that I won't shed a tear over you, when you will be lying here at the feet of the old man you've shamed... Listen! There is great hatred between me and your father, and quite a few grounds for that hatred... It seems to me as if God has chosen your family to be the fire to my thatch, the poison to my well, the gale to uproot my orchards... I have fought, sir, and now I tumble to the dust like an insect, trod upon by someone's foot — My only happiness is to recall that the whole nation is falling apart — what wonder if the house of an old nobleman be buried in the rubble? In the face of such a great catastrophe, the memory of my own misfortune is forgotten. But when I think that my fall, the shaming of my house, is the gift of a traitor...

FELIX
Mr Horsztyński!

HORSZTYŃSKI
I swear to you, the greatest disgrace is to know that my misfortune is brought about by the Kossakowskis! It was not I who nestled my cottage against the walls of your castle, for support. You came here yourselves, in search of my inheritance. Now your father is about to tear the last crumb of bread from the mouth of this old man — and you... you! Worse even than your father, perhaps... It seems to me that you are very base fellows, Count Felix. I must leave you your life.

FELIX
Mr Horsztyński, let us choose our pistols.

HORSZTYŃSKI
Listen! I hold your family in such contempt that if she... loves you, well, I pity her. Because that is real misfortune and shame, a real punishment from God, a Biblical plague, to love a scoundrel. But perhaps you are innocent of this last crime. In such a case, do you know that I have shamed you, mortally, with words? And I have a weapon with which I shall kill you — and your father — and your honour — and the very memory of your having lived — I shall kill you for all time. Choose your pistol, sir!

FELIX
Wait! I'd like to examine, one more time, one thought...

HORSZTYŃSKI
Choose, you traitor!

FELIX
I have chosen.

HORSZTYŃSKI
God! God! I feel the same pistol in my hand as before!
*He turns, and fires into the wall.*
O, God!

SALOMEA
*Through the door.*
Let me in! Jesus and Mary! I'm dying!... Let me in!

HORSZTYŃSKI
Open the door, Felix!

*Salomea falls into his arms, fainting, sobbing.*

SALOMEA
You've killed him!

HORSZTYŃSKI
Wife... Why is it so quiet?

FELIX
She's fainted.

HORSZTYŃSKI
Bring her round... Is it only a fainting fit? Come here, young man... Choose the path that seems best to you... I've chosen mine...

FELIX
You've killed me with your contempt. Now, I'm ready for any villainy. I'll be with them, now.

HORSZTYŃSKI
With whom?

FELIX
With them, who avenge their self-contempt by despising others.

HORSZTYŃSKI
What care I, after all, who you shall become!

FELIX
And I'm just as indifferent as you. Be well, Mr Horsztyński!

HORSZTYŃSKI
Wait! Just let her see that you're still alive. O, how I pity her. What a waste of a woman!

SALOMEA
Where is my husband? Where is my husband!

HORSZTYŃSKI
Bring her over to me. What's wrong with you, my Sally? What were you so afraid of? We were just testing the pistols.

SALOMEA
Husband — it was you who shot — your pistol is warm.

HORSZTYŃSKI
It was only loaded with powder. But it's wrong even to waste powder on sparrows.

SALOMEA
Husband — you've smashed the crucifix that hung over the door.

HORSZTYŃSKI
The crucifix.

SALOMEA
And you, sir, why have you a weapon in your hand?

FELIX
It isn't loaded.
*He pulls the trigger.*

HORSZTYŃSKI
So, Count Felix, you said that you were ready to trade me your Turkish kindjal for these two French pistols — think it over carefully. If you've really determined upon such a trade, I'll agree at last and take advantage of you.

FELIX
As far as I'm concerned, the matter is settled.

HORSZTYŃSKI
I'm very glad. I'll have a souvenir of you — a nice one.

FELIX
I'll also leave you the sheath of my kindjal, in my testament.

HORSZTYŃSKI
Old people die first... But maybe we'll meet again... For I hear that you are going away... to fight... for your fatherland.

FELIX
O! not as quick as all that... I have a father ...

HORSZTYŃSKI
Ha! In that case, we'll be seeing one another... often...

FELIX
I bid you good evening. Just look, madame, how beautifully the sun is setting. The flowers of your garden are taking on a new life... They'll weep with the dew... this evening...

SALOMEA
Where are you going?

FELIX
Home... to my father's house.

SALOMEA
Do you know what those words mean in Holy Scripture?

FELIX
Words have different meanings according to the book in which they're found. The same words that are sacred in Holy Scripture are ungodly in an ungodly book, and they ring with misfortune in a book full of misfortunate events... Be well, both of you!
*Exits.*

[...]

HORSZTYŃSKI
What's with you, Sally? You rushed into my room like a raving woman...

SALOMEA
[...]

HORSZTYŃSKI
[... my little wife], you gave me a proper scare.

SALOMEA
[O my Ksawery!] Do you still love me?

HORSZTYŃSKI
[Why should I not?] — Sally? You were good to me... for a long while. [...I remember] when I left for the Bar expedition with my men — you baked our loaves with your own hands. I saw you myself, kneading the black dough with your sleeves rolled up... and when I came into the kitchen, you hid your hands behind your back and tilted your fresh little, lily-rose face up to my lips for a kiss. I will always remember that scene... Why are you kneeling in front of me? I don't like theatricality, Sally. Why do you kneel before me? I feel your head in my hands... Get up, my child — and go out into the courtyard. When you hear the harvesters returning from the fields, singing that song I like, roll out a barrel of beer for them — and give the harvest girls a red ribbon. Please, Sally — let the peasants relax and have some fun...

SALOMEA
All right, my Ksawery. If you only knew how happy you make me when you ask me to do such things.
*Exits.*

HORSZTYŃSKI
Are you still here?... She's gone. I'm sure that God will set this hour on the balance to my favour, for the absolution of my sins. Yes. Let her not be troubled, and I — after all, I've done some solid work, I have — Of what sort? Well, stepping away from the path over which people tread in such noisy crowds... Misery... or death... I've never seen misery and death so close at hand... What's to do in this world? Sit down at the foot of the roadside cross and croon a beggar's canticle: "Pennies for the blindman!" — At least a beggar has a faithful dog to lead him to that cross, and to the tavern, and back to the village at night... but I... Tomorrow, there'll be licitation in this house... ha! I'll leave them a new item to haggle over — an old man's coffin!... The Old Confederate — the Bar Confederate! How I liked it when people called me that — And before I die, I ought to define myself by my one moment of glory... No need to stain these floors with blood, floors over which I learned to crawl as a baby — no need... Ha! If we

give the Old Confederate some poison — maybe there's poison to be had in the house somewhere... Let's see... *Claps:* Świętosz! Świętosz!

ŚWIĘTOSZ
*Enters.*
My lord...?

HORSZTYŃSKI
Tell me what's going on outside...

ŚWIĘTOSZ
Ah — the wheat's not bad, and there's rye enough, thank God.

HORSZTYŃSKI
They're reaping today?

ŚWIĘTOSZ
They are, my lord. From Szewruk's cottage to Nagolicki's Mound... I don't know why you don't take the horse and go and see for yourself...

HORSZTYŃSKI
Idiot! Don't you remember the candles that blinded these eyes of mine?

ŚWIĘTOSZ
And may the Good Lord pay back those that did it with brimstone!

HORSZTYŃSKI
Listen, Świętosz, would you mind riding into town? There's a pharmacy on Liwska St., run by Josiel the Jew — there's a big sign in front, you can't miss it — Go there and buy a few złotys' worth of acidum prussicum...

ŚWIĘTOSZ
For roaches?* Do we have a problem with them again? Where, blast it? I'll burn the nest when I find it...

---

\*    This exchange turns on an untranslatable pun. In Polish slang, cockroaches were known as *prusaki* — "Prussians."

HORSZTYŃSKI
Maybe you've got some poison on hand?

ŚWIĘTOSZ
Of course. Toadstools for flies* — and there's still some arsenic left with which to season cheese for rats...

HORSZTYŃSKI
Ha! You've got some arsenic? Actually, some rats have made a nest behind the wainscoting in my bedroom. All night long they're rustling the tattered wallpaper...

ŚWIĘTOSZ
I'll bring some spiked doughnuts fried in butter.

HORSZTYŃSKI
No, no, just bring me the bottle... I'll take care of everything myself.

ŚWIĘTOSZ
But you know, my lord, that stuff can blind a person — you've got to be careful with it.

HORSZTYŃSKI
Don't worry, Świętosz my friend. I'll wear glasses.

ŚWIĘTOSZ
O, how stupid I am!

HORSZTYŃSKI
Why? What do you think I've got in mind?

ŚWIĘTOSZ
What? What you've got in mind? ... What do you take me for, my lord?

HORSZTYŃSKI
Nothing, never mind. Just go and get the arsenic for me.

---

\*    In Polish, the word for "toadstool" is *muchomor* — which literally means "fly killer." Powder from toadstools, mixed with sugar, was an old home remedy to get rid of flies.

*Exit Świętosz.*

I was sure he'd caught on and would sound the alarm... Hmm, still need to leave a letter for Fr Procopius... as a posthumous confession. My sin, my death...

ŚWIĘTOSZ
*Re-enters.*
Here you are, my Lord — the bottle with the powder.

HORSZTYŃSKI
Give it here. Is it still a long while until night?

ŚWIĘTOSZ
The sun is setting past Nagolicki's Mound.

HORSZTYŃSKI
Where is that, exactly?

ŚWIĘTOSZ
Oh, over there, where you once went riding with my Lady, in the buggy... Remember? As I drove you past the mound, she sighed out "Stop the horses, Świętosz — Look how many lilies of the valley! I'll cut myself a little bouquet..."

HORSZTYŃSKI
I remember. Here — draw that little table close, and get me pen and paper. Don't let anyone come in here while I'm writing, all right? Now, is my pen inked? Where's the paper? And let me know when I've reached the bottom of the page.

ŚWIĘTOSZ
Go on, sir... From here... Now, up... About face! As God's my witness, how wonderfully you write! Two even rows, like the traces left by wagon wheels in the soft dust! Column right, to the rear... Nice and even now... You know what? It seems to me that you'd still be able to scribble over the moustaches of the Muscovites with your sabre, if they fell on us at night, just like when...

HORSZTYŃSKI
Do you know how to read?

ŚWIĘTOSZ
No.

HORSZTYŃSKI
Tomorrow, at sunrise, take this letter to Fr Procopius' cell... At sunrise, first thing, understand? ... Don't forget — this is a very important matter.

ŚWIĘTOSZ
Of course, my lord.
*Exits.*

HORSZTYŃSKI
I wanted to fling my arms around that man's neck... But then I was afraid, lest he guess that his dying master was bidding him a final farewell... The loneliest man — and who might be lonelier than I? — has so many threads to break before he leaves this world... It's already evening. The crickets begin to chirp in the cracks and crannies of my house... Where will I be tomorrow at this hour? ... My God, my God! Christ, Lord, judge me as you judge the unhappy, the unfortunate... Have mercy on me. Dear God — you might well keep me here upon this earth — That would require no miracle of you... Just speak to my heart; let it tell me that I am still needed... by things, by events... by people; say to my heart "Live!" and I shall live... I would live if there were even the smallest hope of regaining my sight... How am I to take this poison? — I'll wrap it in a wafer.*

*Feeling his way, he goes over to the cupboard and takes out a wafer.*

As blind as I am, I still found a wafer! Who was it directed my hand? I feel the thin bread trembling in my hands — O, how I used to love Christmas! In this very room I used to fashion suns of different colours, and little crèches out of these wafers... and my childish heart was filled with a kind of gladness and... holiness.

---

\*          In Polish: *opłatek*. This is thin, rectangular piece of unleavened bread, identical in material to the communion Host, though in various colours as well as white. Poles traditionally "break this bread" with loved ones at the Christmas Eve meal, exchanging good wishes. The *opłatek* is not consecrated, but religious symbols and inscriptions are often pressed upon its surface.

*He breaks the wafer, sifts the poison onto one piece, and then seals it closed with the other half.*

Even today I don't understand what these sacred letters pressed on the wafer mean. When I was a child, I thought they were words of some angelic song... in some heavenly tongue... It's so hot in here. I'd like to take a little walk around the room, but I'm afraid of striking my forehead against the cold walls.

*The song of the returning harvesters is heard, from afar.*

Shh... The harvesters are singing. O! My village! My village! Tomorrow in this house there will be coffin — and priests — and judgement... Tomorrow, that song will ring in the ears of another master — and no one will have any pity for me. I sacrificed all I had to my country — I squandered that debt on gunpowder and bullets... and tomorrow, had I lived to see it, I would have been as hungry as a stray dog... and no one would have any pity for me. Old and grey — and alone — no children. They won't bury me in consecrated soil. My father must have been a great sinner, for me to suffer so.

HARVESTERS' SONG
*Clearly now.*
We've mown the wheat, we've reaped the rye —
Hey, vodka, lord! Our throats are dry!
The sheaves are stacked on every side,
As broad as the field, as long, as wide!

HORSZTYŃSKI
The wheat is mown — the people flatter me. The wheat, harvested... I see that my wife has had a barrel of beer rolled out for them... What a lot of voices in the courtyard...

HARVESTERS' SONG
We've mown the wheat, the field is clear,
We've chased away both crow and hare;
Don't skimp us ribbons, mistress dear:
Red ribbons to adorn our hair!

HORSZTYŃSKI
In this song, I can see my golden fields, my green woods… At first, the song irritated my heart, and now… it's calmed it, like a nurse's lullaby… like the song my Izabella used to sing… May the perpetual light shine upon her… amen, and — after my death, may it be as peaceful and quiet for me as once it was, at her side, while she was singing… Shh! Someone's coming. It's her — I recognise the rustle of her skirts… She's dressed in silken skirts…

SALOMEA
Husband, come out to the people in the courtyard.

HORSZTYŃSKI
O no, I can't do that, wife.

SALOMEA
But several of the old peasants even came up to the porch and bent down low before my feet, entreating me to kindly lead their master out to them.

HORSZTYŃSKI
Wife — I will not go.

SALOMEA
Why would you make so many people sad?

HORSZTYŃSKI
Why? Because the world is a sad place, and I can't make it happy like some harlequin — Because, because I'm old and blind… Tell me, Sally while I was away from home, did anyone ever deliver any court papers?

SALOMEA
Sometimes, different manifestos were nailed up on the door — Bar manifestos. Targowice manifestos. At first, I read them all through carefully, and then I tossed them all into the chest of drawers in the pantry.

HORSZTYŃSKI
That's good… Do you pray each evening along with the household?

SALOMEA
We always pray together.

HORSZTYŃSKI
Don't forget to pray tonight, my wife... Pray for those who suffered... and lived...

SALOMEA
Pray with us, too, husband.

HORSZTYŃSKI
I'm not well. I have to lie down in bed.

SALOMEA
Right now?

HORSZTYŃSKI
Sally, walk lightly when you're going to your room... No, I don't need to ask you that. But go without a candle, because the light... O, how crazy I am! See? Just like my Świętosz, sometimes I forget that I'm blind... But don't wake me, wife — I feel in great need of sleep... I'd like to sleep well tonight... You take your supper alone.

SALOMEA
Husband, do you want me to stay with you?

HORSZTYŃSKI
Of course not, my pigeon. What, you think I'm sick unto death that you want to sit vigil? Have you forgotten that, just a few months ago, I used to sleep on the wet grass, at the feet of my horse? Ah, what a horse that was! ... I used to feel him lift up his hoof from time to time and nudge my chest — gently, as gently and carefully as Świętosz when he sets a crystal glass down on the table ... That horse had feeling in his hooves — He never scraped my chest roughly, even in sleep.

*Salomea covers her face with her hands.*

Sally, help me with my belt.

*Salomea takes one end of the sash in her hand, while Hosztyński twirls about, as if waltzing, but slowly — and thus he arrives at the other side of the room; the sash remains in Salomea's hands.*

See, Sally — the belt remains in your hands, and the husband has twirled himself free — forever. That's the story of a life — in the morning you held one end of the sash, and I drew near you... and in the evening... What? Are you kneeling before me? My daughter, my dear, Sally — you will never curse me, that's true, right? You'll never curse my memory, whatever falls to your lot through my fault... Give me your hand. Lead me to my bedroom door, and then leave, quietly. 'Cos you know, the blind hear the slightest rustle... Good night, Sally.

SALOMEA
Until tomorrow.

HORSZTYŃSKI
What?

SALOMEA
Tomorrow, husband, you'll be more at peace, perhaps.

HORSZTYŃSKI
More at peace, yes...
*Enters the bedroom.*

SALOMEA
I'll tell the peasants to keep it down outside. O, that the poor old man might fall asleep!


### Scene 2
*The hetman's foyer. A loud ringing. Enter Hetman*

HETMAN
What's going on, for God's sake? Is there no one here? No one?

KSIŃSKI
*Running in.*
What is it, your lordship?

HETMAN
Where are my people? That fellow just had to shoot off his mouth in front of the people about revolution in Warsaw! ... Well, have him shot in the head like a dog! ... It's not true! Warsaw hasn't risen in

revolt; it's calmer in Warsaw than it is in my grey noggin! For God's sake, call the people here — Get the horses harnessed — and then come back here! Where is my son?

KSIŃSKI
He rode out somewhere, on horseback.

HETMAN
Haven't I told you to harness the horses? And fix a chain to the wheel of that emissary from Warsaw! I'll drag him to the governor in Vilnius!

*Exit Ksiński.*

It's collapsing, the mountain is collapsing, but I'll hold it together... The shoemakers are in a ferment... If I wanted to, I could hole myself up in the palace as quiet as a mouse — but those papers! Ha! Mr Horsztyński, those papers of yours will be the doom of Poland! Day after tomorrow the Muscovites will be marching up...

KSIŃSKI
*Re-enters.*
I've passed on your commands.

HETMAN
Mr Ksiński, since I've got you close at hand, I've got to make use of you... Now, as soon as the nobles arrive at the palace, my son ought to stand at their head and march off, at once, armed, to Vilnius, to the Ostrobramska Gate... Word has arrived that Jasiński is planning to enter the city tomorrow night, in secret, just there. He must be nabbed and hanged as a spy, at once, without a trial... you understand... Don't believe a word he says — don't even believe him if he says his name is Jasiński!

KSIŃSKI
Yes, your lordship.

HETMAN
But you know, my son — although it's not at all likely — might not want to stand...

KSIŃSKI
Yes, my lord. Although it is quite unlikely, perhaps he will not wish to stand...

HETMAN
Then you shall.

KSIŃSKI
I will strive to prove to you, my lord, that...

HETMAN
Silence! Silence! — Silence! Words are rubbish! Should my son not wish to stand to the occasion, you will summon my soldiers — the ones being kept in the rear courtyard — to the hall, and you will arrest the little bird! Understand?

KSIŃSKI
I understand.

HETMAN
You'll toss him in some hole, and then — you yourself will take horse to Vilnius... Mr Horda will lead fifty armed me to my palace there, and you will speed with the others to the Ostrobramska Gate.

KSIŃSKI
All will be done according to your will.

HETMAN
Sforka will show you the supply of powder laid up in the tower... Here is my signet... You understand me, sir? Everyone is to heed you as if you were the little finger of my own hand...

KSIŃSKI
I am honoured at the trust...

HETMAN
But my son — I want it to be my son at the head of the troops... Understand?

KSIŃSKI
Yes.
*Enter Amelia.*

HETMAN
Who is this woman? Amelia? What do you want here?

AMELIA
Father, please hear what I have to say —

HETMAN
Tomorrow... tomorrow!

AMELIA
Today, father... Mr Ksiński, please withdraw.

*Ksiński exits.*

HETMAN
What does this mean? You presume too much upon my good will!

AMELIA
Father, dear father — where are you off to?

HETMAN
Vilnius.

AMELIA
I beg you, father — Remain here in the castle! ... A great danger threatens you!

HETMAN
You've had a bad dream.

AMELIA
Father — I was in my room, alone, and I watched as the moon rose, blood red. The dogs began to howl — deep, horrid howls! I turned around ... O, believe me, father! Don't think me some crazy person who sees things! ... I turned around and my mother was there with me!

HETMAN
Your dead mother...

AMELIA
O father, you are so good to believe me! I thought you'd shove me away in contempt — but I see the mist of thought upon your brow. I always knew that, one day, you'd come to love your daughter.

HETMAN
Did she say anything to you?

AMELIA
She stood there silent, a long time. Then the strings of my harp began to vibrate of themselves, and to play a sad and airy sort of melody... Then I seemed to hear a woman's moan, and sobbing, that voice said "Your father is about to die."

HETMAN
Your father...

AMELIA
I was terrified! I ran to your bedroom at once ... I opened the door... and again that white shade was standing before me... It was like I brought her there myself with my eyes.

HETMAN
Your father... That's what she said?!

AMELIA
Father! Why are you looking at me like that? Forgive a poor heart filled with dread. Don't go to Vilnius! Don't spurn me from your knees! Listen to your daughter's plea!

HETMAN
My daughter?

AMELIA
Through my lips, mother is warning you.

HETMAN
Silence!...

AMELIA
Listen! I know that you've never loved me... I'm not complaining, I'm not begging for love, though my poor heart thirsts for it... But have mercy, at least! Have mercy on me!

HETMAN
What is it you want from me?

AMELIA
Swear to me that you'll remain here. O, if only my mother were alive to beg you, as I am doing...

HEMAN
Act your age, madam! You're acting childish... So, off to your room! *Calls.*Ksiński!

AMELIA
Father! Father! O, how horrid!

*Enter Ksiński.*

HETMAN
*To Ksiński.*
Send a message to Mr Horsztyński. Tomorrow the notice will be served! Off with you, for I'm about to leave!

*Exit Ksiński.*

*To Amelia.*
Off with you, too, child. Calm down — no danger threatens me.

AMELIA
Father! I won't let you go! — Listen! She says "Your father shall perish!"

KSIŃSKI
*Enters.*
Your carriage awaits, Lord Hetman.

HETMAN
My cloak, and my pistols!

AMELIA
Mother, my dear! Protect him!]]

[END OF ACT III]

# ACT IV

### Scene 1
*The steward's room in the palace. Sforka — Małgorzata.*

SFORKA
Off with you, woman —Don't disturb me.

MAŁGORZATA
Ah, husband, people put the wildest things in your head, and you believe them! I wish I hadn't put those shards of your skull back in place, when the Hetman shattered your noggin yesterday like a rotten egg!

SFORKA
Be off! Go take care of your hens and your geese! I'm waiting for someone...

MAŁGORZATA
I'm going to lock you up in here, and I won't allow in any of those jokesters who stir up your brains like camomile in a teacup!

SFORKA
It's no jokester, my soul! The wisest man amongst all the Hetman's musicians is on his way here... A man with imagination... First trombone...

MAŁGORZATA
If you want to practise music, it'll be behind a locked door!

SFORKA
It's not me going to play a trombone... Do you take me for an idiot, wife of mine?

MAŁGORZATA
So what are you going to do with a musician?

SFORKA
Work.

MAŁGORZATA
I'll give that head of yours a nice cold dousing if you're going to keep gabbing about those Neapolitan treasures! Keep it close to your chest! And don't get drunk with that trombone player! I'm off to Mass to beg of the Lord an ounce of reason for that head of yours — You're already entering into your second childhood... You must've been a wicked one in your youth, husband, if senility is stealing upon you already at sixty! You'll be fit for sandbox and pebbles... Play, my love!

*She exits.*

SFORKA
Stupid, stupid woman! It's a good thing I copied down the nuncio's questions in the accounts book... Ha! The first trombone!

*Enter Priest.*

Devil take it! — It's Father Procopius!... Greetings, reverend sir... Are you here about the ram?

FR PROCOPIUS
I beg your pardon for interrupting you at work, at your accounts, perhaps? I was looking for Count Felix. I was told that he's been absent from the palace all night long and still hasn't returned... Nobody seems to know where he is... I've got a very important message for him — It concerns the health and welfare of a person dear to him. And so I've come to you, Mr Sforka, to seek your services as a go-between. Let me have a piece of paper and a pen. I'll write a few words to Felix, and ask you, old friend, to get them into his hands as soon as possible.

SFORKA
You were saying, Father...?

FR PROCOPIUS
I asked you for a piece of paper and a pen...

SFORKA
At once... Please, have a seat... Can I get you a small glass of vodka?

**FR PROCOPIUS**
For the love of God, Mr Sforka — Don't slow me down with politesse... I have to return as quickly as possible, to watch over a poor orphan... I can't drink with you, Mr Sforka; I've got a funeral Mass to celebrate.

**SFORKA**
How can I be of assistance?

**FR PROCOPIUS**
Paper, please. And a pen.
*To himself.*
Is the old man gone deaf?

**SFORKA**
Ah — paper, paper — Here you are... Please, sit yourself down and write, Father; you will forgive me for not keeping you company — I've got a very important matter to bring to a conclusion.

*The Priest sits at a desk and writes.*

**SFORKA**
It's an odd thing... Just yesterday I was thinking that this fortune was an improbable matter, and this morning — sheer idiocy, rather. Am I wise in the morning and stupid at night, or wise at night and stupid in the morning?

*Enter the Trombonist.*

Ah, greetings, Garnosz!

**TROMBONIST**
...Servant... What's that priest doing here?

**SFORKA**
I'll send him packing right away, Mr Garnosz — I'm really indebted to you for deigning to come and extend your helping hand to a poor fellow like me... We'll get rid of the priest in short order.

FR PROCOPIUS
Mr Sforka, by the bonds of our old friendship, I beg you, earnestly —
Give this letter to Count Felix as soon as he gets back... It's frightfully
important... The fate of many people depends upon this slip of paper.

SFORKA
Very well, I swear... Fate depending on a slip of paper — That happens
quite often. Have you heard about my story, Father?

FR PROCOPIUS
Peace upon this house...

SFORKA
I fall at your feet, reverend sir.

*Exit Priest.*

TROMBONIST
So, where do we begin?

SFORKA
Mr Garnosz — It often happens that people win at the lottery. Now,
if they chance upon a big sum — they become great lords ... Now ...
What is fate, my dear trombonist, what is fate? Something stupid ...
and not so stupid after all. Because if you risk buying a chance, and
you don't win, people call you stupid. But if you win, well, then they
say that you're clever! Now, what is cleverness, what is reason, my dear
trombonist? What, if not — fate?

TROMBONIST
How about a drink, Mr Sforka — And let's see that paper you were
flapping your gums about. We'll see...

SFORKA
To your health!
*Drinks.*
Even if these questions lead to nothing, Mr Trombonist, drink up!
It'll loosen our tongues... Please — here you go — read...

TROMBONIST
I can read the treble clef, but handwritten Cyrillic... not so much...

SFORKA
Listen...
Easy the tasks,
But the questions it asks
Are tough to solve...

TROMBONIST
Tough to figure out?

SFORKA
They're trying to scare us. Let's read them through. We'll start from the easiest.
*Reads.*
Primo: Why does a stick have two ends?
Secundo: What do I think?

TROMBONIST
Who is it thinking, Mr Sforka?

SFORKA
Nothing's written about that... "What do I think," and that's all. Full stop. But listen further —
Tertio: What's the quickest way to go round the world?
Quarto: Did God create the chicken first, or the egg?
Quinto: Who am — I?

TROMBONIST
Mr Sforka — these are silly questions. Stupid questions!

SFORKA
Sexto: What weighs more — a pound of sand, or a pound of iron?
Septimo: What would a person be, if not a person?
Octavo:

TROMBONIST
Let's write down the answer the first question first, and the others will follow, falling right in line.

SFORKA
We've got to read on to the end.
Octavo: Why do they say — He's got a stud driven in his noggin?

Nono: Why are there only nine questions to answer, no more?
And at the end, there's a postscript in verse:
"Solved it? Since
*Quaestiones, quae pendent,*
*Sforka, intendent,*
He'll be a prince.
    We have a further request of him, to wit: That he should invent a manner of blowing square soap-bubbles, and, when successful, that he should send one such bubble to us, in Milan, as proof. The bubble may be sent here by regular post, or via hot-air balloon." What do you think of that, sir?

TROMBONIST
I think you'd better get started on that bubble; otherwise, your bubble will burst!

SFORKA
The way I see it, we ought to leave the last things for last. Now, tell me, sir — why does a stick have two ends?

TROMBONIST
Why? What do you mean, "why?"

SFORKA
This all seems like such rubbish to me, that, I tell you, I'm ready to spit on it all and that's that!

TROMBONIST
I'm of the opposite opinion. I urge you not to be put off by the difficulties — But let's move on to the second question... What did it say?

SFORKA
What about the first one?

TROMBONIST
Pshaw! The first one is stupid! What's the next one?

SFORKA
Secundo: What do I think?

**TROMBONIST**
That's a very easy one to solve — what do I think...

**SFORKA**
But what do I think?

**TROMBONIST**
What do you mean, what do you think, sir? Am I supposed to know what you're thinking?

**SFORKA**
But who is this I?

**TROMBONIST**
The person asking the question! That's as clear as day!

**SFORKA**
Well, maybe it'll come clear later. Let's move on. What's the quickest way to go round the world?

**TROMBONIST**
That, sir, is the easiest one of all. If there were no oceans, by post-chaise. If there were no land, by boat. But since there is both land and water, then by post-chaise and by boat! Write that down, Mr Sforka: by post-chaise, and by boat!

**SFORKA**
All right — we'll let that be then, even though I don't quite like it... post-chaise and boat — but it'll work,... it'll work!

**TROMBONIST**
I tell you, sir, it'll work splendidly...

**SFORKA**
I'll be in your debt, Mr Trombonist... All right, enough! Let's move on. Drink up, friend.

**TROMBONIST**
You see? The wolf's never as frightening in person as they make him out to be.

SFORKA
Hmmm, hmmm! But you know, we've got to have everything ready before this evening — because if not, it's all just smoke in the face...

TROMBONIST
Well then, let's get a move on, Mr. Sfortia...

SFORKA
Did you call me Sforza, sir?

TROMBONIST
Ha! It's all going on like a well-greased wheel... Read on, Mr Sforka.

SFORKA
Did God create the chicken first, or the egg?

TROMBONIST
How does it seem to you?

SFORKA
The chicken...

TROMBONIST
He might have done, and then again, He might have just as easily created the egg... We've got to be sure before we set anything down.

SFORKA
But if He created the egg first, who would brood over it till it hatched?

TROMBONIST
The chicken.

SFORKA
It seems I rated your imagination a bit too highly, Mr Trombonist. What chicken? That's a stupid answer!

TROMBONIST
I'll prove to you that it's not stupid. I'm certain of the fact that He created the egg first... And, for example, if there was no chicken, you yourself know that the warmth of a a person's body, or a stove, can...

SFORKA
But back then when there were no stoves, my good man...!

TROMBONIST
But there was Eve — She could have hatched it... Nothing could be simpler. Have your wife give it a try. And, if it hatches, then, that's proof. God created the egg first.

SFORKA
I don't want to get my wife involved...

TROMBONIST
So then, just write: the egg... Write it down — the egg. I guarantee it's right.

SFORKA
It seems to me that I'll be changing all this, after some deeper thought... but for now, let it be... Let's read on. Quinto: Who am — I?

TROMBONIST
We've already been over that one.

SFORKA
When?

TROMBONIST
Earlier on. I already figured it out and forgot about it, long ago...

SFORKA
And I guarantee you, that we haven't been over it at all. Who am — I?

TROMBONIST
What a stupid question, "Who am — I!"

SFORKA
You — are a trombonist.

TROMBONIST
Ha! So, write it down. Trombonist.

**SFORKA**
With your permission — Who on earth knows that you were with me, and asked me "who am I?"... And of course, there's no need for anyone to know that you, sir, helped me with the riddles...

**TROMBONIST**
It's quite impossible to get anywhere with you, sir!

**SFORKA**
O! If only the Hetman's dwarf were here! He's got more brains in his little pot than there is in all the Hetman's music!

**TROMBONIST**
The dwarf would not tell you anything different from what I've said, Mr Sforka, sir. Ask him: "What am I?" and he'll tell you: a trombonist. And if he asks me, then I'll say, "you're a dwarf." So, go ahead, Mr Sforka, ask me.

**SFORKA**
I've been asking you for the past hour, for God's sake. Who am I?

**TROMBONIST**
You are Sforka the steward.

**SFORKA**
I know that I'm Sforka the steward!

**TROMBONIST**
So why are you asking me such a stupid question?

**SFORKA**
When it's not me asking, but this paper here!

**TROMBONIST**
What paper?

**SFORKA**
Farewell, Mr Trombonist. You muddle me quite, and then you quarrel with me as if I were a child. I'll read the questions, and answer them myself!

**TROMBONIST**
No, you won't! That you certainly will not do, Mr Sforka!

**SFORKA**
Yes I will, if I die doing it!

**TROMBONIST**
Everything? Before this evening?

**SFORKA**
Before this very evening.

**TROMBONIST**
Everything?

**SFORKA**
Every last one!

**TROMBONIST**
And the soap bubble? What about that?

**SFORKA**
The soap bubble! For God's sake, I'd forgotten about the soap bubble!

**TROMBONIST**
You see? And so, out of the friendship I bear you, Mr Sforka, I'll help you as far as the bubble is concerned. Now, it's supposed to be square?

**SFORKA**
Yes.

**TROMBONIST**
Well, then. You just have to find a square straw.

**SFORKA**
I know! I know! But how to send the proof to them by mail?

**TROMBONIST**
Send some soap along with the square straw, of course, and let the Milanese blow their own bubbles.

SFORKA
That's it... I'll go and look for a square straw out in the fields... Now, where are you off to?

TROMBONIST
To play my trombone.

SFORKA
Come back this evening, sir, to look over the questions again.

TROMBONIST
Your humble servant...

SFORKA
Come, we'll go out together...

*They exit, forgetting the letter on the table.*

SCENE 2
*The depths of the stage are exposed — a large clock room — the tower in the distance — tables covered with green cloth. Young people are playing cards, drinking, smoking pipes. Among them, Ksiński. Some are playing, others are walking around in groups, talking; a constant buzz of conversation and laughter.*

FIRST GROUP
— O, two bottles of champagne!
— On my honour...
— But when I wager with you...
— Enough already, you two! You're betting on something that's quite clear to everyone else!
— Ha, ha, ha!... Did you ever see Kościuszko in person?
— Now, if only he had won the hand of that nobleman's daughter, he'd be sitting peacefully at home right now, sowing barley, instead of chaos!
— I heard that you've been unlucky in love too, is that not so?
— He won! Wschowski won! Here — now you've got to pay for the bubbly.
— What were you wagering on?
— I said that if Kościuszko had married the daughter of that

nobleman, who despised the match because Kościuszko was just a poor engineer, he'd never have gone to America and then become such a terror.
— Just like Cromwell, who had one foot on the deck of a ship to sail to the colonies as a common tar. And then the ship is held in port by royal command, and Cromwell remains behind and becomes a great republican, from sheer boredom.
— What? You compare Kościuszko to Cromwell?
— Listen — Wschowski laid a bet and won, but you can't buy champagne here — it's provided gratis!
— Champagne! We need bettor's champagne!
— Off to Vilnius! We'll buy some in Vilnius!

KSIŃSKI
*Getting up on the table.*
Gentlemen! A moment, if you please! Gentlemen! Your ears, for a moment... Gentlemen! Now, we've spent the whole night happily at cards, waiting on the Hetman's son, who was to lead us — and he did not show up at the castle... And so...

GROUP
— And so, what? Bravo, Ksiński! What now?

KSIŃSKI
Gentlemen — Here I have the Hetman's signet. Your respect, please! Now, in this state of events, I am obliged to assume leadership over you, and lead you to the appointed place.

GROUP
— Let's wait on the Count! Let's wait, wait!

KSIŃSKI
We'll wait on him another quarter hour... Any longer and I'd have hell to pay. Well, I'm finished with my speech.
*Gets down from the table.*

GROUP
— Bravo! Toss him in the air! Toss him in the air!

*They grab Ksiński and start to toss him.*

— Hey! Take down the curtains! Let's use them!

KSIŃSKI
But I've got spurs on — I'll tear them! Enough, gentlemen! That's too high now! Please — you'll make me angry.

GROUP
— Enough of this fooling around with balloons, already!
— Where's our poet? Let's have an improvisation!
— Or let Kleofas sing that song of his beloved who, when she plays the guitar, it sounds like water dripping into a tin bowl.
— Water? What water?
— Dripping from what?
— Sing, poet, Miss Amelia's song!
   "Phyllis went into the rye
   And didn't tell her mother why..."

*Enter Felix, dressed in black. By degrees, the voices die away. Some come up and shake Felix's hand, others bow to him from afar.*

KSIŃSKI
You're here, Count! I'm so happy, that after all... Please, let me introduce you to the heads... You'd like that?

FELIX
Heads? What heads?

KSIŃSKI
Friends! I see that our Hetman is in a good mood... After all, you should be our Hetman, Felix? Where have you been all night? Are those wildflowers in your hair and on your coat? *Whispering.* Well? With Maryna? *Aloud.* Count Felix, that sentimental soul, spent the whole night with the stars, my noble friends, but I wager he won't fall asleep in the saddle.

ONE OF THOSE PRESENT
But, for God's sake, just look at him — how sleepy he looks. What's with him?

FELIX
Please, gentlemen, continue with your revels — Make yourselves at home... MrKsiński, I do apologise for suddenly throwing such a damper on your jollity.

KSIŃSKI
My lord, I beseech you: Wake up and put on the man, already! You can't come with us like that!

FELIX
Whatever...

KSIŃSKI
What do you mean, "whatever?"

FELIX
I mean that I'm quite indifferent to all that... Are you at cards, gentlemen?

VOICE FROM THE CROWD
We're playing faro... Come on, Count — try your luck!

FELIX
My luck?

KSIŃSKI
The hell with faro, by God!

FELIX
Why not? I'll give it a shot.
*Draws near the table.*

ONE OF THE GUESTS
What will my lord wager?

FELIX
Myself — that is, my enterprise. If you win, I'll go with you; if I win, I'll do what I want.

KSIŃSKI
Felix, that's stupid!

FELIX
Not at all! I'm quite serious... King.
*Draws the faro.*

GUEST
King!... You won, Count.

FELIX
And the banker's card?

GUEST
King... How odd...!

FELIX
And in that case...

GUEST
Half the kitty goes to the banker.

FELIX
Half of my will belongs to you. What shall you do with half of my will?

KSIŃSKI
So, half of your will belongs to us, Count! That's already quite a bit...! How about letting us have the second half as well!

FELIX
Ha! And I've forgotten to inquire as to the aim of your expedition?

KSIŃSKI
What? Are you joking, Count Felix? It's your father's cause — your nation's cause!

FELIX
You're all so concerned with the nation's cause? And all of you are noblemen?

VICES
Yes! yes! All of us!

ONE OF THE GUESTS
Except me.

FELIX
Who was it said "except me?"

KSIŃSKI
One of the gentlemen assayed a joke.

FELIX
No — let him, the one who didn't deny his nature, come and stand by me. What? Nobody?

GROUP
—The Count, like Diogenes, is seeking a man with a lantern.

FELIX
How strangely that voice resounded in my heart...! I must discover him, that man... Listen, gentlemen — There's something in the revolutionary atmosphere of this castle that excites my senses and my soul. A horse and a lance! Get me a horse and a lance! I'll go with you — People — ants — insects — stones — I pass them by on my speeding charger... nothing — of which nothing can be made, called "the nation" — all of this has taken on a strange triviality in my eyes. Now, if you don't have enough heat to melt crowns, enough jewels to create others — I'll pour all of my fire into you — I'll sift all of my treasures into your hands. For I swear to you, that your minds have never encompassed such a space as my everyday realm of dreams...!

VOICES
Vivat Felix! Vivat! Vivat!

FELIX
Silence! — Do you not know that we shall create for our country the bronze face of ancient nations? — The sword shall be our chisel. We shall shape the heart of the country upon the mould of Dionysus' iron will. It shall bellow with its horrid fiery maw to the four corners of the world, — with the moans of the imprisoned wretches and martyrs consumed within it as a holocaust... Are your hearts beating with pity? Our fathers possessed the right to kill, and we can't even arrange a gladiatorial show to toughen the hearts of our children. Tell

me — has no one amongst you ever experienced heavenly delight? Never felt himself to be a higher sort of being, when the peasants of the village worshipped him like God and confessed, with bestial instinct, to his natural superiority? — They are madmen, they are lost, damned, who would wish to deprive future generations of the charm of this inheritance granted by a happy fate, begun in the cradle and brought to completion in the glory of the marble tomb! ...

KSIŃSKI
Felix! ...

FELIX
All of your pride is contained in my heart. Long have I striven to poison the vital thought of grandeur with the thin refreshments of feeling! And I couldn't! ... You thought to lead me? Well I, I shall cast you all into such a whirlpool that you will be like drunken men — or like lunatics, you will traipse the high cornices of immense structures! And woe to him, who shall awaken! Whose ears are met with the cry: traitor! For upon awakening, he shall tumble into the abyss. — Have you such pale brows, that they will not grow any paler in the eyes of the world? Or cheeks so ruddy that they shall flame no more when marked with the slap of the hand of the people? If you are men of iron, I shall be yours. For I have searched the earth for something hard, and grand; I shall chew, I shall bend in my hand ingots and bars of iron — and once I have fallen asleep in a horrid dream of inebriation, I shall not awaken until the last of you shall die on behalf of my greatness, my pride. Pride is the soul of my soul. I shall find my happiness in the overthrow of superstition and of law — just as I have been happy at times when winning a match on the ivory chessboard. Pride is harp with a thousand strings — a thousand tones, deep, and thin — a thousand triumphs, elevated, and trivial. Take your place upon the chessboard of the world, [[if you are capable of it — take your place, and I will be yours, and my thought will drive you before me like a furious wind!

VOICES
Vivat Felix! Vivat!

KSIŃSKI
*To himself.*
He's afire — he's ours!

*To Felix.*
Count Felix, that's our boy! You speak like a book. So you belong to us?

FELIX
*Shrugs.*
You all belong to me! Do you understand what it is that I demand of you? What I want, that's my affair, and not your business to know... But come, swear your blind allegiance o me. It's not your empty words, it's not the cheers of the mob that will satisfy the desires of my soul... O, no! The realm of my dreams is so great, so limitless, that the entire world seems but a speck of dust in comparison! Are you all capable of eliciting movement and life from this vacuum? Have you arms of iron to shake the world I show to you?

VOICES
*With ardour.*
We have! Long live Felix! Long live Felix!

FIRST NOBLEMAN
As God's my witness, I can't comprehend any of this.

SECOND NOBLEMAN
What a splendid mind!

VOICES
Shh! ... Quiet!

FELIX
*Unsheathing his sabre.*
Behold the karabela of my ancestors — Let the people approach and swear their unconditional obedience to me on it. Whoever wavers now, let him depart, for woe to him, who will be untrue to his vow! Consider well — the pact that unites you to me is a frightful one, and irrevocable! Well then, will you swear?

VOICES
We swear! We swear!

WSCHOWSKI
I wish to speak.

*The hubbub grows.*

**VOICES**
No! No! Now is the time for action!

**FELIX**
Is there anyone among you who does not have the good of the Fatherland at heart?

**ALL**
Long live Poland! Long live the Fatherland!

**WSCHOWSKI**
Gentlemen, please! But the Golden Freedom — long live the Golden Freedom, too!*

**FELIX**
Amen! — Will you swear?

**ALL**
*Unsheathing their swords.*
We swear!

*At this moment, there is much noise and commotion at the door. Halbardsmen are forbidding entrance to someone.*

**KSIŃSKI**
*Going up to the door.*
What's going on?

---

\* In Polish, *złota wolność*. The Golden Freedom was a peculiarity of the Polish parliamentary system, which traditionally required absolute consent of all (noble) representatives for any motion, however important, to pass into law. Any nobleman had the right to torpedo any legislation, merely by standing and declaring "I disagree." This privilege, which late 18th century Polish legislators abolished just before the final partition of the country, was logically abused by representatives in the pay of Russia, Prussia and Austria — and historians agree that the anarchic policy was much to blame for the decline and fall of the once powerful Polish state.

HALBARDSMAN
It's a young soldier who insists on speaking with my lord Graf Felix. He says that he bears important papers from Vilnius.

KSIŃSKI
*Aside.*
Papers from Vilnius — ah! — Maryna! *Aloud.* Let him in!

*Enter Maryna.*

MARYNA
It's me, my lord, it's me!

FELIX
What is the meaning of this?

MARYNA
*Lowering her eyes.*
Nothing, my lord — I just... sort of came...

FELIX
You have papers for me?

*Maryna hands then over and retreats to the rear.*

STRANGER
*To himself, in the rear.*
Fates are in the balance.

KSIŃSKI
*To himself.*
The brave girl!

FELIX
*Reading in snatches.*
God! All of Poland has arisen! Jasiński's waiting... *Glances feverishly at the papers.* Kościuszko! From the man himself...! *He extracts another paper and reads.* An Act — a Manifest of National Uprising... Am I not mistaken? ... No — it's stated quite clearly... *Cries*: Maryna!

MARYNA
Here I am, my lord!

FELIX
Who gave you these papers? Tell me!

MARYNA
That gentleman dressed in black — I don't know him.

KSIŃSKI
What is it? He's trembling all over!
*Aloud.*
Count Felix, what is it?

FELIX
You'll find out soon enough. To the nobles. I have here some very important news, gentlemen...
All of Poland is up in arms!

VOICES
What? What?

*Great commotion and noise; the noblemen draw near Felix.*

KSIŃSKI
Whence have you this news?

FELIX
From Kraków.
*The noise grows. Felix takes up and displays the Manifesto of National Uprising.*
The hour has finally struck in which word becomes deed; the grave, solemn hour, gentlemen! From this day forward, let us cease to be marionettes animated by an unseen hand. Our country awaits her deliverance — and so, to arms! Whoever is with me, let him stand to!

VOICES
We are all with you! All of us!

WSCHOWSKI
*Somewhat drunkenly.*
I am with the Hetman, and his son!

FELIX
This oath binds you to me. Where I go, you shall go too. In Kraków, Kościuszko has taken his place at the head of the nation. It's not for us to go to Vilnius, but to wait here, upon the outcome of events — Each of you, collect your men, and make yourselves ready for action.

VOICES
Vivat Felix! We are with you!

WSCHOWSKI
And I declare a veto. Where the Hetman goes, there lies our road.

FELIX
Whoever is not with me is against me!

VOICES
Vivat Felix! We are one with Felix!

FELIX
*Takes a pen and signs the Manifesto of National Uprising.*
Who is with me?

VOICES
Bravo! Bravo! Let's sign it! Sign it!

WSCHOWSKI
*To Ksiński, who is speaking with Maryna.*
Mr Ksiński! Mr Ksiński — violence is being done to our Golden Freedom! I disagree!

FELIX
*To Ksiński.*
Sign it, Ksiński!

KSIŃSKI
*Displaying the Hetman's signet.*
Gentlemen! First, I demand your obedience! Listen to me, please!

VOICES
The Fatherland above all! Sign it! Sign it!

*A tumult ensues.*

KSIŃSKI
I shall do no such thing without the express command of my lord!

*An even greater tumult; some unsheathe their sabres.*

WSCHOWSKI
*Unsheathing his.*
Long live the Golden Freedom!

FELIX
*Holding everyone back from Ksiński.*
Ksiński! you don't want to sign]] the document, which I've signed with my own hand.

KSIŃSKI
*Decides to sign, under duress.*
You will answer for this before your father, Count!

FELIX
Have you signed, Mr Ksiński?

KSIŃSKI
I have signed it.

FELIX
Your expenses, gentlemen, will certainly be covered by my father. I now bid you farewell.

*While the above exchange is taking place, the noblemen sign the document, which lies on the middle table.*

WSCHOWSKI
*Calling out a few more times.*
Long live the Golden Freedom!
*Drunk, he jumps up on the table, and, at the moment that Felix is*

*putting away the Manifesto, he cries out:*
I have signed it! But I disagree!

*The noblemen pull him down from the table, amidst cries and commotion, then they each go their own way, taking Wschowski with them, while he continues to cry out:*

I shall not stand for this! I disagree!

*Felix, Maryna, Ksiński and the Stranger remain on stage.*

KSIŃSKI
*To Felix.*
Good God! But you're a tough fellow, Count Felix! You were just mocking us, before!

FELIX
Not at all. I'm quite indifferent to the whole thing. Be well, neighbour!

KSIŃSKI
Recommend me to your friend.

FELIX
I'll introduce you sometime. He's a very worthy fellow, but I don't know his name.

KSIŃSKI
*Exiting.*
Your servant.

FELIX
*To the Stranger.*
Come here! My heart is somehow heavy. Swear to me that you shall tell no one about what you've witnessed here.\* It all seemed so childish to me — back in school, together, we once dreamed of great glory. Now, see? Just as I've been showing you some marionettes, so am I

---

\*    The original Polish reads: *nikomu nie powiesz o tej dzisiejszej scenie* — "you will tell no one about this scene today." The word "scene," which is found time and again in Felix's mouth, emphasises the theatricality of his actions; we're never quite sure when he's being straightforward, and when he's acting.

slain in my heart, as others are slain in their soul. Perhaps my soul will be dead tomorrow, too.

MARYNA
Count Felix, please don't be angry with Maryna, please, my lord.

FELIX
What? You're weeping, girl? As God's my witness, you're pretty — just like a little angel. Come here... *He kisses her on the forehead.* If the sight of this girl did not arouse villainous memories in my heart, who knows what I might have been, at this moment.

MARYNA
You no longer need me, my lord?

FELIX
Go back to your cottage. Put on your homespun skirt and your chaplet of cornflowers, and sit yourself down at the window, to smile at the passing boys. I'll send you a dowry...

MARYNA
But you will always love me, my lord?

FELIX
Go and love your husband, and, later, your children! May your life be a calm and happy one.

MARYNA
You make me want to cry when you talk like that. I was always happy when you smiled at me.

FELIX
You'll forget all about me...

MARYNA
Who knows...? And maybe when I think of you, always... When I think of you... Love me, my lord, for I am a poor girl...!

FELIX
Listen: When I die, will you plant a sprig of rosemary on my grave?

MARYNA
You will not die, my lord! You will not die! When you say such things, my lord — like you once said that you wanted to die — I wept at my spinning wheel like a child...

FELIX
You'll plant me a whole handful of rosemary... But don't pluck any of it later for your bridal chaplet, because that would make me very sad. Go back to your cottage.

MARYNA
Will you come by, my lord?

FELIX
Maybe... Tomorrow... I'll send you a dowry...

MARYNA
But you will come by.
*Exit.*

STRANGER
Felix, you're musing on something sad.

FELIX
I don't know why, but I've grown sleepy. Do you reckon that my father...

STRANGER
Suspicion has fallen upon your father — but fear not for his life. Our people have grown used to respecting men in high places — and the radiance of his wealth has put him beyond the reach of the powerful.

FELIX
My father is suspected of something?

STRANGER
O yes — He is suspected of pride and ambition... They even say... But only among the higher placed...

FELIX
And if they called me the traitor... of a traitor? Are you going to Vilnius?

STRANGER
Yes.

FELIX
Then watch over him! Take the Arabian from my stable — If anything were to happen yet this evening, you will still find me...

STRANGER
What means this "yet," this "still"?

FELIX
When his people do not show up, my father will certainly return to his castle tomorrow morning.

STRANGER
What do you plan to do?

FELIX
Nothing. There will be a pine threshold at the gate, made of four planks...

STRANGER
Felix, do I see you worn out by the first deed of your life? Have you overstrained yourself throwing your first missile at the rotten world?

FELIX
Ask not what is going on in my heart... You heard how I spoke to the people when I was enthused.

STRANGER
You lied to yourself, and to those people.

FELIX
Who knows? Maybe those words contained the most genuine of my thoughts.

STRANGER
I don't believe it! By God I don't!

FELIX
Go to Vilnius and leave me here alone. I've been through so many sad events already, and I have a feeling that it's not all over yet.

[END OF ACT IV]

## ACT V

### Scene 1

*Horsztyński's house. A large room — to the left, open doors lead to another room (Horsztyński's bedroom). The bright light of large tallow candles emerges therefrom. Salomea enters, dressed in white, hair undone, and halts at the door.*

SALOMEA
He's still asleep — O! what a deep sleep, my God! *Pause. She walks about the room, with bowed head.* You silent walls — O, how sad it makes me to look at you! There was once such happiness here... Here! ... And where is it now? — There is no such thing as happiness... Empty word... Illusion. Even a little bird has his nest padded with fluff, and still a storm can cast it down. And even though the little bird has a pair of wings, he can't outfly his fate...

*Steps on the porch are heard. Frightened, Salomea approaches the other door.*

Who's coming? Ah — it's them — the Hetman's people... They're back. I won't let them in. Let him sleep, people! The poor man... He doesn't know...

FR PROCOPIUS
Have mercy on her, Christ the Lord! — Salomea!

SALOMEA
Who was it called me by my name? Ksawery? Is that you?

FR PROCOPIUS
It's me, Father Procopius, your friend.

SALOMEA
I have no more friends. I am an orphan.

FR PROCOPIUS
God is the comforter of orphans.

SALOMEA
*Draws near Father Procopius, takes him by the hand and leads him a few steps near the front of the stage.*
You speak of friends? — O! Yes, I once had a friend. He was handsome... nice... and so sad all the time! When I first laid eyes on him, my heart was seized with fear and unease — I wanted to avoid him, but I couldn't, I felt so sorry for him... He was so unfortunate! I was like a mother to him... a sister... I loved him! He was here just yesterday, in this very room, and, you know? Ksawery killed him... when he smashed the crucifix, he died...

*She takes the shattered crucifix from her bosom.*

Look! The broken crucifix — There is no God! There is no friend any longer.

FR PROCOPIUS
Poor woman, you blaspheme.

SALOMEA
Shh! Did you hear...? Ksawery is calling me... Don't tell him! Don't tell him anything!

FR PROCOPIUS
Calm down, my child... Come... I've come for you.

SALOMEA
No! I'm staying here. He's blind — I have to lead him out. The Hetman is vengeful! His people were here this morning... They'll be back before long. *She goes to the window.* Just look, what a beautiful evening! The sun is sinking lower and lower, the lindens are murmuring, the birds have grown quiet: all of nature is so at peace — It's so blissful, so pleasant, as if it were all a dream, not life! *Short pause.* Look — Do you see that white butterfly? He was once but a worm — love gave him wings, and how he flutters about, in search of his blossom, in search of a drop of dew... — O God! Did you see that?... That black swallow just snatched him! ... How cruel! What did that poor butterfly ever do to deserve that?

**FR PROCOPIUS**
Salomea, my child, I beg you — pull yourself together!

**SALOMEA**
Father! Father! What men are those, on their way here? ... Look! They're carrying a black cross... a pall... a bier... O God! *Her hands fly to her head.* Ah! And so it's death...! Death...

*She faints into the arms of the priest, who sets her down on an armchair. Simultaneously, enter people from the village, along with the funeral procession. The priest makes a sign for them to go away. But, recovering from her swoon, Salomea speaks:*

No, Father, let them stay here and pray. They've come to say their goodbyes. May God reward them their kindness! *To the peasants.* Come near. — It's all clear to my eyes; my hour is approaching... God is calling me, — my mother, and Ksawery, are waiting for me. As God is my witness, I am innocent! All of the threads that linked me to this life are now broken. My soul is longing after her own. Bless me, Father... *Pointing aloft.* Mercy can only be found there.

**FR PROCOPIUS**
God be with you, my daughter!

**SALOMEA**
Pray for me, friends, and for your master. Just yesterday, you sang us a harvest song... And today... a dirge! *To Fr Procopius.* Help me to stand, and lead me to my husband's coffin... There...

*She wants to go, but after a few steps, she staggers and turns back to the window.*

Sun! Sky! O, merciful God!

*Her head falls upon the priest's shoulder, and she dies.*]]

## Scene 2
*A hall in the Hetman's palace, as in Act I.*

AMELIA
*Leading in little Michał by the hand.*
You don't know where your brother Felix is?

MICHAŁ
I saw him, sister, asleep on the green sofa.

AMELIA
Asleep? I can't find out anything about what's going on in this place from anyone! Just now there was so much noise, and now it's so calm and quiet.

MICHAŁ
Amelia, will you tell me a funny story?

AMELIA
We forgot to say our prayers yesterday, Michał.

MICHAŁ
So what, Amelia?

AMELIA
Maybe God will be mad at you.

MICHAŁ
No He won't. I'll give him my drum.

AMELIA
My little sparrow — Come give me a kiss! Hold me tight — tight!

MICHAŁ
Like this!

*He throws his arms around her neck. Enter Felix, lost in thought.*

FELIX
What... Is it night already...? I fell into such a deep sleep — I've been sleeping since the afternoon. *Catching sight of Amelia.* Ah! Amelia

— Good evening. I slept so soundly — just like before a storm. What's it like outside?

AMELIA
The moon is bright — It's a very calm and cool evening.

FELIX
Calm? *Opens the window.* Has father not come back?

AMELIA
No. Off to bed now, Michał. It's late...

MICHAŁ
Not yet! Not yet!... Brother, swing me on your leg!

FELIX
All right. Hold on tight, boy!

MICHAŁ
More — more!

FELIX
That's enough... Tomorrow, we'll go for a horseback ride.

AMELIA
If you say your prayers, like a good boy.

MICHAŁ
I'll say my prayers here with Felix.

AMELIA
All right. Kneel down on the rug and fold your hands. Now, repeat after me. Dear God...!

MICHAŁ
Dear God...

AMELIA
Grant health...

**MICHAŁ**
Grant health...

**AMELIA**
And happiness...

**MICHAŁ**
And happiness...

**AMELIA**
To my Papa...

**MICHAŁ**
To my Papa...

**AMELIA**
And to my brother Felix, and my sister Amelia...

**MICHAŁ**
And to my brother Felix, and my sister Amelia...

**AMELIA**
And to all people...

**MICHAŁ**
And to all people...

**AMELIA**
Have mercy, Lord, upon my Mama...

**MICHAŁ**
Have mercy, Lord, upon my Mama...

**AMELIA**
And upon Amelia's Mama...

**MICHAŁ**
And upon Amelia's Mama...

**AMELIA**
And lead them into Heaven...

MICHAŁ
And lead them into Heaven...

AMELIA
Dear God!

MICHAŁ
Dear God!

AMELIA
Grant wisdom to me, Michał...

MICHAŁ
Grant wisdom to me, Michał...

AMELIA
And love me, Lord, as long as I remain a good boy...

MICHAŁ
And love me, Lord, as long as I remain a good boy...

AMELIA
Amen.

MICHAŁ
Amen.

AMELIA
Felix, how long it has been since we said such quiet prayers...

FELIX
Very long!

AMELIA
Have you heard the sad news? That poor old man Sforka's lost his mind — his wife has had him committed to the Brothers Hospitallers in Vilnius.

FELIX
Committed? To hospital?

AMELIA
They say there's a very good doctor there — And furthermore, she'd rather entrust her husband into the care of good priests than set him up as a laughingstock for the lackeys in the castle.

FELIX
What drove him mad?

AMELIA
When Mr Sforka's wife was returning from church, she found him blowing soap bubbles. He was blowing them and laughing, blowing them and sobbing. In her anger and her shock, the old woman smashed the saucer with the soapy water, and she broke all of his straws. The old man threw himself at her in such fury that he had to be restrained with ropes. I saw them carry him out in that state and place him in the carriage. He kept asking everyone, "Who am I?" "What am I thinking of?" The soldiers were all laughing, and his wife was weeping so, you couldn't help but feel sorry for her...

FELIX
Insanity is a horrible thing! Go put Michał to bed. I'll come by a bit later to speak with you. I have so many sad thoughts in my head; so many have lain in my heart for so long now. I'll come to you, sister — perhaps for a confession of all my past life...

AMELIA
My sweetest; I'll wait for you, and tune my harp. Give your brother Michał a kiss — We're off to bed now.

MICHAŁ
And tomorrow, horses!

AMELIA
I'll be waiting for you, Felix.

*Amelia exits with the child.*

FELIX
How strangely sleep refreshes and toughens the mind. It seems to me that I'm ready now to begin the path of active life. I've thought of death — as a last retreat. No! I will yet begin to struggle with events,

and men — I'll bear up under my father's glare... and will defeat him with the calmness of my brow.

*Enter Servant.*

SERVANT
Strange news, my lord. The Jews in the village are saying that a revolution has broken out in Vilnius!

FELIX
A revolution? ... Today?

SERVANT
They're saying it started at seven this evening. The arsenal's been taken; the whole citizenry's been armed...

FELIX
Saddle my horse! Take whatever men you find in the castle and have them arm themselves at once! At once!

SERVANT
The Jew that leases the tavern, a sober man, said that we should illuminate the castle. The rafts floating to Vilnius will carry word that our master's declared himself.

FELIX
No need! Our master's in Vilnius. And I don't like those lights that toss so pale a light through the windowpanes and into the rooms. Saddle my horse.

SERVANT
The Jews are also saying that there was a revolution in Warsaw a couple of days ago.

FELIX
My horse!

*Exit Servant.*

Warsaw, Vilnius, all of Poland, the nation — Me — A procession of gigantic events is passing before my eyes. How can I mix in with them?

How can I stand to? And where? What am I to become? What will my father become? O! I will cast myself at his feet and weep like an infant, begging him on behalf of the poor people thrashing about in the great net of events. I seem to hear the revolutionary cries of rubble and stone coming to life. Great God! I haven't prayed to You in quite a while, but right now, I can feel my heart crying out from the depths to You: Have mercy upon us!... Upon us? What am I? I did not rise in rebellion...! I am crying out here, safe within these walls, while others are dying in silence... I will look upon the battling people as if upon a gladiatorial slaughter! In the name of God, I go to perish!

*He rises and makes to leave, then the Hetman's ghost enters through the foyer door, stops in the middle of the room, and signs to Felix to remain.*

Father... You've returned? ... Say something! You will stand with the nation, will you not?

GHOST
O! O! O!
*He passes through the hall and enters the office.*

FELIX
Dear God, how quiet and pale... My hair is standing on end!

*He rings. Enter Servant.*

Well? My father's back? What is his will? Did he say anything to you?

SERVANT
The master?

FELIX
Was anyone in the foyer?

SERANT
Four of us were.

FELIX
Then you must have been sleeping! Go into the office and ask your master if he requires anything.

SERVANT
But my lord — I swear to you that the Hetman has not returned. We'd have heard him drive up in the carriage.

FELIX
Maybe he returned on horseback. He's in his office right now — Go see...

*Servant opens the door to the office.*

SERVANT
Count — there's not a living soul in there.

FELIX
You lie! My father! *Glancing into the office.* O! Have I lost my mind too? Give me a glass of water!

HETMAN'S VOICE
A glass of water!

FELIX
Did you hear that? My father's voice — asking for a glass of water!

SERVANT
I heard nothing, my lord.

FELIX
But I swear to you, I heard my father's voice!

SERVANT
Where?

FELIX
*Stamping his foot.*
Here! Maybe he went into one of the rooms on the first floor...

SERVANT
But you said he'd gone into the office — and there's no other exit from there...

FELIX
A servant's logic is a strange thing! Go! Because I must be ill... Don't say anything about this. For God's sake, tell no one! I must be ill...

SERVANT
Shall I call the doctor?

FELIX
No... no! Listen — hoofbeats! Someone is galloping in my head...

VOICE
*In the foyer.*
Where is Count Felix? Where is Felix?

*Enter Stranger.*

STRANGER
Felix! ... Felix! *To Servant.* Leave us!

*Exit Servant.*

FELIX
*Pushes the Stranger away, and stares at him a long while.*
My father must have died... I've seen his ghost...My father must have died...

STRANGER
He has...

FELIX
*Falling into a chair.*
Ha...!

STRANGER
*Aside.*
I don't know what to tell him.

FELIX
Your hand... Help me stand up... I've got to find out all about it... You know... At least let me know, at this unlucky hour, that you take me for a man. Tell me everything... What was it like... in Vilnius... Look

me straight in the eye and hold my mind fast with your stare, for I've lost my moorings. But tell me everything... Because if my imagination must fill in the blanks, I'll be ready to... You understand? What did you see?

STRANGER
Keep seated.

FELIX
No! I will stand. It is easier that way. Now, speak!

STRANGER
Well, then... At seven in the evening Jasiński entered the city through a hole broken in the wall near the Ostrobramska Gate. The moon had not yet risen; a votive lamp was shining at Ostra Brama — as they passed by, the conspirators made the sign of the cross... and quietly slid along toward the guardhouse across from the city hall. Jasiński rushed forward quickly and killed the sentry — he didn't even have time to groan... He grabbed his carbine, and the conspirators denuded the racks of weapons and kettle-drums. Jasiński sent drummers into all the city streets and ordered them to sound a tattoo as soon as eight o'clock struck. He himself took twenty five men and went along the street leading to the castle, to the arsenal. Then eight o'clock struck, and the drums sounded from all sides. In their confusion, the Muscovites thought that there was an armed division in each street. They ran away — from drummer to drummer. Jasiński took the arsenal and set all the bells to ringing. The frightful pealing of the bells stirred the people — they began to collect at the arsenal, which they stripped of weapons, and then they began slaughtering the Muscovites... I was at Jasiński's side. None of the Polish lords who were in Vilnius had anything to fear, because the people had their hands full with the Muscovites... Then some old fellow made his way to Jasiński and handed him a sheaf of papers. Jasiński called for a torch and, after reading them through, spat, and threw them away in contempt. The people began to pass them from hand to hand, grouping themselves around those who knew how to read. For quite some time I couldn't understand what was going on. I thought that the papers were proclamations and manifestos... Then, suddenly, I heard a cry from a thousand throats: "The Hetman is a traitor!" And then, even worse things...

FELIX
Speak on!

STRANGER
"String him up!"

*Felix totters and then makes a gesture with his hand.*

Fighting through the crowd, or, rather, borne on by the tide of people, I resisted until we arrived at the very fence of the palace belonging to your... Hetman... The people crowded the stairs, howling like hyenas... Suddenly, something fell through an open window and split in two on the iron railings... It was the dwarf. He perished, howling like a vermin pierced on a spit.

*Felix shivers.*

A few minutes later, they led him out... He was pale, but calm.

FELIX
Dressed?

STRANGER
In a dressing gown. He was holding something in his hand, gripping it so tightly, that no one could take it from him.

FELIX
Did he say anything?

STRANGER
He asked for a glass of water.

FELIX
Did they give it to him?

STRANGER
Someone in the crowd tried to restrain the impetus of the mob with words — pleading them to hand over the unfortunate man to a judge.

*Felix squeezes his hand.*

Then a priest came up and heard his confession — The penitent was somewhat... enervated, and often looked...

FELIX
Don't torment me! He often looked toward the castle — waiting, waiting!

STRANGER
He was calm... He smiled... Then he opened his palm — It was a cardboard snuffbox. He took some snuff, and gave the box to a man there, who had kept quiet all the while, just looking at him.

*Felix extends his hand, then suddenly retracts it, mechanically.*

He didn't suffer long.

FELIX
How long?

STRANGER
Half a minute, no longer.

*Felix pulls out a watch and looks at it.*

FELIX
But that is long! See how long! ... You see that I am calm... Be well!

STRANGER
Felix! For God's sake! Where are you going?

FELIX
Well... I'm going to take my father down from the gallows.

STRANGER
Calm down — think it all through, my friend.

FELIX
I didn't kill my father. But if I had gone there with some people a few hours ago, my father would still be alive. But I did not kill my father. Do you reckon that I might have been able to defend him?

STRANGER
No, for God's sake, no!

FELIX
Yes! ... I swear that I could have! Convince me that I'm wrong! For I will fall dead here, on the spot!

STRANGER
He can't cry... Felix, give me your hand —

*He places the snuffbox in his hand.*

FELIX
Ah — the snuffbox...
*He covers his eyes; we hear him sobbing.*

STRANGER
Ah, poor man!

FELIX
Look — My portrait is on the lid — Me, when I was a child. Look what a rosy face I had, what a smile... This is the Felix that father would take on his knees to cuddle and kiss. My poor father...! Go, you can't weep for him... I beg you — don't look at me — I want to be a child.

*Enter Servant.*

SERVANT
My lord...! I've ridden here from Vilnius as fast as I could. The mob, in a fury, are on their way here to fire the castle. They'll be at the gate in an hour and a half... Your father has been murdered...

FELIX
Ha! The people are on their way here to fire the castle!

STRANGER
Felix, I urge you: don't defend the place. You need the heart of a Roman now, Felix... You've got to let the wailing mob wear out their frenzy on walls and mirrors. You've got to sacrifice it, Felix!

FELIX
Ha...! You want me to set myself up as a lantern on my castle?

STRANGER
O! For God's sake, don't say such horrible things!

FELIX
Do they know me, that rabble...? Do they not mean to toss in my face a rag stained with the heart-blood of my father?

*Felix rings, enter Servant.*

Everybody!

*He rings, enter many Servants.*

All of you, take all the gold you can find in the treasury and divide it amongst yourselves. Then, go and wait for me on that hilltop, half a mile from here. Don't touch any of the tools or equipment, and do what I ask of you calmly, so that my sister won't hear the slightest rustle! I'll meet up with you at one in the morning. Now this is an order — I am your master now — there mustn't be a single one of you in the castle at midnight.

SERVANTS
As you wish, my lord.

FELIX
I thank you all for your faithful service. Are there any amongst you who have known my father since childhood?

*Several Servants come forward.*

Pray for the soul of your master!

*He shakes the hand of each, then makes a sign that they should depart. Exit Servants. Felix paces the room.*

STRANGER
What are you planning?

FELIX
You said that I've got the heart of a Roman... I shall blow the castle to pieces. No one will lay a hand on it. There is powder enough in the tower.

STRANGER
What? You want to die? Listen: these arms of mine are strong — I will carry you out of here like a child...

FELIX
No! you can blow up a castle without blowing up yourself! I've got a plan. And you will help me carry it out. I don't want to die, no. I've got two stains to wipe clean in the eyes of the nation — Listen! There is powder in the tower. You will place this loaded pistol in a caisson, and you'll take a long string and fasten one end to the trigger, and the other to the mechanism of the clock in the tower. Use the sword of the Lithuanian knight for that. When the clock strikes midnight, the knight raises his sword and strikes the Russian eagle — when that happens, the taut string will pull the trigger, fire the pistol, and then: powder, flash... and nothing. Do that for me!

STRANGER
But you won't be in the castle?

FELIX
Listen — I take it upon myself to deliver my sister and brother to safety. Neither of them know anything about this. You don't think I wish them to die along with me? I'll remain in the castle just a little longer than you — so as to prepare my sister, and not to frighten them with the pain on my face. — And this is why I need a few moments by myself to think a bit, and calm myself down, so that I'll be able to calm the others. Wait for me on the farther bank of the Wilia. But first, make everything ready as I've asked you. Swear that you will!

STRANGER
I swear...

FELIX
Come, give me a hug. ... What a horrid night, is it not?

STRANGER
I will dream of it even in the grave.

FELIX
Hold on... One doesn't dream in the grave. — Or do you think that a thought can be so strong that it can't be completely destroyed by the horrid events of one's life? Is the soul really a lamp that is never snuffed? Can the soil of the grave provide her with new colours, and its dampness vigour, like a flower? Is it for this that the flesh is destroyed, that the soul might dream? And so, I destroy something, for naught? Think it over and place yourself in my shoes, and think — If you could only solve this mystery, which all of the world's religions... I can't take the memory of this night to heaven with me. And if I won't remember what I was, what does it mean, that "I shall be?"

STRANGER
O, how broken you are by misfortune!

FELIX
Of course — I think, therefore I am alive...

FELIX
I'll be waiting for you on the other side of the river.

FELIX
So we will not say goodbye.

*Exit Stranger.*

I see no path before my feet. I seem to be walking along the cornice of the castle. I... and my sister... and the child, who still today was saying his prayers: God grant them health! That child's voice has become the music of my soul... God, grant them health! But what's to do? Tell my staggering mind, what am I to do?

*Enter the Priest.*

## Scene 3

FELIX
Father Procopius! You've come... God has sent you!

*The Priest stands there gloomily and says nothing.*

You behold me today, broken by misfortune. Give me your hand.

FR PROCOPIUS
God has chastised you severely... But trust in His mercy! What are you planning to do, right now?

FELIX
I don't know. Wherever I cast my eyes, I see only an abyss... Do you know how my father died...?

FR PROCOPIUS
I do.

FELIX
I could have saved him, and yet I didn't! I've always underrated the human conscience. I thought it a mere ball to kick around, a plaything. But now I've come to know it! My entire being is howling in pain. Perhaps death will deliver me from the aggressive bugbears of this night. And what is death? The idiotic solution to the riddles of human life...

FR PROCOPIUS
Don't blaspheme. Humble yourself, rather, before God. Make an offering to Him of you suffering. Up until now you've lived aimlessly. Shake off your lethargy now, and become a new man.

FELIX
I can't.

FR PROCOPIUS
You can if you want to. You have a great obligation to fulfil.

FELIX
What obligation?

**FR PROCOPIUS**
To wipe away the stain on your family.

**FELIX**
O, you people! You think the verdicts of your righteousness so omnipotent! ... That, at your command, the son will trample his father's corpse! Strange logic! No, Father! I will not set my foot upon that path... I feel the fresh mark of shame upon my brow. Leave me alone, all of you! Shame has its own pride, and it yearns for loneliness and oblivion.

**FR PROCOPIUS**
So what will become of your brother and sister?

## Scene 4

**AMELIA**
*Runs in.*
O, my brother Felix! ... What horrid news: Horsztyński is dead...

**FELIX**
*To Fr Procopius.*
Horsztyński!!!?

**FR PROCOPIUS**
*With a silent nod.*
Yes...

**FELIX**
*Falling onto a chair, stunned.*
Ha...!

**AMELIA**
Felix! Felix!

**FELIX**
*Coming round.*
Amelia, leave us alone... Go to your room and get Michał dressed. We have to leave the castle within the half hour... Hurry, my child! Hurry...

AMELIA
Felix, my brother! Something frightful has happened... There's so much commotion throughout the castle... unease... You are so pale... changed... Has father returned?

FELIX
No.

AMELIA
Ha! I get it... Felix! Our father is in danger... and you're hastening to Vilnius? O, now I understand!... I'm going, brother, I'm going...
*She throws herself into his arms, sobbing.*
O my Felix! You'll save him, won't you?

FELIX
Don't cry, Amelia.

## Scene 5

FELIX
Father, time is pressing... I entrust my sister and brother into your hands. Get away from here, for death is nigh at hand.

*Rings.*

It seems as if everything were spinning around me.

*Rings again. Enter Servant.*

Harness the wagon, now! Harness it!

*Exit Servant.*

FR PROCOPIUS
You're coming with us?

FELIX
No — I have to wait here for my father's people. Listen, Father — lead my sister and brother to the other bank of the Wilia. I'll be there a midnight... Wait for me there...

FR PROCOPIUS
You'll keep your word?

FELIX
I will.

FR PROCOPIUS
May God keep you in His care...
*Exits.*

## Scene 6

*Felix walks over to the window at the right, at a slow pace. Enter the Stranger.*

FELIX
And so it's come to pass! — A moment more and all will be finished. The people are nearing, thirsty for revenge...

*A tumult is heard, off stage.*

The glow of a horrid inferno. — What horrific moans!... A moment more, and they'll be here.

STRANGER
Felix!

FELIX
*Turns his face in his direction.*
You're here? — Is it still long until midnight?

STRANGER
No — but a few moments more.

FELIX
Have you prepared everything in the tower?

STRANGER
Everything. Let's go!

*Noises off stage.*

**FELIX**
I'm staying here. Farewell, my friend!

**STRANGER**
Are you mad?

*One hears the clatter of swords, as if a fight were taking place off stage.*

**STRANGER**
What's that? They're fighting...!

**FELIX**
Who? My people are not here any longer... I'm alone in the castle.

**STRANGER**
Felix, for God's sake! Let's get out of here!

**FELIX**
Me? And leave them behind? Never!

## Scene 7

**KSIŃSKI**
*Rushes in, sword unsheathed.*
We made it in time!

**FELIX**
What's the meaning of this?

**KSIŃSKI**
You ask what's the meaning of this?
*Goes to the window.*
Just look — the rabble has surrounded the castle. They wanted to burn you alive!

**FELIX**
And what's that to you?

**KSIŃSKI**
Have you forgotten our pact...? You said that you wanted to lead us

on to great deeds. I reckon that being torn apart by the mob does not belong to that number. — Get up and act, Felix!

ALL
Long live Felix! Long live our Hetman!

STRANGER
*Quickly coming near Felix who stands there, lost in thought.*
For God's sake, Felix! Think it over! ... You're not going with them... That's impossible!

KSIŃSKI
Who is he?

FELIX
My friend. I promised to introduce you someday. It's high time, now.

*Ksiński and the Stranger take measure of one another.*

FELIX
*After musing a moment.*
Let it be, then! You've had half of my will; today, you may have it all. You call me to action? Here I am...! But remember — you asked for it. Once more I say: Woe to him who calls his brother a traitor!

*Noises off stage, from afar.*

STRANGER
*Exiting.*
Woe to you, Felix!

FELIX
Like a wave on the sea, so with one's predestination — you can't restrain it. Although we shall find ourselves in different camps, don't curse me... Such is the will of Fate.

*He exits. The curtain begins to fall; the clock in the tower strikes midnight; a gigantic explosion is heard as the curtain reaches the stage — the castle is destroyed.*

[THE END]

# BIBLIOGRAPHY

**Primary Sources for the Translation**

SŁOWACKI, Juliusz. *Dzieła wybrane.* Eugeniusz Sawrymowicz (ed.). Wrocław: Ossolineum, 1983. Vol. 3.

— *Balladyna. Tragedija w 5 aktach.* Paris: W księgarni i drukarni polskiej, 1839.

—*Horsztyński. Dramat zdefektowany w 5 aktach. Uzupełnił dla sceny krakowskiej Juliusz Mien.* Kraków: Księgarnia Gebethnera i Wolffa, 1883.

— *Kordjan. Spisek koronacyjny.* Lwów: Księgarnia polska, 1877.

— *Poezye.* Tom II. Paris: U Teofila Barrois syna; U Hektora Bossange i komp., 1832.

**Secondary Sources**

KRZYŻANOWSKI, Julian. *W świecie romantycznym.* Kraków: Wydawnictwo literackie, 1961.

KURSKA, Anna. "*Balladyna,* czyli o próbie karnawalizacji literatury romantycznej." Łódź: Acta Universitatis Lodziensis, 2015

SAWRYMOWICZ, *Juliusz Słowacki.* Warsaw: Wiedza powszechna, 1973.

STASZEWSKA, Dorota. *O sonetach polskich romantyków.* Łódź: Acta Universitatis Lodzensis, 2005.

WITKOWSKA, Alina. *Literatura romantyzmu.* Warsaw: PIW, 1986.

# ABOUT THE AUTHOR

**Juliusz Słowacki** (1809–1849) is universally recognised as the father of modern Polish drama. His twenty-five plays, many of them inspired by the works of Shakespeare, are the only important dramatic works of the romantic period to be written expressly for the stage. Besides his plays, Słowacki is the author of digressive epics in the style of Lord Byron, prose works of a mystical bent, and some of the most beautiful lyric poems in the Polish language. He travelled to London in 1831 as a courier for the insurrectionist government during the November Uprising against Russia, and elected to remain in exile thereafter, returning to Poland only once, near the end of his life in 1848, to take part in the revolutionary activities of the "Spring of the Peoples." Considered along with Mickiewicz and his friend Zygmunt Krasiński to be one of the "three bards" of Polish Romanticism, Słowacki achieved a great popularity in the early part of the twentieth century, which has only grown with succeeding years.

# ABOUT THE TRANSLATOR

**Charles S. Kraszewski** (b. 1962) is a poet and translator. He is the author of three volumes of original verse (*Diet of Nails; Beast; Chanameed*). Several of his translations of Polish and Czech literature have been published by Glagoslav, among which may be found: Adam Mickiewicz's *Forefathers' Eve* (2016) and *Sonnets* (2018), Zygmunt Krasiński's *Dramatic Works* (2018) and Stanisław Wyspiański's *Acropolis: the Wawel Plays* (2017). His translations of the poetry of T.S. Eliot, Robinson Jeffers, and Lawrence Ferlinghetti into Polish have appeared in the Wrocław monthly *Odra*. He is a member of the Union of Polish Writers Abroad (London) and of the Association of Polish Writers (Kraków).

# Acropolis – The Wawel Plays
# by Stanisław Wyspiański

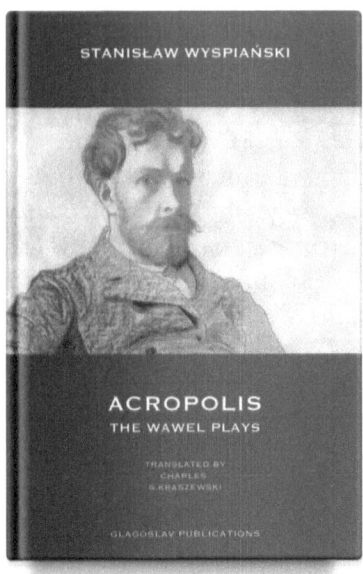

Stanisław Wyspiański (1869-1907) achieved worldwide fame, both as a painter, and Poland's greatest dramatist of the first half of the twentieth century. *Acropolis: the Wawel Plays*, brings together four of Wyspiański's most important dramatic works in a new English translation by Charles S. Kraszewski. All of the plays centre on Wawel Hill: the legendary seat of royal and ecclesiastical power in the poet's native city, the ancient capital of Poland. In these plays, Wyspiański explores the foundational myths of his nation: that of the self-sacrificial Wanda, and the struggle between King Bolesław the Bold and Bishop Stanisław Szczepanowski. In the eponymous play which brings the cycle to an end, Wyspiański carefully considers the value of myth to a nation without political autonomy, soaring in thought into an apocalyptic vision of the future. Richly illustrated with the poet's artwork, *Acropolis: the Wawel Plays* also contains Wyspiański's architectural proposal for the renovation of Wawel Hill, and a detailed critical introduction by the translator. In its plaited presentation of *Bolesław the Bold* and *Skałka*, the translation offers, for the first time, the two plays in the unified, composite format that the poet intended, but was prevented from carrying out by his untimely death.

Buy it > www.glagoslav.com

# Forefathers' Eve
## by Adam Mickiewicz

*Forefathers' Eve* [*Dziady*] is a four-part dramatic work begun circa 1820 and completed in 1832 – with Part I published only after the poet's death, in 1860. The drama's title refers to *Dziady*, an ancient Slavic and Lithuanian feast commemorating the dead. This is the grand work of Polish literature, and it is one that elevates Mickiewicz to a position among the "great Europeans" such as Dante and Goethe.

With its Christian background of the Communion of the Saints, revenant spirits, and the interpenetration of the worlds of time and eternity, *Forefathers' Eve* speaks to men and women of all times and places. While it is a truly Polish work – Polish actors covet the role of Gustaw/Konrad in the same way that Anglophone actors covet that of Hamlet – it is one of the most universal works of literature written during the nineteenth century. It has been compared to Goethe's Faust – and rightfully so...

Buy it > www.glagoslav.com

# A Brown Man in Russia - Perambulations Through A Siberian Winter
## by Vijay Menon

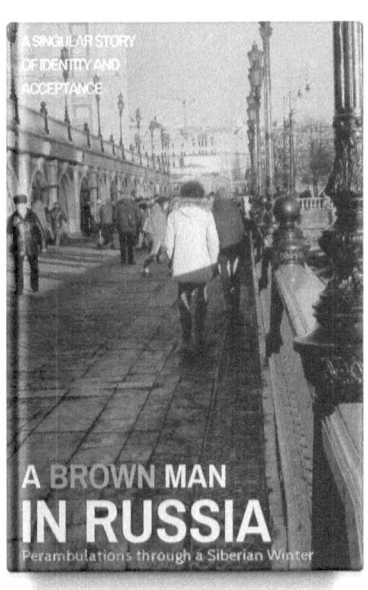

A Brown Man in Russia describes the fantastical travels of a young, colored American traveler as he backpacks across Russia in the middle of winter via the Trans-Siberian. The book is a hybrid between the curmudgeonly travelogues of Paul Theroux and the philosophical works of Robert Pirsig. Styled in the vein of Hofstadter, the author lays out a series of absurd, but true stories followed by a deeper rumination on what they mean and why they matter. Each chapter presents a vivid anecdote from the perspective of the fumbling traveler and concludes with a deeper lesson to be gleaned. For those who recognize the discordant nature of our world in a time ripe for demagoguery and for those who want to make it better, the book is an all too welcome antidote. It explores the current global climate of despair over differences and outputs a very different message – one of hope and shared understanding. At times surreal, at times inappropriate, at times hilarious, and at times deeply human, A Brown Man in Russia is a reminder to those who feel marginalized, hopeless, or endlessly divided that harmony is achievable even in the most unlikely of places.

Buy it > www.glagoslav.com

Dear Reader,

Thank you for purchasing this book.

We at Glagoslav Publications are glad to welcome you, and hope that you find our books to be a source of knowledge and inspiration.

We want to show the beauty and depth of the Slavic region to everyone looking to expand their horizon and learn something new about different cultures, different people, and we believe that with this book we have managed to do just that.

Now that you've got to know us, we want to get to know you. We value communication with our readers and want to hear from you! We offer several options:

– Join our Book Club on Goodreads, Library Thing and Shelfari, and receive special offers and information about our giveaways;

– Share your opinion about our books on Amazon, Barnes & Noble, Waterstones and other bookstores;

– Join us on Facebook and Twitter for updates on our publications and news about our authors;

– Visit our site www.glagoslav.com to check out our Catalogue and subscribe to our Newsletter.

Glagoslav Publications is getting ready to release a new collection and planning some interesting surprises — stay with us to find out!

Glagoslav Publications<br>Email: contact@glagoslav.com

*Glagoslav Publications Catalogue*

- *The Time of Women* by Elena Chizhova
- *Andrei Tarkovsky: The Collector of Dreams* by Layla Alexander-Garrett
- *Andrei Tarkovsky - A Life on the Cross* by Lyudmila Boyadzhieva
- *Sin* by Zakhar Prilepin
- *Hardly Ever Otherwise* by Maria Matios
- *Khatyn* by Ales Adamovich
- *The Lost Button* by Irene Rozdobudko
- *Christened with Crosses* by Eduard Kochergin
- *The Vital Needs of the Dead* by Igor Sakhnovsky
- *The Sarabande of Sara's Band* by Larysa Denysenko
- *A Poet and Bin Laden* by Hamid Ismailov
- *Watching The Russians (Dutch Edition)* by Maria Konyukova
- *Kobzar* by Taras Shevchenko
- *The Stone Bridge* by Alexander Terekhov
- *Moryak* by Lee Mandel
- *King Stakh's Wild Hunt* by Uladzimir Karatkevich
- *The Hawks of Peace* by Dmitry Rogozin
- *Harlequin's Costume* by Leonid Yuzefovich
- *Depeche Mode* by Serhii Zhadan
- *The Grand Slam and other stories (Dutch Edition)* by Leonid Andreev
- *METRO 2033 (Dutch Edition)* by Dmitry Glukhovsky
- *METRO 2034 (Dutch Edition)* by Dmitry Glukhovsky
- *A Russian Story* by Eugenia Kononenko
- *Herstories, An Anthology of New Ukrainian Women Prose Writers*
- *The Battle of the Sexes Russian Style* by Nadezhda Ptushkina
- *A Book Without Photographs* by Sergey Shargunov
- *Down Among The Fishes* by Natalka Babina
- *disUNITY* by Anatoly Kudryavitsky
- *Sankya* by Zakhar Prilepin
- *Wolf Messing* by Tatiana Lungin
- *Good Stalin* by Victor Erofeyev
- *Solar Plexus* by Rustam Ibragimbekov

- *Don't Call me a Victim!* by Dina Yafasova
- *Poetin (Dutch Edition)* by Chris Hutchins and Alexander Korobko
- *A History of Belarus* by Lubov Bazan
- *Children's Fashion of the Russian Empire* by Alexander Vasiliev
- *Empire of Corruption - The Russian National Pastime* by Vladimir Soloviev
- *Heroes of the 90s - People and Money. The Modern History of Russian Capitalism*
- *Fifty Highlights from the Russian Literature (Dutch Edition)* by Maarten Tengbergen
- *Bajesvolk (Dutch Edition)* by Mikhail Khodorkovsky
- *Tsarina Alexandra's Diary (Dutch Edition)*
- *Myths about Russia* by Vladimir Medinskiy
- *Boris Yeltsin - The Decade that Shook the World* by Boris Minaev
- *A Man Of Change - A study of the political life of Boris Yeltsin*
- *Sberbank - The Rebirth of Russia's Financial Giant* by Evgeny Karasyuk
- *To Get Ukraine* by Oleksandr Shyshko
- *Asystole* by Oleg Pavlov
- *Gnedich* by Maria Rybakova
- *Marina Tsvetaeva - The Essential Poetry*
- *Multiple Personalities* by Tatyana Shcherbina
- *The Investigator* by Margarita Khemlin
- *The Exile* by Zinaida Tulub
- *Leo Tolstoy – Flight from paradise* by Pavel Basinsky
- *Moscow in the 1930* by Natalia Gromova
- *Laurus (Dutch edition)* by Evgenij Vodolazkin
- *Prisoner* by Anna Nemzer
- *The Crime of Chernobyl - The Nuclear Goulag* by Wladimir Tchertkoff
- *Alpine Ballad* by Vasil Bykau
- *The Complete Correspondence of Hryhory Skovoroda*
- *The Tale of Aypi* by Ak Welsapar

- *Selected Poems* by Lydia Grigorieva
- *The Fantastic Worlds of Yuri Vynnychuk*
- *The Garden of Divine Songs and Collected Poetry of Hryhory Skovoroda*
- *Adventures in the Slavic Kitchen: A Book of Essays with Recipes*
- *Seven Signs of the Lion* by Michael M. Naydan
- *Forefathers' Eve* by Adam Mickiewicz
- *One-Two* by Igor Eliseev
- *Girls, be Good* by Bojan Babić
- *Time of the Octopus* by Anatoly Kucherena
- *The Grand Harmony* by Bohdan Ihor Antonych
- *The Selected Lyric Poetry Of Maksym Rylsky*
- *The Shining Light* by Galymkair Mutanov
- *The Frontier: 28 Contemporary Ukrainian Poets - An Anthology*
- *Acropolis - The Wawel Plays* by Stanisław Wyspiański
- *Contours of the City* by Attyla Mohylny
- *Conversations Before Silence: The Selected Poetry of Oles Ilchenko*
- *The Secret History of my Sojourn in Russia* by Jaroslav HašekCharles S. Kraszewski
- *Mirror Sand - An Anthology of Russian Short Poems in English Translation* (A Bilingual Edition)
- *Maybe We're Leaving* by Jan Balaban
- *Death of the Snake Catcher* by Ak WelsaparRichard Govett
- *A Brown Man in Russia - Perambulations Through A Siberian Winter* by Vijay Menon
- *Hard Times* by Ostap Vyshnia
- *The Flying Dutchman* by Anatoly Kudryavitsky
- *Nikolai Gumilev's Africa* by Nikolai Gumilev
- *Combustions* by Srđan Srdić
- *The Sonnets* by Adam Mickiewicz
- *Dramatic Works* by Zygmunt Krasiński
- *Zinnober's Poppets* by Elena Chizhova
- *Duel* by Borys Antonenko-Davydovych
- *The Hemingway Game* by Evgeni Grishkovets
- *The Nuremberg Trials* by Alexander Zvyagintsev
- *Mikhail Bulgakov - The Life and Times* by Marietta Chudakova

*More coming soon...*

www.ingramcontent.com/pod-product-compliance
Lightning Source LLC
Chambersburg PA
CBHW031052080526
44587CB00011B/657